Prosocial
Behavior

REVIEW OF PERSONALITY AND SOCIAL PSYCHOLOGY

Editor

Margaret S. Clark, *Carnegie Mellon University*

Prosocial Behavior

Editor
MARGARET S. CLARK

12

REVIEW of PERSONALITY and SOCIAL PSYCHOLOGY

Published in cooperation with the Society for Personality and Social Psychology, Inc.

SAGE PUBLICATIONS
The International Professional Publishers
Newbury Park   London   New Delhi

For information address:

SAGE Publications, Inc.
2455 Teller Road
Newbury Park, California 91320

SAGE Publications Ltd.
6 Bonhill Street
London EC2A 4PU
United Kingdom

SAGE Publications India Pvt. Ltd.
M-32 Market
Greater Kailash I
New Delhi 110 048 India

Printed in the Unites States of America

International Standard Book Number: 0-8039-4071-8
0-8039-4072-6 (pbk.)

International Standard Series Number 0270-1987

Library of Congress Card Number 80-649712

FIRST PRINTING, 1991

Sage Production Editor: Michelle R. Starika

CONTENTS

Editor's Introduction

MARGARET S. CLARK

Margaret S. Clark is Professor of Psychology at Carnegie Mellon University, where she has been since receiving her Ph.D. from the University of Maryland, College Park, in 1977. Her research interests are in the areas of interpersonal relationships and emotions. She has been associate editor of the *Personality and Social Psychology Bulletin* and a representative of Division 8 on the American Psychological Association's Council of Representatives.

This volume includes 11 chapters on prosocial behavior and concludes with a commentary by John Darley. Proposals for the volume were solicited from a wide array of researchers in this field; 23 proposals were received. Although we could select fewer than half of those submitted, I think the contents fairly represent the current breadth of research on prosocial behavior among social and personality psychologists. There are two reviews of research on the development of prosocial behavior (by Grusec and by Eisenberg and Fabes), and a number of chapters examine what individuals' motivations for helping might be (for example, by Batson and Oleson, by Dovidio, Piliavin, Gaertner, Schroeder, and Clark, and by Fiske). Further, evidencing a new trend in the field, a number of chapters emphasize the consequences of providing help for the helper (see, for example, the chapters by Clary and Snyder, by Salovey, Mayer, and Rosenhan, and by Midlarsky). Research in all three of these areas is flourishing. In addition, Nadler's review chapter on help-seeking behavior reveals that we have accumulated a substantial amount of knowledge in that area as well, largely due to Nadler's and his collaborator's efforts. Research on prosocial behavior has not been around for long, yet we have made considerable progress.

Nonetheless, the contents of the volume also reflect some gaps in our research. Particularly noticeable to me (and to John Darley as well) is that we have not fully addressed the different *types* of helping (e.g., giving emotional support versus helping someone perform a physical task versus giving information to someone). Very different processes may in fact drive such different types of helping. Furthermore, it surely is the case that recipient reactions to these different types of helping

7

vary in important ways. As Darley points out, we see *hints* of taxonomies of types of helping being related to theoretical processes in Clary and Snyder's and in Nadler's chapters, but clearly more is needed in this regard. Recipients' reactions to receiving help also remains a relatively neglected area, as does the investigation of the differences for both helper and recipient when help is given in a professional as opposed to a nonprofessional setting. Moreover (with Clary and Snyder's chapter as a welcome exception), we have seen very little work on sustained, long-term helping, particularly long-term helping that occurs in close relationships. Perhaps as social psychologists are influenced by research in other fields (e.g., as we are influenced by and try to influence the type of social support work reviewed by Wills), our own understanding of long-term helping will expand. Finally, despite the biological work described in Buck and Ginsburg's chapter, the anthropological work described in Fiske's chapter, and the epidemiological work reviewed by Wills, social psychological work on prosocial behavior remains somewhat isolated from research in other fields. These are all areas in which I would like to see some progress in the future.

In closing, I thank the members of the editorial board, all of whom helped to evaluate some of the original proposals and/or to critique the original drafts of the chapters included in this volume. Thanks are also due to the authors themselves not only for preparing their own chapters but, in most cases, also for volunteering to critique drafts of other chapters in the volume. Finally, special thanks go to Amy Halberstadt of the board for her careful review of *every* incoming proposal, to John Darley for sending me critical comments on *all* of the original drafts as well as for preparing his own commentary, and to Clyde Hendrick, the outgoing editor of the *Review,* for not only agreeing to serve on the board but also for extensive help in orienting me to my new job as editor of this series.

1

The Socialization of Altruism

JOAN E. GRUSEC

Joan E. Grusec is Professor of Psychology at the University of Toronto. She is the author, with Gary C. Walters, of *Punishment* and, with Hugh Lytton, of *Social Development: History, Theory, and Research.* Her research interests include the role of modeling, character attribution, and assignment of household responsibility in the socialization of altruism, attributional processes and parent disciplinary practices, the impact of discipline on parental belief systems, and features of parenting behavior and discipline in actual practice.

Wilf P. brings 50 loaves of fresh bread every day to geese and ducks at a local pond. He is a Salvation Army officer and often replaces the army jail chaplain. He spends mornings in court cells talking to prisoners and tending to their needs. He has been a St. John Ambulance official for nearly 40 years and is currently a superintendent for St. John cadets between the ages of 8 and 20 years. Although he refers to the geese and ducks as his "flock," Wilf would "like his own Salvation Army church, where he could tend to the sick and the dying, the poor and the lonely" (*Toronto Globe and Mail,* January 13, 1990).

Wilf P.'s behavior is an extreme form of a phenomenon that poses a major and exciting challenge for developmental psychologists. It is relatively easy to understand why individuals act in their own self-interest; displays of concern for the needs of others are less obviously comprehensible. One direction in which developmentalists have looked is at the socialization processes that foster helping, sharing, and consideration for others—that is, altruism. What were Wilf P.'s parents like? What kind of relationship did he have with them? What did they do to develop his impressive sense of caring?

This chapter deals with the socialization of *altruism.* The latter is a term that will be used to refer to acts of concern for others—such as sharing, helping, showing concern and consideration, reassuring, and defending—that are performed independent of hope of reward or fear of punishment from external sources and that may even be of some cost to the altruist. The motivation underlying these behaviors may be varied, including a desire for social interaction, escape from guilt, feelings of pride, a desire to behave in accord with one's self-concept, and the reduction of empathic distress. But what each of these motivations has in common is that its source lies within the individual. This is probably the most frequent way in which developmentalists have conceptualized altruism. It says nothing about altruism motivated by a genuine concern for others that is independent of any sort of personal distress or self-interest, but at least it does require that the behavior occur independent of external consequences, that is, that it appear to be internalized.

Socialization is the second term that requires definitional attention. Generally it is used to refer to those processes by which individuals acquire the values and standards of society, taking them on as their own—that is, internalizing them. More recently, developmentalists have begun to realize that socialization also involves learning about relationships, including concepts of the self and of others.

Interest in the socialization of altruism has a relatively short history, beginning in the early 1970s as developmental psychologists became aware of the work of social psychologists on the topic. Certainly altruism appeared to be related to if not synonymous with *morality* (e.g., honesty, resistance to temptation), whose study had a far longer history, from psychoanalytic conceptions through those of social learning and cognitive developmental theory. And so the tendency was to assume that principles established in connection with the study of morality are the same principles that should guide our understanding of how rules and values in the altruistic domain are imparted. The assumption may be incorrect, however, as there appear to be major differences between acts of morality and acts of altruism. Note, for example, that the story of Wilf P. merited a large amount of space on the third page of one of a major city's leading newspapers. It is difficult to imagine that a highly moral man, who never cheated on his income tax, always told the truth, and never engaged in physical or verbal aggression would attract the same kind of media coverage.

Is Altruism Moral?

Kant (1788) talked about perfect and imperfect duties, that is, duties of omission (e.g., not lying, not harming others) and duties of commission (e.g., showing concern for others). Perfect duties, because they require only that the individual not engage in a certain action, can be followed at all times. Imperfect duties, in contrast, cannot always be performed because one must show some selectivity in time, place, and object of commission. Peterson (1982) demonstrates the necessity of selectivity in the performance of imperfect, or altruistic, duties when she points out that the potential altruist must learn that "I should help or give to *deserving* individuals who are in X level of *need,* and are *dependent* on *me* for help, when I can *ascertain and perform* the necessary behavior and when the *cost* or *risk* to me does not exceed Y *amount* of my currently available resources" (p. 202).

The distinction between perfect and imperfect duties is relevant for any discussion of the difference between the socialization of morality—that is, the maintenance of justice, fairness, and equity—and the socialization of altruism, which, of course, upsets what was an equitable relationship by depriving the altruist and improving the situation of the recipient of altruism. It is difficult to argue that morality, or the maintenance of justice, is ever wrong. Those behaviors that are seen to constitute justice may change, but the principle remains immutable. If we behave in an apparently immoral way, we do not admit it but invent elaborate rationales to justify our acts. Even young children function in this fashion (Much & Shweder, 1978). When they are accused of moral wrongdoing, they deny their transgressions, redefine them ("I didn't take the toy, I borrowed it"), or justify them in terms of someone's prior transgression ("He hit me first") rather than making references to situations and circumstances ("I didn't feel like it"; "The teacher wasn't around"). Behaviors in the altruistic domain are different, however, because there is not always the same compulsion in their performance. Altruism, for example, is not always correct and may often be experienced as a mixed blessing by eliciting feelings of failure, inferiority, and dependency in the recipient (Fisher, Nadler, & Whitcher-Alagna, 1982). There are a number of ways in which this can occur. Help may label the recipient as inferior. Because people are socialized to believe that they should be independent and self-reliant, help may be threatening. As well, help may arouse feelings of obligation that are particularly troubling if the helpful act cannot be reciprocated. It can also restrict the recipient's sense of freedom and self-control. Not only does altruism place the altruist in a disadvantaged position then, by costing time, effort, and/or material resources, but any benefits the recipient may acquire can be offset by possible negative outcomes of having had to be the object of aid.

What are the implications of this for the socialization of altruism? First of all, there may be a degree of ambivalence about altruism on the part of agents of socialization that alters their approach from one they

would use when dealing with Kant's perfect duties. And, second, children's perceptions of the authority that socializing agents have to intervene in the area of altruism may lead to resentment when too much
pressure is applied. These are the kinds of issues that remain to be investigated but that also suggest the socialization of altruism may be
more complex than is the socialization of some other domains of behavior. With these complexities in mind, an attempt will be made in this
chapter to consider research that has dealt specifically with the acquisition of societal values in the area of concern for others and to make it
clear when possibly unwarranted inferences may be drawn from the
results of research addressed to other sorts of values and beliefs.

Overview

The chapter begins with a discussion of the first signs of altruism in
young children and then considers socialization experiences that build
on these initial tendencies. Theories of socialization will be dealt with
next. In the final section, the difficult problem of direction of effect
will be addressed, that is, the extent to which children's characteristics
rather than adult interventions determine child outcomes. A concern
with the impact of children on parents leads naturally into a discussion
of children's effects on parental feelings and belief systems and parents'
subsequent responses, a burgeoning area of inquiry. Until we understand why parents behave as they do, we will not have a complete
picture of the socialization process.

THE FOUNDATIONS OF ALTRUISM

Both psychoanalytic and cognitive developmental theory have little
room for early altruism. Empathic distress and concern for others,
according to traditional formulations of cognitive developmental theory, should not be possible until children grow out of the egocentric
mode of functioning in which they can see no point of view other than
their own. Recent observations, however, indicate that even very young
children are capable of understanding the phenomenal world and points
of view of others, of experiencing their distress empathically, and,
therefore, of recognizing that those individuals are in a state of need.
With the addition of helping skills (learned through observation or
direct tuition), they are then able to respond in an altruistic fashion.

Other motivational systems that also function quite early in the course of development may be responsible, as well, for acts of altruism. These systems appear to revolve around the young child's desire for mastery and social interaction. Much of the work on early altruism is from the laboratories of Rheingold at North Carolina and Radke-Yarrow and Zahn-Waxler at the National Institute of Mental Health. Rheingold, Hay, and West (1976) and Rheingold (1982) have observed that children as early as 12 months of age frequently bring the attention of both parents and strangers to objects by pointing at them as well as actually sharing them. They also observed helping in 18- to 30-month-olds in a structured laboratory situation in which mothers were instructed to carry out a series of household jobs such as setting a table, cleaning up magazines and playing cards, folding laundry, sweeping, and making up a bed. More than half the younger children and all the older children helped with most of these tasks. Rheingold and her colleagues note that children appear to enjoy these activities and are not urged or pressured by their parents to engage in them. She suggests that young children are interested in people and their activities, enjoy imitating them, and take pleasure in companionship and the exercise of skills. Agents of socialization can encourage these natural proclivities in a variety of ways that will be discussed below. They may also discourage early attempts at helping others, preferring, for example, to carry out work themselves in a more efficient manner. Indeed, Rheingold reports that parents often tried to do their chores while young children were asleep to avoid interference from their somewhat inexperienced help giving. Slightly older children also are discouraged from sharing and giving even more than they are discouraged from helping. Thus mothers of 4- and 7-year-olds report that children's offers to give and share are accepted less often than are their offers to help. Rejected offers to give and share are often culturally inappropriate as, for example, in the case of a child who tried to give her father money she had received as a birthday gift from her grandmother (Grusec, in press).

As well as being eager to help and share, young children also respond in positive ways to the distress of others, again in a way that suggests independence from external pressure. Zahn-Waxler, Radke-Yarrow, and King (1979) had mothers report all instances of 10- to 29-month-old children's reactions when they were exposed to some kind of distress. Responses of younger children consisted primarily of looking at the person in distress, crying, whimpering, laughing, and smiling. Over time, however, these responses were replaced by increased seeking of the caretaker, increased imitation, and marked attempts at altruistic intervention, with the latter becoming more sophisticated as the children grew older. Sometimes interventions were inappropriate, as in the case of the child who attempted to soothe her mother who was crying because she was peeling onions. But, frequently, they were impressively appropriate. The root of this particular form of concern for others may lie in the child's early capacity to empathize with distress in others, that is, to vicariously experience their emotional state. Helping and comforting is then carried out to reduce the empathic distress. Zahn-Waxler, Radke-Yarrow, and King also suggest that children were imitating the caring acts of others, of which they themselves, as well as others, would be frequent recipients.

The evidence in very young children of an ability to show concern for others has also been documented in Dunn's work with siblings (e.g., Dunn & Munn, 1986).

SOCIALIZATION TECHNIQUES AND THEIR EFFECTS ON ALTRUISTIC BEHAVIOR

Agents of socialization include parents and siblings, peers, teachers, the school, organizers of extracurricular activities, and the media. In some cases, attempts to foster altruism are deliberate; in others, they are the results of experiences that may not be aimed directly at encouraging prosocial proclivities in the child but that are, nevertheless, potent in their effects.

The Consequences of Altruism: Effects of Reward

The literature on the effects of rewards remains relevant to a survey of the socialization of altruism if only because we know that agents of socialization rely to a major extent on some form of reward in dealing with their children's displays of concern for others. Thus Grusec (in press) trained mothers of 4- and 7-year-olds to observe and report incidents of altruistic behavior that they observed in their children in a home setting. Their reports indicated that spontaneous altruism in young children is most frequently (approximately one-quarter of the time) responded to by other people in the child's environment with some form of social reinforcement—acknowledgment, thanks, smiles, hugs, and praise. Altruism is never followed by material reward.

Laboratory studies indicate that contingent rewards increase the incidence of prosocial behavior (e.g., Azrin & Lindsley, 1956; Gelfand, Hartmann, Cromer, Smith, & Page, 1975). There is a problem, however, when one takes internalization as a central focus of concern. Given that the long-term goals of socialization involve encouraging the child to engage in an act for its own sake, it is difficult to argue that behavior motivated by anticipation of positive consequences can be considered truly altruistic. Does this mean then that parents who respond to their children's prosocial behavior with social approval will be unsuccessful in promoting altruism? This may not, in fact, be the case. Thus Smith, Gelfand, Hartmann, and Partlow (1979) reported that children who received social approval for sharing in a laboratory task were likely to attribute their behavior to internal motives—a desire to help or concern for the welfare of the needy child with whom they had shared. Those who had received material reward attributed their prosocial behavior to an external motive—desire for the reward. This finding certainly suggests that agents of socialization who rely heavily on social rewards and eschew the use of material rewards may, in fact, be acting in an appropriate way if their goal is the internalization of altruistic tendencies.

The undermining effects of material reward have recently been demonstrated in a study by Fabes, Fultz, Eisenberg, May-Plumlee, and Christopher (1989). Fabes and associates first identified two groups of children—those whose mothers reported that they valued the use of rewards in childrearing and those who reported they did not. Children were assigned to these groups on the basis of their mothers' agreement with such statements as these: "The use of rewards to motivate children can be considered a type of bribery" and "The use of rewards to motivate children can help produce desired behavior," as well as their reports of how frequently they administered rewards. The Fabes group then had the children in both groups sort pieces of paper to be taken to the hospital for sick children to play with. Half of those in each group received a material reward for their sorting, and half did not. Subsequently, all children were asked to sort in the experimenter's absence and without the expectation of reward. Children who had been rewarded by the experimenter for helping and whose mothers valued and frequently used rewards subsequently helped less than children in the other three conditions. Thus rewards appeared to undermine helping, but primarily in children who had a past history of expecting them for good behavior. Mothers who valued and used rewards also reported that their children were less likely to be spontaneously prosocial and less likely to comply with requests for helping, sharing, and so on from another child.

If one assumes that these mothers were thinking of the use of material rewards in their responses to the investigators about their child-rearing styles, then an obvious conclusion is that reliance on such an approach to child rearing undermines intrinsic motivation for prosocial acts. Other explanations for these findings cannot be ruled out, of course. It may be, for example, that mothers who make extensive use of rewards across all domains of child rearing have a more "pay for work" approach to social interactions, valuing altruism and self-sacrifice less and, therefore, being less likely to value it in their children. Whatever the explanations, we can conclude that parental emphasis on rewards for good behavior is coupled with a reduction of children's spontaneous altruism.

Character attribution. Character attribution, or dispositional praise, is a variant of reinforcement that appears particularly effective in promoting internalization of altruism. Rather than rewarding a child for a particular act, the agent of socialization instead refers to some personality characteristic of the child as having been responsible for the positive outcome. For example, children who were told that they donated winnings from a game because they were kind and helpful people (character attribution) subsequently donated more when alone and unobserved than those who were told they shared because they were expected to (Grusec, Kuczynski, Rushton, & Simutis, 1979). Grusec and Redler (1980) also found that 8-year-olds (but not 5-year-olds) who were told they had shared because they were kind and helpful people performed better on a number of tests of generalized altruism than did 8-year-olds who were socially reinforced for their sharing by being told that they had done a kind and helpful thing. Thus character attributions seem to be more powerful in their effects than social reinforcement.

Character attributions have to be believable to be effective. Telling a child who has great difficulty with schoolwork that she is really very bright, or suggesting to a miser that he is generous, is unlikely to promote much behavior change. Grusec, Kuczynski, Rushton, and Simutis found an effect of character attribution only when children had originally shared in response to observing a model. When the initial sharing was a result of instruction from the experimenter, character attributions were no different in their effect from attributions to external causes—the experimenter's expectation that they would share. We suggested that children who imitate the altruistic behavior of a model may be less sure why they have behaved as they have than those who donate because they have been told to. In the former case then, character attributions would have a greater effect on their behavior than in the latter.

How do character attributions function? Recent attempts to answer this question (Mills & Grusec, 1989) are only suggestive. Relative to social reinforcement, dispositional attributions appear to enhance self-perceptions of concern for others in boys (but not girls) as well as producing more positive affect in both boys and girls. In certain cases, then, character attributions change a child's self-concept, a situation that could promote altruism as the child begins to behave in accord with that self-concept. We also know that increased positive affect is associated with greater sharing in children (e.g., Barnett, Howard, Melton, & Dino, 1982; Moore, Underwood, & Rosenhan, 1973) so that this particular outcome of the attribution of positive characteristics to the child may also be implicated in an understanding of how prosocial attributions work. It is interesting that self-characterization changes would seem capable of influencing altruism over the long term; mood changes may have only short-term implications for the child's behavior. Unfortunately, Mills and Grusec did not find specific relationships between increased prosocial self-perception, heightened positive affect, and actual sharing behavior. Thus our knowledge about the mechanisms underlying character attributions is still quite limited.

The Consequences for Not Being Altruistic: Effects of Punishment and Reasoning

Now we take up the topic of discipline techniques, or what happens when children fail to behave prosocially. A particularly influential position in this area has been put forward by Hoffman, who proposes that parents who rely on power-assertive discipline techniques (e.g., physical punishment, loss of privileges) will be less likely to produce moral (including altruistic) children than those who reason and, in particular, use a form of reasoning that emphasizes to the child the effect of his or her actions on others (i.e., other-oriented induction). Hoffman (1970a) suggests that power assertion is detrimental to the socialization process because it arouses anger, hostility, and reactance in the recipient. Induction, on the other hand, develops the child's empathic capacities, which are important for understanding, and thereby for being able to respond appropriately to, the plight of others. It also produces guilt about harm to others, which cannot be escaped, unlike external threats of punishment, which lose their motivational effectiveness when the source of threat is removed. Finally, it provides an optimal level of arousal over fear of parental disapproval and can suggest a possible means of reparation for deviant acts as well as providing information about proper behavior that might facilitate accurate generalization to new situations. In Hoffman's analysis, punishment by love withdrawal falls midway in effectiveness between these two others. It arouses nonoptimal levels of anxiety over parental disapproval and so inhibits learning, although it does not produce the hostility and reactance of power assertion.

In trying to establish how disciplinary styles relate to altruism, investigators typically have asked mothers how they would respond to a variety of misdeeds such as their child talking back, disobeying, accidentally damaging something of value, doing poorly at school, destroying a friend's possession with provocation, making fun of another child, and asking why a crippled man walks in a funny way (e.g., Dlugokinski & Firestone, 1974; Hoffman, 1975). Note that, in this procedure, none of the misdemeanors involves a failure to be altruistic, the assumption being that whatever is learned in *any* discipline situation will have implications for *all* categories of behavior, including altruism. The results of the research have been far from conclusive. Among variables apparently mediating the effects of discipline techniques are age and sex of child, sex of parent, child's previous experience with power assertion and induction, and the context of warmth and nurturance in which the discipline technique is used. Thus, after reviewing the relevant research, Radke-Yarrow, Zahn-Waxler, and Chapman (1983) conclude that when power assertion is linked negatively with children's prosocial behaviors it is likely to be administered by parents who are unaccepting of the child and who have authoritarian attitudes to child rearing. Power assertion used by parents who have positive attitudes toward their children and who are responsive to them is much more effective. In other words, strong control, or power assertion, is detrimental when paired with coldness and rejection but not when paired with warmth and affection.

Radke-Yarrow, Zahn-Waxler, and Chapman suggest that the effects of induction are similarly modified by the rearing context in which they occur. In particular, they point to the affective context of reasoning. Thus mothers who respond to toddlers' misdeeds with "dramatic enactments of distress," that is, reasoning delivered in an affectively strong way, are more likely to have altruistic children (Zahn-Waxler, Radke-Yarrow, & King, 1979). As well as the context in which it is delivered, the content and form of reasoning appear to have a differential impact on outcome. The more parents use reasoning that refers to and shows concern for the victim's feelings, the higher their children are rated on indices of moral development (Hoffman & Saltzstein, 1967). And empathic messages ("children will be happy and excited if you share with them") are more likely to produce sharing in third- and fourth-graders in the absence of an observer than are normative ones ("it's good to share"; Eisenberg-Berg & Geisheker, 1979).

Do different forms of discipline have the same effect regardless of domain of misbehavior? In their studies of discipline techniques, investigators tend to have made two assumptions. One is that although parents may show some variation in how they discipline, they can be categorized as leaning more strongly toward one or another particular mode of discipline intervention. The other assumption is that discipline effectiveness is unrelated to the particular misdeed with which it is associated. With respect to the first assumption, we know, in fact, that parents do *not* react in the same way to all misdeeds. Rather, they appear to tailor their discipline to the specific nature of the misdeed (Grusec & Kuczynski, 1980; Hoffman, 1970b; Zahn-Waxler & Chapman, 1982). Indeed, failures of altruism, for example, are *never* followed by power assertion (Grusec, 1989; Grusec, Dix, & Mills, 1982).

That mothers relate their discipline to the child's misdeed suggests that the second assumption—discipline effectiveness is unrelated to the particular misdeed with which it is associated—*may* also be wrong. A rapidly growing literature in developmental social cognition, for example, suggests that children from a very early age differentiate between various domains of social behavior such as moral deeds—concern for the welfare and rights of others, social conventions—rules designed to ensure fluid social interaction and maintain social order (such as forms of address, styles of attire) and personal issues—events that pertain only to the actor and are, therefore, viewed as beyond societal regulation. Thus they differentially react to and reason about transgressions in these areas. Moreover, they have different feelings about the appropriateness of parental rule making in the various domains (Smetana, 1988), seeing it as most appropriate in the moral domain and quite inappropriate in the domain of personal issues. It is not unlikely that reactions to discipline could be determined in part, at least, by how acceptable parental intervention and rule making were perceived to be as well as the extent to which parental reasoning accorded with the child's own reasoning in the area. If parental rule making is deemed less appropriate, for example, for some misdemeanors than for others, then one might expect that the amount of power assertion imposed by parents would be differentially accepted and responded to. And if the kind of reasoning employed by parents to attempt to convince a child to comply with their wishes were foreign to the kind of reasoning the child used, then it might be less convincing.

In our laboratory, we have recently considered children's perceptions of discipline and rule making and their evaluations of the fairness of punishment with respect to morality and altruism (Grusec & Pedersen, 1989). We found that children view rules as more necessary in the moral domain (defined by failures to suppress antisocial acts such as stealing and damaging someone else's property) than in the altruistic domain and that they see punishment as fairer in the former than the latter case. We have suggested, therefore, that, because punishment for failures of altruism is seen as less acceptable than punishment for moral misdeeds, it might be less likely to lead to long-term internalization of concern for others because it would be more likely to arouse anger and reactance to parental wishes. Children also reason differently about why people should behave morally and why they should behave altruistically, with concern for others and stereotyped reasoning predominating in the latter case and authority-related reasoning and reference to internalized rules predominating in the former. From this it would follow that talking about authority and internalized norms should be less conducive to the internalization of concern for others than would reference to other people's feelings and needs. And, as noted above, there is evidence that this is indeed the case (Eisenberg-Berg and Geisheker, 1979).

Modeling and Internal Working Models of Attachment Figures and the Self

The beneficial and long-lasting effects of the modeling of altruism have been demonstrated in many laboratory studies (see Grusec, 1982, for a review). Studies of behavior in naturalistic settings also suggest how potent modeling can be. Rosenhan (1969), for example, found that the parents of civil rights workers who were fully committed to the cause had strong altruistic values that they put into practice, were nurturant and warm with their children, and involved their children in actual altruistic behavior. The negative effects of modeling are demonstrated in work with abusive mothers and their children. Abusive mothers express more anger and annoyance and less sympathy in response to videotapes of crying children than do nonabusive mothers (Frodi & Lamb, 1980). A striking parallel is found in the behavior of abused children. Main and George (1985) report that, while a matched control group of 1- to 3-year-old children responded to one-third of the distress incidents they observed in their day-care setting with concern, empathy, or sadness, not a single abused child reacted in this way. Although the abused children looked at and engaged in mechanical comforting movements in response to distress in their peers, there was no evidence of concerned arousal; in fact, they responded with threats, anger, and actual physical attack.

Although the results of modeling studies generally have been explained by social learning theory principles, the work of attachment theorists provides a new and potentially useful way of conceptualizing the internalization of parental behaviors. According to attachment theory (Ainsworth, Blehar, Waters, & Wall, 1978; Bowlby, 1969), the child, through interactions with other people, constructs increasingly complex internal working models of those other people as well as of the self. Securely attached children, whose mothers are sensitive, responsive, and accepting, will see others in the world as trustworthy and reliable and themselves as worthy of care and concern. Insecurely attached children, who have insensitive and rejecting mothers, will develop a model of others as unloving and the self as unworthy. Thus individuals internalize both sides of a relationship (Sroufe & Fleeson, 1985). Children who trust the parent to provide emotional support will learn the parental role and be able to perform it at later, appropriate times. And centrally involved in the parental role of the securely attached child is concern, responsivity, and care for others.

From attachment theory it follows that securely attached children ought to be more altruistic, that is, caring and concerned, than insecurely attached children because they have internalized this aspect of the parental role. The data base here is not extensive, but it is suggestive. Sroufe (1983) reports that secure attachment at 12 months of age predicts a nursery school child's empathy as measured by teachers'

Q-sort descriptions. Main and Weston (1981) report that securely attached 12-month-olds were more likely to respond to the social overtures of an adult dressed as a clown, as well as showing greater distress when he cried, than were insecurely attached children.

One notable feature of attachment theory is its ability to predict stability of behavior in a way that other theories of socialization cannot. Because working models of relationships, once organized, tend to operate outside conscious awareness, they are relatively resistant to change, and so behavior is maintained even when external circumstances have undergone some degree of modification. It is a compelling feature of this theoretical approach that it is able to predict and explain continuities in behavior over time in a way that other approaches to social and personality development cannot.

THEORIES OF SOCIALIZATION

To the extent that modeling, reasoning, social reinforcement, and other techniques of socialization are effective in promoting altruism, how do they work? Hoffman's suggestions and those of attachment theory have already been presented. Two other approaches that have guided the efforts of researchers are those of social learning and attribution theories. According to the former, altruistic behaviors should be strengthened by positive and negative response consequences as well as the observation of altruistic models. Rather than use the term "internalization," however, the social learning approach talks about *self-regulation,* a designation that makes the distinction between internal and external causes of behavior less sharp.

In attributional analyses (e.g., Grusec, 1983; Lepper, 1983; Walters & Grusec, 1977), the conditions for internalization of standards are seen to be more propitious when external pressures are minimized. Thus blatant forms of reinforcement or punishment should make it too easy for children to attribute the source of their prosocial behavior to external pressures, while more subtle influence techniques such as social reinforcement, rebuke, reasoning, and modeling would render attributions to internal dispositions more likely. Lepper (1983) argues that the techniques of social control most likely to promote subsequent internalization are those that are successful in producing compliance but are, at the same time, sufficiently subtle that the individual is prevented from viewing his or her compliance solely as a function of those extrinsic controls. He refers to this as the "minimal sufficiency principle" of social control. Lepper's thesis is, of course, a relative one. If only strong power assertion can gain compliance, then that is the discipline intervention that must be favored.

Grusec and Dix (1986) also have argued that agents of socialization can affect internalization by the way in which they interpret their children's behavior for them, rather than simply leaving the interpretation up to the children themselves. Even if considerable pressure is needed to induce compliance, the salience of this pressure can be reduced by parental interpretation. Thus a parent who accompanies punishment for a misdeed with compelling (to the child) reasons why that misdeed is socially unacceptable may succeed in masking to some extent the coerciveness of the punishment, thereby promoting internal attributions. Indeed, the data do suggest that successful parents are, in fact, those who combine firm control with power assertion (Baumrind, 1971; Hoffman, 1970b).

Several sets of data support an attributional analysis of altruism. Smith, Gelfand, Hartmann, and Partlow (1979) note that children are more inclined to make internal attributions after social reward and punishment than after material reward and punishment. Dix and Grusec (1983) asked children to make attributions about the altruistic behavior of a child in a series of vignettes in which helping was either spontaneous, resulted from imitation of a model, or was done in response to threats of punishment. Children made external attributions in the latter case, attributing helpful behavior to a desire to please the threatening adult. In the case of spontaneous acts and those carried out after exposure to a model, their attributions were more internal. The work of Grusec, Kuczynski, Rushton, & Simutis (1979) and Grusec and Redler (1980) is, of course, also highly relevant to the attributional argument; the fact that children's altruistic behavior can be increased by labeling them as kind and helpful people suggests that socializing agents can assist their charges in making internal attributions.

Dix and Grusec also report that reasoning paired with punishment was more likely to lead to dispositional attributions than punishment alone for girls, but not boys. Reasoning *alone,* however, led girls (but not boys) to make more external attributions for the protagonist's helpful behavior than in the case of spontaneous helping. It would appear that even reasoning conveys a parental preference for prosocial behavior. Indeed, Henry (1980) has argued that all moral reasoning may be considered authoritarian because it requires the acceptance of moral absolutes that are logically insupportable. Although one might argue that some moral absolutes are more logically supportable than others (see Turiel, 1983, for example), helpfulness and sacrifice may not be among the most compelling moral absolutes, for reasons already discussed.

Although attribution theory seems to provide a useful theoretical framework for understanding the internalization of altruism, Perry and Perry (1983) cite some studies that they believe pose problems for the position, and they offer a modified version. Essentially, the studies that concern them are some in which fairly strong interventions have been necessary to achieve the desired outcome—an experimenter's direct instruction or command or a mother's strong enactments of distress after her child's deviation (Grusec, Kuczynski, Rushton, & Simutis, 1979; Israel & Brown, 1979; Zahn-Waxler, Radke-Yarrow, & King, 1979). Perry and Perry suggest that, at an early age for their child, parents must establish strong habits of concern for others, even if they have to employ obvious external coercion. A similar point is made by Staub (1979) when he argues for the importance of actually performing altruistic acts in strengthening altruistic predispositions. Perry and Perry propose that, once children have been compelled to behave prosocially, they may appear to act as though they have internalized the behavior (for example, by behaving prosocially in the apparent absence of surveillance) but only because they are never sure that their failures to act in accord with the wishes of a socializing agent will go undetected. By the time they are old enough to be reasonably sophisticated about the probability of detection, their habits are so well established that they must now explain them in ways other than those involving fear of punishment. Therefore, they now have no recourse other than to attribute good behavior to internal causes. Even young children must not be dealt with too intrusively, however, because their perceived self-efficacy in the domain of self-regulation (Bandura, 1981) can be undermined if they see acts as the results of continuous intervention by agents of socialization rather than as flowing from their own skills.

Perry and Perry provide, then, a specific developmental approach that is missing from social learning and attributional approaches to socialization. Certainly developmental questions and issues need to form a larger part of attempts to understand socialization effectiveness. For example, there may be developmental changes in the meaning of intervention procedures, with young children perceiving the same intervention quite differently from older children. What may seem a strongly coercive approach to a 12-year-old could be seen as much less so by a 4-year-old. We know very little about developmental changes in children's perceptions of discipline (although we do know something about their changing perceptions of the rights of parents to make rules about behavior in different social domains (e.g., Smetana, 1988). Any theory of socialization must take these into account.

DIRECTION OF EFFECT

For a long time psychologists, guided by psychoanalytic and social learning theory, focused on the parent's effect on the child as central to an understanding of child development. Some 20 years ago, Bell (1968) took formal exception to this position, arguing instead that the child was instrumental in guiding parental interventions. Among other things, he suggested that congenital temperamental differences in children affect their reaction to parent discipline and that parents adjust their behavior accordingly.

Although socialization researchers now are careful to note that the correlations they uncover between parent child-rearing characteristics and child outcomes may be interpreted in a variety of ways, including the possibility that it is the characteristics of the child that have determined the parent's practices, they are, by and large, reluctant to entertain the possibility seriously. This is hardly surprising, given the interest on the part of many researchers in modifying parent behavior to improve child outcomes. Yet Bell's arguments are, given our current state of knowledge, difficult to counter decisively. Certainly we know from experimental studies of the socialization of altruism that children's prosocial behavior can be modified by the actions of others. But Bell and his colleagues also have shown, specifically with respect to altruism, that characteristics of children determine both their altruistic tendencies and the child-rearing techniques employed by agents of socialization. Thus preschool children who are high in person orientation or social adaptability (approach people easily, are adaptable in new situations, have a positive mood) are rated as more helpful at home by their mothers (Stanhope, Bell, & Parker-Cohen, 1987). And Keller and Bell (1979) have demonstrated that the techniques used by socializing agents are affected by characteristics of the child with whom they are dealing. In their study, female undergraduates were instructed to try to get young children to do something helpful for another child. In some cases, the object of their persuasion had been trained to be high in person orientation, attending to the adult's face and answering questions promptly. In other cases, the child was trained to be low in person orientation, looking chiefly at toys and objects in the experimental room and delaying answers to the adult's questions. The persuasive techniques of the undergraduates were accordingly modified, with more reasoning about the consequences of acts for the other child when the child was high in person orientation and more use of bargaining with material rewards in the case of a child low in person orientation.

As researchers do more longitudinal studies in which they can begin to trace pathways and relationships of development, and as correlational findings are supplemented by experimental interventions, we shall begin to sort out some of the issues concerning direction of effect.

PARENTING BELIEF SYSTEMS

A growing recognition of the bidirectionality of effect involved in socialization has oriented developmental psychologists to a greater focus on the parent in that process and to a realization that parents are responsive organisms worthy of study in their own right (Goodnow & Collins, in press; Sigel, 1985). And, in an era in which increasing attention is being paid to the interaction between thinking, affect, and behavior, this new approach has concerned itself with the interrelationships of these three aspects of parent functioning and their ultimate effect on the child's behavior.

There is a difference between the current interest in the relationship between parent cognition and child outcomes and an older interest in parental attitudes as they are related to parental behavior and child outcomes. More traditional approaches concerned themselves with parenting beliefs or styles such as restrictiveness versus permissiveness or warmth versus rejection in child rearing, and it related these general attitudes to certain classes of child behavior. The new approach deals with specific ideas, values, cognitions, and expectations that a child's behavior elicits in a parent and that then lead to certain parental actions. Included among these ideas, values, and so on are the goals parents set for their children and the hopes they have for them, what they want from their children (e.g., status, an expression of themselves, economic help), their notions about the basic nature of children (and, therefore, of how much direction and control they need), their ideas about developmental timetables, and the causal attributions they make for their children's behavior. It is in these differing ideas, as well as their possible effect on emotion, that we can come to understand why parents socialize in the way they do. Moreover, one way of changing the ineffective socialization approaches adopted by some parents is to change their belief systems. Several areas of parenting belief have been addressed; two will be discussed here.

Causal Attributions

Dix and Grusec (1985) have applied attribution theory to an understanding of parent belief systems and their relationship to parental discipline. They suggest that the appraisals parents make of the specific causes of a child's actions will have an impact on their discipline interventions. If parents hold their child responsible for specific antisocial acts, believing that the child caused negative effects that were both foreseen and intended, they will be more likely to punish the behavior than if they believe it was unintentional. This is because, in our legal and ethical system, we believe that punishment is appropriate only when wrongdoers are responsible for their acts and because the belief that an act was intentionally carried out leads to feelings of anger and an accompanying state of arousal that produces a more power-assertive intervention. If, however, a parent believes a child lacks the knowledge that his or her actions will produce negative outcomes, and, therefore, the performance of harm has not been intentional, then reasoning and explanation are more likely to be employed. In this case, the parent is less upset, and so less aroused, and also believes that explanation and reasoning are more effective ways of imparting knowledge than is punishment. Clearly, parents who tend to make dispositional attributions when situational ones are more appropriate will be less effective in their approach to socialization.

In a test of the Dix and Grusec predictions (Dix, Ruble, Grusec, & Nixon, 1986), parents read short descriptions of children's misdeeds—moral transgressions and failures of altruism—and answered a series of questions relating to their beliefs and affect. Dix, Ruble, Grusec, and Nixon report that mothers and fathers, as children grow older (and presumably become more knowledgeable about what is appropriate and inappropriate behavior), believe that their actions are increasingly caused by personality dispositions, are increasingly intentional, and are increasingly under the child's control. In support of hypotheses concerning the relationship between attributions, affect, and outcome, parents' affective reactions to their children's misconduct were related to their assessments of its cause, with increasing perceptions of dispositional attribution correlated with increasing anger, and affect positively related to ratings of the importance of responding to the misdeed. In a later study, Dix, Ruble, and Zambarano (1989) also demonstrated that the more mothers believed that children knew a misdeed was wrong, and the more responsibility they attributed to their children for the negative outcomes of that misdeed, the more upset they reported being, the more sternness and disapproval they said they would express and the longer they thought the child should be punished.

Dix, Ruble, Grusec, and Nixon (1986) were also able to make comparisons between parental reactions to moral transgressions and failures of altruism. Clearly, if the former are perceived to be more frequently dispositionally caused than the latter, this would be one possible explanation for the greater use by parents of power assertion with moral transgressions. The findings were just the opposite, however. Although the relationships between age, dispositional attributions, affect, and ratings of importance of responding were in the same direction for both types of misdeed, failures of altruism overall were seen to be *more* intentional, *more* under the child's control, and *more* dispositionally caused than moral transgressions overall. Even so, parents were more upset by and felt it more important to respond to moral transgressions than to failures of altruism. Clearly, other factors are at work in determining their responses to failures of altruism including, perhaps, some ambivalence about demanding that their children be altruistic at all times.

Expectations About Parenting Efficacy

Bugental (Bugental, 1989; Bugental, Mantyla, & Lewis, 1989) identified two groups of mothers—those who believe they are able to control their children's behavior and those who believe the control resides in the child and that they themselves have little impact. She has shown how children who are difficult to deal with are adversely affected by agents of socialization with low efficacy expectations and thus how the characteristics of the child can interact with the abilities of the parent. When placed with unresponsive children who are not their own and about whom they, therefore, have no preconceived expectations based on actual experience, Bugental finds a distinctive patterning of behavior. Mothers who perceive they have little control over child behavior display a condescending and unconvincing pattern of positive affect marked by inappropriate voice level, smiles without eye involvement, smiles accompanied by eyebrow flashes or a worried brow or frown, tilting of the head to one side, and bringing the head into a lower and closer position than normal. This is a pattern that serves to maintain lack of responsiveness on the part of the child as well as noncompliance because, Bugental suggests, it sends messages that are difficult for the child to decode and so promotes slow responding to and avoidance of the agent of socialization. These mothers also, according to Bugental, are more likely to retrieve problem-focused thoughts such as "Is she doing this on purpose?" as opposed to thoughts such as "Maybe he needs reassurance."

In contrast to mothers with low control attributions, those with high control attributions are able to make unresponsive children more responsive by their more appropriate socializing behavior. And children who are responsive to begin with do not elicit maladaptive behavior even from mothers who have detrimental cognitions about their abilities.

CONCLUSION

Many topics of research investigation wax and wane in popularity. Altruism, however, is one that seems to have elicited a steady interest among psychologists. Probably this is because it has to do with characteristics of behavior that, on the whole, we find extraordinarily laudable and that, at the same time, we find mysterious. This review has presented one researcher's impression of fruitful directions in which solutions to the mystery will be found. These directions include an assessment of the context in which learning about altruism takes place, a concern with the direct effect of early relationships with important figures in the child's environment on subsequent caring for others, an awareness of the way in which altruism is perceived by children and how this affects their reactions to intervention, a concern with developmental changes in perceptions of socialization interventions, and, finally, a focus on the characteristics of socializing agents and the determinants of their behavior.

REFERENCES

Ainsworth, M. D. S., Blehar, M. C., Waters, E., & Wall, S. (1978). *Patterns of attachment: A psychological study of the strange situation.* Hillsdale, NJ: Lawrence Erlbaum.

Azrin, N., & Lindsley, O. (1956). The reinforcement of cooperation between children. *Journal of Abnormal and Social Psychology, 52,* 100-102.

Bandura, A. (1981). Self-referent thought: A developmental analysis of self-efficacy. In J. H. Flavell & L. D. Ross (Eds.), *Social cognitive development: Frontiers and possible futures.* Cambridge: Cambridge University Press.

Barnett, M. A., Howard, J. A., Melton, E. M., & Dino, G. A. (1982). Effect of inducing sadness about self or other on helping behavior in high- and low-empathic children. *Child Development, 53,* 920-923.

Baumrind, D. (1971). Current patterns of parental authority. *Developmental Psychology Monographs, 4*(1, Pt. 2).

Bell, R. Q. (1968). A reinterpretation of the direction of effects in studies of socialization. *Psychological Review, 75,* 81-95.

Bowlby, J. (1969). *Attachment and loss: Vol. 1. Attachment.* New York: Basic Books.

Bugental, D. (1989). *Caregiver conditions as moderators of affect in abusive families.* Paper presented at the biennial meeting of the Society for Research in Child Development, Kansas City.

Bugental, D. B., Mantyla, S. M., & Lewis, J. (1989). Parental attributions as moderators of affective communication to children at risk for physical abuse. In D. Cicchetti & V. Carlson (Eds.), *Current research and theoretical advances in child maltreatment.* New York: Cambridge University Press.

Dix, T., & Grusec, J. E. (1983). Parental influence techniques: An attributional analysis. *Child Development, 54,* 645-652.

Dix, T. H., & Grusec, J. E. (1985). Parent attribution processes in child socialization. In I. Sigel (Ed.), *Parent belief systems: Their psychological consequences for children* (pp. 201-233). Hillsdale, NJ: Lawrence Erlbaum.

Dix, T., Ruble, D. N., Grusec, J. E., & Nixon, S. (1986). Social cognition in parents: Inferential and affective reactions to children of three age levels. *Child Development, 57,* 879-894.

Dix, T., Ruble, D., and Zambarano, R. J. (1989). Mothers' implicit theories of discipline. Child effects, parent effects, and the attribution process. *Child Development, 60,* 1373-1391.

Dlugokinski, E. L., & Firestone, I. J. (1974). Other centeredness and susceptibility to charitable appeals: Effects of perceived discipline. *Developmental Psychology, 10,* 21-28.

Dunn, J., & Munn, P. (1986). Sibling and prosocial development. *International Journal of Behavioural Development, 9,* 265-284.

Eisenberg-Berg, N., & Geisheker, E. (1979). Content of preachings and power of the model/preacher: The effects on children's generosity. *Developmental Psychology, 15,* 168-175.

Fabes, R. A., Fultz, J., Eisenberg, N., May-Plumlee, T., & Christopher, F. S. (1989). Effects of rewards on children's prosocial motivation: A socialization study. *Developmental Psychology, 25,* 509-515.

Fisher, J. F., Nadler, A., & Whitcher-Alagna, S. (1982). Recipient reactions to aid. *Psychological Bulletin, 91,* 27-54.

Frodi, A. M., & Lamb, M. E. (1980). Child abusers' responses to infant smiles and cries. *Child Development, 51,* 238-241.

Gelfand, D., Hartmann, D. P., Cromer, C. C., Smith, C. L., & Page, B. C. (1975). The effects of instructional prompts and praise on children's donation rates. *Child Development, 46,* 980-983.

Goodnow, J. J., & Collins, A. W. (in press). *Development according to parents: The nature, sources, and consequences of parents' ideas.* East Sussex, U.K.: Lawrence Erlbaum.

Grusec, J. E. (1982). Socialization processes and the development of altruism. In J. P. Rushton & R. M. Sorrentino (Eds.), *Altruism and helping behavior.* Hillsdale, NJ: Lawrence Erlbaum.

Grusec, J. E. (1983). The internalization of altruistic dispositions: A cognitive analysis. In E. T. Higgins, D. N. Ruble, & W. W. Hartup (Eds.), *Social cognition and social development* (pp. 275-293). New York: Cambridge University Press.

Grusec, J. E. (in press). Socialization of concern for others in the home. *Developmental Psychology.*

Grusec, J. E., & Dix, T. (1986). The socialization of prosocial behavior: Theory and reality. In C. Zahn-Waxler, E. M. Cummings, & R. Iannotti (Eds.), *Altruism and aggression: Biological and social origins* (pp. 218-237). New York: Cambridge University Press.

Grusec, J. E., Dix, T., & Mills, R. (1982). The effects of type, severity and victim of children's transgressions on maternal discipline. *Canadian Journal of Behavioural Science, 14,* 276-289.

Grusec, J. E., & Kuczynski, L. (1980). Direction of effect in socialization: A comparison of the parent vs. the child's behavior as determinants of disciplinary techniques. *Developmental Psychology, 16,* 1-9.

Grusec, J. E., Kuczynski, L., Rushton, J. P., & Simutis, Z. M. (1979). Modeling, direct instruction, and attributions: Effects on altruism. *Developmental Psychology, 14,* 51-57.

Grusec, J. E., & Pedersen, J. (1989). *Children's thinking about prosocial and moral behavior.* Unpublished manuscript, University of Toronto.

Grusec, J. E., & Redler, E. (1980). Attribution, reinforcement, and altruism: A developmental analysis. *Developmental Psychology, 16,* 525-534.

Henry, R. M. (1980). A theoretical and empirical analysis of "reasoning" in the socialization of young children. *Human Development, 23,* 105-125.

Hoffman, M. L. (1970a). Moral development. In P. H. Mussen (Ed.), *Carmichael's manual of child psychology* (Vol. 2, pp. 261-360). New York: John Wiley.

Hoffman, M. L. (1970b). Conscience, personality, and socialization techniques. *Human Development, 13,* 90-126.

Hoffman, M. L. (1975). Altruistic behavior and the parent-child relationship. *Journal of Personality and Social Psychology, 31,* 937-943.

Hoffman, M. L., & Saltzstein, H. D. (1967). Parent discipline and the child's moral development. *Journal of Personality and Social Psychology, 5,* 45-57.

Israel, A. C., & Brown, M. S. (1979). Effects of directiveness of instructions and surveillance on the production and persistence of children's donations. *Journal of Experimental Child Psychology, 27,* 250-261.

Kant, I. (1788/1956). *Critique of practical reason.* New York: Macmillan.

Keller, B. B., & Bell, R. Q. (1979). Child effects on adult's method of eliciting altruistic behavior. *Child Development, 50,* 1004-1009.

Lepper, M. (1983). Social control processes, attributions of motivation, and the internalization of social values. In E. T. Higgins, D. N. Ruble, & W. W. Hartup (Eds.), *Social cognition and social development: A sociocultural perspective* (pp. 294-330). New York: Cambridge University Press.

Main, M., & George, C. (1985). Responses of abused and disadvantaged toddlers to distress in agemates: A study in the day care setting. *Developmental Psychology, 21,* 407-412.

Main, M., & Weston, D. R. (1981). The quality of the toddler's relationship to mother and to father: Related to conflict behavior and the readiness to establish new relationships. *Child Development, 52,* 932-940.

Mills, R. S. L., & Grusec, J. E. (1989). Cognitive, affective, and behavioral consequences of praising altruism. *Merrill-Palmer Quarterly, 35,* 299-326.

Moore, B. S., Underwood, B., & Rosenhan, D. (1973). Affect and altruism. *Developmental Psychology, 8,* 99-104.

Much, N., & Shweder, R. (1978). Speaking of rules: The analysis of culture in breach. In W. Damon (Ed.), *New directions for child development: Vol. 2. Moral development.* San Francisco: Jossey-Bass.

Perry, D. G., & Perry, L. C. (1983). Social learning, causal attribution, and moral internalization. In J. Bisanz, G. L. Bisanz, & R. Kail (Eds.), *Learning in children: Progress in cognitive development research* (pp. 105-136). New York: Springer-Verlag.

Peterson, L. (1982). Altruism and the development of internal control: An integrative model. *Merrill-Palmer Quarterly, 28,* 197-222.

Radke-Yarrow, M., Zahn-Waxler, C., & Chapman, M. (1983). Children's prosocial dispositions and behavior. In E. M. Hetherington (Ed.), *Handbook of child psychology: Vol. 4. Socialization, personality and social development* (pp. 469-546). New York: Harper & Row.

Rheingold, H. L. (1982). Little children's participation in the work of adults, a nascent prosocial behavior. *Child Development, 53,* 114-125.

Rheingold, H. L., Hay, D. F., & West, M. J. (1976). Sharing in the second year of life. *Child Development, 47,* 1148-1158.

Rosenhan, D. (1969). Some origins of concern for others. In P. H. Mussen, J. Langer, & M. Covington (Eds.), *Trends and issues in developmental psychology.* New York: Holt, Rinehart & Winston.

Sigel, I. (Ed.). (1985). *Parent belief systems: Their psychological consequences for children.* Hillsdale, NJ: Lawrence Erlbaum.

Smetana, J. G. (1988). Concepts of self and social convention: Adolescents' and parents' reasoning about hypothetical and actual family conflicts. In M. R. Gunnar (Ed.), *Minnesota symposium on child psychology* (Vol. 21, pp. 79-122). Hillsdale, NJ: Lawrence Erlbaum.

Smith, C. L., Gelfand, D. M., Hartmann, D. P., & Partlow, M. E. P. (1979). Children's causal attributions regarding help giving. *Child Development, 50,* 203-210.

Sroufe, L. A. (1983). Infant-caregiver attachment and patterns of adaptation in preschool: The roots of maladaptation and competence. In M. Perlmutter (Ed.), *Minnesota symposium on child psychology* (Vol. 16, pp. 41-81). Hillsdale, NJ: Lawrence Erlbaum.

Sroufe, L. A., & Fleeson, J. (1985). Attachment and the construction of relationships. In W. Hartup & Z. Rubin (Eds.), *The nature and development of relationships* (pp. 51-71). Hillsdale, NJ: Lawrence Erlbaum.

Stanhope, L., Bell, R. Q., & Parker-Cohen, N. Y. (1987). Temperament and helping behavior in preschoolers. *Developmental Psychology, 23,* 347-353.

Staub, E. (1979). *Positive prosocial behavior and morality.* New York: Academic Press.

Turiel, E. (1983). *The development of social knowledge: Morality and convention.* Cambridge: Cambridge University Press.

Walters, G. C., & Grusec, J. E. (1977). *Punishment.* San Francisco: Freeman.

Zahn-Waxler, C., & Chapman, M. (1982). Immediate antecedents of caretakers' methods of discipline. *Child Psychiatry and Human Development, 12,* 179-192.

Zahn-Waxler, C., Radke-Yarrow, M., & King, R. A. (1979). Child rearing and children's prosocial initiations toward victims of distress. *Child Development, 50,* 319-330.

2

Prosocial Behavior and Empathy
A MULTIMETHOD DEVELOPMENTAL PERSPECTIVE

NANCY EISENBERG
RICHARD A. FABES

Nancy Eisenberg is Professor of Psychology at Arizona State University. Her research interests are in social development, including the development of altruism, empathy, moral reasoning, and related emotional reactions. She is the author of *Altruistic Emotion, Cognition and Behavior* and *The Roots of Prosocial Behavior in Children* (coauthored with Paul Mussen). She is editor (with Janet Strayer) of *Empathy and Its Development*.

Richard A. Fabes is Associate Professor of Family Resources and Human Development at Arizona State University. His research interests include empathy, altruism, the development and socialization of emotion, and family influences on development. He has written numerous articles on social development.

Philosophers and psychologists (Batson, 1987; Blum, 1980; Eisenberg, 1986; Hoffman, 1982) frequently have argued that empathy and related vicarious emotional reactions (e.g., sympathy) play a role in the performance of prosocial behaviors (voluntary behaviors intended to benefit another). However, the empirical research sometimes has not been consistent with such assertions, particularly the research involving children. The question thus arises: Is existing theory wrong, or are there conceptual and methodological problems with some of the empirical literature?

In this chapter, we review theory and the empirical literature on the role of vicarious emotional responding in prosocial behavior. Because the literature on empathy and altruism among adults is discussed in detail in other chapters in this volume (see Chapter 3 by Batson and Oleson and Chapter 4 by Dovidio, Piliavin, Gaertner, Schroeder, and Clark), we emphasize the developmental literature in our review. However, some of the conceptual and methodological issues and problems

AUTHORS' NOTE: Preparation of this chapter was supported by a grant from the National Science Foundation (BNS-8807784) to both authors and a Research Career Development Award from the National Institute of Child Health and Development (K04 HD00717) to the first author.

in the developmental literature are also relevant in the research with adults; therefore, in our discussion of more general issues, we often refer to the social psychological literature that presents results of work conducted with adults.

This chapter is divided into several sections. First, we briefly define our terminology. Next, theoretical perspectives concerning the relation of empathy to prosocial behavior are reviewed briefly, followed by a discussion of some of the conceptual ambiguities in the literature. In the third section, methodological problems in the research are examined; this section is followed by a review of some of the relevant empirical literature. Finally, relevant issues are summarized and new directions are proposed.

DEFINITIONAL ISSUES

As will become evident, one reason for inconsistent findings in the empirical research seems to be the lack of conceptual differentiation among different vicarious responses and various modes of prosocial behavior. For example, most investigators have used the term *empathy* to encompass a variety of cognitive and emotional constructs. Therefore, it is important that we define our terminology.

We define a vicarious emotional response as an emotional reaction induced by the apprehension of another's emotional state or condition. A vicarious emotional response can be consistent with another's emotional state or condition (e.g., an observer may feel sad when viewing someone who is sad) or inconsistent (e.g., an observer may feel happy when viewing someone who is upset). Vicarious emotional responding is a superordinate category that includes a variety of emotional reactions.

In the past, the term *empathy* has been used to refer to social insight (e.g., Dymond, 1949) or the ability to comprehend the affective or cognitive status of another (Borke, 1971; Deutsch & Madle, 1975). However, more recently, social and developmental psychologists have tended to define *empathy* in more affective terms. Specifically, *empathy* frequently is defined as a vicarious emotional response that is identical or very similar to that of the other person (Eisenberg, 1986). If observers feel sad when viewing someone who is sad, they are experiencing empathy. In our view, empathy involves at least a minimal degree of differentiation between self and other; this sharing of the perceived emotion of another must be somewhat conscious (i.e., observers must be aware of the difference between their own and the other's state). Thus infants who cry in response to hearing another infant cry are not empathizing if they do not differentiate between their own and the other infant's cry.

Sympathy is another vicarious emotional response—one that often may stem from empathy (but also may occur as a consequence of cognitively taking the role of another or accessing information from one's memory; see Eisenberg, Shea, Carlo, & Knight, in press). *Sympathy* refers to feelings of sorrow or concern for another (Eisenberg, 1986; Wispé, 1986) and involves an "other" orientation (Batson, 1987). In contrast, *personal distress* is an aversive reaction, such as anxiety or discomfort, to another's state that leads to the self-focused, egoistic motivation of alleviating one's own aversive state (Batson, 1987). Thus, if a person experiences concern for another person who is sad rather than merely experiencing sadness, he or she is sympathizing. As for sympathy, personal distress sometimes may stem from empathy, especially if the empathic response is experienced as too arousing. However, it is possible that personal distress sometimes stems from other processes (e.g., guilt).

Prosocial behavior—voluntary behavior intended to benefit another—also is a superordinate category. There are different kinds of prosocial behaviors, for example, helping, sharing, and comforting. However, for our purposes, a more important distinction among prosocial behaviors revolves around the actor's motive for his or her behavior. Prosocial behaviors can be motivated by a variety of factors, including egoistic concerns (the desire for reciprocity, a concrete reward, or social approval), practical concerns (e.g., the desire to prevent damage to an object), other-oriented concern (e.g., sympathy), or moral values (e.g., the desire to uphold internalized moral values). We define *altruistic behaviors* as those prosocial behaviors motivated by other-oriented or moral concerns rather than rewards or the desire to reduce aversive affective states (Eisenberg, 1986); some investigators define *altruism* more narrowly (e.g., as not including prosocial behaviors performed to uphold moral principles; Batson, 1989).

The aforementioned distinctions become important when considering the development of vicarious emotional responding and the relation of such responding to prosocial behavior. Not all types of vicarious responding would be expected to be associated with all types of prosocial behaviors. We now turn to conceptual issues of this sort.

THEORETICAL PERSPECTIVES AND CONCEPTUAL ISSUES

A variety of theoretical perspectives have been proposed to account for the role of vicarious emotional responding in prosocial behavior. Due to space limitations, only a few of these perspectives can be considered, and our review of these is brief.

Hoffman (1976, 1982) has proposed an influential developmental model of age-related changes in empathy and the relation of empathy to prosocial behavior. According to Hoffman's model, in the first year of life, before the child has developed the understanding of person permanence (that people are permanent objects that are separate from the self and whose action is independent of the self), distress cues emanating from others elicit global distress reactions. At this stage, it is often unclear to the child who is experiencing the distress; thus the child does not try to help distressed others but may become upset.

As children develop some understanding of person permanence near the end of the second year of life, they increasingly differentiate between their own and others' distresses; however, young children cannot clearly differentiate between their own internal states and those of others and may confuse the two. Thus, as young children start to try to assist distressed others (at about one year of age; Radke-Yarrow, Zahn-Waxler, & Chapman, 1983), their helping behaviors are often "egocentric" in that children will help in ways that are likely to diminish their own distress but may not help the other person. For example, a boy may try to help by alternating between patting the person in distress and patting himself. Hoffman (1976) suggested that these very early prosocial behaviors are "quasi hedonistic" in motive in that a child may assist others to alleviate his or her own distress. At a slightly more advanced stage, children are likely to try to comfort others with means that comfort themselves; for instance, Hoffman (1982) described a 13-month-old boy who responded to a sad adult with a distressed look and then offered the adult his own beloved doll. At this level, although children's helping often is egocentric (i.e., limited by their own cognitive perspective), it would seem that their prosocial behavior may be motivated by empathy, primitive sympathy (labeled "sympathetic distress" by Hoffman), or personal distress.

In the second and third years of life, as children develop the ability to take others' perspectives, Hoffman assumes that children increasingly differentiate between their own and others' perspectives and internal states. As a consequence, children's prosocial actions are more appropriate and responsive to others' particular needs. Moreover, with the development of language, children can derive information about others' states from symbolic cues, rather than just from facial and other physical expressions, and can begin to empathize with a wider range of emotions, including complex emotions like disappointment and feelings of inadequacy (which could be associated with not wanting to be helped). Finally, in late childhood, children's vicarious responding is affected by their developing understanding that the self and others are individuals with different and separate histories and identities and that people have feelings beyond the immediate situation. Children's affective arousal can now be intensified by the knowledge that another's distress may be repeated and chronic, even if there are no immediate cues of distress. Consequently, children can experience empathy (or related reactions) for the poor, the ill, or others with chronic problems, even without immediate information about their distress.

Hoffman's theory is unique because he has tied developmental changes to the emergence of empathy and its relation to prosocial behavior. Although Hoffman appears to be correct regarding his description of early manifestations of empathy, personal distress, and sympathy (see Radke-Yarrow, Zahn-Waxler, & Chapman, 1983), many parts of his theory have not yet been adequately tested (e.g., the role of differentiation of self and other in the development of empathy).

Social psychologists' accounts of the relation between empathy and prosocial behavior focus primarily on adults and do not take into account developmental changes in cognitive and social processes. Because these perspectives are discussed in other chapters, we highlight only a few issues relevant to the differentiation of sympathy and personal distress.

In the Piliavin, Dovidio, Gaertner, and Clark (1981) model of emergency helping, personal distress reactions, as well as the cognitive calculation of costs and rewards in a given situation, are central. Costs for helping may be personal (e.g., costs in time or concrete goods) or empathic (due to the experience of aversive affective states). In their view, bystanders often become aroused from observing an emergency and are motivated to reduce this aversive arousal while incurring as few net costs as possible. Although Piliavin, Dovidio, Gaertner, and Clark (1981) did differentiate between sympathy ("alarm and concern") and personal distress ("disgust and upset"; see pp. 239-240), it is unclear whether sympathetic reactions were believed to lead to helping due to the actor's desire to reduce his or her own distress or that of the other. Piliavin, Dovidio, Gaertner, and Clark seemed to view concern as leading to a lack of differentiation between one's own needs and those of others, producing a "continued and perhaps increased level of unpleasant arousal" (1981, p. 236) and resulting in the needs of others being "incorporated into the bystander's self-interest" (1982, p. 286).

In contrast, Batson (1987) has clearly differentiated between *sympathy* (frequently labeled "empathy" by Batson) and *personal distress* and has proposed differential relations between the two vicarious responses and types of prosocial behavior. In his view, sympathy is associated with the other-oriented goal of reducing the other person's need or distress; thus, unless the costs of helping are quite high, there is little gain for the sympathizer in not assisting. In contrast, personal distress is associated with the egoistic motive of alleviating one's own distress; consequently, if this goal can be reached easily by leaving, the observer experiencing personal distress will leave rather than assist. However, if escape from the aversive cues is not easy, the individual experiencing personal distress is likely to assist as a means of reducing his or her own distress (see Chapter 3).

Thus Batson has delineated a model in which sympathy and personal distress are associated with different motives (other-oriented motives versus egoism) and are differentially related to altruism. This model generally has been supported by research with adults (see Batson's chapter in this volume), although it has seldom been tested with children.

Models such as those of Piliavin, Dovidio, Gaertner, and Clark (1981) and Batson (1987) have been extremely helpful to investigators attempting to conceptualize and study empathy and related responses. However, their models apply only to state-related responses—that is, the relation of emotional responding to prosocial behavior directed toward the target of one's vicarious responding in the given context (in addition, the Piliavin, Dovidio, Gaertner, and Clark model is limited to emergency helping). Their models do not deal with the relation between dispositional empathy (or sympathy and personal distress) and either dispositional prosocial behavior or prosocial behaviors in different contexts.

In fact, patterns of interrelations between vicarious emotional responding and prosocial behavior may differ when focusing on dispositional and state indices. This is for several reasons. First, dispositional empathy (or related emotions) often may be irrelevant for prosocial responding. For example, many prosocial behaviors, especially low-cost behaviors, may be performed rather automatically (Langer, Blank, & Chanowitz, 1978), and emotional responding would not usually be relevant for the performance of habitual prosocial acts. Second, many prosocial behaviors would not be expected to be correlated with individual differences in sympathy. In instances in which a given type of prosocial response typically is associated with nonaltruistic motives, sympathy may be unrelated or even negatively related to prosocial behavior.

Personality characteristics of individuals seem to be related, at least partially, to which types of prosocial behaviors people perform (e.g., Gergen, Gergen, & Meter, 1972). For example, sociable people tend to engage in prosocial behaviors involving social contact whereas less sociable people do not (Hampson, 1984). To the degree that indices of dispositional prosocial behavior tap individual differences in personality characteristics other than those related to vicarious emotional responding (e.g., sociability or other-oriented values), relations between these indices and those assessing dispositional sympathy, empathy, or personal distress are likely to be diluted.

Of course, individual differences in values, social style, perspective-taking abilities, and other sociocognitive skills and traits also influence helping in empathy-evoking situations and may attenuate associations between vicarious emotional responding and prosocial behavior performed in the same context. However, personal characteristics may have more influence on behavior in some settings than in others. According to Snyder and Ickes (1985), in psychologically strong situations—situations that are structured and offer highly salient cues for behavior—situational but not dispositional vicarious emotional responding would be expected to be associated with acts of altruism. However, in psychologically weak situations—less structured and evocative contexts with fewer salient cues—one would predict a stronger relation between dispositional sympathy or personal distress and prosocial behavior (see Eisenberg, Miller, et al., 1989). Nonetheless, assisting in highly evocative helping contexts may be unrelated to even situational emotional responding if the evocative cues are sufficient to elicit sympathy in most people (e.g., if a young child lay sobbing on the sidewalk) and if the cost of helping is low.

In summary, although psychologists' thinking regarding the role of vicarious emotional responding is much more complex than a few years ago, in many studies different modes of vicarious emotional responding or prosocial behavior have not been conceptually differentiated. In addition, investigators frequently have not considered the role of context, the type of emotional response (i.e., situational or dispositional), and the complexity of possible relations between emotional responding and prosocial behavior. These conceptual ambiguities have been reflected in the choice of measures used in relevant research as well in theory. We now turn to the issue of measurement.

METHODOLOGICAL ISSUES

In 1982, Underwood and Moore used meta-analytic procedures to examine the relation between empathy and prosocial behavior. Contrary to theory and the assertions of numerous investigators, they found no relation between the two. This finding seemed to surprise even Underwood and Moore, who suggested that perhaps the relation between empathy and prosocial behavior increases with age (their review included mostly studies involving children).

In a more recent meta-analytic review, Eisenberg and Miller (1987) reexamined the relation between empathy and prosocial behavior. They included studies with children and adults and divided the studies into groups based on the manner in which empathy (which usually was not differentiated from sympathy or personal distress) was assessed. Self-report indices of empathy used with younger children were unrelated to prosocial behavior whereas most other types of indices (e.g., facial indices used with children, physiological indices, self-report indices used with older children and adults, experimental manipulations) were significantly associated with prosocial responding.

This pattern of findings is consistent with the view that different measures of empathy (and related reactions) differ in what they tap. Even more compelling in regard to this issue are the data from Eisenberg and Lennon's (1983) review of gender differences in empathy. They found that gender differences in empathy varied greatly as a function of type of empathy index used; there was a huge gender difference favoring females for self-report questionnaires, a moderate difference favoring females for self-report in experimental contexts (in which people were exposed to empathy-evoking stimuli and asked how they felt), and no gender differences in facial and physiological indices. Eisenberg and Lennon suggested that to the degree it was obvious what was being assessed and subjects had conscious control over their responses, they seemed to respond in a manner consistent with stereotypic gender roles concerning emotionality and sympathetic responding (for reasons related to self-presentation and self-deception). Most obvious from these reviews are the problems with self-report indices of emotional responding for younger children. The commonly used picture-story indices of empathy—in which children are exposed to brief hypothetical scenarios involving protagonists in emotion-evoking stories and are then asked how they themselves feel—frequently have been criticized (see Eisenberg & Lennon, 1983). The brief scenarios may be too short to elicit an emotional response; demand characteristics are strong; and the children are expected to change emotions every few minutes in response to a new story. In addition, gender differences on these indices vary as a function of sex of the experimenter, with children scoring higher if interviewed by same-sex adults (see Eisenberg & Lennon, 1983). Finally, that younger children's self-reported empathic reactions to others in experimental settings (usually involving videotapes of distressed or needy others) were unrelated to prosocial behavior suggests that children may have difficulty assessing or reporting their own emotional reactions.

Another problem with many self-report measures of vicarious emotional responding is that a variety of different types of emotional responses (e.g., fantasy empathy, sympathy, personal distress) and other capabilities (e.g., perspective taking) are included in the index and are considered to be empathy (e.g., Bryant, 1982; Mehrabian & Epstein, 1972). However, in the adult social psychological literature, researchers have recently developed and used indices designed to differentiate among various types of empathy-related capabilities (e.g., Batson, 1987; Davis, 1983). As is discussed shortly, such differentiation is rare in the developmental work.

Despite the demand characteristics of self-report indices and other shortcomings, they do have a place in the work on vicarious emotional responding (see Bryant, 1987a). There are positive aspects of these indices, including the facts that they can be used to assess subjective reactions and are useful for differentiating between sympathy and personal distress, at least for older children and adults. Moreover, new, promising self-report indices are being developed for children (Strayer & Schroeder, 1989). Thus we would argue that self-report indices should not be dismissed but are best used in combination with other types of indices.

Indeed, all types of measures of vicarious emotional responses have shortcomings. Although facial and physiological indices of sympathy and empathy have been positively associated with prosocial behavior (see later sections in this chapter) and probably are less susceptible than self-report measures to contamination due to social desirability effects, both have unique problems (Eisenberg, Fabes, Bustamante, & Mathy, 1987; Marcus, 1987). For example, physiological responses such as heart rate and skin conductance are affected by myriad factors, including cognitive processing, body movement, and speaking. In addition, physiological reactions are difficult to interpret because people have different baseline responses and reaction rates, and various physiological indices do not always interrelate in the expected manner (see Eisenberg, Fabes, Schaller, & Miller, 1989). With regard to facial indices, the ability and tendency to mask and monitor facial reactions, and the understanding of this ability, clearly increase with age (Saarni, 1982; Shennum & Bugenthal, 1982). Thus, given the potential problems with the measurement and interpretation of all measures of vicarious emotional responding, we frequently have used multiple indices of response in our work.

EMPIRICAL FINDINGS

The types of measures most commonly used to assess children's vicarious emotional responses are facial, physiological, and self-report indices. In the following section, each of these is discussed in turn, with an emphasis on our own work. Because our work centers on studies involving children, we do not review the experimental manipulations commonly used to assess empathy in studies involving only adults (see Eisenberg & Miller, 1987).

The Relation of Facial Indices of Empathy to Prosocial Behavior

In the last decade, a number of researchers have used facial expressions as an index of people's reactions to others in need or distress and have related these measures to prosocial behavior. These studies, most of which have involved only children, can be divided into two groups: (a) those in which children's facial reactions were examined while they were responding to hypothetical picture-story indices of empathy (e.g.,

Howard, 1983) and (b) studies in which children's facial reactions were assessed while they were viewing videotapes of other people, usually portrayed as real people, in affect-laden situations (e.g., Eisenberg, Fabes, Miller, et al., 1989; Periano & Sawin 1981).

Eisenberg and Miller (1987) recently reviewed the relation of different types of indices of empathy to prosocial behavior using meta-analytic procedures. They found no consistent relation between facial reactions to picture-story indices of empathy and prosocial behavior. In contrast, the relation between facial reactions to videotaped stimuli and prosocial behavior was positive and significant. Because of the lack of a relation between picture-story indices and prosocial behavior, and due to questions concerning the validity of these indices (see Eisenberg & Lennon, 1983), further critique and discussion are limited to those studies involving facial reactions to tapes of others in emotionally distressing situations.

Although Eisenberg and Miller (1987) reported a positive relation between facial reactions to others' distress and prosocial behavior, there are two characteristics of the relevant studies that, in our opinion, limit their interpretation. First, in most of these studies, researchers did not distinguish between sympathy and personal distress (e.g., Lennon, Eisenberg, & Carroll, 1986; Periano & Sawin, 1981). Thus, when vicarious negative emotional reactions have been linked with prosocial behavior, it has been impossible to determine what type of emotional response (e.g., sympathy or personal distress) is involved in the relation. Second, in some studies, researchers did not attempt to distinguish altruistically motivated behavior from those prosocial behaviors that were performed for more egoistic motives.

The need for the aforementioned conceptual and empirical distinctions is evident in recent research in which investigators have tried to build upon the findings in the adult social psychological literature (e.g., Batson, 1987). Eisenberg, McCreath, and Ahn (1988) found that children's sad/concerned facial responses were positively associated with prosocial behavior in situations in which children's prosocial actions were likely to be altruistically motivated (i.e., spontaneous sharing). However, anxious expressions (believed to be indicative of personal distress) were positively related to prosocial behavior in response to a peer's request—a situation in which escape from another's request for sharing was difficult. Thus some of the inconsistencies among prior developmental studies involving facial indices may have occurred because sympathetic and personal distress facial reactions were not differentiated and/or were not assessed in situations in which they would be expected to be differentially related to prosocial behavior (e.g., when escape is possible and easy).

In the Eisenberg, McCreath, and Ahn (1988) study, sad and concerned facial reactions were not differentiated and the facial ratings were global. Recently, we have begun to differentiate among a variety of empathy-related facial reactions in children and adults. In our first two studies, children (ranging in age from preschoolers to sixth graders) and adults were exposed to either (a) short videotapes designed to elicit personal distress or sympathy and empathic sadness (Eisenberg, Fabes, et al., 1988) or (b) a mood induction procedure designed to induce emotional responses akin to personal distress (i.e., subjects described a time when they were concerned about their own welfare) or sympathy (subjects described a time when they were concerned about another's welfare; Eisenberg, Schaller, et al., 1988). In general, the results of both studies confirmed the validity of our facial indices. For example, facial sadness and sympathy were highest during the overtly sad videotape or the sympathy mood induction and lowest during the distressing film or the distressing mood induction. In contrast, facial distress and fear were highest in the distressing tape or in the distress mood induction (but only when distress was induced first and there were no carryover effects from another induction). Thus these studies provided evidence that facial indices of sympathy and personal distress reactions were valid and could be used to examine the relation between vicarious responding and prosocial behavior.

In our next studies, we examined the relation of our facial indices of sympathy and personal distress to prosocial behavior. For example, in one study, children and adults viewed a purported pilot television show about local people who had been in an automobile accident (Eisenberg, Fabes, Miller et al., 1989). In the tape, a mother described the problems her two children were having because of injuries they had suffered in the accident. The subjects' facial reactions were recorded while they watched the videotape and when they read (or were read) a letter in which the mother in the film requested assistance. Then they were given an opportunity to help the children in the tape (in a context in which they believed they would have no further contact with the needy family if they refused to help). For adults, both facial sadness and concerned attention (believed to be correlated with sympathetic concern) exhibited while viewing the tape were positively correlated with helping. For children, personal distress reactions were negatively related to helping or donating (especially for older children and for boys), whereas facial concerned attention was positively related to prosocial behavior (especially for younger children and for boys). Thus the relations between facial reactions believed to reflect sympathy or empathic sadness and willingness to help in an easy-escape situation were clear for adults. For children, the findings were not as clear and were dependent on the age and the sex of a child. However, those associations that were found were consistent with expectations based on Batson's (1987) theorizing about the relations of sympathy and personal distress to prosocial behavior in an easy-escape context.

In a recent study (Eisenberg, Fabes, et al., in press), we used procedures similar to those just described to examine the relation of preschoolers' facial reactions to both their situational and their dispositional prosocial tendencies (i.e., helping the distressed others or general prosocial proclivities). Children were given an opportunity to help hospitalized children in a videotape, and their naturally occurring prosocial and defensive behaviors in the classroom were assessed. Consistent with predictions, facial sadness was associated with situational helping whereas facial distress was inversely related to situational helping (but only for boys). For the dispositional measures of children's classroom behaviors, concerned facial expressions were positively associated with assertive defensive behaviors (especially for girls) and negatively correlated with compliant, requested prosocial behaviors (especially for boys). The pattern for personal distress facial reactions was the reverse of that for sympathetic reactions.

These results, in combination with those of Eisenberg, McCreath, and Ahn (1988), have interesting implications. According to these studies, children who exhibited concerned attention in response to others' distress were relatively assertive (particularly girls) and non-compliant, whereas those children who were prone to personal distress tended to be more compliant (particularly boys). We interpret these findings as supportive of the view that children who tend to react with personal distress when exposed to needy or distressed others frequently engage in compliant prosocial behaviors to reduce their peer-related distress reactions. In contrast, children who are less compliant and more assertive tend to be those children who exhibit sympathetic facial reactions and help for more altruistic motives. These findings are consistent with research indicating that children who engage in high levels of spontaneous prosocial behavior use more other-oriented moral reasoning (Eisenberg, Pasternack, Cameron, & Tryon, 1984) and are relatively assertive and sociable, especially in comparison with children who engage in high levels of compliant prosocial behaviors (Eisenberg, Cameron, Tryon, & Dodez, 1981; Eisenberg, Pasternack, Cameron, & Tryon, 1984). In addition, the data are consistent with the general finding of a positive relation between children's social competence and both empathy and prosocial behavior (Bryant, 1987b; Eisenberg & Miller, 1987).

The Relation of Heart Rate to Prosocial Behavior

Heart rate (HR) is one physiological index that has provided valuable information regarding emotional states and emotionally charged behaviors. Most relevant to the study of empathy and prosocial behavior is work in which emotional reactions have been vicariously rather than directly induced. For example, researchers have found that subjects who viewed another person who was sad or crying (Campos, Butterfield, & Klinnert, 1985) or who viewed another receiving noxious stimulation (Craig & Lowery, 1969) exhibited relatively large HR decelerations if the situation was not threatening to the subject. Because sympathetic concern involves other-oriented attention and processing of information about someone aside from oneself, these findings are consistent with psychophysiological research in which the intake of information and an outward focus have been associated with HR deceleration (Cacioppo & Sandman, 1978; Lacey, Kagan, Lacey, & Moss, 1963). In contrast, HR acceleration has been associated both with vicariously induced fear or anxiety and with being placed in anxiety-evoking situations (e.g., Kutina & Fischer, 1977; Lacey, Kagan, Lacey, & Moss, 1963). This acceleration may be due to cognitive elaboration (about one's own situation) or active coping (Lazarus, 1974; Smith, Allred, Morrison, & Carlson, 1989).

Based on the research just reviewed, one might expect HR deceleration during presentation of information relevant to another's welfare to be associated with an other-oriented sympathetic response and, consequently, with helping. Contrary to this prediction, Gaertner and Dovidio (1977) found that acceleration was related to shorter latencies before assisting someone in need and that deceleration was correlated with longer latencies. However, HR was measured shortly before the subjects stood up to assist (because they were going to help someone in an emergency in another room). Thus HR acceleration may have been associated with assisting because preparation for physical mobilization (as well as mobilization itself) has been found to increase HR (Obrist, Webb, Sutterer, & Howard, 1970). Moreover, those subjects who exhibited HR acceleration may have been experiencing personal distress, not sympathy, and felt they could reduce their distress by ascertaining what had happened in the next room. Consistent with this suggestion, Sterling and Gaertner (1984) noted a positive correlation between HR acceleration and helping when an emergency was unambiguous but a nonsignificant reversal of the pattern when the emergency was ambiguous and subjects could escape assisting by concluding that no one was injured.

Because of the contradictions in the literature, we sought to determine whether we could use HR to differentiate between emotional reactions in situations designed to elicit either primarily sympathy or primarily personal distress. In addition, we examined the relation of HR trends to prosocial behavior. In general, the results from these studies support the validity of HR as an indirect marker of vicarious emotional responding. HR acceleration was observed when children were exposed to anxiety-provoking stimuli (Eisenberg, Fabes, et al., 1988), and HR was relatively high when children and adults talked about distressing events (i.e., during a personal distress mood induction; Eisenberg, Schaller, et al., 1988). In contrast, HR decelerated during the evocative parts of sad and sympathy-inducing stimuli and was relatively low during a sympathetic mood induction. With regard to the relation of HR to prosocial behavior, HR deceleration during the most sympathy-inducing portion of the film featuring the family involved in the automobile accident (see previous description) was associated with relatively high levels of helping (Eisenberg, Fabes, Miller, et al., 1989).

In another study involving only adults (Fultz et al., 1987), we reexamined the relation between HR and prosocial behavior in a situation similar to that used in the Eisenberg, Fabes, Miller, et al. (1989) study. In this study, HR acceleration was associated with lower levels of helping.

If heart rate is viewed as a marker of "other" orientation, the aforementioned data can be viewed as supporting the notion that sympathy frequently motivates altruistic behavior. However, one could also interpret the findings as indicating that people who are merely more attentive to others are more likely to assist. Although the latter explanation may, in general, be true, in our studies the other person's needs were quite salient; therefore, differences in recognition of the needy other's condition were unlikely to mediate the relation between heart rate and prosocial behavior. However, it is quite likely that people who are more other-oriented in a given situation are more likely to attend to details regarding another's distress or need and, consequently, are more likely to perspective take, empathize, and sympathize. People who experience personal distress when viewing others in distress may be expected to try to reduce their own arousal by diverting attention away from the arousal-inducing situation (Field, 1982).

In a recent study, Eisenberg, Fabes, et al. (1990) examined the relation of HR trends during exposure to sympathy-evoking films to dispositional as well as situational prosocial behavior (in the previously discussed studies, HR was only related to helping the person who produced the vicarious emotional response). In this study, HR acceleration was associated with no helping of the person in need in the empathy-evoking context, whereas HR deceleration was associated with higher levels of situational helping. However, HR trends exhibited while children viewed videotapes of others in distressing situations generally were not related to children's dispositional prosocial behaviors (i.e., sharing and helping in their preschool class).

To summarize the findings in regard to HR, our data generally are consistent with the view that HR can be used as an indirect marker of sympathy and personal distress and also can be used to predict prosocial behavior directed toward the object of one's sympathy. However, HR acceleration and deceleration did not, in general, relate to dispositional indices of prosocial behavior. This might be due to HR, as we have used it, being used primarily as an index of focus of attention and being highly situationally dependent. We return to discussion of this point shortly.

The Relation of Self-Report Measures of Vicarious Emotional Responding to Prosocial Behavior

According to the previously mentioned review (Eisenberg & Miller, 1987), the degree of association between self-reported empathy (or sympathy) and prosocial behavior is quite low for younger children but moderate and positive for older children and adults. The difference in the pattern of findings for children and adults probably is due in part to children having more difficulty than adults identifying and communicating internal states. Another possible reason for the clearer findings in studies with adults is that researchers often have tried to distinguish between reports of adults' sympathy and personal distress but seldom have tried to do so with children (although children may not be capable of making the distinction).

Some new self-report indices for children are promising, however. For example, in a recent study, Strayer and Schroeder (1989) used self-report measures to examine whether the presence of shared empathy motivates children's willingness to help needy others. Children (ranging from 4.5 to 13.5 years) viewed emotionally evocative videotaped vignettes and were then asked to identify the emotions and the intensity of the emotions felt by the vignette characters and by themselves. Empathy was scored in two ways: (a) as a function of the match between the type and intensity of the emotions reported and (b) according to the attribution provided by the child for his or her emotional reactions. Consistent with their expectations, Strayer and Schroeder found that empathy was correlated with reported willingness to help. Moreover, when children reported empathy, willingness to help increased with age; however, there were no significant age differences in helping when empathy was not reported. Thus, although helping may occur when no empathy is reported, with increasing age, willingness to help appears to become more aligned with reported empathy.

Feshbach and Feshbach (1986) also have examined the relation between self-reported empathy (based on the degree of correspondence between children's self-reported responses to emotionally evocative videotapes and the affect experienced by the stimulus child) and children's prosocial behavior. They reported that, when empathy was based solely on the match between the child's and the character's affective response, prosocial behavior was positively associated with empathy, but only for girls. When empathy was scored so that the intensity of the child's feelings was considered, boys who reported intense dysphoric feelings when viewing children in dysphoric situations were likely to be helpful, to perceive themselves as helpful, and to be sensitive to others' feelings and motives. For girls, the relation between empathy and prosocial behavior remained fairly constant regardless of whether affective intensity was considered. However, because gender differences in affective empathy favoring females have been found for picture-story and other self-report indices but not for physiological or unobtrusive observations of nonverbal behavior (Eisenberg & Lennon, 1983), more research is needed prior to drawing firm conclusions based on the Feshbachs' instrument.

In our previously described research, we examined the validity of self-report indices of sympathy and personal distress as well as HR and facial measures. The results from our first study with preschoolers and second graders suggested that children's self-reports of sympathy and personal distress varied as a function of the age of the child (Eisenberg, Fabes, et al., 1988). Although the self-reports of both groups of children differed across the distressing and sympathy-evoking films, the older children's self-reports of feeling scared, sorry, sad, and happy, in comparison with those of younger children, were more clearly differentiated across films and appropriate to the content of the films. For example, older children were more likely than younger children to report feeling sympathy in reaction to viewing the film of a child with spina bifida (unpublished data). In fact, preschoolers frequently verbally reported happiness in reaction to the films.

In the previously discussed mood induction study (Eisenberg, Schaller, et al., 1988), verbal reports of emotional reactions to neutral, sympathetic, and personal distress mood inductions were collected from elementary school children and adults. Both children and adults reported more sympathy in the sympathy induction than in the neutral or distress inductions and the most happiness in the neutral inductions. More distress was reported in the sympathy and distress inductions than in the neutral inductions, and females reported more distress in the distressing induction than in the sympathy function. In addition, in the distress induction, third graders reported more sympathy than did sixth graders, a finding that suggests that the younger children may not have reported their sympathetic responding (which should have been relatively low in the distress induction) as accurately as the older children.

Thus the results from the two studies just reviewed indicated that self-reports of vicariously induced emotion generally were consistent with the content of the stimulus tapes or the mood inductions. However, younger children's self-reports were less differentiated and less contextually appropriate than were those of older children and adults.

The relations of self-reports of sympathy and personal distress to prosocial behavior were assessed in our next set of studies (Eisenberg, Fabes, Miller, Fultz, et al., 1989; Eisenberg, Fabes, Miller, Shell, et al., in press). For adults, reports of sympathy were positively related to helping. Adults' reports of personal distress were marginally related to helping. For children (controlling for age), reports of positive mood were negatively related to helping, whereas reports of negative mood (girls only), sympathy (boys only), and personal distress (boys only) were positively related to helping (Fabes, Eisenberg, & Miller, 1990).

Summarizing the findings concerning the use of self-reports as an index of vicarious emotional responding, we have found that even preschoolers' self-reports of emotion differ reliability across contexts, although their responses are less differentiated (and perhaps more influenced by their initial mood) than are those of older children and adults. Moreover, young children's self-reports appear to be less consistently related to their prosocial behavior than are those of older persons (also see Eisenberg & Miller, 1987). In addition, although reports of sympathy and negative emotion generally have been positively correlated with older children's and adults' prosocial behavior, verbal reports of personal distress also have been positively related to helping (e.g., Eisenberg, Fabes, Miller, et al., 1989; Fabes, Eisenberg, & Miller, 1990). Verbal reports of personal distress appear to be somewhat ambiguous in meaning and sometimes seem to tap sympathy rather than personal distress (Batson et al., 1988). Furthermore, adults' reports of sympathy and personal distress have been found to be positively correlated with each other (Batson, 1987) and with indices of social desirability (Eisenberg, Fabes, Miller, et al., 1989). Thus self-report indices probably reflect, in part, a person's general willingness and ability to report negative emotional states.

Summary of the Empirical Data

Overall, the empirical data are consistent with theoretical perspectives in which sympathy and empathy are viewed as a source of altruistically motivated prosocial behavior. Findings regarding the relations of personal distress and sympathy to children's prosocial behavior generally were not as clear as those for adults; perhaps this is because of children's difficulty in distinguishing and reporting various emotional reactions and/or a weaker link between felt emotion and some modes of behavior in children. Nonetheless, based on the larger literature involving facial indices of vicarious emotional response (see Eisenberg & Miller, 1987), observational research with young children (Radke-Yarrow, Zahn-Waxler, & Chapman, 1983), and our recent multimethod research, it seems reasonable to conclude that even young children sometimes help others because of sympathetic concern and sometimes avoid helping due to feelings of personal distress. In addition, however, feelings of personal distress appear to frequently motivate nonaltruistic prosocial behaviors such as preschoolers' compliant prosocial behaviors.

FUTURE DIRECTIONS

In this final section of the chapter, we address many interesting issues concerning the relation of vicarious emotional responding to prosocial behavior. Some related issues are discussed in other chapters in this volume; others have yet to be addressed. We now present a few of the issues and problems that seem provocative to us and are guiding our research efforts.

Methodological Issues

In our various studies, we have been using heart rate (HR) primarily as a measure of focus of attention and mode of processing and not as a measure of arousal or emotional intensity. If we are correct in our assumption that patterns of acceleration and deceleration during short, evocative portions of films do not reflect intensity of emotional arousal, then it may be useful to use another physiological measure that is somewhat more likely to tap such arousal (although all physiological measures are influenced by multiple factors). One logical candidate for use is skin conductance (SC), which, in some settings, appears to reflect emotional arousal (see Lanzetta & Englis, 1989). Thus, in some of our ongoing research, we have included skin conductance as a possible marker of the intensity of a vicariously induced emotional response. In an initial study conducted with adults, we have found that SC was higher for a distressing film than for a more mild, sympathy-inducing film. Moreover, SC responses in reaction to viewing film clips likely to elicit vicarious reactions were associated with individual differences in emotional arousability and the tendency to empathize with fantasy characters (as in movies), particularly for females. Therefore, based on these initial findings, SC seems to be a promising measure of intensity of emotional response.

In most of the recent research concerning the relation of sympathy and personal distress to prosocial behavior, HR, facial, and self-report measures have been used primarily to predict helping directed toward the object of subjects' vicarious response. Thus, in most of our work, as well as in most of the recent social psychological literature, the focus has been on situationally induced personal distress and sympathy—and their relation to prosocial behavior—not on dispositional sympathy and personal distress or the relation of vicarious emotion to dispositional prosocial behavior. Based on our studies, we have found e evidence suggesting that HR, as least as we have used it, is associated with dispositional prosocial behavior or even with dispositional empathy, sympathy, and personal distress as assessed with self-report questionnaire measures of empathy (see Eisenberg, Fabes, et al., 1988; Eisenberg, Fabes, et al., in press; Eisenberg, Schaller, et al., 1988). Because we typically assessed linear trends in HR during very specific, evocative portions of films (we have not used HR as a general measure of arousability or some related construct), it is not surprising that HR has seldom been related to any of our dispositional measures. However, given the associations that we have found between SC and dispositional measures of emotional intensity and fantasy empathy, SC may, in combination with other measures (e.g., facial indices) that assess other relevant cognitive processes, motives, or values, be more useful than HR trends in predicting dispositional prosocial behavior.

Two other physiological measures that may prove useful in future research concerning empathy are electromyography (EMG) and vagal tone. EMG involves the measurement of muscle actions (e.g., on the face). With EMG, it is possible to measure muscle actions associated with facial expressions, including muscle movements too small to be detected by the human eye. Moreover, according to recent research, different patterns of EMG can be used as markers of negative and positive emotions, although some negative emotions such as anxiety may be difficult to measure using EMG (Cacioppo, Martzke, Petty, & Tassinary, 1988; Cacioppo, Petty, Losch, & Kim, 1986). Consequently, it may be fruitful to include EMG in studies of vicariously induced emotion, although EMG would be difficult to use with children because it is rather invasive and may be frightening (e.g., electrodes are put in various places on the face).

With regard to vagal tone (believed to reflect autonomic nervous system functioning), Fox and his colleagues (Fox, 1989) have found that children with low vagal tone (high and stable heart rates) appear to be relatively anxious and distressed by mildly stressful events and tend not to engage their peers in spontaneous social interaction. Fox argued that infants with high vagal tone (more HR variability and lower HR) were better able to regulate their own arousal and were more sociable and responded positively to novel events. Similarly, Kagan (1982) found that children with high and stable heart rates were more likely to display shy, fearful, or introverted social behaviors. These children were distressed by mildly stressful events and tended not to engage in spontaneous social interaction. Thus children with high vagal tone may be better able to cope with vicariously induced emotional reactions and, therefore, more likely to experience sympathy rather than overarousal in empathy-inducing contexts. Indeed, Fox's and Kagan's descriptions of children with low vagal tone sound like the preschool children in our research who exhibited personal distress reactions to others' distresses and also engaged in high levels of compliant prosocial behaviors (whereas more sociable, assertive children tend to engage in spontaneously emitted prosocial behaviors; Eisenberg, Cameron, Tryon, & Dodez, 1981).

Socialization and Developmental Issues

Although the concepts of sympathy and empathy are of considerable importance to the study of prosocial behavior, fundamental questions remain concerning the processes through which empathy-related responses develop and are socialized. The limited existing data suggest that parents who are responsive, inductive, warm, and accepting of children's emotional reactions have offspring who are emotionally responsive to others (e.g., Barnett, 1987) and who are socially competent (Roberts & Strayer, 1987). However, in most of these studies, different vicarious emotional responses were not differentiated. Thus it is difficult to draw firm conclusions regarding sympathy and personal distress from these studies.

Recently, we have used a more differentiated approach to examining the interrelations between parents' reported vicarious emotional responsiveness and their children's empathic and prosocial behaviors (e.g., Fabes, Eisenberg, & Miller, 1990). In our work, we have found that measures of mothers' vicarious emotional responding were related to their children's vicarious emotional responsiveness and prosocial behavior. Mothers' scores on a self-report measure of sympathy and cognitive role taking were positively correlated with children's verbal reports of sympathy and negative affect after viewing a needy other, and they were inversely related to reports of positive affect (these relations were stronger for girls than for boys). In contrast, these patterns were reversed for mothers' scores on a measure of personal distress. Moreover, mothers' sympathy and role-taking scores were positively correlated with their children's helpfulness (but helpfulness was not correlated with mothers' personal distress; Fabes, Eisenberg, & Miller, 1990).

Generally, our data are consistent with those presented by Feshbach (1987), who found that mothers who reported being empathic to distress in others had children who evidenced greater self-control and less negative affect during laboratory tasks. These mothers also were more emotionally expressive than mothers who were lower on self-reported empathy. Bryant (1987b) also reported that mothers' expressiveness in response to children's distress predicted children's self-reported empathy.

Together, these data suggest some important avenues for future research. First, they provide evidence that parents' response to children's distress are related to the development of their children's vicarious emotional responding and social competence. Parents who respond with concern may foster the development of sympathy by being more willing to acknowledge and sustain a focus on the child's feelings. Children who learn to accept and deal effectively with their own emotional responses may be more capable than other children of responding with sympathy rather than self-concern to vicariously induced emotion. In contrast, parents who respond to children's distress with anxiety and discomfort (e.g., personal distress) may be more likely to focus on their own feelings of distress and may be relatively unresponsive to their children's emotional needs. However, to date, the research in this area is limited both in quantity and in scope. Thus there is a need to further examine the role of parents reactions to children's distress in the development of empathic and prosocial tendencies.

Moreover, there is a need to examine how empathy-related socialization practices change as children age. For example, whereas Bowlby (1982) regarded comforting a crying infant as an effective response to the infant's distress, Roberts and Strayer (1987) reported that older children were comforted by parents primarily when parents were at a loss for an effective response. Further research is needed to examine these age-related changes and how such changes are associated with empathic and prosocial development.

One important limitation of most of the existing studies of the relation between sympathy in parents and their offspring is that most researchers have relied primarily on parents' self-reported empathy and/ or child-rearing practices (e.g., Fabes, Eisenberg, & Miller, 1990; Feshbach, 1987). Because of the problems associated with self-report indexes, as noted earlier, concerns must be raised regarding bias due to social desirability and demand characteristics in these data. To provide more robust and valid measures, multiple measures of parents' responses to distress situations (e.g., combining self-reports with observational and physiological data) may be needed.

Coping and Vicarious Emotional Responding

A new and potentially important topic of research is the role of coping mechanisms in individuals' responses to others' negative emotional states and situations (see Eisenberg, Bernzweig, & Fabes, in press). Although there has been a great increase in interest in studying stress and coping, most of this work has focused on cognitive mechanisms (e.g., Lazarus & Folkman, 1984) with little attention devoted to interpersonal coping mechanisms.

We suggest that coping processes may be involved in empathic and prosocial responses. For example, individuals who are unable to adequately cope with feelings of arousal and distress when exposed to others' negative emotional states or situations (i.e., experience personal distress) may respond in self-focused ways that address their own needs rather than those of the needy other. Thus those persons who become overly distressed and aroused when exposed to another's plight are more likely to employ coping strategies that deny, distract, or shield themselves from the source of the distress (Miller & Green, 1985) and are, therefore, less likely to help when escape is easy. In contrast, individuals who become moderately aroused (but not overwhelmingly so) would be expected to be more likely to experience sympathy and to cope with others' distress by employing problem-focused strategies (e.g., helping) that directly address the needs of the other person.

In summary, we propose that sympathetic reactions are those that are associated with moderate levels of arousal and the ability to cope with one's own arousal. Individual differences in both arousability and coping skills (and their interaction) are, therefore, viewed as relevant to sympathetic responding. In addition, coping skills both may influence one's level of vicarious arousal (i.e., they may play a role in modulating arousal) and may be influenced by the individual's level of arousability (e.g., individuals who are optimally aroused would be expected to use more adaptive coping strategies and to be more sympathetic and other-oriented in their behavior). Clearly, the interrelations among coping, vicarious emotional responding, and social behavior are complex and are a topic of potential importance to the study of sympathy and prosocial behavior.

REFERENCES

Barnett, M. A. (1987). Empathy and related responses in children. In N. Eisenberg & J. Strayer (Eds.), *Empathy and its development* (pp. 146-162). Cambridge: Cambridge University Press.

Batson, C. D. (1987). Prosocial motivation: Is it ever truly altruistic? In L. Berkowitz (Ed.), *Advances in experimental social psychology* (Vol. 20, pp. 65-122). New York: Academic Press.

Batson, C. D. (1989). Personal values, moral principles, and a three-path model of prosocial development. In N. Eisenberg, J. Reykowski, & E. Staub (Eds.), *Social and moral values: Individual and societal perspectives* (pp. 213-228). Hillsdale, NJ: Lawrence Erlbaum.

Batson, C. D., Dyck, J. L., Brandt, J. R., Batson, J. G., Powell, A. L., McMaster, M. R., & Griffitt, C. (1988). Five studies testing two new egoistic alternatives to the empathy-altruism hypothesis. *Journal of Personality and Social Psychology, 55,* 52-77.

Blum, L. A. (1980). *Friendship, altruism and morality.* London: Routledge & Kegan Paul.

Borke, H. (1971). Interpersonal perception of young children: Egocentrism or empathy. *Developmental Psychology, 5,* 262-269.

Bowlby, J. (1982). *Attachment and loss: Vol. 1. Attachment.* New York: Basic Books.

Bryant, B. K. (1982). An index of empathy for children and adolescents. *Child Development, 53,* 413-425.

Bryant, B. K. (1987a). Critique of comparable questionnaire methods in use to assess empathy in children and adults. In N. Eisenberg & J. Strayer (Eds.), *Empathy and its development* (pp. 361-373). Cambridge: Cambridge University Press.

Bryant, B. K. (1987b). Mental health, temperament, family, and friends: Perspectives on children's empathy and social perspective taking. In N. Eisenberg & J. Strayer (Eds.), *Empathy and its development* (pp. 245-270). Cambridge: Cambridge University Press.

Cacioppo, J. T., Martzke, J. S., Petty, R. E., & Tassinary, L. G. (1988). Specific forms of facial EMG response index emotions during an interview: From Darwin to the continuous flow hypothesis of affect-laden information processing. *Journal of Personality and Social Psychology, 54,* 592-604.

Cacioppo, J. T., Petty, R. E., Losch, M. E., & Kim, H. S. (1986). Electromyographic activity over facial muscle regions can differentiate the valence and intensity of affective reactions. *Journal of Personality and Social Psychology, 50,* 260-268.

Cacioppo, J. T., & Sandman, C. A. (1978). Physiological differentiation of sensory and cognitive tasks as a function of warning processing demands and reported unpleasantness. *Biological Psychology, 6,* 181-192.

Campos, J. J., Butterfield, P., & Klinnert, M. (1985, April). *Cardiac and behavioral differentiation of negative emotional signals: An individual differences perspective.* Paper presented at the biennial meeting of the Society for Research on Child Development, Toronto.

Craig, K. D., & Lowery, H. J. (1969). Heart-rate components of conditioned vicarious autonomic responses. *Journal of Personality and Social Psychology, 11,* 381-387.

Davis, M. H. (1983). Measuring individual differences in empathy: Evidence for a multidimensional approach. *Journal of Personality and Social Psychology, 44,* 113-126.

Deutsch, F., & Madle, R. A. (1975). Empathy: Historic and current conceptualizations, measurement, and a cognitive, theoretical perspective. *Human Development, 11,* 112-113.

Dymond, R. F. (1949). A scale for the measurement of empathic ability. *Journal of Consulting Psychology, 13,* 27-33.

Eisenberg, N. (1986). *Altruistic emotion, cognition and behavior.* Hillsdale, NJ: Lawrence Erlbaum.

Eisenberg, N., Bernzweig, J., & Fabes, R. A. (in press). Coping and vicarious emotional responding. In T. Field, P. McCabe, & N. Schneiderman (Eds.), *Stress and coping in childhood.* Hillsdale, NJ: Lawrence Erlbaum.

Eisenberg, N., Cameron, E., Tryon, K., & Dodez, R. (1981). Socialization of prosocial behavior in the preschool classroom. *Developmental Psychology, 17,* 773-782.

Eisenberg, N., Fabes, R. A., Bustamante, D., & Mathy, R. M. (1987). Physiological indices of empathy. In N. Eisenberg & J. Strayer (Eds.), *Empathy and its development* (pp. 380-385). Cambridge: Cambridge University Press.

Eisenberg, N., Fabes, R. A., Bustamante, D., Mathy, R. M., Miller, P. A., & Lindholm, E. (1988). Differentiation of vicariously induced emotional reactions in children. *Developmental Psychology, 24,* 237-246.

Eisenberg, N., Fabes, R. A., Miller, P. A., Fultz, J., Mathy, R. M., Shell, R., & Reno, R. R. (1989). The relations of sympathy and personal distress to prosocial behavior: A multimethod study. *Journal of Personality and Social Psychology, 57,* 55-66.

Eisenberg, N., Fabes, R. A., Miller, P. A., Shell, R., Shea, R., & May-Plumee, T. (in press). *The relation of preschoolers' vicarious emotional responding to situational and dispositional prosocial behavior.* Merrill Palmer Quarterly.

Eisenberg, N., Fabes, R. A., Schaller, M., & Miller, P. A. (1989). Developmental change, sex differences, and interrelations in indices of vicarious emotional responding. In N. Eisenberg (Ed.), The development of empathy and related vicarious responses. *New Directions in Child Development, 44,* 107-126.

Eisenberg, N., & Lennon, R. (1983). Sex differences in empathy and related capacities. *Psychological Bulletin, 94,* 100-131.

Eisenberg, N., McCreath, H., & Ahn, R. (1988). Vicarious emotional responsiveness and prosocial behavior: Their interrelations in young children. *Personality and Social Psychology Bulletin, 14,* 298-311.

Eisenberg, N., & Miller, P. (1987). The relation of empathy to prosocial and related behaviors. *Psychological Bulletin, 101,* 91-119.

Eisenberg, N., Miller, P. A., Schaller, M., Fabes, R. A., Fultz, J., Shell, R., & Shea, C. (1989). The role of sympathy and altruistic personality traits in helping: A re-examination. *Journal of Personality, 57,* 41-67.

Eisenberg, N., Pasternack, J. F., Cameron, E., & Tryon, K. (1984). The relation of quantity and mode of prosocial to moral cognitions and social style. *Child Development, 55,* 1479-1485.

Eisenberg, N., Schaller, M., Fabes, R. A., Bustamante, D., Mathy, R., Shell, R., & Rhodes, K. (1988). The differentiation of personal distress and sympathy in children and adults. *Developmental Psychology, 24,* 766-775.

Eisenberg, N., Shea, C. L., Carlo, G., & Knight, G. (in press). Empathy-related responding and cognition: A "chicken and the egg" dilemma. In W. Kurtines (Ed.), *Advances in moral development* (Vol. 1). New York: John Wiley.

Fabes, R. A., Eisenberg, N., & Miller, P. A. (1990). Maternal correlates of children's vicarious emotional responsiveness. *Developmental Psychology, 26,* 639-648.

Feshbach, N. D. (1987). Parental empathy and child adjustment/maladjustment. In N. Eisenberg & J. Strayer (Eds.), *Empathy and its development* (pp. 271-291). Cambridge: Cambridge University Press.

Feshbach, S., & Feshbach, N. D. (1986). Aggression and altruism: A personality perspective. In C. Zahn-Waxler, E. M. Cummings, & R. Iannotti (Eds.), *Altruism and aggression: Biological and social origins* (pp. 189-217). Cambridge: Cambridge University Press.

Field, T. (1982). Affective displays of high-risk infants during early interactions. In T. Field & A. Fogel (Ed.), *Emotion and early interaction* (pp. 101-125). Hillsdale, NJ: Lawrence Erlbaum.

Fox, N. A. (1989). Psychophysiological correlates of emotional reactivity during the first year of life. *Developmental Psychology, 25,* 364-372.

Fultz, J., Fabes, R. A., Miller, P. A., Eisenberg, N., Shell, R., & Shea, C. (1987). *Focus of attention, sympathy, and helping behavior.* Unpublished manuscript.

Gaertner, S. L., & Dovidio, J. F. (1977). The subtlety of White racism arousal and helping behavior. *Journal of Personality and Social Psychology, 35,* 691-707.

Gergen, K. J., Gergen, M. M., & Meter, K. (1972). Individual orientations to prosocial behavior. *Journal of Social Issues, 8,* 105-130.

Hampson, R. B. (1984). Adolescent prosocial behavior: Peer group and situational factors associated with helping. *Journal of Personality and Social Psychology, 46,* 153-162.

Hoffman, M. L. (1976). Empathy, role-taking, guilt, and development of altruistic motives. In T. Lickona (Ed.), *Moral development and behavior: Theory, research and social issues* (pp. 124-143). New York: Holt.

Hoffman, M. L. (1982). Development of prosocial motivation: Empathy and guilt. In N. Eisenberg (Ed.), *The development of prosocial behavior* (pp. 218-231). New York: Academic Press.

Howard, J. A. (1983). Preschoolers' empathy for specific affects and their social interaction (Doctoral dissertation, Kansas State University, Manhattan). *Dissertation Abstracts International, 44,* 3954B.

Kagan, J. (1982). Heart rate and heart rate variability as signs of a temperamental dimension in infants. In C. E. Izard (Ed.), *Measuring emotions in infants and children* (pp. 38-66). Cambridge: Cambridge University Press.

Kutina, J., & Fischer, J. (1977). Anxiety, heart rate and their interrelation at mental stress in school children. *Activitas Nervosa Superior, 19,* 89-95.

Lacey, J. I., Kagan, J., Lacey, B. C., & Moss, H. A. (1963). The visceral level: Situational determinants and behavioral correlates of autonomic response patterns. In P. H. Knapp (Ed.), *Expression of the emotions in man* (pp. 161-196). New York: International Universities Press.

Langer, E. J., Blank, A., & Chanowitz, B. (1978). The mindlessness of ostensibly thoughtful action. *Journal of Personality and Social Psychology, 36,* 635-642.

Lanzetta, J. T., & Englis, B. G. (1989). Expectations of cooperation and competition on observers' vicarious emotional responses. *Journal of Personality and Social Psychology, 56,* 543-554.

Lazarus, R. S. (1974). A cognitively oriented psychologist looks at biofeedback. *American Psychologist, 30,* 553-561.

Lazarus, R. S., & Folkman, S. (1984). *Stress, appraisal, and coping.* New York: Springer.

Lennon, R., Eisenberg, N., & Carroll, J. (1986). The relation between empathy and prosocial behavior in the preschool years. *Journal of Applied Developmental Psychology, 7,* 219-224.

Marcus, R. F. (1987). Somatic indices of empathy. In N. Eisenberg & J. Strayer (Eds.), *Empathy and its development* (pp. 374-379). Cambridge: Cambridge University Press.

Mehrabian, A., & Epstein, N. A. (1972). A measure of emotional empathy. *Journal of Personality, 40,* 523-543.

Miller, S. M., & Green, M. L. (1985). Coping with stress and frustration: Origins, nature, and development. In M. Lewis & C. Saarni (Eds.), *The socialization of emotions* (pp. 263-314). New York: Plenum.

Obrist, P. A., Webb, R. A., Sutterer, J. R., & Howard, J. L. (1970). Cardiac deceleration and reaction time: An evaluation of two hypotheses. *Psychophysiology, 6,* 695-706.

Periano, J. M., & Sawin, D. B. (1981, April). *Empathic distress: Measurement and relation to prosocial behavior.* Paper presented at the biennial meeting of the Society for Research in Child Development, Boston.

Piliavin, J. A., Dovidio, J. F., Gaertner, S. L., & Clark, R. D., III. (1981). *Emergency intervention.* New York: Academic Press.

Piliavin, J. A., Dovidio, J. F., Gaertner, S. L., & Clark, R. D., III. (1982). Responsive bystanders: The process of intervention. In V. J. Derlega & J. Grzelak (Eds.), *Cooperation and helping behavior: Theories and research* (pp. 279-304). New York: Academic Press.

Radke-Yarrow, M., Zahn-Waxler, C., & Chapman, M. (1983). Prosocial dispositions and behavior. In P. Mussen (Ed.), *Manual of child psychology* (Vol. 4, E. M. Hetherington, Ed.), *Socialization, personality, and social development* (pp. 469-545). New York: John Wiley.

Roberts, W., & Strayer, J. (1987). Parents' responses to the emotional distress of their children: Relations with children's competence. *Developmental Psychology, 23,* 415-432.

Saarni, C. (1982). Social and affective functions of nonverbal behavior: Developmental concerns. In R. S. Feldman (Ed.), *Development of nonverbal behavior in children* (pp. 123-147). New York: Springer-Verlag.

Shennum, W. A., & Bugenthal, D. B. (1982). The development of control over affective expression. In R. S. Feldman (Ed.), *Development of nonverbal behavior in children* (pp. 101-121). New York: Springer-Verlag.

Smith, T. W., Allred, K. D., Morrison, C. A., & Carlson, S. D. (1989). Cardiovascular reactivity and interpersonal influence: Active coping in a social situation. *Journal of Personality and Social Psychology, 56,* 209-218.

Snyder, M., & Ickes, W. (1985). Personality and social behavior. In G. Lindzey & E. Aronson (Eds.), *Handbook of social psychology* (3rd ed., pp. 883-948). New York: Random House.

Sterling, B., & Gaertner, S. L. (1984). The attribution of arousal and emergency helping: A bi-directional process. *Journal of Experimental Social Psychology, 20,* 286-296.

Strayer, J., & Schroeder, M. (1989). Children's helping strategies: Influences of emotion, empathy, and age. In N. Eisenberg (Ed.), *New directions in child development: Empathy and related emotional responses* (Vol. 44, pp. 85-106). San Francisco: Jossey-Bass.

Underwood, B., & Moore, B. (1982). Perspective-taking and altruism. *Psychological Bulletin, 91,* 143-173.

Wispé, L. (1986). The distinction between sympathy and empathy: To call forth a concept, a word is needed. *Journal of Personality and Social Psychology, 50,* 314-421.

3

Current Status of the Empathy-Altruism Hypothesis

C. DANIEL BATSON
KATHRYN C. OLESON

C. Daniel Batson received his Ph.D. in psychology from Princeton University in 1972 and is now Professor of Psychology at the University of Kansas. He studies motivators of prosocial and antisocial behavior, focusing on vicarious emotion and personal values as sources of such motivation. He has a forthcoming book, *The Altruism Question: Toward a Psychological Answer* (Lawrence Erlbaum).

Kathryn C. Oleson is a graduate student in social psychology at Princeton University. Currently, her research examines the effect of biases on decision-making strategies and the process of self-presentation leading to self-concept change. Other interests include the impact of emotion, moral principles, and religious orientation on prosocial motivation.

Why do we help others? Most of us have asked ourselves this question. Often, of course, the answer is easy. We help because we have no choice, because it is expected, or because it is in our own best interest. We do a friend a favor because we do not want to lose the friendship or because we expect to see the favor reciprocated. But it is not for such easy answers that we ask ourselves why we help; it is to press the limits of these answers. We want to know whether our helping is *always and exclusively* motivated by the prospect of some benefit for ourselves, however subtle. We want to know whether anyone ever, in any degree, transcends the bounds of self-benefit and helps out of genuine concern for the welfare of another. We want to know if altruism exists.

Advocates of *universal egoism* claim that everything we do, no matter how noble and beneficial to others, is really directed toward the ultimate goal of self-benefit. Advocates of *altruism* do not deny that the motivation for much of what we do, including much that we do for others, is egoistic. But they claim there is more. They claim that, at least under some circumstances, we are capable of a qualitatively different form of motivation, motivation with an ultimate goal of benefiting someone else.

AUTHORS' NOTE: Preparation of this chapter was supported by National Science Foundation grants BNS-8507110 and BNS-8906723 to C. Daniel Batson (Principal Investigator).

Over the centuries, the most frequently proposed source of altruism has been what we shall call *empathy*—an other-oriented emotional response congruent with the perceived welfare of another person. If the other is in need, then empathic emotions include sympathy, compassion, tenderness, and the like. These empathic emotions can and should be distinguished from the more self-oriented emotions of discomfort, anxiety, and upset, often called "personal distress" (Batson, Fultz, & Schoenrade, 1987). The *empathy-altruism hypothesis* claims that feeling empathy evokes motivation with an ultimate goal of benefiting the person for whom empathy is felt.

If true, this empathy-altruism hypothesis seems quite important. Not only does it contradict the common assumption in psychology that all motivation is ultimately directed toward the egoistic goal of increasing our own welfare, but it also contradicts the underlying assumption that human nature is fundamentally self-serving (Wallach & Wallach, 1983). It suggests that we may be more interconnected with one another than we have imagined. Rather than others simply being sources of reward and punishment, of facilitation and inhibition as we each pursue our own welfare, the empathy-altruism hypothesis claims that we are actually capable of caring about the welfare of others for their sakes and not simply for our own. But is this hypothesis true?

DISCERNING THE MOTIVES UNDERLYING THE EMPATHY-HELPING RELATIONSHIP

There is considerable evidence that feeling empathy for a person in need leads to increased helping of that person (Batson, Duncan, Ackerman, Buckley, & Birch, 1981; Coke, Batson, & McDavis, 1978; Fultz, Batson, Fortenbach, McCarthy, & Varney, 1986; Krebs, 1975; Toi & Batson, 1982; and see Eisenberg & Miller, 1987, for an extensive review). To observe an empathy-helping relationship, however, tells us nothing about the nature of the motivation that underlies this relationship. It gives us a phenomenon to explain, not an explanation. The motivation could be altruistic or egoistic: Increasing the other person's welfare could be the ultimate goal, or it could be merely an instrumental goal on the way to the ultimate goal of increasing our own welfare.

There are obvious self-benefits that result from helping a person for whom we feel empathy. We reduce our empathic arousal, which may be experienced as aversive; we avoid social and self-punishments for failing to help when we feel we should; and we gain social and self-rewards for doing what we feel is good and right. Egoistic explanations of the empathy-helping relationship assume that one or more of these self-benefits is the ultimate goal of the empathically aroused helper. But it is possible that these self-benefits are unintended consequences of the helper reaching the ultimate goal of reducing the other's suffering. And if they are, then the underlying motivation is altruistic.

To determine the validity of the empathy-altruism hypothesis we must ascertain the empathically aroused helper's ultimate goal. The most fruitful strategy for doing this seems to be to consider possible egoistic ultimate goals in turn, conducting experiments that vary helping situations in ways that disentangle the confounding of the benefit to other and the benefit to self.

In 1987, Batson reviewed evidence from a series of studies that employed this strategy to test one major egoistic alternative to the empathy-altruism hypothesis: aversive-arousal reduction. He also identified two other major egoistic alternatives that still needed to be tested: empathy-specific punishment and empathy-specific reward. Over the past five years, more than a dozen experiments have been conducted to test these other two alternatives. To provide a comprehensive assessment of the current status of the empathy-altruism hypothesis, we shall consider evidence for each of these major egoistic alternatives.

TESTING EGOISTIC ALTERNATIVES TO THE EMPATHY-ALTRUISM HYPOTHESIS

Aversive-Arousal Reduction

The most frequently proposed egoistic explanation of the empathy-helping relationship has long been aversive-arousal reduction. This explanation claims that the goal of empathically aroused helpers is to reduce their own empathic emotion, which—as a congruent response to the perceived suffering of another—is experienced as aversive. Hoffman (1981b) put this aversive-arousal reduction explanation in a nutshell: "Empathic distress is unpleasant and helping the victim is usually the best way to get rid of the source" (p. 52; see also Dovidio, 1984; Krebs, 1975; Piliavin & Piliavin, 1973). According to this explanation, empathically aroused individuals help to benefit themselves by reducing their empathic arousal.

To test this aversive-arousal reduction explanation against the empathy-altruism hypothesis, experiments have been conducted varying the ease of escaping further exposure to the suffering victim without actually helping. Because aversive empathic arousal is a result of witnessing the victim's suffering, either terminating this suffering by helping or terminating exposure to it by escaping should serve to reduce the arousal. Escape is not, however, a viable means of reaching the altruistic goal of relieving the victim's distress; it does nothing to promote that end.

The difference in viability of escape as a means to these two goals produces competing predictions in an Escape (easy versus difficult) × Empathy (low versus high) design. Among individuals experiencing low empathy for the person in need, both the aversive-arousal reduction explanation and the empathy-altruism hypothesis predict more helping when escape is difficult than when it is easy. This is because both explanations assume that the motivation of individuals feeling low empathy is egoistic. Among individuals feeling high empathy, the aversive-arousal reduction explanation predicts a similar difference; it assumes that empathically induced motivation is also egoistic. But the empathy-altruism hypothesis predicts high helping even when escape is easy among individuals feeling high empathy for the person in need. Across the four cells of an Escape × Empathy design, then, the aversive-arousal reduction explanation predicts less helping under easy escape in each empathy condition; the empathy-altruism hypothesis predicts a 1 versus 3 pattern: relatively low helping in the easy-escape/low-empathy cell and high helping in the other three cells.

In a typical experiment employing an Escape × Empathy design, participants observe a "worker" whom they believe is reacting badly to a series of uncomfortable electric shocks; they are then given a chance to help the worker by taking the shocks themselves. To manipulate ease of escape, some participants are informed that, if they do not help, they will continue observing the worker take the shocks (difficult escape); others are informed that they will observe no more (easy escape). Empathy has sometimes been manipulated, sometimes measured, and sometimes both.

Batson (1987) summarized evidence from five different studies that have used an Escape × Empathy design to test the aversive-arousal reduction explanation. Results consistently conformed to the 1 versus 3 pattern predicted by the empathy-altruism hypothesis and not to the main-effect pattern predicted by the aversive-arousal reduction explanation. Only among individuals experiencing a predominance of personal distress rather than empathy did the chance for easy escape reduce helping. In spite of the longstanding popularity of the aversive-arousal reduction explanation of the empathy-helping relationship, a popularity that continues in a number of social psychology textbooks, this explanation appears to be wrong.

Empathy-Specific Punishment

The empathy-specific punishment explanation claims we learn through socialization that an additional obligation to help, and so additional guilt and shame for failure to help, are attendant on feeling empathy for someone in need. As a result, when we feel empathy, we are faced with impending social or self-censure above and beyond any general punishment associated with not helping. We say to ourselves, "What will others think—or what will I think of myself—if I don't help when I feel like this?" We help out of an egoistic desire to avoid these empathy-specific punishments.

In recent years, two versions of this empathy-specific punishment explanation have been proposed. One is based on social evaluation and anticipated social punishments; the other, on self-evaluation and self-punishment.

Socially Administered Empathy-Specific Punishments

According to the first version, empathy leads to increased helping only when empathic individuals anticipate negative social evaluation for failing to act in a manner consistent with their expressed feelings of concern (Archer, 1984; Archer, Diaz-Loving, Gollwitzer, Davis, & Foushee, 1981). To test this version, Fultz et al. (1986) confronted female undergraduates induced to feel more and less empathy for a lonely young woman with an opportunity to help her. To manipulate anticipation of negative social evaluation, research participants were led to believe either that both the experimenter and the young woman would know if they decided not to help (high social evaluation) or that no one else would know (low social evaluation). The latter was accomplished by having information about the need and about the opportunity to help come from two independent and unrelated sources.

Fultz et al. reasoned that, if social-evaluative circumstances are a necessary condition for the empathy-helping relationship, then, under low social evaluation, the empathy-helping relationship should disappear. However, if empathy evokes altruistic motivation to reduce the victim's need, then even under low social evaluation the empathy-helping relationship should remain.   . In each of two studies, Fultz et al. found an empathy-helping relationship even under low social evaluation. Results of these two studies cast serious doubt on the first version of the empathy-specific punishment explanation. They instead support the empathy-altruism hypothesis.

Self-Administered Empathy-Specific Punishments

The second version of the empathy-specific punishment hypothesis claims that empathically aroused individuals help not to avoid social censure but to avoid self-administered punishments and negative self-evaluation (Batson, 1987; Dovidio, 1984; Schaller & Cialdini, 1988). Testing this version is more difficult than testing the previous one, for it requires a procedure in which potential helpers can escape anticipated self-punishment (guilt, shame) for not helping.

What might allow individuals to escape expectations of self-punishment? If these expectations have been internalized to the degree that they are automatic and invariant across all helping situations, then nothing will allow escape. But it seems unlikely that many people, if any, have internalized expectations of self-punishment to such a degree. Even those who feel guilty whenever they do wrong are likely to be sensitive to situational cues in determining when they have done wrong. And, given the discomfort produced by self-recrimination, it seems likely that most people will not automatically self-punish. Instead, they will, if possible, overlook their failures to do good, doling out self-punishments only in situations in which their failures are salient and inescapable. Where there is leeway in interpreting a failure to help as unjustified and hence deserving of self-punishment, the expectation of self-punishment can be reduced by providing individuals with information that justifies not helping. Batson et al. (1988) used a different technique to provide justification for not helping in each of three studies.

(1) *Providing justification for not helping through the inaction of others.* Research on social influence and norms (Moscovici, 1985; Sherif, 1936) suggested using information about the inaction of other potential helpers to provide justification. If most people asked have said

no to a request for help, then one should feel more justified in saying no as well. Following this logic, Batson et al. (1988, Study 2) gave individuals feeling either low or high empathy for a young woman in need an opportunity to pledge time to help her. Information on the pledge form about the responses of previously asked peers indicated that either five or seven had pledged (low justification) or two of seven had pledged (high justification). The young woman's need was such that others' responses did not affect her need for help.

Results revealed more helping in the low-justification condition than in the high for participants induced to feel little empathy, but high helping in both justification conditions for participants induced to feel high empathy. This was the pattern predicted by the empathy-altruism hypothesis, not the pattern predicted by the empathy-specific punishment hypothesis. The empathy-specific punishment explanation had predicted more helping in the low-justification condition than in the high by participants induced to feel high empathy.

(2) *Providing justification for not helping through attributional ambiguity.* Research by Snyder, Kleck, Strenta, and Mentzer (1979) suggested a second technique for providing justification: attributional ambiguity. If individuals can attribute a decision not to help to helping-irrelevant features of the decision, then they should be less likely to anticipate self-punishment. Following this logic, Batson et al. (1988, Study 3) gave research participants a chance to work on either or both of two task options. For each correct response on Option A, participants would receive one raffle ticket for a $30.00 prize for themselves; for each correct response on Option B, they would reduce by one the shocks a peer was to receive. Information about helping-irrelevant attributes of the two task options indicated either that the two tasks were quite similar and neither was typically preferred (low justification) or that one task involved numbers, the other letters, and most people preferred to work on the numbers or on the letters—whichever was paired with the nonhelpful Option A (high justification).

Once again, among individuals reporting low empathy for the peer, participants helped more in the low-justification condition than in the high. Among individuals reporting high empathy, helping was high in both justification conditions, supporting the empathy-altruism hypothesis and not the empathy-specific punishment explanation.

(3) *Providing justification for not helping through difficulty of the performance standard on a qualifying task.* As a third technique, Batson

et al. (1988, Study 4) gave participants a chance to help a peer, whom they watched reacting intensely to a series of uncomfortable electric shocks, by taking the remaining shocks themselves. But, even if they volunteered, participants had to meet the performance standard on a qualifying task before they could help. Justification for not helping was manipulated by varying the difficulty of the performance standard on this task. In the low-justification condition, the standard was described as relatively easy: 70% of college students qualify. In the high-justification condition, the standard was quite difficult: only 20% of college students qualify. Dependent variables were (a) volunteering to help and (b) performance on the qualifying task by those volunteering.

Batson et al. (1988) reasoned that performance on the qualifying task should provide a behavioral measure of motivation to reduce the peer's suffering (which requires qualifying) or to avoid self-punishment (which does not). This should be true, however, only if poor performance could be justified, which it could if the performance standard on the qualifying task was so difficult that most people would fail. If the standard was this difficult, a person could not be blamed—either by him- or herself or by others—for not qualifying. In this case, individuals motivated to avoid self-punishment could either (a) decline to help because of the low probability of qualifying or (b) offer to help but not try very hard on the qualifying task, ensuring that they did not qualify: Put bluntly, they could take a dive. In contrast, altruistically motivated individuals should try even harder when the standard was difficult. Only by both volunteering to help and qualifying could they reach the altruistic goal of relieving the peer's suffering.

Helping responses in this study patterned as in the two previous studies, once again supporting the empathy-altruism hypothesis. The performance measure also patterned as predicted by the empathy-altruism hypothesis: Performance of low-empathy individuals was lower when the qualifying standard was difficult than when it was easy; performance of high-empathy individuals was higher when the qualifying standard was difficult. This interaction pattern suggested that the motivation of low-empathy individuals was at least in part directed toward avoiding self-punishment; whereas, contrary to the empathy-specific punishment explanation, the motivation of high-empathy individuals was not. The motivation of these individuals appeared to be directed toward the altruistic goal of relieving the other's suffering.

Implications. In each of these three studies then, justification for not helping dramatically reduced the helping of low-empathy individuals, but it had very little effect on the helping of high-empathy individuals. The relatively high rate of helping by high-empathy individuals, even when justification for not helping was high, is precisely what we would expect if feeling empathy for the person in need evokes altruistic motivation to have that person's need reduced. It is not what we would expect if feeling empathy evokes increased egoistic motivation to avoid anticipated self-punishment.

In sum, all attempts to date to find evidence for either the social evaluation version or the self-evaluation version of the empathy-specific punishment explanation have failed to provide supporting evidence. This second egoistic explanation of the empathy-helping relationship is, it seems, also wrong.

Empathy-Specific Reward

The final major egoistic alternative to the empathy-altruism hypothesis, the empathy-specific reward explanation, claims we learn through socialization that special rewards in the form of praise, honor, and pride are attendant on helping a person for whom we feel empathy. As a result, when we feel empathy, we think of these rewards and help out of an egoistic desire to gain them.

Two versions of this empathy-specific reward explanation have been proposed. The first claims that we learn through prior reinforcement that, after helping those for whom we feel empathy, we can expect a special mood-enhancing pat on the back—either from others in the form of praise or from ourselves in the form of enhanced self-image. When we feel empathy, we think of this good feeling and are egoistically motivated to obtain it (Batson, 1987; Thompson, Cowan, & Rosenhan, 1980; also see Meindl & Lerner, 1983). In contrast to this first version, the second claims that it is not the social or self-reward that is empathy specific, it is the *need* for this reward that is. Feeling empathy for a person who is suffering involves a state of temporary sadness, and this sadness can be relieved by any mood-enhancing experience, including obtaining the social and self-rewards that accompany helping. According to this second version, the egoistic desire for negative-state relief accounts for the increased helping of empathically aroused individuals (Cialdini et al., 1987; Schaller & Cialdini, 1988).

Social and Self-Rewards Associated with the Empathy-Helping Relationship

Batson et al. (1988) reported two studies designed to test the first version of the empathy-specific reward explanation. In the first, they assessed the effect on mood of depriving high-empathy individuals of the opportunity to help.

Effect on mood of not being allowed to help. Because social and self-rewards for helping are given only to the helper, the empathy-specific reward explanation predicts that empathically aroused individuals will feel worse if deprived of an anticipated opportunity to help (assuming that helping is low cost and effective). In contrast, the empathy-altruism hypothesis predicts that empathically aroused individuals will feel as good when the victim's need is relieved by other means as when it is relieved by their own action. The empathy-altruism hypothesis also predicts that, when empathically aroused individuals are deprived of the opportunity to help, they will feel better when the victim's need is relieved by other means than when it is not relieved. The empathy-specific reward explanation does not predict a difference in mood across these two conditions, because neither relief of the need nor lack of relief per se is relevant to the egoistic goal of obtaining mood-enhancing rewards for helping.

To test these predictions, Batson et al. (1988, Study 1) led individuals feeling either low or high empathy for a person about to receive electric shocks to believe that they would have a no-cost, no-risk opportunity to help the person avoid the shocks. Later, half of the individuals learned that by chance they would not have the opportunity to help after all. Moreover, both among the individuals who would have the opportunity to help and those who would not, half learned that the person still was scheduled to receive the shocks, and half learned that by chance this threat had been removed. These variations produced an Empathy (low versus high) × Prior Relief of Victim's Need (no prior relief versus prior relief) × Perform Helping Task (perform versus not perform) design. The major dependent measure was change in self-reported mood after participants were or were not allowed to help.

The pattern of mood change for individuals reporting high empathy was as predicted by the empathy-altruism hypothesis and not the empathy-specific reward explanation. There was more positive mood change in the three cells in which the victim's need was relieved than in the one in which it was not; prior relief of the victim's need did not lead to the negative mood change predicted by the empathy-specific reward explanation. Moreover, this pattern of results was specific to high-empathy individuals; it did not approach statistical reliability among low-empathy individuals.

Goal-relevant cognitions associated with empathy-induced helping. In a second study, Batson et al. (1988, Study 5) examined the goal-relevant cognitions associated with empathy-induced helping. They reasoned that if the goal of high-empathy helpers is to obtain social and self-rewards such as praise, honor, and esteem, as the empathy-specific reward explanation claims, then reward-relevant cognitions should be associated with high-empathy helping; if the goal is to relieve the victim's need, as the empathy-altruism hypothesis claims, then victim-relevant cognitions should be associated with high-empathy helping. These predictions were tested using a Stroop (1938) procedure, which detects the salience of cognitions by assessing the time taken to name the color of the ink in which words expressing these cognitions are printed. Stroop (1938) had found that color-naming latency for a word increases when respondents are thinking about cognitions related to that word.

Batson et al. (1988) led research participants to feel either low or high empathy for a young woman who had lost her parents in a tragic automobile accident and was struggling to avoid having to put her younger brother and sister up for adoption. While deciding whether to volunteer to help her, participants performed a reaction-time task (ostensibly to provide a baseline control for assessing cognitive reactions to the broadcast tape that informed them of the young woman's need). On this task, they named as quickly as possible the color of the ink in which a series of words appeared. Some words were reward relevant *(nice, proud, honor, praise),* some were victim relevant *(loss, needy, adopt, tragic),* and some were neutral *(pair, clean, extra, smooth).* To provide a further test of the empathy-specific punishment hypothesis, some words were also punishment relevant *(duty, guilt, shame, oblige).*

The only positive association in the high-empathy condition was between helping and color-naming latency for the victim-relevant words. This was the association predicted by the empathy-altruism hypothesis. There was no evidence that the helping of high-empathy individuals was positively associated with thoughts of either empathy-specific rewards or empathy-specific punishments. Once again, the first version of the empathy-specific reward explanation (and the empathy-specific punishment explanation) failed to receive support.

A Variant on Version 1 of the Empathy-Specific Reward Explanation: Empathic Joy

Smith, Keating, and Stotland (1989) have recently suggested an interesting variant on the first version of the empathy-specific reward explanation. Rather than helping to gain the rewards of seeing oneself or being seen by others as a helpful person, Smith, Keating, and Stotland propose that empathically aroused individuals help to gain the good feeling of sharing vicariously in the joy of the needy individual's relief. "It is proposed that the prospect of empathic joy, conveyed by feedback from the help recipient, is essential to the special tendency of empathic witnesses to help. . . . The empathically concerned witness to the distress of others helps in order to be happy" (Smith, Keating, & Stotland, 1989, p. 641).

Unlike other forms of Version 1 of the empathy-specific reward explanation, the rewards at issue here are contingent on the victim's need being relieved and not on the empathically aroused individual being the agent of this relief. The agent might be another person, time (which, it is said, heals all wounds), or chance, and the empathic joy would be as sweet. Therefore, none of the evidence against the first version of the empathy-specific reward explanation reviewed thus far counts against the empathic-joy hypothesis. All of the preceding evidence deals with rewards from helping, not from seeing the victim's need relieved.

Effect of feedback on the empathy-helping relationship. To test their empathic-joy hypothesis, Smith, Keating, and Stotland (1989) manipulated the expectation of feedback concerning the effect of one's helping efforts. They reasoned that if the empathic-joy hypothesis is correct, the empathy-helping relationship should be found only when prospective helpers anticipate receiving feedback on the effect of their helping efforts: "When feedback is assured, the empathic person can expect to move from a state of empathic concern to empathic joy by helping, and we would expect the familiar positive relation between empathic concern and helping" (Smith, Keating, & Stotland, 1989, pp. 642-643). But when prospective helpers do not anticipate receiving feedback, "helping is a goal-irrelevant response, and we would expect empathic witnesses to refuse to help as often as their non-empathic counterparts" (p. 643). If, however, the empathy-altruism hypothesis is correct, then the empathy-helping relationship should be found even under no-feedback conditions; helping can still relieve the victim's need.

In a 2 (feedback versus no feedback) × 2 (low versus high empathy) design, Smith, Keating, and Stotland (1989) found an empathy-helping relationship in both feedback conditions. This was the pattern predicted by the empathy-altruism hypothesis, and not the empathic-joy hypothesis. Because their empathy manipulation did not have a significant effect on self-reported empathy (it did have a significant effect on helping), Smith, Keating, and Stotland (1989) chose to disregard these results and focus instead on an internal analysis in which low- and high-empathy conditions were created by a median split on a measure of self-reported empathy minus self-reported distress. In this internal analysis, there was no relationship between relative empathy and helping in the no-feedback condition, as predicted by the empathic-joy hypothesis. But there are reasons to doubt the validity of self-reports of empathy and, especially, self-reports on a difference measure in the particular research procedure used by Smith, Keating, and Stotland (see Batson, in press). Therefore, their experimental manipulation seems to us to have been the better operationalization of empathy. And, if it was, then the results of this experiment support the empathy-altruism hypothesis and not the empathic-joy hypothesis. We do not, however, place much confidence in this conclusion. A more appropriate conclusion is that the empathic-joy hypothesis needs more testing.

Effect of likelihood of improvement on desire for further exposure to a person in need. Batson, Batson, Slingsby, et al. (1990) recently completed two studies designed to test the relative merits of the empathic-joy and empathy-altruism hypotheses using a different technique. In these studies, research participants presented with a person in need were not given a chance to help the person. Instead, they were given a choice of whether to hear a second interview with that person or an interview with someone else. Before choosing, participants received information (ostensibly from experts) on the likelihood that the needy person's situation would be substantially improved by the time of the second interview. Some participants were told the likelihood was only 20%; some were told it was 50%; and some were told it was 80%. Perspective-taking instructions were used to manipulate empathy, producing a 2 (low versus high empathy) × 3 (20%, 50%, 80% likelihood of improvement) factorial design.

Batson et al. (1990) reasoned that if empathically aroused individuals are egoistically motivated to gain empathic joy, then their desire to hear from the needy person again should be a function of the likelihood of obtaining empathic joy. Accordingly, in the high-empathy condition, there should be a linear relation between the likelihood the needy person would be better and the choice to hear from this person again: Few participants should make this choice in the 20% condition, more should make this choice in the 50% condition, and the most should make this choice in the 80% condition. In the low-empathy condition, there should be little incentive to choose to hear from the needy person again regardless of the likelihood of improvement. Thus, overall, the empathic-joy hypothesis predicted an interaction between the empathy and likelihood-of-improvement manipulations.

If, however, empathically aroused individuals are altruistically concerned for the needy person's welfare, then there should be a main effect for empathy. Participants in the high-empathy condition, because they are more concerned about the person's welfare, should have more interest in hearing about how she is doing than participants in the low-empathy condition. In the high-empathy condition, there should not be the linear increase predicted by the empathic-joy hypothesis.

Batson et al. (1990) tested these competing predictions in two different experiments. Results of each were patterned as predicted by the empathy-altruism hypothesis, not the empathic-joy hypothesis. Participants in the high-empathy condition were more likely than participants in the low-empathy condition to choose to hear from the person in need again. In neither experiment was there any evidence of the linear trend in the high-empathy condition predicted by the empathic-joy hypothesis or evidence of the predicted Empathy × Likelihood of Improvement interaction.

Considering the results of these two experiments and the results of the Smith, Keating, and Stotland (1989) experiment, there is not considerable evidence that empathically aroused individuals are now motivated simply to gain the pleasure of sharing vicariously in the needy person's relief. The empathic-joy hypothesis, like the earlier form of the first version of the empathy-specific reward explanation, does not appear capable of accounting for the empathy-helping relationship.

Negative-State Relief and the Empathy-Helping Relationship

We turn now to the second version of the empathy-specific reward explanation. Cialdini and his colleagues (Cialdini et al., 1987; Schaller

& Cialdini, 1988) have argued that it is *the need for the rewards of helping, not the rewards themselves,* that is empathy specific. They claim that individuals who experience empathy when witnessing another person's suffering are in a negative affective state—one of temporary sadness or sorrow—and help in order to relieve this negative state. "Because helping contains a rewarding component for most normally socialized adults . . . , it can be used instrumentally to restore mood" (Cialdini et al., 1987, p. 750).

The empathy-altruism hypothesis does not dispute the Cialdini et al. (1987) claim that individuals feeling empathy for someone in need are likely to feel sad. Indeed, expressions of sadness at learning of another's suffering have been used as an index of empathy by some researchers (Eisenberg et al., 1989). The empathy-altruism hypothesis also does not dispute the claim that, following helping, empathically aroused individuals are likely to feel better (see Batson et al., 1988, Study 1). What it disputes is the claim that empathically aroused individuals help *in order to* feel better. Disagreement is over the nature of the motivation underlying the empathy-helping relationship, not over the presence of or even mediation by feelings of sadness.

As Cialdini et al. (1987) point out, negative-state relief can explain why more empathy leads to more helping even when physical escape is easy and not helping is justified. According to a negative-state relief explanation, the empathy-helping relationship remains even under these conditions because the empathically aroused individual is in special need of a positive, mood-enhancing experience, and the self-rewards associated with helping are the only such experience available. Escape may reduce one's aversive arousal, and justification may enable one to avoid social and self-punishment, but these conditions do not provide positive mood enhancement.

Effect of mood enhancement on the empathy-helping relationship. Cialdini et al. (1987) sought to test their negative-state relief explanation of the empathy-helping relationship by conducting two studies. In the first, they used an experimental procedure that included essentially the same need situation, opportunity to help, and escape manipulation used by Batson, Duncan, Ackerman, Buckley, and Birch (1981) to provide support for the empathy-altruism hypothesis. Into this procedure they introduced perspective-taking instructions to manipulate empathy (Stotland, 1969; Toi & Batson, 1982) and mood-enhancing experiences (payment or praise) to provide negative-state relief (Cialdini, Darby, & Vincent, 1973).

Results of this initial experiment patterned in some ways as predicted by the negative-state relief explanation, but they were neither very strong nor very consistent. Although the rate of helping was somewhat lower for easy-escape/high-empathy individuals who had an interposed rewarding experience, as predicted by the negative-state relief explanation, the decrease was clear only for those paid, not for those praised. Moreover, payment decreased the rate of helping in the difficult-escape condition as much as in the easy-escape condition, suggesting the presence of processes other than negative-state relief, such as reactance (Brehm & Cole, 1966).

Effect of mood fixing on the empathy-helping relationship. In their second experiment, Cialdini et al. (1987) did not interpose a mood-enhancing experience between exposure to the victim's suffering and the opportunity to help; instead, they interposed information designed to convince some participants that, because they had taken a mood-fixing drug (a manipulation used previously by Manucia, Baumann, & Cialdini, 1984), helping would not enhance their mood. Perspective-taking instructions similar to those in the previous experiment were used to manipulate empathy.

For a scaled measure of helping (amount of help offered), results of this experiment patterned as predicted by the negative-state relief model, not the empathy-altruism hypothesis. The increased helping of high-empathy individuals disappeared when they were informed that helping would not enhance their mood. For a dichotomous measure of helping (proportion of participants agreeing to help), however, this pattern was weaker and did not approach statistical reliability.

Cialdini et al. (1987, p. 757) concluded that the results of their two experiments "appear to support an egoistic (Negative-State Relief model) interpretation over a selfless (Empathy-Altruism model) interpretation of enhanced helping under conditions of high empathy." They were careful to point out, however, that their case was not airtight because distraction could have been a confound in each experiment: "The reward procedures of Experiment 1 or the placebo-drug procedures of Experiment 2 may have turned subjects' attention away from their empathic emotions" (Cialdini et al., 1987, p. 757). Cialdini et al. recognized that their results offered no strong disconfirmation of a distraction explanation, and they called for subsequent research to address this issue.

A distraction confound in the Cialdini et al. (1987) experiments? The possibility that distraction produced the apparent support for the negative-state relief explanation in the Cialdini et al. (1987) experiments was underscored by the results of an experiment by Schroeder, Dovidio, Sibicky, Matthews, and Allen (1988). Working at the same time as Cialdini et al., but independently, Schroeder et al. also tested the relative merits of the negative-state relief and empathy-altruism explanations using a perspective-taking manipulation of empathy and the Manucia, Baumann, and Cialdini (1984) mood-fixing manipulation. But Schroeder et al. obtained quite different results. They failed to find the drop in helping in the fixed-mood/high-empathy condition predicted by the negative-state relief model, and they concluded that their results were more supportive of the empathy-altruism hypothesis than of the negative-state relief explanation.

The conflicting results of the Schroeder et al. (1988) experiment and Cialdini et al.'s (1987) Experiment 2 may be due to an important procedural difference. In the Schroeder et al. experiment, participants were informed of the drug's effects (no mood fixing versus mood fixing) before they were exposed to the person in need. After exposure, those in the fixed-mood condition were simply reminded that the drug should fix their present mood "for the next 20 minutes or so." In the Cialdini et al. experiment, the mood-fixing side effect was introduced for the first time after participants had been exposed to the victim's need. The Schroeder et al. procedure seems far less likely to cause distraction.

Effect of anticipated mood enhancement on the empathy-helping relationship. Schaller and Cialdini (1988), recognizing that both of the Cialdini et al. (1987) experiments were subject to a distraction explanation, conducted a study in which they used the same need situation and empathy manipulation as Cialdini et al. (1987) in Experiment 2. But, rather than interposing mood-enhancing or mood-fixing information between the empathy induction and the opportunity to help, Schaller and Cialdini led some participants to expect that their mood would be enhanced shortly even if they chose not to help: They would listen to an audiotape of comedy routines. Other participants did not expect a mood-enhancing experience. To keep distraction to a minimum, information about the upcoming tape was presented at the beginning of the study; only a brief reminder was inserted between the empathy induction and the opportunity to help. Combined with the perspective-taking manipulation of empathy, this information produced an Anticipated Mood Enhancement (no anticipated mood enhancement versus anticipated enhancement) × Empathy (low versus high) design.

The negative-state relief explanation made two predictions in this design: In the no anticipated mood-enhancement condition, helping by high-empathy individuals would be higher than helping by low-empathy individuals. Among high-empathy individuals, helping would be lower in the anticipated mood-enhancement condition than in the no mood-enhancement condition. The empathy-altruism hypothesis predicted a main effect for empathy: Helping by high-empathy individuals would be higher than helping by low-empathy individuals in each mood-enhancement condition.

Schaller and Cialdini's (1988) results did not provide unambiguous support for either the negative-state relief explanation or the empathy-altruism hypothesis. On the scaled measure (amount of help offered), the results seemed more consistent with the negative-state relief explanation, but they were not statistically reliable except using an unadjusted post hoc analysis including time of semester. On the dichotomous measure (proportion of participants helping), results seemed at least as consistent with the empathy-altruism hypothesis.

In an independent effort to assess the relative merits of the negative-state relief explanation and the empathy-altruism hypothesis, Batson et al. (1989) conducted two studies using an Anticipated Mood Enhancement × Empathy design much like the one used by Schaller and Cialdini (1988). Results of these two studies were highly consistent. In each, there was a significant main effect for empathy; empathy produced relatively high helping even among individuals who anticipated mood enhancement without helping. This was the pattern predicted by the empathy-altruism hypothesis and not the negative-state relief explanation.

Clearly, there has been some disagreement about the status of the negative-state relief version of the empathy-specific reward explanation. Cialdini and his colleagues have claimed support for this version, although they have noted ambiguities and inconsistencies in their evidence. Other researchers using procedures less subject to interpretational ambiguity have found support for the empathy-altruism hypothesis and not the negative-state relief explanation. We believe that an objective assessment of the evidence to date suggests that the negative-state relief explanation of the empathy-helping relationship is probably wrong, but, of course, we may be the ones who are wrong.

A TENTATIVE CONCLUSION

If this second version of the third major egoistic alternative is wrong, then the case for the empathy-altruism hypothesis seems very strong indeed. In the words of Sherlock Holmes, "When you have eliminated the impossible, whatever remains, *however improbable,* must be the truth." It seems impossible for any of the three major egoistic explanations of the empathy-helping relationship to account for the research evidence we have reviewed. What remains is the empathy-altruism hypothesis. Pending new evidence or a plausible new egoistic explanation of the existing evidence, this hypothesis must, we believe, be tentatively accepted as true.

If the empathy-altruism hypothesis is true, there are broad implications. As noted at the outset, we must radically revise our views about human nature and the human capacity for caring. To say that we are capable of altruistic motivation is to say that we can care about the welfare of others for their sakes and not simply for our own. And if this is true, then we are far more social animals than our psychological theories, including virtually all of our social psychological theories, would lead us to believe.

LIMITS ON THE EMPATHY-ALTRUISM RELATIONSHIP

Having reviewed the evidence that leads us tentatively to accept the empathy-altruism hypothesis, let us add two qualifiers. One concerns the scope of empathy; the other, competing concerns.

The Scope of Empathy

All of the research we have reviewed suggests that the human capacity for altruism is limited to those for whom we feel empathy. In study after study, when empathy for the person in need is low, the pattern of helping suggests underlying egoistic motivation. It is not that we never help people for whom we feel little empathy; we often do—but, the research suggests, only when it is in our own best interest.

Other sources of altruistic caring, aside from empathic feeling for the person in need, have been proposed, including an "altruistic personality" (Rushton, 1980; Staub, 1974), principled moral reasoning (Kohlberg, 1976; Staub, 1974), and internalized prosocial values (Batson, 1989; Schwartz & Howard, 1984; Staub, 1989). But, although some evidence suggests that these potential sources are associated with increased helping, there is, as yet, no clear evidence that the underlying motivation is altruistic. Instead, what little experimental evidence exists suggests that the care for others associated with these sources is instrumental and not terminal (see Batson, Bolen, Cross, & Neuringer-Benefiel, 1986). If there are sources of altruistic caring other than empathy, they have yet to be found.

Given this first qualifier, a question immediately arises: How easy is it for us to become empathically aroused by another person's plight? We know of no clear answer to this question. But, if empathy is a source—perhaps *the* source—of altruistic motivation, it seems clear that we need careful and extensive investigation to provide an answer.

Upon reflection, there certainly seem to be strong forces working against the arousal of empathy. These include anything and everything that makes it difficult for us to attend to or value another person's welfare (Batson, 1990): self-preoccupation or absorption in an ongoing task; seeing the other as an object or "thing," as a statistic and not a person who cares about his or her own welfare; seeing the other as a person but as different from ourselves, as one of "them" not "us," as Black not White, male not female, Arab not Jew, Catholic not Protestant. Under the influence of such forces, we can find ourselves, like Rousseau's princess, responding to those who have no bread by coolly suggesting they eat cake instead.

In spite of these pressures against empathy, we still seem to have a remarkable capacity to get involved and invested in the welfare of others. The research we have reviewed in this chapter reveals that undergraduates facing no pressing demands can feel considerable empathy for a suffering peer whom they have not seen before and need never see again. And think about our capacity to feel for characters in novels, in movies, and on television. We may have known these characters only for minutes, and we know they are fictitious. Still, we find ourselves churning inside when they are in danger, yearning when they are in need, weeping over their losses and successes.

Some psychologists have suggested that our empathic emotions have a genetic base in the response of mammalian parents to their helpless offspring (e.g., Hoffman, 1981a; MacLean, 1973). If this is true, then it is apparently also true that we can cognitively adopt a wide range of "non-kin," bringing them under our umbrella of empathic concern. Indeed, it often seems that we must take steps to avoid feeling empathy, whether for the homeless, those starving in Africa and Cambodia, or refugees from Central America. Lest we become empathically aroused, we turn the corner, switch channels, flip the page, think of something else. This apparent necessity to defend ourselves against feeling empathy suggests that our potential for such feelings is strong indeed.

Competing Concerns

The second qualifier to our general conclusion is that although we humans seem capable of experiencing concern for others, we clearly also care for ourselves. Batson, O'Quin, Fultz, Vanderplas, & Isen (1983, Study 3) found that if the cost of helping was high (taking high-level shocks that were "clearly painful but of course not harmful"), the motivation even of individuals who had previously reported high empathy for the person in need appeared to be egoistic. This finding suggests that our concern for others is "a fragile flower, easily crushed by self-concern" (Batson, O'Quin, Fultz, Vanderplas, & Isen, 1983, p. 718). There seems little doubt that even if we have empathic concern for others, we often do not act on it. It is overridden by other, more pressing concerns.

Of course, this is not all bad. Our lives would be decidedly awkward if we were only looking out for others' concerns and not our own. It would be, as one philosopher has suggested, like a community in which everyone tried to do each others' washing. No one's washing would get done.

The ease with which self-concerns can override altruistic concern for another is almost certainly a function of the strength of the altruistic motivation. In the study just mentioned, the potential helper and the person in need were undergraduate students who had never met before; the empathic response was based on watching through closed-circuit television as the person in need reacted with obvious discomfort to a series of electric shocks. With strong emotional attachment between the helper and the person in need, altruistic motivation may be less fragile. Think, for example, of a father's response at seeing his daughter toddling into the path of an oncoming car. Even though the situation involves considerable personal danger, the father's focus of concern may well remain riveted on the child and her needs, with relatively little attention paid to the threat to his own life.

Clearly, even if empathy-induced altruistic motivation exists, it is not a panacea. The range of people and problems that evoke empathy and hence altruistic motivation is limited, and altruistic concerns can be and often are overridden by self-concerns. These observations set bounds on the practical usefulness of empathy-induced altruism. Still, just as it would be wrong to try to bottle such altruism as a patent medicine that is "good for whatever ails you," it would be wrong to conclude that it is good for nothing. Empathy-induced altruistic motivation is a potentially important psychological resource that, if harnessed and put to work, may yield important practical as well as theoretical benefits.

REFERENCES

Archer, R. L. (1984). The farmer and the cowman should be friends: An attempt at reconciliation with Batson, Coke, and Pych. *Journal of Personality and Social Psychology, 46,* 709-711.

Archer, R. L., Diaz-Loving, R., Gollwitzer, P. M., Davis, M. H., & Foushee, H. C. (1981). The role of dispositional empathy and social evaluation in the empathic mediation of helping. *Journal of Personality and Social Psychology, 40,* 786-796.

Batson, C. D. (1987). Prosocial motivation: Is it ever truly altruistic? In L. Berkowitz (Ed.), *Advances in experimental social psychology* (Vol. 20, pp. 65-122). New York: Academic Press.

Batson, C. D. (1989). Personal values, moral principles, and a three-path model of prosocial motivation. In N. Eisenberg, J. Reykowski, & E. Staub (Eds.), *Social and moral values: Individual and societal perspectives* (pp. 213-228). Hillsdale, NJ: Lawrence Erlbaum.

Batson, C. D. (1990). How social an animal? The human capacity for caring. *American Psychologist, 45,* 336-346.

Batson, C. D. (in press). *The altruism question: Toward a Social-Psychological Answer.* Hillsdale, NJ: Lawrence Erlbaum.

Batson, C. D., Batson, J. G., Griffitt, C. A., Barrientos, S., Brandt, J. R., Sprengelmeyer, P., & Bayly, M. J. (1989). Negative-state relief and the empathy-altruism hypothesis. *Journal of Personality and Social Psychology, 56,* 922-933.

Batson, C. D., Batson, J. G., Slingsby, J. K., Harrell, K. L., Peekna, H. M., & Todd, R. M. (1990). *Empathic joy and the empathy-altruism hypothesis.* Unpublished manuscript, University of Kansas.

Batson, C. D., Bolen, M. H., Cross, J. A., & Neuringer-Benefiel, H. (1986). Where is the altruism in the altruistic personality? *Journal of Personality and Social Psychology, 50,* 212-220.

Batson, C. D., Duncan, B., Ackerman, P., Buckley, T., & Birch, K. (1981). Is empathic emotion a source of altruistic motivation? *Journal of Personality and Social Psychology, 40,* 290-302.

Batson, C. D., Dyck, J. L., Brandt, J. R., Batson, J. G., Powell, A. L., McMaster, M. R., & Griffitt, C. (1988). Five studies testing two new egoistic alternatives to the empathy-altruism hypothesis. *Journal of Personality and Social Psychology, 55,* 52-77.

4

The Arousal: Cost-Reward Model and the Process of Intervention
A REVIEW OF THE EVIDENCE

JOHN F. DOVIDIO
JANE A. PILIAVIN
SAMUEL L. GAERTNER
DAVID A. SCHROEDER
RUSSELL D. CLARK III

John F. Dovidio is Professor of Psychology at Colgate University. His research interests involve helping and altruism, prejudice and intergroup bias, and the nonverbal communication of social power.

Jane A. Piliavin is Professor of Sociology at the University of Wisconsin—Madison. Her past research was on emergency intervention; her current work focuses on blood donation as an example of more sustained helping behavior.

Samuel L. Gaertner is Professor of Psychology at the University of Delaware. His current research interests involve the reduction of intergroup bias and conflict.

David A. Schroeder is currently Professor and Chair of the Department of Psychology at the University of Arkansas. His research interests include the study of the motivation for helping and the facilitation of cooperation in social dilemmas.

Russell D. Clark III is Professor and Chair of the Department of Psychology at the University of North Texas. His current research interest is in minority influence.

This chapter provides an integrative overview of current theoretical perspectives on helping and altruism that is organized around the "arousal: cost-reward" model. There have been several versions of this model over the past 20 years. It was introduced by I. Piliavin, Rodin,

AUTHORS' NOTE: Preparation of this chapter was supported by the Colgate University Research Council and the Marie Wilson Howells Research Fund. We express our appreciation to Hong-Wen Charng, Craig Johnson, Diantha Joiner, Kristen Kling, and Hayley Thompson for their assistance with the preparation of this chapter. In addition, we gratefully acknowledge the very helpful suggestions offered by the reviewers and the editor on an earlier version of the chapter.

and J. Piliavin (1969) as a "heuristic device" and was more fully developed as a model of emergency intervention by J. Piliavin and I. Piliavin (1973). The model was more recently revised and expanded to consider nonemergency helping, as well as emergency helping, by J. Piliavin, Dovidio, Gaertner, and Clark (1981, 1982).

THE AROUSAL: COST-REWARD MODEL

The arousal: cost-reward model identifies two conceptually separate but functionally interdependent components that influence helping. The first factor, arousal in response to the need or distress of others, is an emotional response and is the fundamental motivational construct of the model. The model proposes that this arousal, when attributed to the other person's need, is experienced as unpleasant. The bystander is, therefore, motivated to reduce it. Arousal mobilizes bystanders for action that could lead to intervention and helping. The second factor is a cost-reward component. This factor involves the cognitive processes by which bystanders assess and weigh anticipated costs and rewards associated with action and inaction. Although the arousal and cost-reward components are conceptually distinct, they are often functionally related (see Figure 4.1). Many of the situational, social, and personality variables that increase arousal also affect perceived costs. Variation in arousal can also produce changes in the perceptions or assessment of costs; the recognition of potential costs can, in turn, influence arousal.

The arousal: cost-reward model, as presented by Piliavin, Dovidio, Gaertner, and Clark (1981), consisted of five propositions:

Proposition I: Observation of another's problem or crisis arouses bystanders. The degree of arousal is directly related to the clarity, severity, and duration of need and to bystanders' physical and psychological closeness to the person in need.

Proposition II: In general, arousal occasioned by observation of a problem or crisis and attributed to that event becomes more unpleasant as it increases, and bystanders have greater motivation to reduce it.

Proposition III: Bystanders will choose responses that most rapidly and completely reduce the arousal and that incur as few net costs (costs minus rewards) as possible.

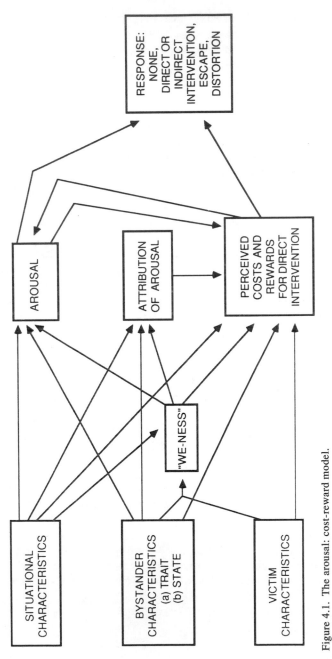

Figure 4.1. The arousal: cost-reward model.
SOURCE: From Piliavin, Dovidio, Gaertner, and Clark (1981). Reprinted by permission of Academic Press.

Proposition IV: There will be (a) special circumstances that give rise to, and (b) specific personality types who engage in, rapid, impulsive, noncalculative, "irrational" helping or escape behavior following observation of an emergency.

Proposition V: On termination of contact with the situation, arousal will decrease monotonically with time, whether or not the victim is helped.

We believe that this model is a particularly useful framework for conceptually organizing helping research because, first, it can generate testable hypotheses, and, second, it attempts to be a comprehensive model. Piliavin, Dovidio, Gaertner, and Clark (1981) note that the revised model was developed as a "meta-model" to organize previous studies, present new research and ideas, and encourage the orderly theoretical development of the area. In this chapter, we assess how well the model has fulfilled the potential envisioned a decade ago by discussing and evaluating the basic propositions and processes of the revised model. Because the model has previously been used to review the helping literature up to 1980 (Piliavin, Dovidio, Gaertner, & Clark, 1981), we primarily emphasize the empirical and theoretical work of the 1980s.

AROUSAL

According to the arousal: cost-reward model, bystanders are motivated to help because intervention is perceived as being an effective way to reduce unpleasant arousal generated by and attributed to another person's plight. This arousal is a function of the clarity and severity of the crisis and of the psychological and physical closeness of the bystander to the victim. The central role of arousal and affect as motivational constructs is shared by several theorists who adopt very diverse perspectives on helping (see, for example, Chapter 3 by Batson and Oleson and Chapter 2 by Eisenberg and Fabes).

Vicarious Emotional Response

The first proposition of the model, that bystanders are aroused by the problems and crises of others, has received considerable support. Studies using self-report (Batson, 1987), behavioral measures (Vaughan & Lanzetta, 1980, 1981), and physiological measures (Gaertner & Dovidio, 1977) converge on the same conclusion: People are aroused by the distress of others and exhibit emotionally empathic reactions to the problems and crises of others. Also consistent with the first proposition of the model, the severity and clarity of another person's emergency and the relationship to the victim systematically influence arousal. Emergencies of greater clarity and severity generate higher levels of arousal (e.g., as indexed by heart rate acceleration; Sterling & Gaertner, 1984). Furthermore, the distress of others with whom one is closer generates a stronger empathic reaction (as indexed by heart rate, skin conductance, and electromyographic responses; Lanzetta & Englis, 1989). These affective reactions appear quite early developmentally (see Eisenberg and Fabes's chapter). The findings are sufficiently strong and compelling that Hoffman (1981), Cunningham (1986), and MacDonald (1984) all implicate empathy as a candidate for an inherited capacity closely allied with the evolution of altruistic tendencies.

Arousal, Empathy, and Helping

There is also much support for the second proposition of the model, that arousal attributed to the other person's problem, crisis, or emergency motivates helping. Correlations between physiological arousal and speed of helping across six samples in which the bystander was the only witness to an emergency range between .47 and .77 (Dovidio, 1984), producing a highly significant and strong meta-analytic effect ($z = 5.67$, $p < .001$; mean effect size based on Fisher's $z = .635$).[1]

More recently, Eisenberg and Miller (1987) conducted a meta-analytic review of the literature on the relationship between empathy and prosocial behavior. Across seven studies involving nine samples, they found that facial, gestural, and vocal indices of empathy to movies and "lifelike enactments" were positively related to helping. Across 13 different studies involving 20 individual comparisons, observational sets intended to facilitate emotional reactions to the need of another person (e.g., "Imagine how the other person feels") significantly increased helping. We repeated this meta-analysis with seven more recent tests (from Batson, Batson, et al., 1989; Batson, Dyck, et al., 1988; Cialdini et al., 1987; Schaller & Cialdini, 1988; Schroeder, Dovidio, Sibicky, Matthews, & Allen, 1988; K. Smith, Keating, & Stotland, 1989). The effect of observational set remained significant ($z = 6.27$, $p < .001$) and became slightly stronger when all 27 tests are considered (mean effect size of .15 as compared with the .11 reported by Eisenberg & Miller, 1987).

Additional research supporting the causal link between arousal and helping suggests that arousal generated by an independent source can, if it becomes associated with the person in need, increase helping. In experiments based on excitation transfer theory, arousal generated by aggressive films (Mueller, Donnerstein, & Hallam, 1983), erotic films (Mueller & Donnerstein, 1981), and exercise (Sterling & Gaertner, 1984) facilitated later helping. Conversely, misattribution of arousal generated by another person's problem, crisis, or emergency to an unrelated source reduced helping (Eisenberg & Miller, 1987, based on five samples).

Summary

Consistent with the first proposition of the arousal: cost-reward model, over the past decade, evidence indicating that the problems, crises, and emergencies of others do generate arousal and emotional reactions in bystanders, even very young children, has continued to mount. In addition, consistent with the second proposition of the model, research demonstrates that emotional reactions to others' distress play an important *causal* role in motivating helping.

COST AND REWARD CONSIDERATIONS

The third major proposition of the arousal: cost-reward model states that bystanders choose responses that most rapidly and completely reduce arousal, in the process incurring as few net costs (costs minus rewards) as possible. Within this framework, there are two general categories of potential costs and rewards: (a) those contingent upon making a direct helping response (costs or rewards for helping) and (b) those that would result if the person in need were to receive no help (costs for no help to the victim).

Costs for Helping

The first category, personal costs/rewards for helping, involves direct outcomes for the benefactor. Costs for helping involve, for example, effort, physical danger, and rewards forgone. Rewards for helping include feelings of efficacy, admiration from others, fame, and awards. We hypothesize that as net costs for helping increase, intervention decreases.

Earlier reviews of the literature on costs for helping revealed strong support for this hypothesis (Dovidio, 1984; Piliavin, Dovidio, Gaertner, & Clark, 1981). More recent research provides further evidence. As costs for helping increase, helping decreases, even though costs may be operationalized in diverse ways: psychological aversion based on physical stigma (Edelmann, Evans, Pegg, & Tremain, 1983; Walton et al., 1988), potential embarrassment for the bystander associated with helping (Edelmann, Childs, Harvey, Kellock, & Strain-Clark, 1984), fear of disapproval (Midlarsky & Hannah, 1985), relative unfamiliarity with the helping task (Ladd, Lange, & Stremmel, 1983), and pain associated with helping (Batson, O'Quin, Fultz, Vanderplas, & Isen, 1983; Doede-Anderson & Kaplan, 1977). These results complement earlier findings of decreases in helping as a function of higher personal costs for helping, operationalized in terms of effort and time (e.g., Darley & Batson, 1973), money expended or forgone (Bleda, Bleda, Byrne, & White, 1976), and threat to personal freedom (Berkowitz, 1973).

Conversely, as the potential rewards associated with helping increase, intervention increases. For example, praise and monetary compensation facilitate helping (e.g., Deutsch & Lamberti, 1986; Katz, Farber, Glass, Lucido, & Emswiller, 1978; McGovern, Ditzian, & Taylor, 1975). In addition, the greater the reward associated with feedback from effective helping, the more helpful bystanders are. Utne and Kidd (1980) concluded that help was more likely when it was perceived as effectively improving the other's condition, and K. Smith, Keating, and Stotland (1980) found more helping when feedback about the effectiveness of helping was possible than when it was not.

Costs for No Help to the Victim

The second category of costs, costs associated with the bystander's knowledge that the victim has received no help, has two conceptual subcategories. There are personal costs for not helping, which are negative outcomes imposed directly on the bystander for failure to intervene. Examples of these costs are self-blame for inaction and public censure. The second subcategory, empathy costs for the victim receiving no help, depends upon the knowledge that the victim is continuing to suffer. In particular, empathy costs involve internalizing the need or suffering of the victim.

We hypothesize that the effects of the person in need receiving no help depend on the level of costs for helping. As can be seen in Figure 4.2, when costs for helping are low to moderate, helping should increase as the costs for the victim receiving no help increase. With high costs for helping, however, persons in need are predicted to receive indirect help or no help at all. In the latter case, the arousal engendered by observing the victim's distress will likely be handled through derogation of the victim or through other reinterpretations of the situation as "not an emergency" or as one in which helping is not the bystander's personal responsibility (i.e., diffusion of responsibility).

Consistent with the model, when costs for helping are low to moderate, helping generally increases as the costs for no help to the victim increase. With respect to personal costs for not helping, helping increases (a) with stronger and more immediate appeals for help (Steele, Critchlow, & Liu, 1985), (b) with focusing responsibility on the bystander verbally (Moriarty, 1975; Shaffer, Rogel, & Hendrick, 1975) or nonverbally (Paulsell & Goldman, 1984), and (c) when the need for helping a person of another race is legitimatized by a third party's request (Frey & Gaertner, 1986).

One manipulation relating to personal costs for *not* helping is the easy-difficult escape factor used in a number of recent tests of Batson's (1987) empathy-altruism hypothesis (see Batson and Oleson's chapter). In studies employing this manipulation, the easy-escape condition minimizes costs for not helping by limiting exposure to the victim (e.g., Batson, Duncan, Aderman, Buckley, & Birch, 1981), decreasing the likelihood of future contact with the person in need (e.g., Toi & Batson, 1982), providing a justification for not helping (Batson, Dyck, et al., 1988, Studies 2 and 4), varying attributional ambiguity (Batson, Dyck, et al., 1988, Study 3), or eliminating the possibility for negative social evaluation for not helping (e.g., Batson, Bolen, Cross, & Neuringer-Benefiel, 1986). In general, helping in these studies involved low to moderate costs (e.g., making telephone calls for the person in need). We performed a meta-analysis involving 13 hypothesis tests (from nine research reports) that used these paradigms for varying personal costs for not helping. As expected, helping was higher when the personal costs for not helping were greater ($z = 6.38$, $p < .001$, effect size based on Fisher's $z = .23$) across these studies involving low to moderate costs for helping.

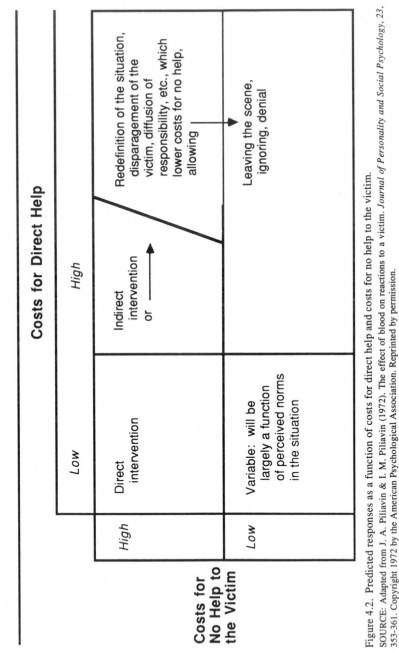

Figure 4.2. Predicted responses as a function of costs for direct help and costs for no help to the victim.

SOURCE: Adapted from J. A. Piliavin & I. M. Piliavin (1972). The effect of blood on reactions to a victim. *Journal of Personality and Social Psychology, 23,* 353-361. Copyright 1972 by the American Psychological Association. Reprinted by permission.

Research also supports the hypothesis that, as empathic costs for no help to the victim (i.e., costs based primarily on the bystander's awareness of the victim's continued distress) increase, helping increases. Consistent with the earlier review of the literature by Piliavin, Dovidio, Gaertner, and Clark (1981), recent studies have found that people are more helpful when the person is perceived to be in greater need (e.g., Juhnke et al., 1987; Ladd, Lange, & Stremmel, 1983; Midlarsky & Hannah, 1985; Sinha & Jain, 1986) or distress (Levin & Arluke, 1982) or is seen as more dependent (Walton et al., 1988) or deserving of help (Frey & Gaertner, 1986).

Costs for No Help to the Victim and Costs for Helping Combined

As the model predicts, the impact of costs for no help to the person in need depends on the level of costs for helping. After a review of 12 emergency and nonemergency experiments, Dovidio (1984, p. 386) concluded that costs for helping have a greater impact than do costs for the victim receiving no help: "Across all of these studies, helping decreased as costs for helping increased. The effects of cost for the victim receiving no help were weaker, more inconsistent, and often appeared only in interactions with other variables." In general, consistent with the arousal: cost-reward model, costs for *not* helping affect intervention primarily when the costs *for* helping are low.

Because many real-life emergencies involve high costs both for helping and for not helping, the upper-right hand quadrant of the cost matrix presented in Figure 4.2 is of particular interest. Piliavin, Dovidio, Gaertner, and Clark (1981) reviewed 14 studies that examined both direct and indirect helping (e.g., seeking the assistance of a third person) and concluded that, although indirect helping does occur more frequently when the costs for helping are high, indirect helping is relatively infrequent when the costs for helping are low. More recent research supports this conclusion (Cramer, McMaster, Bartell, & Dragna, 1988; Shotland & Heinold, 1985).

Cognitive reinterpretation seems to be an even more common way of resolving the high cost for helping/high cost for not helping dilemma. Reinterpretation may involve redefining the situation as one in which help is not needed, diffusing responsibility, or denigrating the victim—all with the consequence of reducing the perceived costs for not helping. Supportive of this proposed process, Otten, Penner, and Waugh (1988) found, in a path analytic test of the model, that higher perceived costs for helping led to lower perceived costs for not helping. With high costs for helping and lower costs for not helping, bystanders are hypothesized to become less likely to intervene. Consistent with this prediction, the presence of others, who may provide social information that help is not needed or the opportunity to diffuse responsibility, has a robust effect on intervention in emergencies (Darley & Latané, 1968; Latané & Darley, 1970). In their meta-analytic review of almost 50 tests in the literature, Latané and Nida (1981, p. 290) concluded, "With very few exceptions, individuals faced with a sudden need for action exhibit a markedly reduced likelihood of response if other people actually are, or are believed to be available."

Also directly supportive of the cost-reward formulations within the model is the finding that cognitive reinterpretation in the form of diffusion of responsibility is a function of the costs for helping. Across 14 experiments, Piliavin, Dovidio, Gaertner, and Clark (1981) found that diffusion of responsibility effects were greater when the costs for helping were higher. Recent research continues to support this conclusion. Walton et al. (1988) found that a bystander was more likely to diffuse responsibility when the person in need was facially disfigured; when the subject was the only bystander, however, he or she was as likely to help the disfigured person as the nondisfigured person (replicating Piliavin, Piliavin, & Rodin, 1975). Cramer, McMaster, Bartell, and Dragna (1988) demonstrated that, although competence did not relate to helping when subjects were the only bystander in an emergency situation, subjects who were lower in competence were more likely to diffuse responsibility when they had the opportunity.

Impulsive Helping

The fourth basic proposition of the model states that there are certain *specifiable* circumstances in which helping will take the form of a rapid, impulsive, "irrational" response; cost factors will have no impact on helping. Piliavin, Dovidio, Gaertner, and Clark (1981) compared 23 studies in which impulsive helping occurred with 26 studies in which helping was not impulsive and found systematic differences. Impulsive helping was more likely in emergencies that were clearer, were more realistic, and involved a prior relationship between bystander and victim. Piliavin et al. noted that these same factors also have been demonstrated to be related to bystander arousal. Thus they speculated that high levels of arousal in impulse-generating situations, through narrowing of the focus of attention (Easterbrook, 1959), could interfere with a broad and rational consideration of costs. Because in recent years there has been little research on impulse-generating situations, the empirical status of this proposition is essentially unchanged.

Summary

Conceptualizing helping as the outcome of a decision-making process in which costs and rewards are weighed provides a parsimonious account for the effects of diverse manipulations on helping. A weakness of this approach, however, is that post hoc cost interpretations too often become circular arguments. In addition, because costs are presumably based on an individual's perceptions, it is often difficult to generate unequivocal predictions. Thus, although most researchers use manipulations for which most people have a common perception, it is also important that measures of individuals' idiosyncratic perceptions be included in these experimental designs. Nevertheless, cost-reward analysis, as a heuristic aid, adds to our understanding of the processes involved in decisions about whether to help.

FACTORS MODERATING THE EFFECTS OF
AROUSAL AND COSTS AND REWARDS

In *Emergency Intervention*, Piliavin, Dovidio, Gaertner, and Clark (1981) hypothesized that trait and state characteristics of the bystander and the nature of the bystander-victim relationship could influence both arousal and cost-reward processes (see Figure 4.1). This section examines individual differences, moods, and the bond between bystander and victim as they relate to the model.

Individual Differences

Within the model, individual differences are hypothesized to influence the process of intervention through the level of arousal experienced, the interpretation of arousal, cost-reward considerations, or some combination of these factors. For example, persons who are characteristically more sensitive to the needs of others might experience greater arousal in response to another's plight, experience this arousal more negatively, and perceive greater costs for no help to the needy person. Other individuals, such as sociopaths, may experience lower levels of arousal and perceive lower costs for not helping (Marks, Penner, & Stone, 1982). Indeed, Piliavin et al. (1981, p. 203) concluded that "helpers are generally more 'other-oriented' (versus 'self-oriented') than non-helpers," for example, on dimensions such as social responsibility, extraversion, need for social approval, social interest, and attractiveness as a friend. More recently, Eisenberg and Miller's (1987) meta-analysis of 41 samples found that dispositional empathy was positively related to helping. Oliner and Oliner (1988) compared 231 gentiles who saved Jews in Nazi Europe with 126 nonrescuers and found that rescuers had stronger beliefs in equity and greater empathy. Also, Allen and Rushton (1983) found that mental health volunteers were generally higher on empathy and prosocial standards (relating to both arousal and cost factors) than were nonvolunteer control subjects.

The model further proposed that individual differences would have their primary impact in the low cost for helping, low cost for no help to the victim quadrant of the 2 × 2 cost matrix presented in Figure 4.2 when the situation is ambiguously structured (Mischel, 1973) and "psychologically weak" and less "evocative" (Snyder & Ickes, 1985). In this regard, Piliavin, Dovidio, Gaertner, and Clark (1981) proposed a theoretically important contextual distinction between emergency situations, which are attention capturing and highly arousing, and non-emergency helping situations, in which cognitive factors may be more influential.

Because of the compelling and evocative nature of emergencies, Piliavin et al. (1981, p. 185) hypothesized "person variables to have less potency in determining bystander response as the situation becomes more emergency-like." Indeed, a number of studies have failed to find personality differences in helping in emergency situations (see Krebs & Miller, 1985, p. 33). The personality variables that do have an influence in emergency situations are, however, the ones directly related to processes hypothesized by the arousal: cost-reward model. Individuals more likely to help in emergencies are those who are less preoccupied in determining what is real or unreal (Denner, 1968), who are highly emotional (Huston, Geis, & Wright, 1976), who are relatively high on "sympathetic identification" and "disposition to take instrumental action for relief of one's own distress" (Liebhart, 1972), who are less safety oriented (Wilson, 1976), and who have stronger feelings of social responsibility (Cramer, McMaster, Bartell, & Dragna, 1988).

In less arousing situations, personality factors relating to cost-reward considerations and other cognitive aspects seem to be effective predictors of helping. For example, both children and adults relatively high on task-specific and general competence (Midlarsky, 1984; Peterson, 1983) and self-esteem (Batson, Bolen, Cross, & Neuringer-Benefiel, 1986) tend to be more helpful in nonemergency situations. Presumably, people who feel higher in competence and self-esteem perceive helping as less difficult (costly); they may also be more likely to expect helping to be successful and to anticipate positive outcomes (rewards) for the other and the self (Midlarsky, 1984). Similarly, people higher on acceptance of responsibility (Briggs, Piliavin, Lorentzen, & Becker, 1986) and who have a more salient self-image as a helper (J. Piliavin & Callero, in press; Smith & Shaffer, 1986) are more helpful. Individual differences that may be associated with differential personal costs for not helping and potential rewards for helping also relate to nonemergency, premeditated helping. People higher in need for social approval are more likely to help when they anticipate social rewards for helping and are less likely to help when they expect social punishments for helping (Deutsch & Lamberti, 1986). When compensation for helping is expected, "receptive givers" (subjects relatively high on nurturance and succorance) are likely to help; when compensation is not anticipated, "altruists" (subjects high on nurturance but low on succorance) are more likely to help (Romer, Gruder, & Lizzadro, 1986).

Within the arousal: cost-reward framework, personality factors that broadly and systematically affect both arousal and cost-reward factors are considered good candidates for general "prosocial traits"; personality variables that are focused in their impact on one particular component in the process are more likely to manifest an effect under some circumstances but not others (i.e., person × situation interactions). The model can thus be used to organize personality variables according to those related to arousal factors (e.g., empathy) and those related to cost-reward factors and to identify "a limited number of personal characteristics that account for a significant amount of variance, to define the nature of relevant situational influences, and to provide a specification of their joint influence . . . to successfully . . . increase our understanding of how personality and situations jointly determine (positive) behavior" (Staub, 1984, p. 31).

The model can be applied similarly to understanding gender differences in helping. Piliavin and Unger (1985) proposed that sex and gender can relate to both arousal and cost-reward processes. With respect to arousal, women may experience greater empathy in response to another person's need than men (Hoffman, 1977; see Eisenberg & Lennon, 1983, for a critical examination of this issue). With respect to cost-reward considerations, men and women may be attentive to different aspects of the social environment and, as a consequence, may assess and weigh costs and rewards differently.

If women, compared with men, are more attentive to the needs of others (Austin, 1979) and respond more empathically, the model predicts greater helping by women. Eagly and Crowley (1986), however, found that, across 172 studies, men were significantly more helpful than were women. This finding challenges the arousal: cost-reward model. The model must assume that, because women have greater arousal but help less than men, sex and gender have particularly strong and direct influences on cost-reward considerations that outweigh women's greater empathy. The results of Eagly and Crowley's (1986) analysis of the literature provided substantial evidence that men and women do view the costs for helping differently. Furthermore, they found that the tendency for women to help less than men was most pronounced in situations in which women perceived higher costs for helping than did men.

Eagly and Crowley's (1986) findings also suggest that cost-reward considerations associated with deviating from or complying with traditional gender roles may mediate sex differences in helping. The female gender role involves caring for others. Consistent with this role, women report providing their friends with more personal favors, emotional support, and counseling about personal problems than men (Aries & Johnson, 1983; Berg, 1984; Johnson & Aries, 1983). Women also report that they would be more likely to visit a friend who "needed someone to talk to" and would feel worse if they did not (Otten, Penner, & Waugh, 1988). The male gender role involves heroism and chivalry. Consistent with this role, Eagly and Crowley (1986) found that men were more helpful than women when an audience witnessed the helping act and other potential witnesses were available. These gender roles, which are reflected to some extent in helping behaviors presented in children's picture books (Barnett, 1986), affect helping even among younger children. Larrieu and Mussen (1986) observed that, among fourth-graders, the predominant prosocial responses of girls reflected empathy, expressiveness, and caring, whereas the most common prosocial behaviors of boys were active and instrumental.

In summary, despite the pessimism of earlier reviews of this area (e.g., Krebs, 1970), a growing body of literature suggests the importance of individual differences in helping, which operate through arousal and cost-reward mechanisms. In general, we propose that a theory-guided approach can productively organize past research and suggest topics and strategies for future research. The arousal: cost-reward model, even when used in this post hoc fashion, seems to provide a reasonable framework for integrating the results of studies that may appear to be pursuing independent objectives.

Moods

Like Morris (1989), we conceptualize mood as a diffuse regulatory state serving, even without his or her awareness, to orient a potential benefactor's attention outward toward others or inward toward aspects of the self. Attention is hypothesized to influence both arousal and cost-reward factors. To the extent that a mood focuses a bystander on others, bystanders may be more sensitive to others' needs, perceive others more positively, and produce a more inclusive social outlook such that the other person is more likely to be categorized as a "we" than as a "they" (Hornstein, 1982). An attentional focus on another could facilitate helping by stimulating an empathy response (Thompson, Cowan, & Rosenhan, 1980) or by increasing the personal costs for not helping (e.g., through guilt). (See also Chapter 8 by Salovey, Mayer, and Rosenhan.)

We hypothesize that whether a mood that focuses attention inward inhibits or facilitates helping depends on the aspect of the self to which the bystander attends. Helping should be facilitated if self-focus makes personal standards relating to prosocial behavior more salient (which may increase personal costs for not helping or rewards for helping) or results in deeper processing of the other's plight (which may increase arousal attributed to the other's situation or may increase the salience of costs to the other person for not receiving help). Helping should be inhibited if inward attention involves self-absorption at the expense of sensitivity to the needs of others (inhibiting an arousal response or increasing the salience of perceived costs for helping; see also Carlson & Miller, 1987).

According to Piliavin, Dovidio, Gaertner, and Clark (1981), good moods may facilitate helping by increasing attraction toward the other person and expectations that helping will be rewarding (thereby increasing the costs for not helping and rewards for helping) or by increasing the salience of personal prosocial standards (which also will increase the costs for not helping). Consistent with these expectations, research has demonstrated that people in good moods perceive objects, people, and helping opportunities in more favorable ways (Clark & Teasdale, 1985; Forgas, Bower, & Krantz, 1984; Isen, Shalker, Clark, & Karp, 1978). Clark and Waddell (1983) found that positive moods increase positive associations with potential helping situations and with people subjects imagine meeting. Across the 34 articles included in Carlson, Charlin, and Miller's (1988) meta-analysis, positive moods significantly facilitated helping.

With respect to negative moods, Carlson and Miller's (1987, p. 101) review of 47 articles found that "more helping occurs when the target of concern in the negative-mood induction is another person as opposed to oneself." An inward, self-absorbed focus produced by negative states decreases helpfulness in situations in which the request for help is not salient. (See also Chapter 8.)

In sum, the predictions we made nearly a decade ago concerning how moods relate to helping have received support from a wide variety of studies. We acknowledge that our predictions, however, are far from unique. Researchers adopting a variety of different perspectives have developed similar hypotheses (see Carlson, Charlin, & Miller, 1988; Carlson & Miller, 1987). Indeed, most research on this topic has been generated by other perspectives. Thus, we recognize these studies do not provide direct support for the underlying processes of our model.

We-ness

One of the major changes in the Piliavin, Dovidio, Gaertner, and Clark (1981) elaboration of the arousal: cost-reward model from earlier versions was the inclusion of the concept of "we-ness," which connotes a sense of connectedness or the categorization of another person as a member of one's own group, as an important mediating process (see Figure 4.1). As subsequent research has demonstrated, categorization of persons as members of one's own group or as members of other groups has a profound impact on a broad range of social behaviors (see Hogg & Abrams, 1988; Messick & Mackie, 1989; Tajfel, 1978, 1982; Turner, 1987; Wilder, 1986). The categorization of individuals as members of the ingroup ("we") results in feelings of greater closeness, more positive attitudes, and the perception that they share attitudes that are more similar to one's own (e.g., Brewer, 1979; Brown & Abrams, 1986). Conversely, helping can play important roles in establishing and strengthening group bonds and facilitating the achievement of group goals (Worchel, Wong, & Scheltema, 1989).

We hypothesize that because of shared identity, extended sense of self, perception of similarity, and attraction, the sense of we-ness can have multiple and simultaneous effects. Within the model, these closer relationships to the person in need may increase arousal and costs for not helping and, because of greater familiarity, decrease costs for helping. In addition, the categorization of a person as an ingroup member rather than as an outgroup member establishes very different interpersonal relationships. These differences may parallel Clark and Mills's (1979) distinction between communal and exchange relationships (see also Clark, Ouellette, Powell, & Milberg, 1987). In communal relationships, such as those between friends, family members, and romantic partners, people feel responsible for the other's welfare and desire to help the other person when he or she has a need. In contrast, in exchange relationships, such as those between strangers or in business, people do not feel a special responsibility for the other person's needs. They give benefits conditionally and reciprocally, in response to past help or with the expectation of receiving future benefits.

Although much of the research on family relations and helping has been derived from sociobiology, the findings are consistent with the hypothesized effects of ingroup classification within the arousal: cost-reward model. For example, across two anthropological studies, Essock-Vitale and McGuire (1980, 1985) found that exchanges (both giving and receiving) were more common among kin than among non-kin, that help between kin was less conditional (i.e., less tied to reciprocity), and that costly and important types of help (e.g., large gifts) were much more frequent among kin than among non-kin.

The degree of closeness among relatives is also associated with helping. Cunningham (1986) concluded in his review of the literature that closeness of kinship was related to willingness to provide aid and with expectations that aid would be given. In addition, Segal (1984) demonstrated that, on an initial experimental task, there was greater cooperation between monozygotic than between dizygotic twins. In a second task in which twins worked once for their own benefit and once for their co-twin's benefit, monozygotic twins worked harder for their partner than did dizygotic twins. Simmons, Klein, and Simmons (1977) had potential kidney recipients rate their closeness to a range of potential donors (relatives). Recipients reported feeling very close to 63% of eventual donors but only to 42% of eventual nondonors. Furthermore, when only siblings were considered, donors were closer in age and more likely to be of the same sex as the recipient. Finally, feelings of family solidarity, independent of degree of relationship, are positively correlated with helping extended family members (Atkinson, Kivett, & Campbell, 1986). Thus, considering family relationship as a group boundary, helping is greater for ingroup than for outgroup members, and the stronger the we-ness, the greater the helping.

Research comparing interactions between friends and strangers also provides results consistent with role of we-ness in the model and support for Clark, Ouellette, Powell, and Milberg's (1987) predictions for established communal relations. Friends are more attentive to their partner's need for help than are strangers (Clark, Mills, & Corcoran, 1989). They are also more likely to take need into account when dividing money (Lamm & Schwinger, 1980, 1983) and are expected to be more helpful to one another than are strangers (Bar-Tal, Bar-Zohar, Greenberg, & Herman, 1977). In addition, friends are more helpful than strangers, except when the situation poses a direct threat to one's self-image (Tesser, Millar, & Moore, 1988; Tesser & Smith, 1980). Strangers, in comparison, monitor more closely their partner's contributions to joint tasks potentially involving a reward (Clark, 1984; Clark, Mills, & Corcoran, 1989).

Even among individuals without a previous relationship, perceptions of similarity can establish a sense of group identity and feelings of we-ness (Sole, Marton, & Hornstein, 1975). Consistent with the model, the effect of similarity on helping is robust. Dovidio (1984) reviewed 34 separate tests of the similarity-helping relationship, and 82% of these tests demonstrated that subjects helped similar others significantly more than they helped dissimilar others. Furthermore, helping as a function of similarity increases when the interactants face an external threat (Dovidio & Morris, 1975; Hayden, Jackson, & Guydish, 1984), which increases the salience of group boundaries (Campbell & Levine, 1972). Batson, Pate, et al. (1979) found that under situations of threat, subjects showed uniformly high levels of helpfulness to similar others, but subjects helped dissimilar objects only when they anticipated the need for reciprocal help. Thus helping toward similar others, who were presumably seen as ingroup members, was more unconditional and "selfless" under conditions of mutual threat than was helping toward dissimilar others.

In summary, the arousal: cost-reward model provides a relatively parsimonious account of how a variety of different factors (e.g., similarity, family relationship, relationship orientation) can influence helping. Again, our hypotheses are not unique. A variety of perspectives (e.g., sociobiology, reinforcement theory) could account for parts of the overall pattern, but the strength of the model is that it provides an overriding framework for examining the interface of what have often been considered separate and unrelated theoretical approaches. We recognize that most of this research has been generated from frameworks other than our model. Although the outcomes are consistent with our hypotheses, there is no direct evidence that arousal, attribution of arousal, or cost-reward considerations are relevant mechanisms. We can conclude, however, that the results of research in this area are consistent with the arousal: cost-reward model, if not directly supportive of it.

EVALUATION OF THE MODEL

It has been almost a decade since Piliavin, Dovidio, Gaertner, and Clark (1981) presented the detailed reformulation of the arousal: cost-reward model in *Emergency Intervention*. The model was consistent with the data up until 1980, in part because it was revised to account for these research findings. How well has the model stood the test of time? Overall, we believe that the numerous and diverse studies have produced results largely consistent with the model.

Arousal and Helping

With respect to the first proposition of the model, bystanders do react with arousal to the distress of another person. Studies of physiological responses, facial expressions, and self-reports demonstrate that both children and adults exhibit empathic arousal in response to another person's need. Consistent with the second proposition of the model, greater arousal is associated with more helping. In unambiguous emergency situations, degree of heart rate acceleration (e.g., Sterling & Gaertner, 1984) and level of self-reports of negative affect (Cramer, McMaster, Bartell, & Dragna, 1988) positively correlate with helping.

Across a variety of nonemergency situations, self-reports of empathy relate to helping (Eisenberg & Miller, 1987). In addition, in non-emergency situations, heart rate and facial distress predict helping (Eisenberg et al., 1989).

Different situations, different arousal. Because the model was developed in the context of emergency situations, we generally conceptualized this arousal as the strong autonomic activation involved in a "defense reaction" (Sokolov, 1963). The defense reaction

> occurs to sudden and/or intense stimuli . . . and physiologically it is characterized by heart-rate *increase,* negative feedback to the reticular activating system and the cortex (leading to a blocking of much external stimulation), signals the limbic system and the sympathetic nervous system to prepare for "flight or fight," an increase in skin conductance, peripheral vasoconstriction, and pupillary constriction. Subjectively, the defense reaction is experienced as negative. (J. Piliavin, Dovidio, Gaertner, & Clark, 1982, p. 283)

Indeed, clear emergencies do produce strong defense reactions in bystanders (e.g., Sterling & Gaertner, 1984).

Most of the studies in the 1980s, however, have used nonemergency situations (e.g., a film presentation of a mother describing the needs of her children injured in a car accident). Such situations are unlikely to produce strong defense reactions. Nevertheless, they do elicit a physiological response: Eisenberg and her colleagues (see Chapter 2 by Eisenberg and Fabes) have found heart rate *deceleration* in these situations. Heart rate deceleration reflects a different type of physiological activation, which "is associated with the intake of information concerning the needy other, interest in the other, and an outward attention" (Eisenberg et al., 1989, p. 56). Thus to apply the arousal: cost-reward model to nonemergency and nonspontaneous helping situations seems to require a broader conceptualization of arousal, one that is not restricted to a defense reaction.

Because of profound differences between emergency and nonemergency situations (Pearce & Amato, 1980; Shotland & Huston, 1979), the emotional experience of arousal that motivates helping in such situations may be different. In emergency situations, autonomic arousal experienced as an unpleasant state (e.g., upset) motivates helping. In less emergencylike situations, when a defense reaction is less likely, the emotions of sadness or empathic concern (characterized by heart rate deceleration and feelings of compassion and warmth) provide the primary motivation for helping.

The type of emotional reaction to another's need has further been linked to the fundamental nature of the motivation to help (Batson, 1987). The arousal: cost-reward model has been characterized as an egoistic model because it proposes that the motivation for helping is related to the desire to improve *one's own* welfare. Piliavin, Dovidio, Gaertner, and Clark (1981, pp. 239-240) note that

> to the extent that arousal is interpreted as alarm and concern rather than disgust and upset . . . , the motive for helping has a sympathetic rather than selfish tone. Thus, the needs of another can become one in the same or coordinated with those of the bystander. Nevertheless, there are many instances in which the bystander's motive is more selfish. How marvelous, though, that another's distress could instigate arousal which, even egoistically, impels us to action.

The model also considers, however, the possibility that there are *empathic* costs for not helping associated with the recognition of another person's continued distress. Thus, although bystanders are motivated to reduce their own arousal, the needs of the other are closely linked to the bystanders' own needs and goals.

Other theoretical approaches to the nature of the motivation to help. A more purely egoistic approach is exemplified by Cialdini, Kenrick, and Baumann's (1982) negative-state relief model. Cialdini, Kenrick, and Baumann (1982) suggest that arousal states that are labeled negatively can motivate helping because helping can be perceived as a positive act that will relieve these negative feelings. Research has demonstrated that helping is perceived to have mood-elevating consequences (Harris, 1977) and may actually improve the mood of the benefactor (Williamson & Clark, 1989; Yinon & Landau, 1987). Consistent with Cialdini et al.'s model, research has demonstrated that helping is facilitated by causing or witnessing harm to another person (Cialdini, Darby, & Vincent, 1973) or by feeling sadness (Schaller & Cialdini, 1988), except when people experience or anticipate experiencing a mood-enhancing event (e.g., receiving money or listening to a comedy tape) before the opportunity to help. Furthermore, consistent with the hypothesized link between helping and relief from one's own negative state, negative moods facilitate helping only if people believe that their moods are manageable (Manucia, Baumann, & Cialdini, 1984).

Despite some surface similarities between the arousal: cost-reward model and the negative-state (sadness) relief model, there are important conceptual distinctions. First, attribution of arousal plays a central role in the arousal: cost-reward model: Arousal *attributed to the plight of the other person* will motivate helping. In contrast, the negative-state relief model posits that, *regardless of their attributed source,* negative states (particularly sadness; see Cialdini et al., 1987) can motivate helping.

A second major distinction between the two models is that the arousal: cost-reward model is a tension-reduction model that assumes (a) that the victim's need produces an arousal state in the potential bene-factor and (b) that helping is directed toward relieving this unpleasant state. The classical analogue for this process is an escape-conditioning paradigm in which a rat presses a bar to terminate a shock. In contrast, the negative-state (sadness) relief model assumes that seeing the victim suffer creates a negative mood (sadness) that increases the potential helper's need for mood-enhancing self-rewards, which may be associ-ated with helping. The classical analogue for this process is a depriva-tion paradigm, in which a rat below normal body weight bar-presses for food.[2] Although these distinctions are subtle, they are important: They define the fundamental nature of the motivation underlying helping.

In contrast to the egoistic models of helping, Batson and his col-leagues (see Chapter 3 by Batson and Oleson) present an empathy-altruism model. According to this model, witnessing another person in need can produce either of two different emotional reactions: personal distress (e.g., upset, worry, alarm) and empathic concern (e.g., sympa-thy, compassion). Batson (1987) further proposes that personal distress and empathic concern lead to two qualitatively distinct motivations to help: Personal distress generates an egoistic desire to reduce *one's own* distress; empathic concern produces an altruistic desire to reduce the *other person's* distress.

Much of the support for the empathy-altruism hypothesis resides in findings that subjects experiencing empathic concern help even when costs for helping apparently outweigh the costs for not helping. Subjects who feel personal distress, however, do not help as much under these circumstances, presumably because escape is a less costly way of reducing distress (see Chapter 3). It should be noted, though, that, even if altruistic motivation can be demonstrated, that finding would not disprove the arousal: cost-reward model. Batson (1987) acknowledges the existence of motivations to reduce one's own distress and recognizes that, most of the time, helping may relate to egoistic motivation. What the demonstration of a truly altruistic motivation may do, however, is indicate a boundary condition of the arousal: cost-reward model.

Costs, Arousal, and Helping

The review of the recent literature on costs for helping provides additional support for our third proposition that bystanders choose responses that reduce arousal and incur as few net costs as possible. As costs for helping increase, helping decreases; as costs for no help to the victim increase, helping increases. In addition, individual differences and moods that may affect the perception and salience of costs for helping or costs for not helping relate predictably to intervention. With respect to traits, feelings of greater competence reduce the perceived costs for helping; individuals who perceive they are highly competent are more likely to help. Individuals higher in social responsibility may perceive the costs for not helping as higher; they are also more likely to help a person in need. With respect to temporary states, moods that focus attention on the needs of others or on the bystander's own prosocial standards—thereby increasing the costs for not helping—consistently facilitate helping.

The relationship between the potential benefactor and the person in need may also affect perceived costs. With respect to a sense of weness, the categorization of another person as an ingroup member increases the evaluation of the other person, brings that person closer to the self, and increases the salience or level of costs for not helping. Across a variety of experimental and naturalistic groups, people are more likely to help ingroup than outgroup members.

Because of the decline in empirical interest in emergency helping (perhaps because of ethical concerns), there is little new evidence bearing on impulsive helping, as described in our fourth proposition. The general finding of that body of literature is that factors (e.g., clarity, relationship to the victim) that facilitate high levels of arousal are the ones that are most predictive of impulsive helping. Thus much of the recent data on helping from a variety of areas can be interpreted as consistent with the role of costs and the hypothesized relationship between arousal and perceived costs within the model.

The last proposition of the arousal: cost-reward model seems to be important to Batson's (1987) demonstration of an altruistic motivation independent of the motivation hypothesized in our model. This proposition states that, on termination of contact with an emergency, the bystander's arousal decreases monotonically with time, whether or not the victim is helped. Actually, we know of no direct evidence supporting this proposition, and we now question its validity. It is quite possible that, as long as the plight of the victim is psychologically salient, bystanders continue to experience a negative arousal state. To the extent that empathic concern positively relates to the psychological salience of another person's need and the costs for not helping, the work of Batson and his colleagues suggests this is probably the case. If, however the victim's plight decreases in salience over time (e.g., through cognitive reappraisal of the situation, successful rationalization, denial, or forgetting), arousal will likely decrease with time. The conditions that influence arousal, and its dissipation after leaving the scene, are obviously a topic requiring further study.

Testing the Model

As noted earlier, although there are substantial data consistent with the model, true tests of the underlying theory require direct measurement of intervening processes. Because a variety of other frameworks generated much of the data in this area, there is less direct evidence for the processes central to our model than one would prefer. The fact that research based on these diverse frameworks provides *convergent* support for the predictions of the arousal: cost-reward model is, however, reassuring.

Methodological constraints impose further limitations. For example, it is difficult to operationalize focus of attention or, in emergency situations, to obtain self-reports of emotional experience from bystanders before they intervene. Nevertheless, studies that have attempted to measure intervening processes have produced support for the model. For example, Otten, Enner, and Waugh (1988) applied the arousal: cost-reward model to helping a psychologically distressed friend. Subjects read scenarios that systematically varied aspects of the situation relating to costs for helping (amount of help needed) and to costs for not helping (opportunity to diffuse responsibility). In two studies, estimates of costs for helping and costs for not helping and measures of willingness to help were obtained. Using path analysis, Otten, Penner, and Waugh found direct support for the model. Thus we believe that, as a model for generating hypotheses and integrating the results of studies, the arousal: cost-reward framework has been, on the whole, effective.

CONCLUSION

We have used the arousal: cost-reward model to organize and critically examine the literature on helping over the past decade. Overall, we feel that the model has proven useful for identifying areas of inquiry and generating testable hypotheses. Although the model does not provide a complete account of helping behavior, it is relatively comprehensive. As a consequence, it may serve as backdrop for other models of helping that are more focused (e.g., Batson's empathy-altruism hypothesis). We acknowledge that the model is relatively complex, but it should be recognized, after more than 1,000 studies investigating helping, that the processes involved in intervening in the problems, crises, and emergencies of others are also complex. We hope that as research on helping continues to move from a simple input-output/independent variable-dependent variable approach to a deeper appreciation for intervening processes, the arousal: cost-reward model will continue to offer valuable insights and suggestions. We expect that the research of the 1990s will encourage us to continue our critical reappraisals of the model and to contribute materially to the further evolution of the model.

NOTES

1. Details of this and all other meta-analyses reported in this chapter can be obtained from the first author.
2. We express our appreciation to C. Daniel Batson, who first suggested this analogy.

REFERENCES

Allen, N., & Rushton, J. P. (1983). The personality of community volunteers. *Journal of Voluntary Action Research, 12,* 36-49.
Aries, E. J., & Johnson, F. L. (1983). Close friendship in adulthood: Conversational content between same-sex friends. *Sex Roles, 9,* 1183-1196.

Atkinson, M. P., Kivett, V. R., & Campbell, R. T. (1986). Intergenerational solidarity: An examination of a theoretical model. *Journal of Gerontology, 41*, 408-416.

Austin, W. (1979). Sex differences in bystander intervention in a theft. *Journal of Personality and Social Psychology, 37*, 2110-2120.

Barnett, M. A. (1986). Sex bias in helping behavior presented in children's picture books. *Journal of Genetic Psychology, 147*, 343-351.

Bar-Tal, D., Bar-Zohar, Y., Greenberg, M. S., & Herman, M. (1977). Reciprocity behavior in the relationship between donor and recipient and between harm-doer and victim. *Sociometry, 40*, 293-298.

Batson, C. D. (1987). Prosocial motivation: Is it ever truly altruistic? In L. Berkowitz (Ed.), *Advances in experimental social psychology* (Vol. 20, pp. 65-122). New York: Academic Press.

Batson, C. D., Batson, J. G., Griffitt, C. A., Barrientos, S., Brandt, J. R., Sprengelmeyer, P., & Bayly, M. J. (1989). Negative-state relief and the empathy-altruism hypothesis. *Journal of Personality and Social Psychology, 56*, 922-933.

Batson, C. D., Bolen, M. H., Cross, J. A., & Neuringer-Benefiel, H. E. (1986). Where is the altruism in the altruistic personality? *Journal of Personality and Social Psychology, 50*, 212-220.

Batson, C. D., Duncan, B., Ackerman, P., Buckley, T., & Birch, K. (1981). Is empathic emotion a source of altruistic motivation? *Journal of Personality and Social Psychology, 40*, 290-302.

Batson, C. D., Dyck, J. L., Brandt, J. R., Batson, J. G., Powell, A. L., McMaster, M. R., & Griffitt, C. (1988). Five studies testing two new egoistic alternatives to the empathy-altruism hypothesis. *Journal of Personality and Social Psychology, 55*, 52-77.

Batson, C. D., O'Quin, K., Fultz, J., Vanderplas, M., & Isen, A. (1983). Influence of self-reported distress and empathy on egoistic versus altruistic motivation to help. *Journal of Personality and Social Psychology, 45*, 706-718.

Batson, C. D., Pate, S., Lawless, H., Sparkman, P., Lambers, S., & Worman, B. (1979). Helping under conditions of threat: Increased "we-feeling" or ensuring reciprocity? *Social Psychology Quarterly, 42*, 410-414.

Berg, J. H. (1984). Development of friendship between roommates. *Journal of Personality and Social Psychology, 46*, 346-356.

Berkowitz, L. (1973). Reactance and the unwillingness to help others. *Psychological Bulletin, 79*, 310-317.

Bleda, P. R., Bleda, S. T., Byrne, D., & White, L. A. (1976). When a bystander becomes an accomplice: Situational determinants of reaction to dishonesty. *Journal of Experimental Social Psychology, 12*, 9-25.

Brewer, M. B. (1979). In-group bias in the minimal intergroup situation: A cognitive-motivational analysis. *Psychological Bulletin, 86*, 307-324.

Briggs, N., Piliavin, J. A., Lorentzen, D., & Becker, G. A. (1986). On willingness to be a bone marrow donor. *Transfusion, 26*, 324-330.

Brown, R. J., & Abrams, D. (1986). The effects of intergroup similarity and goal interdependence on intergroup attitudes and task performance. *Journal of Experimental Social Psychology, 22*, 78-92.

Campbell, D. T., & Levine, R. A. (1972). *Ethnocentrism.* New York: John Wiley.

Carlson, M., Charlin, V., & Miller, N. (1988). Positive mood and helping behavior: A test of six hypotheses. *Journal of Personality and Social Psychology, 55*, 211-229.

Carlson, M., & Miller, N. (1987). Explanation of the relation between negative mood and helping. *Psychological Bulletin, 102,* 91-108.

Cialdini, R. B., Darby, B. K., & Vincent, J. E. (1973). Transgression and altruism: A case for hedonism. *Journal of Experimental Social Psychology, 9,* 502-516.

Cialdini, R. B., Kenrick, D. T., & Baumann, D. J. (1982). Effects of mood on prosocial behavior on children and adults. In N. Eisenberg (Ed.), *The development of prosocial behavior* (pp. 339-359). New York: Academic Press.

Cialdini, R. B., Schaller, M., Houlihan, D., Arps, K., Fultz, J., & Beaman, A. L. (1987). Empathy-based helping: Is it selflessly or selfishly motivated? *Journal of Personality and Social Psychology, 52,* 749-758.

Clark, D. M., & Teasdale, J. D. (1985). Constraints on the effects of mood on memory. *Journal of Personality and Social Psychology, 48,* 1595-1608.

Clark, M. S. (1984). Record keeping in two types of relationships. *Journal of Personality and Social Psychology, 47,* 549-557.

Clark, M. S., & Mills, J. (1979). Interpersonal attraction in exchange and communal relationships. *Journal of Personality and Social Psychology, 37,* 12-24.

Clark, M. S., Mills, J., & Corcoran, D. M. (1989). Keeping track of needs and inputs of friends and strangers. *Personality and Social Psychology Bulletin, 15,* 533-542.

Clark, M. S., Ouellette, R., Powell, M., & Milberg, S. (1987). Recipient's mood, relationship type, and helping. *Journal of Personality and Social Psychology, 53,* 94-103.

Clark, M. S., & Waddell, B. A. (1983). Effects of moods on thoughts about helping, attraction and information acquisition. *Social Psychology Quarterly, 46,* 31-35.

Cramer, R. E., McMaster, M. R., Bartell, P. A., & Dragna, M. (1988). Subject competence and minimization of the bystander effect. *Journal of Applied Social Psychology, 18,* 1133-1148.

Cunningham, M. R. (1986). Levites and brother's keepers: Sociobiological perspective on prosocial behavior. *Humboldt Journal of Social Relations, 13,* 35-67.

Darley, J. M., & Batson, C. D. (1973). From Jerusalem to Jericho: A study of situational and dispositional variables in helping behavior. *Journal of Personality and Social Psychology, 27,* 100-108.

Darley, J. M., & Latané, B. (1968). Bystander intervention in emergencies: Diffusion of responsibility. *Journal of Personality and Social Psychology, 8,* 377-383.

Denner, B. (1968). Did a crime occur? Should I inform anyone? A study of deception. *Journal of Personality, 36,* 454-465.

Deutsch, F. M., & Lamberti, D. M. (1986). Does social approval increase helping? *Personality and Social Psychology Bulletin, 12,* 149-157.

Doede-Anderson, P., & Kaplan, M. F. (1977, May). *Actual, self-predicted, and predictions of others' helping as social judgments.* Paper presented at the 49th meeting of the Midwestern Psychological Association, Chicago.

Dovidio, J. F. (1984). Helping behavior and altruism: An empirical and conceptual overview. In L. Berkowitz (Ed.), *Advances in experimental social psychology* (Vol. 17, pp. 361-427). New York: Academic Press.

Dovidio, J. F., & Morris, W. N. (1975). Effects of stress and commonality of fate on helping behavior. *Journal of Personality and Social Psychology, 31,* 145-149.

Eagly, A. H., & Crowley, M. (1986). Gender and helping behavior: A meta-analytic review of the social psychological literature. *Psychological Bulletin, 100,* 283-308.

Easterbrook, J. A. (1959). The effect of emotion on cue utilization and the organization of behavior. *Psychological Review, 66,* 183-201.

Edelmann, R. J., Childs, J., Harvey, S., Kellock, I., & Strain-Clark, C. (1984). The effect of embarrassment on helping. *Journal of Social Psychology, 124,* 253-254.

Edelmann, R. J., Evans, G., Pegg, I., & Tremain, M. (1983). Responses to physical stigma. *Perceptual and Motor Skills, 57,* 294.

Eisenberg, N., Fabes, R. A., Miller, P. A., Fultz, J., Shell, R., Mathy, R. M., & Reno, R. R. (1989). Relation of sympathy and personal distress to prosocial behavior: A multi-method study. *Journal of Personality and Social Psychology, 57,* 55-66.

Eisenberg, N., & Lennon, R. (1983). Sex differences in empathy and related capacities. *Psychological Bulletin, 94,* 100-131.

Eisenberg, N., & Miller, P. A. (1987). The relation of empathy to prosocial and related behaviors. *Psychological Bulletin, 101,* 91-119.

Essock-Vitale, S. M., & McGuire, M. T. (1980). Predictions derived from the theories of kin selection and reciprocation assessed by anthropological data. *Ethology and Sociobiology, 1,* 233-243.

Essock-Vitale, S. M., & McGuire, M. T. (1985). Women's lives viewed from an evolutionary perspective. II. Patterns of helping. *Ethology and Sociobiology, 6,* 155-173.

Forgas, J. P., Bower, G. H., & Krantz, S. E. (1984). The influence of mood on perceptions of social interactions. *Journal of Experimental Social Psychology, 20,* 497-513.

Frey, D. L., & Gaertner, S. L. (1986). Helping and the avoidance of inappropriate interracial behavior: A strategy that perpetuates a nonprejudiced self-image. *Journal of Personality and Social Psychology, 50,* 1083-1090.

Gaertner, S. L., & Dovidio, J. F. (1977). The subtlety of white racism, arousal, and helping. *Journal of Personality and Social Psychology, 35,* 691-707.

Hayden, S. R., Jackson, T. T., & Guydish, J. (1984). Helping behavior of females: Effects of stress and commonality of fate. *Journal of Psychology, 117,* 233-237.

Harris, M. B. (1977). Effects of altruism on mood, *Journal of Social Psychology, 102,* 197-208.

Hoffman, M. L. (1977). Sex differences in empathy and related behaviors. *Psychological Bulletin, 84,* 712-720.

Hoffman, M. L. (1981). Is altruism part of human nature? *Journal of Personality and Social Psychology, 40,* 121-137.

Hogg, M. A., & Abrams, D. (1988). *Social identifications: A social psychology of intergroup relations and group processes.* London: Routledge & Kegan Paul.

Hornstein, H. A. (1982). Promotive tension: Theory and research. In V. J. Derlega & J. Grzelak (Eds.), *Cooperation and helping behavior: Theories and research* (pp. 129-248). New York: Academic Press.

Huston, T. L., Geis, G., & Wright, R. (1976, June). The angry samaritans. *Psychology Today, 85,* 61-64.

Isen, A. M., Shalker, T. E., Clark, M., & Karp, L. (1978). Affect, accessibility of material in memory, and behavior. *Journal of Personality and Social Psychology, 36,* 1-12.

Johnson, F. L., & Aries, E. J. (1983). Conversational patterns among same-sex pairs of late-adolescent close friends. *Journal of Genetic Psychology, 142,* 225-238.

Juhnke, R., Barmann, B., Vickery, K., Cunningham, M., Hohl, J., Smith, E., & Quinones, J. (1987). Effects of attractiveness and nature of request on helping behavior. *Journal of Social Psychology, 127,* 317-322.

Katz, I., Farber, J., Glass, D. C., Lucido, D., & Emswiller, T. (1978). When courtesy offends: Effects of positive and negative behavior by the physically disabled on altruism and anger in normals, *Journal of Personality, 46,* 506-518.

Krebs, D. L. (1970). Altruism: An examination of the concept and a review of the literature. *Psychological Bulletin, 73,* 258-302.

Krebs, D. L., & Miller, D. T. (1985). Altruism and aggression. In G. Lindzey & E. Aronson (Eds.), *Handbook of social psychology* (Vol. 2, pp. 1-71). New York: Random House.

Ladd, G. W., Lange, G., & Stremmel, A. (1983). Children's helping behavior: Factors that mediate compliant helping. *Child Development, 54,* 488-501.

Lamm, H., & Schwinger, T. (1980). Norms concerning distributive justice: Are needs taken into account in allocation decisions? *Social Psychology Quarterly, 43,* 425-429.

Lamm, H., & Schwinger, T. (1983). Need consideration in allocation decisions: Is it just? *Journal of Social Psychology, 119,* 205-209.

Lanzetta, J. T., & Englis, B. G. (1989). Expectations of cooperation and competition and their effects on observers' vicarious emotional responses. *Journal of Personality and Social Psychology, 56,* 543-554.

Larrieu, J., & Mussen, P. (1986). Some personality and motivational correlates of children's prosocial behavior. *Journal of Genetic Psychology, 147,* 529-542.

Latané, B., & Darley, J. M. (1970). *The unresponsive bystander: Why doesn't he help?* New York: Appleton-Century-Crofts.

Latané, B., & Nida, S. (1981). Ten years of research on group size and helping. *Psychological Bulletin, 89,* 308-324.

Levin, J., & Arluke, A. (1982). Embarrassment and helping behavior. *Psychological Reports, 51,* 999-1002.

Liebhart, E. H. (1972). Empathy and emergency helping: The effects of personality, self-concern, and acquaintance. *Journal of Experimental Social Psychology, 8,* 404-411.

MacDonald, K. (1984). An ethological-social learning theory of the development of altruism: Implications for human sociobiology. *Ethology and Sociobiology, 5,* 97-109.

Manucia, G. K., Baumann, D. J., & Cialdini, R. B. (1984). Mood influences in helping: Direct effects or side effects? *Journal of Personality and Social Psychology, 46,* 357-364.

Marks, E. L., Penner, L. A., & Stone, A. V. W. (1982). Helping as a function of empathic responses and sociopathy. *Journal of Research in Personality, 16,* 1-20.

McGovern, L. P., Ditzian, J. L., & Taylor, S. P. (1975). The effect of one positive reinforcement on helping behavior. *Bulletin of the Psychonomic Society, 5,* 421-423.

Messick, D. M., & Mackie, D. M. (1989). Intergroup relations. *Annual Review of Psychology, 40,* 45-81.

Midlarsky, E. (1984). Competence and helping: Notes toward a model. In E. Staub, D. Bar-Tal, J. Karylowski, & J. Reykowski (Eds.), *Development and maintenance of prosocial behavior* (pp. 291-308). New York: Plenum.

Midlarsky, E., & Hannah, M. E. (1985). Competence, reticence, and helping by children and adolescents. *Developmental Psychology, 21,* 534-541.

Mischel, W. (1973). Toward a cognitive social learning reconceptualization of personality. *Psychological Review, 80,* 252-283.

Moriarty, T. (1975). Crime, commitment, and the responsive bystander: Two field experiments. *Journal of Personality and Social Psychology, 31,* 370-376.

Morris, W. N. (1989). *Mood: The frame of mind.* New York: Springer-Verlag.

Mueller, C. W., & Donnerstein, E. (1981). Film-facilitated arousal and prosocial behavior. *Journal of Experimental Social Psychology, 17,* 31-41.

Mueller, C. W., Donnerstein, E., & Hallam, J. (1983). Violent films and prosocial behavior. *Personality and Social Psychology Bulletin, 9,* 83-89.

Oliner, S. P., & Oliner, P. M. (1988). *The altruistic personality: Rescuers of Jews in Nazi Europe.* New York: Free Press.

Otten, C. A., Penner, L. A., & Waugh, G. (1988). That's what friends are for: The determinants of psychological helping. *Journal of Social and Clinical Psychology, 7,* 34-41.

Paulsell, S., & Goldman, M. (1984). The effect of touching different body areas on prosocial behavior. *Journal of Social Psychology, 122,* 269-273.

Pearce, P. L., & Amato, P. R. (1980). A taxonomy of helping: A multidimensional scaling analysis. *Social Psychology Quarterly, 43,* 363-371.

Peterson, L. (1983). Role of donor competence, donor age, and peer presence on helping in an emergency. *Developmental Psychology, 19,* 873-880.

Piliavin, I. M., Piliavin, J. A., & Rodin, J. (1975). Costs, diffusion, and the stigmatized victim. *Journal of Personality and Social Psychology, 32,* 429-438.

Piliavin, I. M., Rodin, J., & Piliavin, J. A. (1969). Good Samaritanism: An underground phenomenon? *Journal of Personality and Social Psychology, 13,* 289-299.

Piliavin, J. A., & Callero, P. C. (in press). *Giving blood: The development of an altruistic identity.* Baltimore, MD: Johns Hopkins University Press.

Piliavin, J. A., Dovidio, J. F., Gaertner, S. L., & Clark, R. D., III. (1981). *Emergency intervention.* New York: Academic Press.

Piliavin, J. A., Dovidio, J. F., Gaertner, S. L., & Clark, R. D., III. (1982). Responsive bystanders: The process of intervention. In V. J. Derlega & J. Grzelak (Eds.), *Cooperation and helping behavior: Theories and research* (pp. 279-304). New York: Academic Press.

Piliavin, J. A., & Piliavin, I. M. (1973). *The Good Samaritan: Why does he help?* Unpublished manuscript, Department of Sociology, University of Wisconsin.

Piliavin, J. A., & Unger, R. K. (1985). The helpful but helpless female: Myth or reality? In V. E. O'Leary, R. K. Unger, & B. S. Wallston (Eds.), *Women, gender, and social psychology* (pp. 149-189). Hillsdale, NJ: Lawrence Erlbaum.

Romer, D., Gruder, C. L., & Lizzadro, T. (1986). A person-situation approach to altruistic behavior. *Journal of Personality and Social Psychology, 51,* 1001-1012.

Schaller, M., & Cialdini, R. B. (1988). The economics of empathic helping: Support for a mood management motive. *Journal of Experimental Social Psychology, 24,* 163-181.

Schroeder, D. A., Dovidio, J. F., Sibicky, M. E., Matthews, L. L., & Allen, J. L. (1988). Empathy and helping behavior: Egoism or altruism? *Journal of Experimental Social Psychology, 24,* 333-353.

Segal, N. L. (1984). Cooperation, competition, and altruism within twin sets: Reappraisal. *Ethology and Sociobiology, 5,* 163-177.

Shaffer, D. R., Rogel, M., & Hendrick, C. (1975). Intervention in the library: The effect of increased responsibility on bystanders' willingness to prevent a theft. *Journal of Applied Social Psychology, 5,* 303-319.

Shotland, R. L., & Heinold, W. D. (1985). Bystander response to arterial bleeding: Helping skills, the decision-making process, and differentiating the helping response. *Journal of Personality and Social Psychology, 49,* 347-356.

Shotland, R. L., & Huston, T. L. (1979). Emergencies: What are they and how do they influence bystanders to intervene? *Journal of Personality and Social Psychology, 37,* 1822-1834.

Simmons, R. G., Klein, S. D., & Simmons, R. L. (1977). *The gift of life: The social and psychological impact on organ transplantation.* New York: John Wiley.

Sinha, A. K., & Jain, A. (1986). The effects of benefactor and beneficiary characteristics on helping behavior. *Journal of Social Psychology, 126,* 361-368.

Smith, J. D., & Shaffer, D. R. (1986). Self-consciousness, self-reported altruism, and helping behaviour. *Social Behavior and Personality, 14,* 215-220.

Smith, K. D., Keating, J. P., & Stotland, E. (1989). Altruism reconsidered: The effect of denying feedback on a victim's status to empathic witnesses. *Journal of Personality and Social Psychology, 57,* 641-650.

Snyder, M., & Ickes, W. (1985). Personality and social behavior. In G. Lindzey & E. Aronson (Eds.), *Handbook of social psychology* (Vol. 2, pp. 883-947). New York: Random House.

Sokolov, P. N. (1963). *Perception and the conditioned response.* Oxford: Pergamon.

Sole, K., Marton, J., & Hornstein, H. A. (1975). Opinion similarity and helping: Three field experiments investigating the bases of promotive tension. *Journal of Experimental Social Psychology, 11,* 1-13.

Staub, E. (1984). Notes toward an interactionist-motivational theory of the determinants and development of (pro)social behavior. In E. Staub, D. Bar-Tal, J. Karylowski, & J. Reykowski (Eds.), *Development and maintenance of prosocial behavior* (pp. 29-50). New York: Plenum.

Steele, C. M., Critchlow, B., & Liu, T. J. (1985). Alcohol and social behavior II: The helpful drunkard. *Journal of Personality and Social Psychology, 48,* 35-46.

Sterling, B., & Gaertner, S. L. (1984). The attribution of arousal and emergency helping: A bidirectional process. *Journal of Experimental Social Psychology, 20,* 286-296.

Tajfel, H. (1978). *Differentiation between social groups: Studies in the social psychology of intergroup relations.* London: Academic Press.

Tajfel, H. (1982). The social psychology of intergroup relations. *Annual Review of Psychology, 33,* 1-39.

Tesser, A., Millar, M., & Moore, J. (1988). Some affective consequences of social comparison and reflection processes: The pain and pleasure of being close. *Journal of Personality and Social Psychology, 54,* 49-61.

Tesser, A., & Smith, J. (1980). Some effects of friendship and task relevance on helping: You don't always help the one you like. *Journal of Experimental Social Psychology, 16,* 583-590.

Thompson, W. C., Cowan, C. L., & Rosenhan, D. L. (1980). Focus of attention mediates the impact of negative affect on helping. *Journal of Personality and Social Psychology, 38,* 291-300.

Tice, D. M., & Baumeister, R. F. (1985). Masculinity inhibits helping in emergencies: Personality does predict the bystander effect. *Journal of Personality and Social Psychology, 49,* 420-428.

Toi, M., & Batson, C. D. (1982). More evidence that empathy is a source of altruistic motivation. *Journal of Personality and Social Psychology, 43,* 281-292.

Turner, J. C. (1987). *Rediscovering the social group: A self-categorization theory.* Oxford: Basil Blackwell.

Utne, M. K., & Kidd, R. F. (1980). Equity and attribution. In G. Mikula (Ed.), *Justice and social interaction* (pp. 63-93). New York: Springer-Verlag.

Vaughan, K. B., & Lanzetta, J. T. (1980). Vicarious instigation and conditioning of facial expressive and autonomic response to a model's expressive display of pain. *Journal of Personality and Social Psychology, 38,* 909-923.

Vaughan, K. B., & Lanzetta, J. T. (1981). The effect of modification of expressive displays on vicarious emotional arousal. *Journal of Experimental Social Psychology, 17,* 16-30.

Walton, M. D., Sachs, D., Ellington, R., Hazelwood, A., Griffin, S., & Bass, D. (1988). Physical stigma and the pregnancy role: Receiving help from strangers. *Sex Roles, 18,* 323-331.

Wilder, D. A. (1986). Social categorization: Implications for creation and reduction of intergroup bias. In L. Berkowitz (Ed.), *Advances in experimental social psychology,* (Vol. 19, pp. 291-355). Orlando, FL: Academic Press.

Williamson, G., & Clark, M. S. (1989). Effects of providing help to another and of relationship type on the provider's mood and self-evaluation. *Journal of Personality and Social Psychology, 56,* 722-734.

Wilson, J. P. (1976). Motivation, modeling, and altruism: A person × situation analysis. *Journal of Personality and Social Psychology, 34,* 1078-1086.

Worchel, S. W., Wong, F. Y., & Scheltema, K. E. (1989). Improving intergroup relations: Comparative effects of anticipated cooperation and helping on attraction for an aid-giver. *Social Psychology Quarterly, 52,* 213-219.

Yinon, Y., & Landau, M. O. (1987). On the reinforcing value of helping behavior in a positive mood. *Motivation and Emotion, 11,* 83-93.

5

A Functional Analysis of
Altruism and Prosocial Behavior
THE CASE OF VOLUNTEERISM

E. GIL CLARY
MARK SNYDER

E. Gil Clary is Associate Professor of Psychology and the current holder of the Endowed Professorship in the Sciences at the College of St. Catherine. He received his Ph.D. in 1980 from the University of Georgia. In addition to his interests in dispositional and motivational factors related to volunteer activity, his research is concerned with the social climate of organizations utilizing volunteers, the meanings people attach to the concept of helpfulness, and methods of promoting ethically informed decision making.

Mark Snyder is Professor of Psychology at the University of Minnesota, where he has been a faculty member since 1972. He received a B.A. from McGill University in 1968 and a Ph.D. from Stanford University in 1972. His research interests include theoretical and empirical issues associated with the motivational foundations of individual and social behavior and the applications of basic theory and research in personality and social psychology to addressing practical problems confronting society. He is the author of *Public Appearances/Private Realities: The Psychology of Self-Monitoring.*

"And who is my neighbor?" Jesus replied, "A man was going down from Jerusalem to Jericho, and he fell among robbers, who stripped him and beat him, and departed, leaving him half dead. Now by chance a priest was going down the road; and when he saw him he passed by on the other side. So likewise a Levite, when he came to the place and saw him, passed by on the other side. But a Samaritan, as he journeyed, came to where he was; and when he saw him, he had compassion, and went to him and bound his wounds, pouring on oil and wine; then he set him on his own beast and brought him to an inn, and took care of him. And the next day he took out two dennarii and gave them to the innkeeper, saying, 'Take care of him; and whatever more you spend, I will repay you when I come back.' Which of these three, do you think, proved neighbor to him who fell among the robbers?" He said, "The one who showed mercy on him." And Jesus said to him, "Go and do likewise." (Luke 10:29-37, RSV)

AUTHORS' NOTE: We wish to acknowledge the support of the Gannett Foundation. Preparation of this chapter was facilitated by the appointment of the first author to the Endowed Professorship in the Sciences at the College of St. Catherine. The chapter was written while the second author was a Fellow at the Center for Advanced Study in the Behavioral Sciences, supported in part by a fellowship from the James McKeen Cattell Fund.

This well-known parable has served as an inspiration for countless generations of Sunday school students—and for at least one generation of social psychologists. For, in this elegant story, we have the basis for several important questions surrounding helping behavior (see Darley & Batson, 1973): Does the salience of religious and ethical beliefs promote helpfulness? Is the pressure of time responsible for failures to help? Are some types of religious people particularly likely to render aid? The parable can also be viewed as exemplary of a particular form of helping behavior, that which occurs in *spontaneous helping* situations. The situation was one in which potential helpers—the priest, Levite, and Samaritan—were exposed to an unexpected opportunity to help and required to quickly and immediately decide whether to offer assistance. The parable, however, contains another component, one that we draw on for our inspiration. In the story, the Samaritan not only experienced compassion, approached the victim, and attended to his wounds, but he also transported him to an inn, stayed with him for a period of time, and saw to his needs for the immediate future. The Samaritan, in other words, also engaged in *sustained helpfulness* and exhibited a *continued commitment* to the victim's care, and these latter acts, we might reasonably assume, occurred under *nonspontaneous* conditions.

SPONTANEOUS AND NONSPONTANEOUS HELPING

The parable of the Good Samaritan then might be taken as exemplary of two major types of helping behavior—spontaneous and nonspontaneous helpfulness. Psychological research on helping behavior has largely focused on spontaneous situations, where subjects, most often college students in laboratory settings, are first exposed to situations (the independent variables manipulated in these studies) in which they must quickly decide whether to engage in a brief and limited act of help (the dependent variable measured in these studies). The emphasis in this research, as noted by several reviewers (Bar-Tal, 1984; Benson et al., 1980; Krebs & Miller, 1985), has been on highly salient situational cues that affect the spontaneous decision to help for a relatively brief and limited period of time. This approach to studying helping behavior has successfully identified several important situational influences on helping behavior, including the presence of others (Latané & Darley, 1970), the pressure of time (Darley & Batson, 1973), and exposure to helpful models (Bryan & Test, 1967). At the same time, it has not provided much evidence of dispositional influences on helping behavior (e.g., Darley & Batson, 1973). In comparison, *nonspontaneous helping* situations have quite different characteristics. They are marked by circumstances in which potential helpers have time to decide whether and how to help. Very often, in such cases, helpers actually seek out, rather than react to, an opportunity to help. Moreover, these situations frequently involve giving aid for an extended time (Benson et al., 1980). Perhaps the best examples of nonspontaneous helping activity are found in people involved in *volunteer work* on an ongoing basis, for example, providing leadership to youth groups, health care and companionship to the sick or elderly, or counseling to those with psychological difficulties.

For whatever reason, nonspontaneous helping situations have not received the same empirical scrutiny that spontaneous ones have (see Smithson, Amato, & Pearce, 1983). Nevertheless, there are several reasons that examination of nonspontaneous helping situations might just be of interest to personality and social psychologists. First, there has been some question about the influence of dispositional factors on helping behavior, as research (at least that conducted in spontaneous helping situations) has generally not supported dispositional approaches. However, it has been argued that relations between dispositions and helping will be obtained if one examines nonspontaneous situations. As Benson et al. (1980, p. 89) observed, the nonspontaneous helping situation "calls for considerably more planning, sorting out of priorities, and matching of personal capabilities and interests with the type of intervention." If this is the case, then we should find dispositional factors exerting a much greater influence on decisions in nonspontaneous situations, relative to their influence in spontaneous situations. For now, suffice it to say that there is some support for this proposition (e.g., Allen & Rushton, 1983; Benson et al., 1980); later sections of this chapter consider this literature in more detail.

A second reason for examining nonspontaneous helping situations derives from the fact that interest in causal factors located within the person (e.g., dispositions) eventually leads to a concern with motivation. Certainly, much of the research on helping behavior is directed at motivational questions, as the questions "why do people help?" and "why do people fail to help?" are, at heart, questions of motivation. Yet, by focusing on spontaneous situations, questions of motivation tend to be limited to asking why people help in response to unexpected need situations. Nonspontaneous helping situations force us to address additional questions. For example, why didn't the Good Samaritan stop after giving immediate aid? Why did he continue and take the victim to the inn? Why did the Samaritan then stay with the victim until the next day? And why did he ensure continued care for the victim? Thus nonspontaneous helping situations raise a whole host of motivational questions and signal the complexity of the motivational factors that may come into play in helping behavior that is sustained and continuing over time.

Third, nonspontaneous helping behavior generally, and participation in volunteer work as a prototypic instance of nonspontaneous helping behavior, are important events in their own right. Volunteer activity is a significant social phenomenon—the most recent Gallup Poll on volunteer activity estimated that 80 million American adults engaged in volunteering in 1987, with approximately 21 million giving five or more hours per week (Independent Sector, 1988). Further, volunteer work encompasses a wide variety of specific activities, ranging from baby-sitting the children of one's neighbor to delivering meals to the homebound to tutoring illiterate adults. Volunteerism, it should also be emphasized, involves one of those discrepancies between beliefs and actions so familiar to personality and social psychologists, as volunteer work is an activity that nearly everyone favors but in which a considerably smaller number actually participates (Independent Sector, 1988). In other words, the motives for nonspontaneous help are apparently present and widespread, but less frequently are those motives translated into action.

In sum, examination of nonspontaneous help, and particularly participation in volunteer work, promises to provide new perspectives on helping behavior, as it poses some fundamentally important questions about the nature of helpfulness. What processes guide people when they seek out helping opportunities? Are these processes different from the processes involved in reacting to an unexpected helping situation? What factors are implicated in decisions to offer one's help over extended periods of time? And, having engaged in an initial helping act, what leads to continued and sustained helpfulness? In this chapter, we will examine some of these questions and issues, both theoretically and empirically, by focusing on the specific case of volunteer work. We will do so from a particular perspective, that of functional analysis, whose defining features we will now present.

A FUNCTIONAL ANALYSIS OF NONSPONTANEOUS HELP

Clearly, the questions that arise in thinking about volunteer work as continued, sustained, nonspontaneous help are fundamentally motivational in nature. That is, they ask about the motives that are involved when one decides whether to commit oneself to an ongoing task and then must regularly decide whether or not to continue to participate in it. How then are questions such as these, which concern the motivational foundations of volunteerism, to be addressed? One approach we have found promising builds on the strategy of *functional analysis*. By definition, a functional analysis is concerned with the reasons and purposes that underlie and generate psychological phenomena—the personal and social needs, plans, goals, and functions being served by people's beliefs and their actions (e.g., Snyder, 1988). Accordingly, a functional analysis of volunteerism is concerned with the needs being met, the motives being fulfilled, and social and psychological functions being served by the activities of those people who engage in volunteer work.

In personality and social psychology, the functional approach is most strongly identified with theories of attitudes and persuasion (e.g., Herek, 1987; D. Katz, 1960; M. B. Smith, Bruner, & White, 1956; Snyder & DeBono, 1987, 1989). To the question, "Of what use to people are their attitudes?" the functional theorists responded by addressing the means by which attitudes might help meet needs, execute plans, and achieve goals and by proposing that people may hold the same attitudes or engage in apparently similar behaviors for very different motivational reasons and to serve quite different psychological functions.

Although functional theorists have tended to emphasize their own preferred sets of functions, certain ones occur with some regularity across diverse functional approaches to attitudes and persuasion. Some attitudes are thought to serve a knowledge function, bringing a sense of understanding of the social world. Other attitudes may help people fit into important social situations; as such, they are thought to serve a social-adjustive function. Attitudes serving a value-expressive function are thought to help a person express deeply held values, convictions, and dispositions. And attitudes serving an ego-defensive function are said to help protect the person from accepting undesirable or threatening truths about the self.

This list is by no means exhaustive of the personal and social functions that have been ascribed to attitudes, because other functions have been proposed, and even some on this list have received other labels. Nevertheless, the functions on this list have both theoretical roots (e.g., D. Katz, 1960, has argued that they embody the themes of the major theoretical views of human nature) and empirical foundations (e.g., Herek, 1987, has asserted that they emerge empirically from his studies of attitudes). At the very least, though, this set of functions does provide some sense of the flavor of the functional approach. To be sure, researchers have experienced some difficulties in testing functional theories of attitudes (see Kiesler, Collins, & Miller, 1969). Many of these problems were empirical ones, often having to do with the assessment devices used to measure functions, problems that largely have been overcome by new and emerging approaches to studying the functional bases of attitudes and persuasion (e.g., Herek, 1987; Shavitt, 1989; Snyder & DeBono, 1987, 1989).

To students of attitudes and persuasion, the functional theories have been appealing for a host of reasons. Foremost among these reasons are (a) the functional theories' explicit concern with the motivational infrastructure of attitudes, (b) their assertion that the same attitude may serve different functions for different people, and (c) their implication that attempts to influence attitudes and change behavior will be successful to the extent that they address the function being served by the current attitude.

Each of these considerations has its counterpart in a functional analysis of volunteerism, and each promises to reveal the personal and social motivational foundations of volunteer activity. Acts of volunteerism that appear to be quite similar on the surface may reflect markedly different underlying motivational processes, that is, they may be serving differing personal, social, and psychological functions (see Omoto & Snyder, 1990). Let us illustrate by using the list of functions we have abstracted as a *heuristic* device to consider the diversity of motivations that may contribute to volunteerism. In doing so, we make no claim that this set of functions contains the only ones relevant to volunteerism. Rather, we take them as a point of departure and see our task as one of assessing just how good a heuristic device they are for understanding volunteerism.

Consider, first, the often discussed notion that helping behavior generally, and volunteer work specifically, is motivated by a helper's concern for the recipient of help. Frequently, this type of motivation is discussed in terms of altruism (e.g., Batson, 1987), although other theorists use different labels and somewhat different conceptualizations, for example, Staub's (1978, 1984) prosocial orientation as a personal goal and Schwartz's (1977) moral obligation as a personal norm. When volunteer activity is based on altruistic concern for others in need, humanitarian values, and/or desires to contribute to society, the functional model conceives of such behavior as serving a *value-expressive function* for the individual. The idea of a value-expressive function thus incorporates the general hypothesis that values about other people's well-being influence helping behavior. At the same time, the functional model suggests that volunteering is not only guided by the values themselves but also helps individuals remain true to their conception of self and allow the expression of deeply held values, convictions, and personality dispositions.

At other times and for other people, the act of volunteering may serve a *social-adjustive function,* reflecting the normative influences of friends, family, and other significant associates who themselves are volunteers. This type of motivation also has figured prominently in several accounts of helpfulness, including Rosenhan's (1970) normative altruism that is controlled by social rewards and punishments. From the functional perspective, volunteering may help one fit in and get along well with important members of one's reference group. It is, in this case, a response to social pressure coming from one's existing social network. Additionally, some people may perceive volunteering as providing a way of expanding their social circles, that is, to make new social contacts or for new social opportunities.

There also may be cases where volunteering serves an *ego-defensive function,* helping people to cope with inner conflicts, anxieties, and uncertainties concerning personal worth and competence. Ekstein (1978) discussed several psychoanalytic accounts of helping behavior, noting that those writers have focused on the mechanisms of guilt, reaction formations (as defenses against greed and sadism), or narcissism, exhibitionism, and masochism. We might also include here Zuckerman's (1975) hypothesis that those with a strong belief in a just world would, in a time of personal need, help another in order to make themselves deserving of desirable outcomes. In general, in the case of the ego-defensive function, some people may look upon volunteering as a way of providing self-protection—to protect themselves from accepting the undesirable or threatening conclusions about the self that might be warranted in the absence of the good works of their volunteerism, to work on their own psychological problems, or to ensure that they will deserve, and, therefore, receive, good things in the future.

Finally, for other people and at other times, service as a volunteer may fulfill a *knowledge function*, whereby greater understanding is achieved through this kind of activity. For these people, volunteer work may provide new insights into the people they have contact with, thereby satisfying an intellectual curiosity about the world in general and the social world in particular. Volunteer activity might also provide the opportunity to exercise, and/or practice, knowledge and skills that otherwise could not be used. In addition to gaining an improved understanding of the world they live in, or honing specific skills, volunteer work may provide opportunities to acquire new skills and competencies, skills that represent ends in themselves or skills that might prove useful for a career. In general, it seems that very little work on this kind of motivation has been conducted in relation to helping behavior. In the case of volunteer activity, however, this motivation that focuses on gaining new understanding (which may be specific in content or general) may be especially relevant in the case of volunteer activities that have "joblike" characteristics and where volunteer and paid versions of the work coexist (e.g., volunteer and paid firefighters).

Thus a functional analysis incorporates and continues several trends already present in the literature. Some of the functions share some features with other theoretical constructs, and the notion that the same activity may, for different people, serve very different functions has also been expressed in the literature. It should be clear, then, that participation in volunteer activity is a complex phenomenon. And not only may the same act serve different functions for different people, the same act may serve more than one psychological function for the same individual. Analyzing volunteer work in terms of the functions it serves points to this complexity and encourages us to consider the wide range of personal and social motivations that promote this form of helping behavior. To be sure, the set of functions we have focused on may or may not be precisely *the* set of functions. Nevertheless, this set of functions may serve productively as a guiding framework for examining and organizing the literature on volunteerism.

RESEARCH ON VOLUNTEER WORK

To date, there is little published research that has *explicitly* tested the functional model. There is, nevertheless, a considerable body of research concerned with voluntary action. Researchers have been interested in relations between various factors, quite often sociological in nature, and involvement in neighborhood block organizations (e.g., Wandersman, Florin, Friedmann, & Meier, 1987), self-help groups (e.g., A. H. Katz, 1981), and social movements (e.g., Zald & McCarthy, 1987).

In this chapter, however, we will concern ourselves with research that addresses the *motivational* foundations of involvement in the more traditional, service-oriented volunteer work—activities where one assists another directly, often on an individual basis (D. H. Smith, 1974). We do so because it is this type of service-oriented voluntary action that most clearly fits with conceptions of "helping behavior." Furthermore, we believe that such research on motivations ultimately speaks, albeit at times indirectly, to the utility of an analysis of *psychological* functions.

In the review that follows, we will be considering four kinds of investigations of participation in volunteer work. One kind has relied on surveys in which respondents have identified themselves as volunteers or nonvolunteers and researchers have then compared these groups on sociological and/or psychological variables. A second kind has examined volunteers working within organizations (and hence did not rely on self-reported volunteer status) and then provided descriptions of the sample without comparisons to a nonvolunteer group. A third kind of investigation has explicitly compared a group of volunteers with one of nonvolunteers. And, finally, a fourth kind has focused on a group of volunteers and compared committed volunteers with less committed volunteers, with commitment often operationalized by length of service. The first three kinds of studies attempt to answer the question of why people volunteer and how volunteers differ from nonvolunteers motivationally, and the fourth kind addresses the question of why people continue to volunteer, or, more specifically, the matter of whether levels of motivation are related to amounts of service. Below, we discuss studies representative of these four types and their findings and place them within the framework of a functional analysis.

National Surveys of Volunteers

For several years now, the Gallup organization has been surveying the American public about their participation in volunteer activities (Gallup organization, 1981, 1986; Independent Sector, 1988). Using a broad definition of volunteer work (one that included informally help-ing one's friends and neighbors as well as working within a service organization), the 1981 survey revealed that 52% of the population had performed some volunteer work during the previous 12 months; the 1985 survey found 48% participation; and the 1988 poll found 45% involvement. Further, the three surveys have consistently found the greatest percentages of volunteers in the activity areas of religious organizations, informal helping, and education. Finally, in terms of specific tasks, the 1985 and 1988 surveys revealed that the most fre-quently reported tasks were assisting the elderly or handicapped, acting as an aide or assistant to a paid employee, baby-sitting, fund-raising, and serving on committees. Demographic information also has been obtained from respondents, and people most likely to be involved in volunteer work are those who are female, White, and under the age of 50; those who are employed, especially those in part-time jobs; and those who live in suburban and rural environments. Participation also tends to be positively related to socioeconomic status, as volunteering increases with education, income, and occupational prestige.

The Gallup surveys also ask respondents to indicate their reasons for volunteering. Consider, now, the motivations reported in Table 5.1 from the perspective of our functional analysis. Although the surveys were not conducted with this framework in mind, there is some indication that at least some of the functions are involved in volunteers' participa-tion. For example, the most frequently indicated reason, "do something useful; help others," as well as "religious concerns," seem consistent with the value-expressive function. The item "had someone who was involved or would benefit from it" (e.g., a family member or friend also was participating or is one of the recipients of the activity) may well reflect social-adjustive concerns. Further, from the functional perspective, knowledge concerns may be tapped by the item "wanted to learn, get experience." Finally, we wonder if the "feel needed" part of the item "enjoy the work; feel needed" may be tapping some part of the ego-defensive function.

Studies of Volunteers

A second attempt at answering questions about the motivations of volunteers has proceeded by obtaining samples of volunteers through volunteer organizations. Thus, unlike the national surveys, these studies do not have to rely on self-reported volunteer status. This kind of study,

TABLE 5.1 Percentage of Volunteers Reporting Various Reasons for Volunteering: National Surveys[a]

Reasons	1981	1985	1988
Do something useful; help others	45.0	52.0	55.8
Had an interest in activity, working	35.0	36.0	NI[b]
Enjoy the work; feel needed	29.0	32.0	33.5
Religious concerns	21.0	27.0	21.8
Had someone who was involved in the activity, or would benefit from it	23.0	26.0	27.2
Wanted to learn, get experience; work experience; help get a job	11.0	10.0	9.4
Had a lot of free time	8.0	10.0	8.6
Previously benefited from activity	NI	NI	9.9

a. From the Gallup organization's national surveys of volunteering conducted for the Independent Sector in 1981, 1985, 1988 (Gallup organization, 1986, Independent Sector, 1988). The survey item was as follows: "For what reasons did you first become involved in your volunteer activities" and the above reasons were response alternatives. Multiple responses were allowed.
b. NI = question was not included on that year's survey.

however, has focused on a particular group of volunteers, and comparisons to nonvolunteers are made only implicitly. Finally, the studies discussed below have all included measures intended to reflect volunteers' motives, with the measures ranging from the relatively simple to the more sophisticated.

Jenner (1982), for example, asked women in the Junior League to indicate their reasons for volunteering by selecting one of four response options. The most frequently chosen option was belief in the organization's purpose (46%), followed by the opportunity to do interesting work (25%), a friend's request to join (16%), and respect for the people in the organization (14%). Somewhat similarly, Anderson and Moore (1978) had volunteers (obtained from volunteer recruitment and referral centers) respond to a 10-item list of reasons, indicating as many reasons as applied: 75% reported that helping others was involved in their volunteering, followed by feeling useful and needed (50.6%), self-fulfillment (39.3%), personal development (34%), and improving the community (32.7%). Fitch's (1987) volunteers in college community service organizations rated the importance of 20 items designed to reflect altruism, egoism, or social obligation reasons for volunteering. Here, the highest rated item was an egoistic one ("It gives me a good feeling or sense of satisfaction to help others"), followed by altruistic ("I am concerned about those less fortunate than me"), egoistic, and social obligation ("I would hope someone would help me or my family if I/we were in similar situations") reasons.

Other investigations have focused less on separate items and more on classes of items, often in terms of altruistic and egoistic motives. Wiehe and Isenhour (1977) assessed the importance of four motivational categories (for volunteers obtained through a recruitment and referral center) and found that the order of importance (in descending order) was altruism, personal satisfaction (spend free time in a personally gratifying manner), self-improvement (upgrade job skills), and external demands (club or class requirement). Gidron (1978) asked volunteers in health and mental health institutions to report the extent to which they expected to receive several types of extrinsic rewards (rewards the organization controls) and intrinsic rewards (rewards associated with volunteers' subjective interpretation). While two-thirds of the sample expected two extrinsic rewards (training, contact with other volunteers), the vast majority expected the intrinsic reward of "stressing one's other-orientation." Also with respect to intrinsic rewards, just under 80% expected "self-development, learning, and variety in life" rewards as well as "opportunities for social interaction" rewards. Finally, in a study of Red Cross policymaking, administrative, and operational volunteers, Frisch and Gerrard (1981) factor-analyzed their motivational items and obtained an altruistic and an egoistic factor; further, they found that altruistic motives were the primary ones.

Similarly, based upon surveys that used extensive batteries of open-ended and structured items to ascertain people's motives for doing AIDS-related volunteer work, Omoto and Snyder (1990) found that value-expressive considerations figure prominently in most AIDS volunteers' motivations. Participation in AIDS volunteer work gave them a chance to act on personal values, convictions, and beliefs—to do something important to them. Moreover, these functional motivations occurred against the background of relevant personality dispositions. For example, AIDS volunteers motivated by value-expressive concerns also scored high on measures of nurturance, empathy, and social responsibility. To be sure, value-expressive functions were not the only ones served by AIDS-related work. Consistent with the functional analysis, other motives were present in varying degrees, suggesting that the same acts of volunteerism may serve quite different psychological functions. Functions other than the value-expressive ones, however, were relatively less important overall.

Clearly, these studies have relied on different kinds of volunteers and have used different measuring instruments. Some consistencies, however, have emerged and are interpretable within the functional framework. First, the volunteers in these investigations report the importance of altruism, or the value-expressive function, as a factor in their involvement. Second, these investigations also found evidence for other motives, many lumping these together under the egoistic label, although some did make distinctions among self-oriented motives (e.g., Gidron, 1978). Finally, several studies reported relations between age and some of the motives. Volunteers who were younger, relative to the other age groups, were more likely to report that the motives of gaining career-related experiences, making social contacts, and learning and self-development were moderately important (Anderson & Moore, 1978; Frisch & Gerrard, 1981; Gidron, 1978; Wiehe & Isenhour, 1977); older volunteers (over 55 years) in Gidron's study (1978) were somewhat more likely to view volunteering as a way of maintaining contact with their community. It is interesting that these findings suggest the importance of some needs and functions may well vary with one's life situation and/or stage of development. At the same time, these studies argue that value-expressive needs are a consistent feature of volunteer activity.

Comparisons of Volunteers and Nonvolunteers

A third type of study has proceeded by explicitly comparing volunteers with nonvolunteers on several dimensions. For example, in a comparison of male members of rescue squads and Big Brothers with male nonvolunteers on responses to the 16 PF (an omnibus personality inventory), B.M.M. Smith and Nelson (1975) found that volunteers were more extraverted, lower on need for autonomy, and (for older volunteers) had greater ego strength. And Pearce (1983) compared volunteer and paid employees engaged in the same kind of activity (newspaper, poverty relief, family planning, or fire department) and found the volunteers to have higher levels of service (e.g., "a chance to make a real contribution") and social (e.g., "working with people I like") motivations than paid workers; the two groups of workers did not differ on intrinsic motivation (e.g., "enjoyment of just doing the work").

One investigation deserving particular attention is Oliner and Oliner's (1988) extensive comparison of (authenticated) rescuers of Jews in Nazi-occupied Europe and nonrescuers. They found that rescuers were higher on social responsibility and prosocial action orientation measures, more internal in their locus of control, and more responsive to the pain and suffering of others than nonrescuers. Overall, rescuers exhibited what Oliner and Oliner call the capacity for extensive relationships (stronger feelings of attachment to and responsibility for others, including nonfamily and nonfriends), whereas nonrescuers were marked by constrictedness (centered on themselves and their small circle of family and friends). Rescuers' actions also appeared to be rooted in different developmental experiences and catalyzed by different factors. Specifically, some rescuers' (37%) first act of rescue illustrated an empathic orientation (i.e., motivated by a direct connection to a victim, tied to an emotional reaction to an external event); for others (11%), their first act reflected a principled orientation (i.e., motivated by the violation of fundamental principles, such as justice and care); however, the majority (52%) of rescuers acted out of a normocentric orientation (i.e., motivated by obligations to a significant social group).

Other studies have gone beyond a dichotomous volunteer-nonvolunteer distinction and obtained overall indices of participation in volunteer activity, then correlated this continuous measure with measures of dispositional factors. Benson et al. (1980), for example, had people recall their involvement in specific types of helping during the past year. A multiple regression analysis revealed that number of hours spent helping was predictable from social responsibility, locus of control, and intrinsic religion; the number of types of helping reported was predicted by intrinsic religion, size of town where the person grew up, and church attendance. More recently, Amato (1985) developed a measure of planned help, which includes both formal organized activities (many of which involve volunteer work) and informal activities (items about planned help to family and friends). His investigation revealed that the best predictors of formal planned help were high scores on social responsibility and low scores on authoritarianism; the best predictors of the informal subscale were (being lower on) internal locus of control and experiencing generally positive mood states.

Perhaps the most extensive examination of volunteers and nonvolunteers is Allen and Rushton's (1983) review of 19 published studies comparing community mental health volunteers with nonvolunteers.

Their review indicated that volunteers, compared with nonvolunteers, possessed more internalized moral standards, positive attitudes toward self and others, a greater degree of self-efficacy, more emotional stability, and greater empathy. Overall, Allen and Rushton concluded that community mental health volunteers possessed several characteristics associated with what may be thought of as an "altruistic personality."

Clearly, the investigations comparing volunteers with nonvolunteers have focused on several types of volunteer tasks and relied on a variety of dispositional measures. We can, nevertheless, consider these studies from the perspective of a functional analysis. Perhaps the most apparent function to surface is the value-expressive one. Whether operationally defined by social responsibility, the value of helpfulness, moral or ethical principles, or service motivation, the evidence is generally consistent with respect to the existence of value-expressive needs. Other functions also appear, especially the social-adjustive function. For example, the social-adjustive function may be reflected by the extraversion of rescue squad and Big Brother volunteers (B.M.M. Smith & Nelson, 1975), the social motives of volunteer employees (Pearce, 1983), and the normocentric orientation of some rescuers of Jews (Oliner & Oliner, 1988).

Partially Versus Fully Committed Volunteers

In this section we consider studies that address the question of the factors, especially motivational ones, that are influential in determining how long volunteers engage in an activity. Here, the comparison is not between volunteers and nonvolunteers but between volunteers who exhibit different levels of commitment. Several studies previously discussed did include some measures of volunteers' commitment. In the 1988 Gallup survey (Independent Sector, 1988), for example, the reported reasons and frequencies for continuing to participate were quite comparable to reasons for volunteering in the first place (reported in Table 5.1). Similarly, Jenner (1982) asked respondents about their reasons for maintaining membership in the Junior League; 48% cited their belief in the organization's purpose and 42% cited the personal rewards of their work.

Other investigations have more directly, and in greater detail, addressed questions about continued participation by comparing volunteers with different levels of participation. In a study of participants in the civil rights movement, Rosenhan (1970) observed that activists could be classified as partially committed (participating in one or two "freedom rides") or fully committed (participating in various ways for at least one year). The two types of activists reported different socialization experiences, which, in turn, produced motivational differences. Fully committed volunteers were autonomous altruists, intrinsically motivated by a concern for others, while the partially committed were normative altruists, motivated more by self-concerns, often involving social rewards and punishments.

In their work with crisis-counseling volunteers, Clary and Miller (1986) examined the interaction of socialization experiences and the social rewards provided by training group cohesiveness. As expected, autonomous volunteers (those reporting socialization experiences similar to Rosenhan's fully committed activists) had a high commitment to the volunteer work regardless of group cohesiveness. The commitment of normative volunteers (those with experiences similar to Rosenhan's partially committed activists) varied with the training group experience; for these volunteers, having received this socially rewarding experience increased their commitment to a level comparable to the autonomous group.

In addition to the Rosenhan and Clary and Miller studies, which were concerned with socialization antecedents of help-related motivations, other investigations have focused more directly on the motivation-commitment relationship. Clary and Orenstein (in press) found that volunteer crisis counselors who terminated their participation early had reported fewer altruistic reasons for volunteering in the first place than did either volunteers who completed the expected period of service or those who were terminated for lack of ability. Further, Rohs (1986) reported that length of service as a 4-H volunteer leader was directly related to the role of significant others (the influence was positive in some cases, negative in others) and indirectly related (via the positive influence of others) to beliefs about the value of 4-H to society.

Two additional studies have also examined altruistic motives but, contrary to the studies cited above, failed to find a relationship with commitment. Rubin and Thorelli (1984) found, as predicted, that length of participation with a Big Brother/Big Sister program was inversely related to the number of egoistic reasons motivating entry into this work but unrelated to the number of altruistic motives. (It should be noted, however, that the category of egoistic reasons included eleven items, but the altruistic reasons category contained only four; hence considerations of differential reliability may cloud interpretation of these findings.) Pierucci and Noel's (1980) study of correctional volunteers found no differences among committed, partially committed, and uncommitted groups on measures of altruistic, personal reward, or interest motivations. Also relevant to the issue of commitment to volunteer activities are the comparisons between rookie and veteran blood donors reviewed by Piliavin, Evans, and Callero (1984). According to the authors, there are five motivational categories relevant to blood donation: external social motives, community or social group responsibility, personal moral obligation, self-based humanitarian concern, and hedonic motives. Among rookie donors, there appeared to be two subgroups. The initial donation of the "externals" seemed to be determined by strong social pressure and that of the "internals" by a personal decision or the simple suggestion of friends. With repeated donations, community responsibility and moral obligation motives gain in strength (the "internal" rookies appear to be further along in this regard). Eventually, with enough donations, "role-person" mergers may occur where the blood donor role is viewed as a part of the self (Callero, Howard, & Piliavin, 1987).

Investigations of volunteer behavior that have examined duration of participation can readily be viewed within the functional framework. Once again, evidence for the value-expressive function emerges, with positive relations between this function and continued participation being observed. Two studies, however, did not provide confirming evidence, and one even suggested that duration was related to the absence of egoistic motives and not to the presence of value-expressive ones (Rubin & Thorelli, 1984). There also was some evidence for the social-adjustive function, with Rohs (1986), for example, finding that significant others had an impact on the duration of service of volunteer leaders. Rosenhan's concept of normative altruism can profitably be viewed in social-adjustive terms, and it appears that the commitment of these volunteers can be increased by providing desired social experiences (Clary & Miller, 1986). Finally, the initial and continual donations of Piliavin, Evans, and Callero's (1984) "external" blood donors seem to reflect social-adjustive concerns.

Methodological Considerations

We have, up to this point, considered several types of studies that have examined the issue of volunteers' motivations and its relations to various aspects of volunteer behavior. Now consider the studies as a group from a methodological standpoint. Our review has presented the research on its own terms and provided very few comments about the methods used in these investigations. There are, however, a number of methodological questions that apply to most, if not all, of the studies. Overall, these investigations have relied on field methodologies, have applied correlational approaches, and have examined people who have selected themselves into volunteer or nonvolunteer categories. These features of the research are potential sources of concern, in particular, regarding the possibility of demand characteristics, the timing of the motivational measures, and the adequacy of the measures themselves.

In their review of research on community mental health volunteers, Allen and Rushton (1983) considered the possible operation of demand characteristics. To the extent that volunteers are aware of the interest that researchers have in their motives, they may perceive a "demand" to adopt a "good volunteer" role. Allen and Rushton argued that the demand characteristics explanation is rendered less plausible by the fact that studies have failed to find correlations with social desirability measures. Moreover, one study they reviewed (Knapp & Holzberg, 1964) examined relations between dispositional factors obtained during subjects' freshman year (as part of the college's testing program) and participation in a volunteer act that occurred one to three years later; this lengthy separation between the measurements of dispositions and participation renders a demand interpretation rather unlikely.

A second related concern arises when dispositional measures are measured along with, or even after, measures of volunteer activity. Quite simply, the volunteer experience may change the volunteer and his or her motivations, and, rather than motivations influencing volunteering, it may be a case of volunteering influencing motivations. Both Allen and Rushton (1983) and Clary and Miller (1986) cite several studies that have found positive personality and motivation-relevant changes as a result of volunteering. Still, there are investigations that have used prospective methods, assessing dispositional factors at the beginning of the volunteer experience and then tracking volunteers' participation. Such prospective studies (e.g., Clary & Miller, 1986; Clary & Orenstein, in press) have found initial motivational differences related to later behavioral differences in volunteers and suggest that these motivational factors may have causal significance and influence subsequent aspects of the volunteer experience.

A final concern centers on the measures that have been used to assess motivations, particularly the psychometric properties of those measures. Many of the investigations have relied on separate items without regard to larger groupings, some have grouped items according to some rational scheme (often, altruistic versus egoistic), others have grouped items empirically, still others have provided practically no information about the measures, and some have utilized previously developed scales (often, Berkowitz & Lutterman's, 1968, social responsibility scale). Clearly, the widespread use of measures of unknown reliability and validity is troublesome and suggests the need for the development of adequate measures of volunteer motivation. Nevertheless, in spite of the methodological concerns, different studies, using a variety of measurement procedures, have revealed some consistencies.

THE FUNCTIONAL ANALYSIS: HOW WELL DOES IT FARE?

As we have argued all along, a functional analysis offers one scheme for understanding the motivations of volunteers and incorporates many of the consistent findings. Taking the literature on volunteers' motivation as a whole, the evidence is consistent with the fundamental tenets of the functional approach, namely, that the same action may involve different motives and that different motivations will require different satisfactions. But what about the specific motives identified by the functional approach? Perhaps the one consistent finding throughout this literature on the motivations of volunteers is that implicating the value-expressive function. Whether referred to in these terms, or as altruistic motivation or humanitarian concern, the desire to help others has been found time and again to be characteristic of volunteers, to distinguish volunteers from nonvolunteers, and to discriminate between partially and fully committed volunteers. Thus there seems to be a pervasive value-expressive component that is central to volunteer activity.

There is evidence for other functional motivations as well, but it is certainly not as clear and consistent as that for the value-expressive function. Clearest, perhaps, is the evidence for the operation of the social-adjustive function. Piliavin, Evans, and Callero's (1984) studies of blood donors have found that donations, and especially the initial one, were affected by social pressure. Similarly, Oliner and Oliner (1988) found that the initial involvement of the majority of rescuers of

Jews was in response to perceived pressure from members of one's social circle. Pearce's (1983) volunteer employees reported higher levels of social motivation than did the paid employees, although in this case the motivation centered more on the friendship aspect of social motives. Finally, there are the normative altruists (e.g., Clary & Miller, 1986; Rosenhan, 1970) who responded with the social consequences of their actions in mind.

Several studies suggest the knowledge function may be involved in the participation of some volunteers. Some blood donors, for example, reported curiosity about the donation experience as one factor in deciding to make an initial donation (Piliavin, Evans, & Callero, 1984), and Gidron's (1978) volunteers in institutional settings reported that they expected to learn from their experience. Other volunteers apparently desire more specific, job-related skills. Thus, when Jenner's (1982) Junior League volunteers indicated the role that volunteering played in their lives, 15% perceived it as preparation for a new career or as a way of maintaining career-relevant skills.

Of the functions we have examined, the ego-defensive function seems to have the least amount of evidence for its operation in volunteerism. Several studies did, however, present findings relevant to the ego-defensive function. Both Rosenhan (1970) and Clary and Miller (1986) examined the psychoanalytic idea that altruistic behavior is related to the presence of inner conflicts (and thus helping others provides a way of defending one's ego) by considering differences between "normative" and "autonomous" altruists in their experience with psychological treatment. It is interesting, and contrary to the psychoanalytic hypothesis, that both studies found it was the less committed normative volunteers who reported more experience. Finally, in Omoto and Snyder's (1990) studies of AIDS volunteers, although ego-defensive motivations tended to be relatively unimportant to AIDS volunteers overall, when they were present, they occurred in a meaningful context of relevant personality dispositions. The AIDS volunteers who were motivated by ego-defensive concerns were also the ones with relatively low self-esteem, high need for social recognition, and high death anxiety. There is then some evidence that *some* volunteers may volunteer out of ego-defensive needs, although at this point this does not appear to characterize a large number of people.

That some functions seem to be more prevalent than others in volunteers' motivations may say something about the types of volunteer opportunities that have been the focus of research. In other words, volunteer opportunities may well differ in the functions they are likely to engage. If so, then we need not only a functional analysis of persons who volunteer but also a *functional analysis of the situations* in which people volunteer. Consider two recent advertisements for volunteers: "*Writer*—Write a column about volunteer opportunities for suburban newspapers. Determine column content from information retrieved from a computer." "*Special event driver*—Play an important role in the third annual Jail and Bail fundraiser for a nonprofit agency that provides jobs for disabled and disadvantaged people. Pick up celebrities, local business personalities and other donors. Drive jailees to mock jail site in downtown Minneapolis." ("You Can Help," 1989, p. 5T) It may be the case that the writer activity will satisfy some knowledge functions (e.g., to practice and exercise one's writing skills as well as gain some job-related experience) while the driver activity may well fulfill social-adjustive motivations (e.g., allowing one to make new, and here, high-status, social contacts). Thus these two volunteer opportunities represent situations that engage differing psychological functions.

IMPLICATIONS OF A FUNCTIONAL ANALYSIS

It remains for us to consider some of the implications of a functional analysis of helping. Let us begin with the specific case of volunteerism, which has served as the vehicle for our analysis, and consider how the functional perspective offers some prescriptive advice for the practice of volunteerism. Let us then broaden the scope to consider implications for the conceptualization of helping behavior and consider such fundamental issues as the integration of both dispositional and situational perspectives on helping behavior and the long-running egoism versus altruism debate.

The Practice of Volunteerism

The functional analysis of volunteer activity should have significant applications to the work of organizations that rely on the unpaid help of volunteers for providing services to people in need. A functional analysis points to the critical importance of the match or mismatch between an individual's motives for volunteering and the ability of volunteer activities and volunteer organizations to satisfy those motives. One implication of this proposition is that attempts at *recruiting* volunteers will be successful to the extent that they tailor persuasive appeals to potential volunteers' motives. A second implication is that individuals' *self-selecting* (or initiating) certain volunteer activities as opposed to others can profitably be viewed from the standpoint of the functions that guide the selection and initiation process. Finally, our analysis implies that *commitment* to a volunteer activity and continued service as a volunteer will occur to the extent that volunteer work serves the psychological functions of volunteers.

Given the links between a functional analysis of volunteerism and the functional approaches to attitudes and persuasion, it's quite natural that there are implications for the issue of volunteer recruitment. For effective recruitment, one would first need to know something about potential volunteers' needs and motives. This may be at the level of individual volunteers (in one-to-one recruitment) or of groups of potential volunteers (e.g., giving advertisements to engage the common motivations of readers of a certain periodical). Following this, the persuasive attempt, either face-to-face or in media advertisements, should be tailored to the motives and goals of the individual. Persuasive communications then might demonstrate how particular needs and goals could be satisfied through volunteering generally, through association with a particular organization, or through a specific activity (e.g., telephone counseling volunteer work provides experience and skills relevant for a career as a therapist).

Similar notions apply to placing volunteers in specific tasks and encouraging continuing, sustained service. One such attempt has been reported in the literature on volunteering. Francies (1983), based on his experience with social service volunteers, developed a measure of seven volunteer needs and then used the measure to match volunteers to activities. Volunteers matched with the needs profile, relative to a control group assigned tasks without the profile, received more suitable assignments; further, volunteers with better matches exhibited greater job satisfaction and longer tenure. Similarly, Clary and Miller (1986) found that "normative" crisis-counseling volunteers (who may be high in social-adjustive motivations) exhibited greater commitment if they participated in a cohesive training group experience; the same experience had no impact on "autonomous" (perhaps value-expressive) volunteers.

The Egoism Versus Altruism Debate

The debate over the selflessness versus selfishness of a helper's motives has been vigorous, both in the psychological literature (see Batson, 1987, and see Chapter 3) and in the literature on the motivations of volunteers (see Van Til, 1988). In both literatures, the argument centers on whether the motivations underlying a helpful act are ever truly altruistic (based on concern for the other) as opposed to egoistic (based only on concern for the self). The issue also arises in connection with the functional approach, where the value-expressive function is akin to altruistic motivation, and, in fact, the two have been linked in the literature (e.g., Frisch & Gerrard, 1981); the remaining functions have a much more self-serving or egoistic flavor to them.

Careful consideration of the functional approach, however, leads us to question the "purity of motives" idea. At the level of the individual helper, the functional analysis encourages the notion that a volunteer's action may be guided by multiple motives. While our review suggests that the value-expressive component is an important one, the literature also suggests that this function is often combined with other functions. Surveys, for example, find respondents reporting multiple reasons for volunteering, and it appears that many volunteers report both egoistic and altruistic reasons (e.g., Anderson & Moore, 1978). Also, recall Pearce's (1983) finding that volunteer employees reported higher levels of service *and* social motivation than did paid employees. Thus the functional analysis and research on volunteers both suggest that individuals have a multiplicity of motives for volunteering.

Some of the constructs used in the functional approach also question the "purity" idea, suggesting that a function may not be either altruistic or egoistic but may actually consist of a mixture. This raises the question of whether altruistic motives can truly be teased apart from egoistic motives. This is readily apparent in the very meaning of the value-expressive function, where values (in this case, altruistic ones) are thought to become part of one's identity and self-concept, and "the reward is not so much a matter of social recognition or monetary advantage as of establishing one's self-identity, confirming one's notion of the sort of person one sees oneself to be, and expressing the values appropriate to this self-concept" (D. Katz & Kahn, 1978, p. 361). Hence, actions taken in the service of altruistic and humanitarian concerns may also be sources of personal rewards and self-affirmation. A similar point is made in Callero, Howard, and Piliavin's (1987) application of role-person merger to veteran blood donors—self and altruistic roles of the blood donor merge, incorporating both social and personal norms. Thus the most seemingly "altruistic" construct within the functional approach, the value-expressive function, may well consist of both a concern for a needy other (an altruistic element) *and* a need to express or act on that value (an egoistic element).

Just as one can question whether altruistic motives are purely altruistic, we can wonder whether egoistic constructs are themselves purely egoistic. Consider, for example, the social-adjustive function. Snyder and DeBono (1987, 1989) have suggested that one way to think about and investigate the social-adjustive function is in terms of its association with the interpersonal orientation characteristic of the high self-monitor, and it has been argued that the high self-monitoring/ social-adjustive individual is interested in facilitating smooth and pleasing social functioning. Obviously, the desire for smooth social intercourse has its self-serving component, but it may also have an element of concern for the other. That is, smooth interactions benefit not only the self but also others participating in the interaction. Daniels's (1985) discussion of the various manifestations of sociability among women volunteers who organize "benefits" illustrates this point, as these hostesses often strive to minimize the social distance among guests from very different social strata.

The Study of Helping Behavior

In this final section, we consider nonspontaneous help, volunteer activity, and the functional approach within the larger context of research on helping behavior. Specifically, what does the work covered in this review contribute to our understanding of helping behavior? Most obvious, perhaps, is the support this approach offers for the relations between dispositional variables and helping behavior. In comparison with studies of helping in spontaneous situations, studies on volunteering (studies conducted on a variety of volunteer activities, with a variety of methods) have found an important role for dispositional forces in understanding many aspects of this kind of helping behavior.

This finding about when dispositions affect helping behavior seems to be quite consistent with the distinction made by personality and social behavior theorists between strong and weak situations (Snyder & Ickes, 1985). "Strong situations" are those that are highly structured and provide highly salient cues for behavior, while "weak situations" are less structured and offer fewer guidelines regarding behavior. It seems that participation in volunteer activity, *at least with respect to initial involvement,* constitutes a "weak situation"—potential helpers can, more "coolly" perhaps, decide whether or not to act, choose their specific volunteer tasks, and decide how long to maintain their involvement. Moreover, they may be able to do all these things in ways that take into account their personal motivations and psychological functions. Spontaneous helping situations, by comparison, surprise potential helpers with opportunities to help and provide very little time for reflection upon whether and how to act; action then is guided by situational cues (e.g., the presence or absence of others).

More broadly, however, our functional analysis and the literature on volunteerism suggest that one adopt a "disposition-by-situation" interactionist approach to understanding helping behavior. This is apparent from the argument that the role of dispositions in helping behavior varies with the psychological strength of the situation (that is, strong, spontaneous versus weak, nonspontaneous situations). The functional approach also encourages the interactive approach by arguing for the *match* between a helper's motives and the kinds of satisfactions available in the situation. Thus, on the person side we need to consider potential helpers' personal needs, plans, and motives; on the situation side we need to examine the opportunities offered by helping situations and the way in which these opportunities satisfy or stymie personal motivations.

Clearly, this approach has some utility in dealing with volunteerism as a prototypic form of nonspontaneous, sustained helping behavior. What, however, does the functional approach offer to helping behavior conceptualized in the broadest of terms? First, as mentioned before, the functional approach suggests that a variety of motives may underlie helping activities, in terms of both different motives being important for different people and even two or more psychological functions being important for one individual. Second, these functions may also be involved in spontaneous situations, as particularly strong needs may "prime" a person to react in certain ways in an emergency situation (see Wilson, 1976). Third, several motivations that are central to the functional approach have their counterparts in the helping literature generally, especially the value-expressive and social-adjustive functions. The functional analysis, however, suggests that other functions may also be involved, and it behooves us to determine whether these other functions exist and how they might influence helpfulness. Finally, the functional analysis, along with Piliavin's research on motivational changes in blood donors (e.g., Piliavin, Evans, & Callero, 1984) and research on the development of prosocial reasoning (see Eisenberg, 1986), suggest that we attend to changes in the functional foundations of helping that may occur with age and/or those that occur as people have experience with helping other people.

All of the benefits cited above for understanding the motivational foundations of both voluntary action and helping behavior are predicated on the assumption that one can measure the motivations underlying volunteer activity. And, as previously noted, there is a pressing need for a psychometrically sound measure of volunteers' motivations. To explore the ideas generated by our functional analysis, we have recently begun work on an inventory designed to assess the several psychological functions served by volunteer work (Clary & Snyder, 1990). The initial form of the inventory consisted of several scales, each measuring a specific function (based initially on the value-expressive, social-adjustive, ego-defensive, and knowledge constructs as well as a measure of career-oriented motivation). Early indications are that each of the scales is reliable, and a factor analysis of volunteers' responses to the scale revealed that multiple factors are involved, and the factors are generally consistent with a functional analysis. Thus some of the first steps toward investigating the functional approach to volunteer work are currently being taken.

The potential uses of such an inventory of the functions served by volunteering are considerable, and, here, the objectives of researchers and practitioners merge. Researchers, such as ourselves, can use it to test key propositions about the functional foundations of volunteering, propositions that provide the foundation for both theory development and practical application. We would expect, for instance, that recruitment of people into volunteer work will be more effective when persuasive messages appeal to their psychological motives for volunteering. Further, people should be more effective and satisfied when they are placed in volunteer opportunities that engage psychological functions important to them. And, finally, volunteers' commitment to the volunteer activity is expected to depend on the match of volunteers' motivations and the ability of the volunteer opportunity to satisfy those psychological needs.

In sum, a functional analysis offers a framework for examining the motivational foundations of helping behavior, one that emphasizes the personal and social needs and goals, and plans and motives, served by helping and prosocial behavior. At the very least, a functional framework does perform the useful heuristic function of organizing the diverse literature on the societally significant topic of nonspontaneous, sustained volunteerism. But, in a more general sense, this approach, we have every reason to hope, may help set the agenda for theoretical and empirical inquiries into helping behavior.

REFERENCES

Allen, N., & Rushton, J. P. (1983). Personality characteristics of community mental health volunteers: A review. *Journal of Voluntary Action Research, 12,* 36-49.
Amato, P. R. (1985). An investigation into planned helping behavior. *Journal of Research in Personality, 19,* 232-252.
Anderson, J. C., & Moore, L. (1978). The motivation to volunteer. *Journal of Voluntary Action Research, 7,* 51-60.
Bar-Tal, D. (1984). American study of helping behavior: What? Why? And where? In E. Staub, D. Bar-Tal, J. Karylowski, & J. Reykowski (Eds.), *Development and maintenance of prosocial behavior: International perspectives on positive morality.* New York: Plenum.
Batson, C. D. (1987). Prosocial motivation: Is it ever truly altruistic? In L. Berkowitz (Ed.), *Advances in experimental social psychology* (Vol. 20). New York: Academic Press.
Benson, P., Dohority, J., Garman, L., Hanson, E., Hochschwender, M., Lebold, C., Rohr, R., & Sullivan, J. (1980). Intrapersonal correlates of nonspontaneous helping behavior. *Journal of Social Psychology, 110,* 87-95.
Berkowitz, L., & Lutterman, K. (1968). The traditionally socially responsible personality. *Public Opinion Quarterly, 32,* 169-185.
Bryan, J. H., & Test, M. A. (1967). Models and helping: Naturalistic studies in aiding behavior. *Journal of Personality and Social Psychology, 6,* 400-407.
Callero, P., Howard, J., & Piliavin, J. (1987). Helping behavior as role behavior: Disclosing social structure and history in the analysis of prosocial action. *Social Psychology Quarterly, 50,* 247-256.
Clary, E. G., & Miller, J. (1986). Socialization and situational influences on sustained altruism. *Child Development, 57,* 1358-1369.
Clary, E. G., & Orenstein, L. (in press). The amount and effectiveness of help: The relationship of motives and abilities to helping behavior. *Personality and Social Psychology Bulletin.*
Clary, E. G., & Snyder, M. (1990, March). *A functional analysis of volunteers' motivations.* Paper presented at Independent Sector's Spring Research Forum, Boston.
Daniels, A. K. (1985). Good times and good works: The place of sociability in the work of women volunteers. *Social Problems, 32,* 363-374.
Darley, J. M., & Batson, C. D. (1973). "From Jerusalem to Jericho": A study of situational and dispositional variables in helping behavior. *Journal of Personality and Social Psychology, 27,* 100-108.

146 *Volunteerism*

Eisenberg, N. (1986). *Altruistic emotion, cognition, and behavior.* Hillsdale, NJ: Lawrence Erlbaum.

Ekstein, R. (1978). Psychoanalysis, sympathy, and altruism. In L. Wispé (Ed), *Altruism, sympathy, and helping: Psychological and sociological principles.* New York: Academic Press.

Fitch, R. T. (1987). Characteristics and motivations of college students volunteering for community service. *Journal of College Student Personnel, 28,* 424-431.

Francies, G. R. (1983). The volunteer-needs profile: A tool for reducing turnover. *Journal of Volunteer Administration, 1,* 17-33.

Frisch, M. B., & Gerrard, M. (1981). Natural helping systems: A survey of Red Cross volunteers. *American Journal of Community Psychology, 9,* 567-579.

Gallup Organization. (1981). *Americans volunteer 1981.* Washington, DC: Independent Sector.

Gallup Organization. (1986). *Americans volunteer 1985.* Washington, DC: Independent Sector.

Gidron, B. (1978). Volunteer work and its rewards. *Volunteer Administration, 11,* 18-32.

Herek, G. (1987). Can functions be measured? A new perspective on the functional approach to attitudes. *Social Psychology Quarterly, 50,* 285-303.

Independent Sector. (1988). *Giving and volunteering the United States: Findings from a national survey.* Washington, DC: Author.

Jenner, J. R. (1982). Participation, leadership, and the role of volunteerism among selected women volunteers. *Journal of Voluntary Action Research, 11,* 27-38.

Katz, A. H. (1981). Self-help and mutual aid: An emerging social movement? *Annual Review of Sociology, 7,* 129-155.

Katz, D. (1960). The functional approach to the study of attitudes. *Public Opinion Quarterly, 24,* 163-204.

Katz, D., & Kahn, R. L. (1978). *The social psychology of organizations* (2nd ed.). New York: John Wiley.

Kiesler, C. A., Collins, B. E., & Miller, N. (1969). *Attitude change: A critical analysis of theoretical approaches.* New York: John Wiley.

Knapp, R. H., & Holzberg, J. D. (1964). Characteristics of college students volunteering for service to mental patients. *Journal of Consulting Psychology, 28,* 82-85.

Krebs, D. L., & Miller, D. T. (1985). Altruism and aggression. In G. Lindzey & E. Aronson (Eds.), *The handbook of social psychology* (3rd ed., Vol. 2). New York: Random House.

Latané, B., & Darley, J. M. (1970). *The unresponsive bystander: Why doesn't he help?* New York: Appleton-Century-Crofts.

Oliner, S. P., & Oliner, P. M. (1988). *The altruistic personality: Rescuers of Jews in Nazi Europe.* New York: Free Press.

Omoto, A. M., & Snyder, M. (1990). Basic research in action: Volunteerism and society's response to AIDS. *Personality and Social Psychology Bulletin, 16,* 152-166.

Pearce, J. L. (1983). Job attitude and motivation differences between volunteers and employees from comparable organizations. *Journal of Applied Psychology, 68,* 646-652.

Pierucci, J., & Noel, R. C. (1980). Duration of participation of correctional volunteers as a function of personal and situational variables. *Journal of Community Psychology, 8,* 245-250.

Piliavin, J. A., Evans, D. E., & Callero, P. (1984). Learning to "give to unnamed strangers": The process of commitment to regular blood donation. In E. Staub, D. Bar-Tal, J. Karylowski, & J. Reykowski (Eds.), *Development and maintenance of prosocial behavior: International perspectives on positive morality.* New York: Plenum.

Rohs, F. R. (1986). Social background, personality, and attitudinal factors influencing the decision to volunteer and level of involvement among adult 4-H leaders. *Journal of Voluntary Action Research, 15,* 87-99.

Rosenhan, D. L. (1970). The natural socialization of altruistic autonomy. In J. Macauley & L. Berkowitz (Eds.), *Altruism and helping behavior* (pp. 251-268). New York: Academic Press.

Rubin, A., & Thorelli, I. M. (1984). Egoistic motives and longevity of participation by social service volunteers. *Journal of Applied Behavioral Science, 20,* 223-235.

Schwartz, S. H. (1977). Normative influences on altruism. In L. Berkowitz (Ed.), *Advances in experimental social psychology* (Vol. 10). New York: Academic Press.

Shavitt, S. (1989). Functional imperative theory. In A. R. Pratkanis, S. J. Breckler, & A. G. Greenwald (Eds.), *Attitude structure and function.* Hillsdale, NJ: Lawrence Erlbaum.

Smith, B.M.M., & Nelson, L. (1975). Personality correlates of helping behavior. *Psychological Reports, 37,* 307-310.

Smith, D. H. (1974). Research and communication needs in voluntary action. In J. Cull & R. Hardy (Eds.), *Volunteerism: An emerging profession.* Springfield, IL: Charles C Thomas.

Smith, M. B., Bruner, J. S., & White, R. W. (1956). *Opinions and personality.* New York: John Wiley.

Smithson, M., Amato, P., & Pearce, P. (1983). *Dimensions of helping behavior.* Oxford: Pergamon.

Snyder, M. (1988, August). *Needs and goals, plans and motives: The new "new look" in personality and social psychology.* "State of the Art" address presented at the meeting of the American Psychological Association, Atlanta.

Snyder, M., & DeBono, K. G. (1987). A functional approach to attitudes and persuasion. In M. P. Zanna, J. M. Olson, & C. P. Herman (Eds.), *Social influence: The Ontario symposium* (Vol. 5). Hillsdale, NJ: Lawrence Erlbaum.

Snyder, M., & DeBono, K. G. (1989). Understanding the functions of attitudes: Lessons from personality and social behavior. In A. R. Pratkanis, S. J. Breckler, & A. G. Greenwald (Eds.), *Attitude structure and function.* Hillsdale, NJ: Lawrence Erlbaum.

Snyder, M., & Ickes, W. (1985). Personality and social behavior. In G. Lindzey & E. Aronson (Eds.), *The handbook of social psychology* (3rd ed., Vol. 2). New York: Random House.

Staub, E. (1978). *Positive social behavior and morality: Vol. 1: Social and personal influences.* New York: Academic Press.

Staub, E. (1984). Notes toward an interactionist-motivational theory of the determinants and development of (pro)social behavior. In E. Staub, D. Bar-Tal, J. Karylowski, & J. Reykowski (Eds.), *Development and maintenance of prosocial behavior: International perspectives on positive morality.* New York: Plenum.

Van Til, J. (1988). *Mapping the third sector: Voluntarism in a changing social economy.* New York: Foundation Center.

Wandersman, A., Florin, P., Friedmann, R., & Meier, R. (1987). Who participates, who does not, and why? An analysis of voluntary neighborhood organizations in the United States and Israel. *Sociological Forum, 2*, 534-555.

Wiehe, V. R., & Isenhour, L. (1977). Motivation of volunteers. *Journal of Social Welfare, 4*, 73-79.

Wilson, J. P. (1976). Motivation, modeling, and altruism: A person × situation analysis. *Journal of Personality and Social Psychology, 34*, 1078-1086.

You can help. (1989, October 15). *Minneapolis Star Tribune*, p. 5T.

Zald, M. N., & McCarthy, J. D. (1987). *Social movements in an organizational society: Collected essays*. New Brunswick, NJ: Transaction.

Zuckerman, M. (1975). Belief in a just world and altruistic behavior. *Journal of Personality and Social Psychology, 31*, 972-976.

6

Spontaneous Communication and Altruism
THE COMMUNICATIVE GENE HYPOTHESIS

ROSS BUCK
BENSON GINSBURG

Ross Buck is Professor of Communication Sciences and Psychology at the University of Connecticut. He received his M.A. from the University of Wisconsin, Madison, and his Ph.D. from the University of Pittsburgh. He was a Research Associate at the University of Pittsburgh Medical School and taught at Carnegie-Mellon University before coming to Connecticut. He has been a Visiting Scholar at Harvard University and the Aphasia Research Unit of the Boston Veterans Administration Hospital; a Visiting Fellow at Wolfson College, Oxford; and is a 1990-1991 Visiting Faculty Fellow at Yale University. His books include *Human Motivation and Emotion* (1976, second edition, 1988) and *The Communication of Emotion* (1984).

Benson Ginsburg is Professor of Biobehavioral Sciences and Psychology at the University of Connecticut, Storrs, and Professor of Psychiatry at the University of Connecticut Health Center, Farmington. He was previously the William Rainey Harper Professor of Biology at the University of Chicago and the Scheinfeld Professor of Human Genetics in the Social Sciences at the Hebrew University of Jerusalem. His publications have been in the field of behavior genetics.

The phenomenon of altruism is remarkable in that it is of great interest to investigators at widely differing levels of analysis in the behavioral sciences: At the level of behavioral genetics, on one hand, and of complex social behavior, on the other. *Altruism* broadly defined is the tendency of one organism to act to increase the welfare of another organism, with no obvious benefit and often at a cost to the actor. Social psychologist C. Daniel Batson (1983, p. 1381) defined *altruism* as "a desire within one organism to increase the welfare of another organism as an end-state goal." Sociobiologist E. O. Wilson (1975) defined it as "the surrender of personal genetic fitness for the enhancement of personal genetic fitness in others" (p. 106), or "when a person (or animal) increases the fitness of another at the expense of his own fitness" (p. 117). Altruism was put into evolutionary perspective by Hamilton

AUTHORS' NOTE: We gratefully acknowledge the support of the University of Connecticut Research Foundation, of NIMH Grant MH40753 to the first author, and of the Harry Frank Guggenheim Foundation and NIMH Grant MH35908 to the second author.

(1964), who found that the recipients of altruistic acts often are genetic relatives of the actor(s), who thereby pass on their genes indirectly, and by Trivers (1971), whose views on reciprocal altruism, in which recipients and actors each benefit over time, extend and modify the concept. The understanding of these tendencies is central to the understanding of prosocial behavior, antisocial behavior, and their roles in social organization.

One of the complexities in the definition of *altruism* and other social behaviors (such as aggression) is that they are often described as qualities of the individual when they are perhaps more properly conceived as at least dyadic concepts requiring both actor(s) and partner(s). Both Batson's and Wilson's definitions place altruism within an individual organism, but both also note that other organisms are necessary for altruism to occur. Implicitly, there must also exist communication of some sort between the altruistic individual and the other(s) (e.g., see Wilkinson, 1990).

Several investigators have suggested that emotional communication is sufficient to activate feelings of attachment, altruistic impulses, and prosocial behaviors (Batson, 1983; Batson & Oleson, Chapter 3 of this volume; Hoffmann, 1977, 1981). Observation of the distress or joy of others appears to be sufficient to directly release empathic emotions of warmth, sympathy, and compassion, and these, in turn, evoke responses reducing the other's distress or maximizing the other's joy (Buck, 1988a, 1988b, 1989). The result is an affectively based prosocial bond.

This chapter will argue that altruism and other kinds of social behaviors involve species-specific behavior systems that derive from and are based upon affective bonds or affinities, often hierarchically structured, that characterize the social system of the species. Such bonds are species typical and range from those involved in mating, parenting, and peer coalitions to the more complex social roles that are central to the formation and maintenance of socially cohesive groups. These bonds, in turn, are based upon experiences with spontaneous affective communication over the course of development.

We begin with a brief overview of the history of the concept of altruism from Darwin and Spencer to the sociobiologists, suggesting that the kin selection explanation of altruism favored by the latter underestimates the complexity of the relationship between genotype (the underlying genetic system) and phenotype (the expression of the genetic system in the characteristics of the individual organism). We then propose that the social cement that characterizes all of life, from its simplest to most complex forms, is spontaneous affective communication. The role of affective communication in the social behavior of a variety of species is described, culminating in the *communicative gene hypothesis:* that communicative genetic systems are at the root of altruism and, indeed, of all social behavior.

HISTORICAL OVERVIEW

Darwin

Theories concerning the evolutionary roots of altruism have undergone a remarkable transformation in the interval between their Darwinian inception and their resurrection by sociobiologists. Darwin assigned a primary role to behavior as an agent of evolutionary change, often preceding structure and providing the basis for the selective advantage of structural changes that further enhanced behavioral adaptations. The latter became incorporated as instincts, leaving their physical imprint on the brain. Instincts, for Darwin, derived from habit over generational time and, like morphological features, served as grist for the mill of natural selection. Darwin saw a continuity among living forms, such that more advanced forms drew upon the evolutionary legacy of their less advanced forebears. He extended this approach to higher mental faculties, including reasoning and the development of moral and ethical capacities. The "guilty" demeanor of his dog following an unwitnessed transgression was, for Darwin, evidence of a sense of guilt and, therefore, of right and wrong. He saw in such actions the basis for the development of moral instincts and even of religiosity. Clearly, the behavior on the dog's part involved displays that seemed understandable to the human observer.

In *The Expression of the Emotions in Man and Animals*, Darwin (1872) amassed an impressive array of observations and reports on the expressive behaviors of dogs, cats, monkeys, and humans as well as other species. He did not, however, attribute the evolutionary *origins* of their behaviors to their adaptive values as communicative signals or as indicators of affect, although, secondarily, they fulfilled these functions. For him, the homologies between organisms were in the structures and the physiology of the body. That is, the organs of expression are primarily in the musculature, and the "nerve force" resulting from excitement or from other "feelings" (which he felt we can only intuit anthropomorphically) is selectively channeled to homologous structures in the various species to produce the characteristic expressions. It is the underlying homologies of structure that, for Darwin, were basic and served to identify the evolutionary relationships between species. Darwin felt that some expressive displays arose through convergence to serve as social adaptations due to similar environmental circumstances, much as the similarities in the body shapes of the shark and the dolphin served as physical adaptations to similar demands of the environment. For example, the aggressive displays of lizards, fish, and primates are alike in that they produce an apparent increase in body size, albeit in these instances by different mechanisms. To Darwin, the communicative functions of expressive behaviors did not, in themselves, constitute primary evidence of evolutionary relationships.

Spencer

Regarding the evolution of moral and ethical behavior, and, in particular, the origin of the concept of altruism as a social construct in evolutionary theory, we owe much to Spencer's contributions. For Spencer (1893), altruism, and, in particular, reciprocal altruism, constituted evidence for a biology of ethics and morality and pointed to the ultimate perfectability of human nature. Because an altruistic act can often lead to the demise of the actor, it would be difficult to reconcile the notion of altruism as an evolutionary "good" with the principle of natural selection. Here, Spencer fell back on the idea of community selection proposed by Darwin to account for the occurrence of neuter castes among insects. The neuter castes of social insects perform self-sacrificing acts on behalf of the group to which they belong. Because they leave no progeny and are replaced in later generations, their loss has no direct effect on the genetic potential of the group from which they originated but indirectly promotes its survival (see also Richards, 1987). In these terms, groups containing altruistic individuals would have an advantage over those that do not. Richards (1987, pp. 309-311) provides a concise summary of Spencer's views, foreshadowed in Darwin's time, in which he credits Spencer with having put forward the concept of kin selection as well as that of reciprocal altruism, both of which figure prominently in the sociobiological theories of today.

Sociobiology

In genetically less differentiated populations, where each individual is a potential reproductive unit, behaviors involving self-risk but promoting the chances for the survival of others would appear to involve negative selection. The seeming paradox of the survival value of altruistic behaviors for the group at the expense of those individuals exhibiting the behaviors for which they presumably have a genetic predisposition is resolved in the reasoning of sociobiology by the concept of "kin selection" hinted at by Spencer (Hamilton, 1964; Williams, 1966). If one saves the life of a genetic relative, one makes it more likely that the relative's genes, which have features in common with one's own, are passed on to new generations. The degree to which an individual's genes are passed on when a genetic relative reproduces is termed *inclusive fitness,* and the number of one's genes passed on, either directly or via relatives, determines the overall *reproductive success* of the individual.

Altruism may enhance reproductive success by maximizing inclusive fitness, according to these arguments. Because related individuals share the same genes in proportion to their degrees of genetic relatedness, the loss of an individual from the reproductive pool because of behaviors enabling close kin to survive maintains and enhances the occurrence of those genes within the population. Because of the occurrence of such behaviors, "altruistic" genes have been postulated—but not found. In fact, we argue that the kin selection hypothesis underestimates the complexity of the relationship between the genes or genotype and their expression in the characteristics of the individual (phenotype).

THE LOCI OF NATURAL SELECTION

The Phenotype-Genotype Relationship

Selection operates within a species by changing gene frequencies. It functions by favoring some phenotypes over others. Such phenotypes do not necessarily bear a one-to-one relationship to an underlying genotype. In the fruit fly, for example, the phenotype of white eyes may be due genetically to a single sex-linked mutation. However, there are other genotypes that produce white eyes. Because the normal eye color is due to a combination of two pigments, each of which is formed via a series of enzymatically controlled genetic steps, white eyes also can be produced by a number of genetic combinations that block the formation of each of these pigments at one or another step. Selection involving this phenotype of white eyes will affect the various underlying genotypes in proportion to their occurrence in the population. This complex relationship of phenotypes and genotypes is not an atypical or isolated instance parochial to fruit fly genetics. Phenotypic selection within a population will differentially affect the underlying genotypes. Those recessive autosomal genes that, in certain combinations, will give rise to white eyes will have different phenotypic effects in other combinations and, in addition, will remain hidden from selective forces in the heterozygous condition, where the dominant and recessive members of a gene pair appear together and only the dominant phenotype is expressed.

The supposition that altruism, if it has a definitive genetic basis, can be maintained by kin selection oversimplifies the complexities of genotype-phenotype relations. None of the siblings of the altruistic individual who, by virtue of altruism, is removed from the reproductive pool, thereby permitting two or more sibs to remain in the pool, may carry the particular adaptive genes he or she would have contributed. The construct of altruism and the assumption of its genetic basis, coupled with the supposition that individuals within a sibship or a close kinship group would share the postulated gene(s) are, in our view, a compounding of improbable, unproven postulates. What is more probable is that the affective communication and bonding that characterize the group result in a variety of behaviors, some of which are agonistic and seem aggressive and hostile, others of which are prosocial and appear to be altruistic.

Herbert Simon (personal communication, January 1990) argues that the "ability to accept social influence," which he equates with the ability to learn from others, is both a product of natural selection and a means by which selection can act at the level of the social group, as well as the individual, to increase Darwinian fitness (i.e., success in leaving progeny). While agreeing with this position, we would emphasize that it is not the mere number of progeny but the number of *well-adapted* progeny that themselves survive to reproduce that count. Organized social groups constitute one means of enhancing the chances for survival through cooperation at a variety of behavioral levels varying from care and protection of the young, defense of territory and against predation, courtship and mating, securing food and other resources, and partitioning the gene pool (Ryan, 1990). What appear to be altruistic acts on the part of the individual depend upon recognition signals that are genetically based and that serve to enhance the survival value of the group (Wilkinson, 1990).

Implications: The Concept of Altruism

The concept of altruism has unfortunate and misleading connotations when applied to animal groups because it is based on the analogy of the way it is conceptualized in human society, where it has a learned, cultural overlay. It is a beguiling anthropomorphic construct because we think we understand it by analogy and because it fills a void in a formal structure that requires a cohesive force in a biological world where agonistic (aggressive) forces prevail. The biological reality of agonistic behaviors is grounded in solid evidence based on studies of dominance hierarchies in various vertebrate species (Jenks & Ginsburg, 1987; Schotté & Ginsburg, 1987; Scott, 1983, 1989, pp. 196-199). Aggressive behaviors creating and enforcing dominance are, by themselves, destructive of social cohesiveness. This has given rise to the embrace of a concept of altruism as the essential and primary social cement and to the evolutionary rationalizations that speculate about the genetic roots of altruism. We argue that these rationalizations, which have come to dominate a major segment of the literature of sociobiology, are circular and without support.

We are not merely setting forth a counterrationalization but are presenting evidence that there are demonstrable cohesive social forces that have actual rather than speculative roots in biology and genetics and that constitute the actual evolutionary legacy for our own species (Moyer, 1968). We argue that these roots support the social structures that have come to exist and that "altruism" is, therefore, a derivative epiphenomenon.

What then constitutes the social cement that is such a prominent phylogenetic feature encompassing all animal life? In our view, it is *communication,* whether at the protozoan level or at that of the insect, mammal, or human mammal.

SPONTANEOUS COMMUNICATION

Definition

Spontaneous communication is defined as nonintentional, non-propositional, affective communication about feelings and desires or emotions and motives (Buck, 1984, 1988a; Ginsburg, 1976). It is represented on the individual level by tendencies to display one's feelings and desires (sending tendencies) and preattunements to such displays in others (receiving tendencies). Such displays are social affordances in the Gibsonian sense and are directly perceived.

Spontaneous communication is defined as having the following qualities:

(1) Spontaneous communication is based upon *biologically structured sending and receiving mechanisms.* The basic function of spontaneous communication is social coordination, and it evolves because the transmission of certain kinds of motivational-emotional information are adaptive to a given species.

(2) The elements of spontaneous communication are *signs,* which are externally accessible aspects of the referent. Dark clouds are a sign of rain because the darkness of the clouds is an externally accessible aspect of the rain. Just so, spontaneous signals involving pheromones, vocalizations, facial expressions, and so on are externally accessible aspects of certain important motivational-emotional states.

(3) Spontaneous communication is *in no way intentional,* although it can be suppressed or inhibited intentionally.

(4) The content of spontaneous communication is *nonpropositional,* because it cannot be false. Propositions must be capable of being subjected to logical analysis, such as tests for truth or falsity. Because spontaneous communication is composed of signs, if the sign is present, the referent by definition must be present. The content of spontaneous communication instead involves motivational-emotional states.

Because it is biologically structured in both its sending and its receiving aspects, spontaneous communication is *direct* in that it requires no process of intention on the part of the sender or inference on the part of the receiver. It is a way in which the receiver has direct access to the motivational-emotional state of the sender. In this way, the individuals involved in spontaneous communication constitute a biological unit.

In contrast to spontaneous communication, "symbolic" communication is defined as being (a) learned and culturally patterned, (b) based upon symbols that have an arbitrary relationship with their referent, (c) at some level intentional; and (d) composed of propositions (Buck, 1984). Spontaneous communication constitutes a conversation between limbic systems, a conversation between brainstems, and so on, which goes on simultaneously with the symbolic stream of communication. In effect, communication proceeds in two simultaneously occurring and interactive "streams:" one biologically structured and nonvoluntary, and the other intentional and structured by learning and experience.

Genetic Bases: Communication Genes

Sending and receiving tendencies are phenotypic readouts of encoded genes. We do not have to postulate that such communication genes exist; they are demonstrably present. We cite three compelling examples of this at widely different phylogenetic points. For insects, there is now the classic work of Bentley and Hoy (1974) demonstrating a genetic basis for cricket "songs," where the genetics of the sending and receiving capacities overlap, constituting a fail-safe mechanism for effective signaling. Work with amphibians has shown that anurans (frogs, toads) will respond to the calls of their own species and that hybrids will selectively respond to hybrid calls (Bogert, 1961; Ryan, 1990). At the mammalian level, coyotes have been hybridized with beagles into coyote-dog crosses, or "coy-dogs." The defensive threat gesture of the coyote, consisting of a U-shaped body posture accompanied by a wide oral gape and a sibilant hiss, is not within the genetic repertoire of the domestic dog (Moon & Ginsburg, 1985). In coy-dogs, in which the genes of the two species are recombined, both genetic systems are present, and it has been shown that, around puberty, the threat behavior can be switched from the repertoire of the dog to that of the coyote by social stress mediated by an elevation of plasma cortisol.

An interesting case of reciprocal altruism involves the sharing of regurgitated blood by vampire bats (Wilkinson, 1990). The regurgitated blood is a valuable commodity to the bats, for a bat who fails to feed for two nights in a row will die of starvation. The process of soliciting blood begins by grooming and licking a potential donor under the wing and on the lips. Such grooming may facilitate recognition.

The sharing of blood seems to occur only between close relatives and those who have had a long-term association. This tends to assure that the sharing of blood is reciprocal, involving a "buddy system" in which the roles of donor and solicitor reverse on a regular basis. Wilkinson speculates that the bats recognize their relatives and close associates through their vocalizations. We argue that it is the vocalizations and the grooming that have the genetic basis. Given proper experience, these result in behaviors that in this context are labeled as examples of "reciprocal altruism."

We argue that the clear evidence that genetic systems underlie spontaneous communication, combined with the evidence that such communication is sufficient to activate feelings of attachment, altruistic impulses, and prosocial behaviors, make a simpler and clearer argument for the biological basis of altruism than alternative hypotheses. Without communicative genes there would be neither prosocial behavior nor a mechanism for the variety of social behaviors characterizing the range of animal species to be initiated, developed, and maintained. In our own species, it is through communication that we achieve altruism. We respond empathically to the smile of an infant and to facial expressions and vocalizations denoting emotional states, and we signal our own, often unconsciously, by virtue of our phylogenetic heritage. This heritage also permits us to interpret the signals of our dogs, as Darwin did, and those of other species that have distinctive expressive behaviors.

The Development of Spontaneous Communication

Experience affects genetic readouts. The phenotypic readout for a given individual may be changed during vulnerable points in development by events that regulate which genes come to expression. Disruptions in the normal course of development can result in "antisocial" individuals who lack the capacity for normal affective communication and, therefore, the capacity for altruism and other prosocial behaviors. Evidence of this phenomenon in wolves, monkeys, and humans provides examples of the effects of such disruptions and also points to the robustness of the evolved genetic potential to achieve species-typical norms, such that remediation is possible during the earlier, labile periods of development. Remediation can even occur later in some cases, especially where serious disruptions of affect appear to induce lability and to restore the capability for reestablishing normal behavior under favorable conditions. Thus Suomi and Harlow (1972), working with monkeys reared in isolation during the first six months of life, showed that their otherwise abnormal social behaviors and impaired cognitive abilities could be remediated by placing them with younger monkeys over a 26-week period.

Ginsburg and coworkers (Ginsburg, 1987; Rabb, Woolpy, & Ginsburg, 1967) have shown that wolf pups from separate litters placed together in a large study area with no adults develop the social roles and behaviors of a natural pack in the wild out of their own interactions. Moreover, wolves reared in isolation until six to ten months of age and placed with each other as behavioral pacemakers can also achieve a similar end point. Carter (1988) has shown this for chimpanzees as well, and Koluchova (1972, 1976) has provided a striking example of the same phenomenon in a pair of "isolate" human twins who had been kept confined with no social contacts and had no experience of language until they were 6-7 years of age. They too were restored to social normality that followed into adulthood. The genetic potential for species-typical social behavior, therefore, exists in genetically unimpaired individuals of more advanced species on the phylogenetic scale, including our own. The key to actualizing this potential lies in social interactions that lead to affective bonding and consequent group identification.

That the "normal" social structure of each of these groups includes hierarchies, coalitions, and other interactions requiring communication to initiate and maintain various social roles, coupled with the fact that the capacity for achieving species-appropriate communication is latent in all normal members, argues for a phylogenetic primacy of communication capped by the capacity of the human infant for language of whichever sort occurs in its social milieu. Among the diversity of social roles are those that put some individuals at risk in fulfilling their functions as members of a cooperating group. This "altruistic" behavior is here viewed as derivative. It derives from the species-specific social organization based upon affective communication. Altruistic behavior thus inheres *contingently* in the genes in that it is dependent upon appropriate social experience. To call it *altruism* does not constitute a differentiating genetic description. Genetic selection has resulted in the capacity for the differentiation of many social roles within a species, but the actors are not preprogrammed for these roles qua individuals. Instead, the actors are preprogrammed to communicate. From this spontaneous affective communication, combined with social experience, arises the diversity of social roles that characterizes a given species.

Therapeutic implications. As previously mentioned, there are genetic set points that characterize the individual and the species that are robust and can be attained even when serious developmental disruptions have occurred (Carter, 1988; Ginsburg, 1974; Koluchova, 1972, 1976; MacDonald & Ginsburg, 1981; Suomi & Harlow, 1972). The capacity for altruism and communication, having an affective foundation, requires, if impaired, an affective approach to restoration that precedes the rational-cognitive in both human and animal therapy.

A common feature shown by the isolate wolves, monkeys, chimps, and children mentioned earlier is that, although they are capable of emitting social signals, they do not appear to understand them. This can be explained in part by the extreme fear they exhibit when newly thrust into social situations and by their lack of the affective bonding that occurs naturally in normally reared individuals. To evaluate the ability of the isolate to "understand" or respond appropriately to species-typical signals and to use them appropriately, it is first necessary to overcome their affective opacity. In the case of the isolate wolves, this was accomplished in one study (MacDonald & Ginsburg, 1981) by exposing them to age-matched isolates in round-robin fashion for 24 hours at a time, one on one, by housing the group together and finally by introducing a normally reared adult into the group. At each stage there first was a reduction of fear, followed by tentative contacts, play, and occasional aggression. By the end of the experiment, the group was communicating normally, forming preferences, and initiating hierarchies.

In the case of the Carter chimpanzees, each had individually formed an affective bond with her but were fearful or hostile to each other. Over a lengthy period, she succeeded in introducing various ones to each other, and the work was crowned by their forming a normal social group, at which time the affective bonds with her were broken. Perhaps this may be seen as a prototype of human therapy and transference.

For the Koluchova twins, apart from language therapy, the situation was similar. They first showed extreme fear, followed by the gradual establishment of affective bonds with their foster parents. Then, over the years, they were exposed to a series of behavioral pacemakers. First, these were retarded children, and then younger, normal children. Under these conditions, they completed normal schooling, achieved age-appropriate IQs, and were judged to be psychologically normal.

Thus, in all three species, the communication and establishment of affect was prerequisite to establishing normal social relations and achieving the species-typical set points.

The Social Structuring of Spontaneous Communication

We have seen that the typical social environment of the infant and child tends to be structured to encourage, via spontaneous communication, the development of affective bonds and social behaviors. Larger social units also tend to structure spontaneous communication, and thereby affective bonds, in specific adaptive directions. An example is in the structuring of kin relationships.

The structuring of kin relationships. The sociobiologists have argued that it can be directly adaptive from the point of view of the survival of one's genes to behave in a fashion that benefits the group when the group includes close kin. How do humans and other animals know who is a genetic relative and who is not? The social system is sometimes organized so that relatives and nonrelatives tend to be sorted out in an appropriate way. For example, the social system of chimpanzees is characterized by female exogamy: The female leaves her home group at sexual maturity and mates in a different group, whereas the male usually stays in the same group all of his life (Ghiglieri, 1985). This tends to ensure that males within a group are genetic relatives, and it also provides the males with a cue—familiarity—that tends to sort out genetic relatives from "strangers." The aggressive behavior of male chimpanzees is characteristically moderated within the group, and within-group cooperation is high, even when access to rare mating opportunities is involved. Arguably, this is because a male chimpanzee's inclusive fitness tends to be enhanced when a familiar male succeeds and to be compromised when a familiar male fails. For this reason, a communication system has evolved as a phylogenetic adaptation that moderates aggression and enhances altruism within the chimpanzee group. Such a group may consist of pseudo-kin as well as actual kin—the actual kinship status is not important. Behavior is based on group membership.

Pseudospeciation. This state of affairs does not, however, apply to male chimpanzees from *different* groups. Here, there is no sign of altruism; indeed, Goodall and her colleagues have observed evidence of chimpanzee "wars" in which groups of males have entered the territory of a weaker group, systematically killed the males and older females, and incorporated the younger females within their own group (Goodall, 1986). Brutal and merciless aggressive behaviors occur in these group attacks that are not observed in aggressive interchanges within the group. Instead, the attackers showed behaviors seen during the killing of large prey, such as the twisting of limbs, the tearing of flesh, and the drinking of blood pouring from the victim's wounds. The victim gave up after initial resistance and crouched or lay passively during the attack and, at the end, was not only badly wounded but immobilized. Its cries were unheeded. Goodall suggests that the outgroup member is treated as if it were, in effect, a member of a different species; such behavior is termed by ethologists *pseudospeciation* (Eibl-Eibesfeldt, 1979; Goodall, 1986).

This system tends to ensure that one is more "altruistic" with familiar group members, who are usually genetic relatives, than one is with the unfamiliar members of different groups, who tend to be non-kin; again, it is group membership that is important, rather than actual kinship status, and it is communication vis-à-vis familiar or nonfamiliar others, not altruism per se, that has the genetic basis. It is interesting that chimpanzee social organization differs from that of other nonhuman primates, but it is similar to the characteristic human social organization at the hunting and gathering stage of human culture (Ghiglieri, 1985). Humans certainly show evidence of pseudospeciation in their warfare. The use of dehumanizing terms for one's enemies, for example, seems to be a distinguishing characteristic of human warfare (Eibl-Eibesfeldt, 1979; Ginsburg, 1979). On the other hand, this very effort to dehumanize the enemy implies that there is something about human qualities per se that tends to discourage killing and promote bonding (Buck, 1988b). We suggest that this quality is spontaneous communication: that spontaneous communication in and of itself is sufficient to activate empathic impulses and altruistic behavior.

THE COMMUNICATIVE GENE HYPOTHESIS

To recapitulate, in the preceding section we defined and discussed the nature of *spontaneous affective communication* and presented compelling evidence that the capacity for such communication has a genetic basis. Next, we described how there are degrees of freedom mediating between these encoded capacities and our ability to develop and use them and illustrated how, although these capacities do not develop under aberrant conditions of rearing, they can still be attained using methods involving affective communication. The establishment of affective communication and consequent bonding is primary and necessary before any cognitive social skills can be developed. Finally, we showed how larger social units tend to structure spontaneous communication, and thereby affective bonds, in specific adaptive directions. This seems to us to have profound implications for behavioral geneticists and social psychologists alike and brings us to the central feature of this chapter, the *communicative gene hypothesis,* which posits that there are communicative genetic systems at the root of spontaneous affective communication, which, in turn, form the basis of all social behaviors, including empathic emotions and altruism.

We suggest that this view of social organization as an affective system cemented by communication belies the selfish gene hypothesis advanced by Dawkins (1976). Dawkins argued that communicative displays are means by which the central nervous system of one animal controls the muscles of a second; that communication is "a means by which one animal makes use of another's muscle power" (Dawkins & Krebs, 1978, p. 283). Dawkins and Krebs (1978, p. 285) write: "As an inevitable by-product of the fact that animals are selected to respond to the environment in ways that are on average beneficial to themselves, other animals can be selected to subvert this responsiveness to their own ends. This is communication."

We argue that Dawkins misses the reality and importance of the powerful affective bonds fostered by affective communication that underlie altruism, prosocial behavior, and, ultimately, social organization. We suggest that the origin of the controversy involves disagreement about the unit of natural selection. Often, this unit is seen to be the individual or social group; Dawkins regards the unit as the gene (Redican, 1982). We suggest that, in any organism that communicates spontaneously, the *communicative relationship,* which depends upon the genetic fit between sender and receiver, is a biological unit transcending the individuals involved that can participate in the process of natural selection. The individuals in spontaneous communication thus constitute a biological unit. In any organism that communicates spontaneously, the coordination of behavior for mutual benefit is a fundamental principle.

Spontaneous Communication in Nonvertebrates

In advanced vertebrates, including humans, the relationship of spontaneous communication and altruism is conditioned on social experience: Altruism depends on affective bonds that normally are formed in early communicative exchanges. In nonvertebrates, the story is the same, but it is simpler in that the communication-altruism relationship is rigid and reflexive. In considering these simple creatures we can draw back the curtain of language and complex learning and cognitive processing that in human beings obscures this fundamental relationship.

It is clear that the coordination of behavior via spontaneous communication systems is not limited to the vertebrates. In fact, coordination via spontaneous communication systems can be identified and analyzed in species as simple as algae (Maier & Muller, 1986) and slime mold (Bonner, 1969, 1977; Davis, 1978). For example, Maier and Muller (1986) note that living organisms are open systems that depend upon energy and nutrient intake from the environment and that they have, therefore, evolved highly sensitive antennae for detecting relevant signals. These include chemical signals, or pheromones, from other organisms. The authors describe in detail how the activity in the sexual cells of green and brown algae are regulated by pheromones from other organisms, resulting in a coordination of activity, the mixing of genetic material, and reproduction.

W. C. Allee spent a scientific lifetime searching for altruism by studying the tendencies of life forms to aggregate, to form social structures, and to cooperate. His *principle of cooperation* was as close as he could come to identifying altruism as a social cement (Allee, 1931, 1938, 1951). Simple unicellular forms tend to aggregate and appear to condition the medium in which they live so that it becomes more favorable as a habitat for others of the same species. Indeed, proximity is necessary for forms such as the paramecium in which conjugation involving an exchange of nuclear materials must take place at intervals. Simple multicellular forms such as sponges have been fractionated into their cellular elements, and these will reaggregate to form the organism if placed together in a supportive medium. Other colonial forms consist of cooperating semi-independent cellular elements—and so on up the ladder of complexity. For vertebrates, and particularly for mammals, species-typical forms of social organization occur, which, as we have argued, are structured by communication and consequent social bonding.

At every level, there is a communicative link involved. Single-celled paramecia must not only find each other but identify particular sub-types for conjugation to occur. The disaggregated cells of the sponge must recognize each other according to type to reaggregate as an organism. Social insects are differentiated physically according to function and cooperate as groups using complex communication systems, such as odor trails in termites and the dancing language of the honey bee that informs others in the hive of the exact location and type of food source. According to Allee, these served as examples of phylogenetic continuity of cooperative behavior and demonstrations of a biological impetus toward sociality. At every level, the foundations of even the possibility of such necessary social tendencies depend upon cellular and organismic recognition, which all involve spontaneous communication.

For Allee, the quest for the grail of altruism ended with the principle of cooperation. The different roles assumed by members of a social group, whether insect or primate, relate to a species-typical group structure amounting to a social genetics.

The Social Psychology of the Slime Mold

The slime mold constitutes an interesting case in point, for here single-celled organisms coordinate their behaviors via chemical signals to construct a multicelled organism. The slime mold begins life as a one-celled amoeba that feeds on bacteria. In times of famine, individual amoebas congregate and aggregate into a composite sluglike creature that moves through the soil. Eventually, the slug converts itself into a fruiting body, a long-stemmed creature topped with a globe of spores. In the process, the amoebas at the front end of the slug become trapped in the cellulose structure that constitutes the stem, and they die. The amoebas in the tail become encased in hard capsules and become spores that are released, scattered, and, given favorable conditions, eventually wind up again as one-celled individual amoebas (Davis, 1978). The community of amoebas thus acts as an organism, which depends upon coordination and communication among the aggregated individuals. The evolution from organismic aggregate to organism constitutes an example of community selection.

The processes that control the aggregation of the individual amoebas into the slug and the differentiation of the slug into the fruiting body are regulated by chemical signals. They are spontaneous communication processes in which the tendencies to give off the appropriate chemical and to respond appropriately constitute sending and receiving tendencies, which, in turn, are phenotypic readouts of communicative genes or genetic systems. The process occurs in single-celled creatures even simpler than the slime mold: myxobacteria, which are prokaryotes (see below), also form fruiting bodies when food is scarce (Margulis, 1982). The slime molds have been studied in some detail, in part because of the insights they might give into the process by which cells become differentiated in a fetus. Bonner (cited in Davis, 1978) has termed the chemical signal involved in aggregation *acrasin,* after the witch Acrasia, who attracted men and turned them into beasts in Edmund Spenser's *The Faerie Queen.* In one species of slime mold, the acrasin appears to be cyclic AMP, which, significantly, is a fundamental "messenger substance" in human cells and in the human hormonal system (Davis, 1978).

When analyzed in such simple creatures, the fundamental importance of spontaneous communication in the evolution of differentiation and complexity in biological systems becomes apparent. Specifically, one could argue that spontaneous communication systems must have been involved in the differentiation of the primordial cell and in the construction of multicelled organisms. Spontaneous communication is, in effect, the bootstrap by which simple life forms were able to attain higher levels of organization.

THE PALEOBIOLOGY OF
SPONTANEOUS COMMUNICATION

The best place to begin a discussion of spontaneous communication in microbes is, perhaps, at the beginning: in this case, the beginning of life on the Earth. Such an analysis benefits from important advances made in recent years in the understanding of this early story of life. New discoveries in several fields, including geology, biochemistry, and microbiology, have contributed to a new realization that the evolution of complex multicelled plants and animals over the past 600 million years was preceded by a much longer period—3 billion years—in which the only life forms were primitive microorganisms. These early single-celled creatures established the basic features of life on the Earth, including basic biochemical systems and the oxygen-enriched atmosphere upon which more complex life forms depend (Margulis, 1982; Schopf, 1980).

The Beginning of Life

For generations, the fossil record was thought to begin rather suddenly, about 600 million years ago at the beginning of the Cambrian period. All over the world there was an explosion of well-developed fossils of marine animals that seemed to have no precursors, and many thought that the beginning of the Cambrian represented a major discontinuity in the history of the Earth that may have been preceded directly by the origin of life. These apparent discontinuities led to the concept of "punctuated evolution" (Gould & Eldridge, 1977). However, it is now recognized that the sudden appearance of fossils was due to the evolution by invertebrates of hard shells of calcium carbonite or calcium phosphate, which left better fossil evidence than did the soft bodies of their precursors (Margulis, 1982). This conclusion is supported by the discovery of microfossils and other fossil evidence of life beginning 3 billion years earlier than the beginning of the Cambrian. The oldest fossil-like objects appear to be nearly 3.5 billion years old, and the first evidence of photosynthesis is more than 3 billion years old. This is not so long after the formation of Earth's crust: The oldest terrestrial sedimentary rocks are about 3.8 billion years old (Schopf, 1980).

There is thus an enormous span of time between the origin of life on the Earth and the appearance of fossils visible to the naked eye. In that period, there evolved in single-celled organisms the chemical and biological strategies that are basic to more complex forms of life (from Margulis, 1982, p. 1):

During those first three billion years, the cell . . . was engaged, quite literally, in evolving its working parts. By the time marine algae and animals appeared, microbes had developed all the major biological adaptations: diverse energy-transforming and feeding strategies, movement, sensing, sex, and even cooperation and competition. They had invented nearly everything in the modern repertoire of life except, perhaps, language and war.

The discovery and analysis of microfossils were enhanced by the use of the electron microscope, which also contributed to the detailed study of the fine structure of cells and thereby revolutionized our knowledge of the functioning of the single cell. One result has been a greatly increased ability to determine the similarities and differences between cells, to classify them, and thereby to determine their evolutionary relationships.

One of the most conspicuous differences between organisms is that some stay put and derive energy from sunlight, while others move in search of energy; this is the basis of the traditional distinction between plants and animals. However, many organisms are difficult to classify; some, for example, use both means of deriving energy. Also, since the 1960s, it has become apparent that there is a more fundamental distinction in the living world: that between prokaryotes and eukaryotes. Eukaryotes contain intracellular structures, or organelles, that are associated with specific cellular functions. For example, the genetic material (DNA) is carried in a membrane-bounded nucleus. Such a nucleus is the defining feature of a eukaryote as opposed to a prokaryote. Also, such organelles as mitochondria (involved in the generation of energy within the cell) and plastids (involved in photosynthesis) are present and attached to the nucleus via an intricate web of membranes called the endoplasmic reticulum. Much of the latter is covered with ribosomes, small bodies that produce specific proteins using genetic information from the nucleus. In contrast, prokaryotes are relatively undifferentiated in that they lack a membrane-bounded nucleus that carries genetic information, have no organelles or endoplasmic reticulum, and have only small ribosomes (Margulis, 1982; Schopf, 1980).

The cells of all elaborate organisms—all plants and animals—are eukaryotes, while prokaryotes consist of bacteria, cyanobacteria, and similar microbes. The earliest life forms on Earth were prokaryotes, and there is much debate about the timing and sequence of events by which eukaryotes evolved from prokaryote ancestors. One theory is that eukaryotes arose via symbiosis: that originally independent microbes of different species came together and lived intimately as separate guest and host cells and that eventually the guests became the organelles of a new kind of cell (Margulis, 1982).

Spontaneous Communication in the Differentiation of Life Forms ·

The story of the evolution of life has been a story of increasing differentiation and complexity added to a basic theme: According to Dawkins, the theme is that of preserving the DNA, of preserving the gene. Prokaryotes evolved into eukaryotes, eukaryotes evolved into complex multicelled organisms, multicelled organisms evolved patterns of social organization. In each of these transformations, the original forms of life were not lost but continued to live much as they always had. Their activities were, however, reorganized.

Prokaryotes to eukaryotes. It is a fundamental tenet of current evolutionary theory that selection pressures act on the level of the individual organism. If this is the case, how is it that individual prokaryotes were able to combine into eukaryotes, eukaryotes into multicelled organisms, and so on? We suggest that this increasing differentiation occurred because spontaneous communication tendencies—tendencies to send information to and receive information from others and to respond appropriately—were selected on the individual level. In the case of prokaryotes, symbiotic relationships could have been established via spontaneous communication mechanisms that first attracted the protohost and protoguest to one another and then regulated their behavior once together. The individuals with the most efficient spontaneous communication between themselves, and thus the most finely tuned symbiotic relationship, would have been selected. Eventually, the need for separate sources of genetic information in host and guest would be obviated, and, in fact, the existence of separate sources might tend to disrupt spontaneous communication and, therefore, be subjected to negative selection pressures. Eventually, the DNA of both individuals was organized into a bounded nucleus from which the genes took over the construction and maintenance of both individuals. The spontaneous communication system would endure but as an intracellular communication system rather than one linking two individual cells of different species.

Multicelled life. A similar case can be made for the evolution of multicelled life. Multicelled organisms are formed by prokaryotes, as in the case cited above of the fruiting bodies formed by myxobacteria. In the slime mold, the spontaneous communication system of sending and receiving mechanisms involves chemical substances, or pheromones, that function first to aggregate individual cells when food is scarce and then to regulate their activities so that the fruiting body is formed. In the process, some of the individuals die, so that the formation of the fruiting body is in Wilson's (1975) sense an altruistic act on the part of those individuals.

In the case of fruiting bodies, there are no permanent structural connections formed between cells. However, physical communicative connections could be established and maintained genetically, and, once this happened, individual cells would be able to become differentiated and specialized into permanent multicelled systems. The more complex and sophisticated the communicative connections between cells, the more they could be able to differentiate into specialized tissue and organ systems. Again, the packaging of the genetic information into a single form capable of constructing and maintaining the whole organism would have obvious advantages, and the evolution of advanced eukaryotic sexuality made this possible while still allowing for genetic variation from generation to generation. Also again, the spontaneous communication system would endure but as an intraorganismic communication system.

Social systems. The spontaneous communication systems linking individual organisms into a social system follow a similar pattern, and it is here that the social psychological analysis of altruism becomes most relevant. Biologically based sending and receiving tendencies link individual organisms directly, regulating their behavior in ways that have proved adaptive. The individuals involved in spontaneous communication constitute a biological unit just as real as the units formed by eukaryotes and multicelled organisms. Such spontaneous communication systems are most obvious when they regulate relatively rigid social systems such as those of insects—bees, ants, termites—but, as we have seen, they regulate the more complex social systems of animals, including human animals, as well. It is also the basis, both phylogenetically and ontogenetically, of general-purpose symbolic—and, in humans, linguistic—communication (Buck, 1984, 1988a).

This analysis implies that the genes mediating interindividual behavior for most forms of life must be communicative genes. The exception is the viciously exploitative virus, which survives by expropriating the genetic material of prokaryotes or eukaryotes. Communicative genes, in their own self-interest, are able to send and receive information vis-à-vis other genes to coordinate activities and, ultimately, cooperate. These sending and receiving mechanisms are phylogenetic adaptations that are genetically determined and maintained.

The Social Psychology of Spontaneous Communication

To recapitulate, we have argued that there is a direct, spontaneous stream of communication that mediates interindividual behavior for most forms of life and that this is based upon communicative genetic systems. In nonvertebrates, this system is simple and reflexive, while, in vertebrates, it requires, by way of communicative experience, the formation of affective bonds. Although a detailed discussion of the nature of these affective bonds is beyond the scope of this chapter, it may be noted that Panksepp (1982) has suggested that mechanisms involving the endorphins are involved in basic social motivation (see Buck, 1988a, pp. 110-112). Hormones and other neural transmitters have been implicated as well.

Our position is relevant to the debate between social psychologists who advocate "universal egoism" and those who argue for "true altruism" in the analysis of human behavior (see Batson and Oleson, Chapter 3 of this volume). The egoistic position, like Dawkins's selfish gene hypothesis, seems more realistic and hard-headed, and it is sometimes suggested that "true" altruism, if it exists at all, must be a product of an evolved human capacity based upon reason and the social contract. For example, in *Leviathan* (1651), Hobbes described human life in the state of nature as "nasty, brutish, and short" and suggested that the social contract was arrived at out of fear, to end the war of all against all. In contrast, John Locke (1632-1704) argued that, in the state of nature, people lived together without leaders according to reason and natural law, which had a divine origin.

In this volume, Batson and Oleson carefully review the social psychological evidence for egoistic explanations of altruistic behavior and conclude that the evidence supports the empathy-altruism hypothesis: that the needs of the other evoke emphatic emotions of sympathy and compassion that motivate altruistic responses. We agree with this position, adding that the capacity for empathic emotion has a basis in early experiences with affective communication and that, given appropriate experience, the necessary and sufficient condition for the arousal of empathic emotion is spontaneous communication. The implications, as Batson and Oleson (in Chapter 3 of this volume) note, are considerable, suggesting not only that "we are far more social animals than . . . our social psychological theories . . . would lead us to believe," but that this social nature has its roots in communicative genetic systems that have from the beginning directly involved life forms with one another.

CONCLUSIONS: THE COMMUNICATIVE GENE HYPOTHESIS

We have argued that altruism and other prosocial behaviors in vertebrates are based upon prosocial affects that, in turn, are based upon experiences during development involving spontaneous emotional communication. For this reason, spontaneous communication normally is sufficient to produce social bonds such that individuals act in concert and individuate social roles that are beneficial to the group but not necessarily to each individual within it. Furthermore, we suggest that the roots of the phenomenon of spontaneous communication activating altruistic impulses go back to the fundamental nature of the communicative gene and that altruism is a derivative phenomenon based on social roles that characterize the organization of the species. It might be objected that we are talking here about qualitatively different phenomena and that to compare the processes by which prokaryotes evolved into eukaryotes, eukaryotes evolved into multicelled organisms, and multicelled organisms evolved social organization is nonsense. However, we see an essential link between these phenomena—that they all have come about through genetically based spontaneous communication systems.

We find no evidence for the existence of genes for altruistic behavior as such but consider this to be a derivative aspect of social behavior based on social bonding and communication. Affective social bonding precedes and is necessary for cognitive learning to occur. The social fabric that characterizes each species is initiated, maintained, and altered by affect-laden communication, the capacity for which is genetically based. We, therefore, conclude that the genetics of communication form the primary basis for all forms of sociality, from loose and occasional aggregations to highly diversified social systems.

REFERENCES

Allee, W. C. (1931). *Animal aggregations: A study in general sociology.* Chicago: University of Chicago Press.
Allee, W. C. (1938). *Social life of animals.* New York: Norton.
Allee, W. C. (1951). *Cooperation among animals with human implications.* New York: Henry Schuman.
Batson, C. D. (1983). Sociobiology and the role of religion in promoting prosocial behavior: An alternative view. *Journal of Personality and Social Psychology, 45,* 1380-1385.
Bentley, D. R., & Hoy, R. R. (1974). The neurobiology of cricket song. *Scientific American, 231*(2), 34-44.

Bogert, C. M. (1961). The influence of sound in the behavior of amphibians and reptiles. In W. E. Lanyon & W. N. Tavdga (Eds.), *Animal sounds and communication* (Publication No. 7). Washington, DC: American Institute of Biological Sciences.

Bonner, J. T. (1967). *The cellular slime molds.* Princeton, NJ: Princeton University Press.

Bonner, J. T. (1969). Hormones in the social amoebae and mammals. *Scientific American, 220,* 78-91.

Bonner, J. T. (1977, May-June). Some aspects of chemotaxis using the cellular slime mold as an example. *Mycologia.*

Buck, R. (1984). *The communication of emotion.* New York: Guilford.

Buck, R. (1988a). *Human motivation and emotion* (2nd ed.). New York: John Wiley.

Buck, R. (1988b). Emotional education and mass media: A new view of the global village. In R. P. Hawkins, J. M. Weimann, & S. Pingree (Eds.), *Advancing communication science: Merging mass and interpersonal processes: Vol. 16. Sage annual reviews of communication research.* Newbury Park, CA: Sage.

Buck, R. (1989). Emotional communication in personal relationships: A developmental-interactionist view. In C. Hendrick (Ed.), *Close relationships: Vol. 10. Review of personality and social psychology.* Newbury Park, CA: Sage.

Carter, J. (1988). Survival training for chimps. *Smithsonian, 19,* 36-49.

Darwin, C. (1872). *The expression of the emotions in man and animals.* Chicago: University of Chicago Press. (Reprinted in 1965)

Davis, F. (1978). *Eloquent animals.* New York: Coward, McCann, & Geoghegan.

Dawkins, R. (1976). *The selfish gene.* New York: Oxford University Press.

Dawkins, R., & Krebs, J. R. (1978). Animal signals: Information or manipulation? In J. R. Krebs & N. B. Davies (Eds.), *Behavioural ecology: An evolutionary approach* (pp. 282-309). Oxford: Blackwell Scientific.

Eibl-Eibesfeldt, I. (1979). Human ethology: Concepts and implications for the science of man. *The Behavioral and Brain Sciences, 2,* 1-57.

Ghiglieri, M. P. (1985). The social ecology of chimpanzees. *Scientific American, 252,* 102-113.

Ginsburg, B. E. (1974). Nonverbal communication: The effect of affect on individual and group behavior. In P. Pliner, L. Krames, & T. Alloway (Eds.), *Nonverbal communication of aggression* (pp. 161-173). New York: Plenum.

Ginsburg, B. E. (1976). Evolution of communication patterns in animals. In M. E. Hahn & E. C. Simmel (Eds.), *Communicative behavior and evolution* (pp. 59-79). New York: Academic Press.

Ginsburg, B. E. (1979). The violent brain: Is it everyone's brain? In C. R. Jeffery (Ed.), *Biology and crime: Vol. 10. Sage research progress series in criminology* (pp. 47-64). Beverly Hills, CA: Sage.

Ginsburg, B. E. (1987). The wolf pack as a socio-genetic unit. In H. Frank (Ed.), *Man and wolf* (pp. 401-413). Amsterdam: Dr. W. Junk.

Goodall, J. (1986). *The chimpanzees of Gombe: Patterns of behavior.* Cambridge, MA: Belknap.

Gould, S. J., & Eldridge, N. (1977). Punctuated equilibria: The tempo and mode of evolution. *Paleobiology, 3,* 115-151.

Hamilton, W. D. (1964). The genetical theory of social behaviour, I, II. *Journal of Theoretical Biology, 7,* 1-52.

Hoffmann, M. (1977). Empathy: Its development and prosocial implications. In C. B. Keasy (Ed.), *Nebraska symposium on motivation* (Vol. 25). Lincoln: University of Nebraska Press.

Hoffmann, M. (1981). Is altruism part of human nature? *Journal of Personality and Social Psychology, 40,* 121-137.

Jenks, S. M., & Ginsburg, B. E. (1987). Socio-sexual dynamics in a captive wolf pack. In H. Frank (Ed.), *Man and wolf* (pp. 375-399). Amsterdam: Dr. W. Junk.

Koluchova, J. (1972). Severe deprivation in twins: A case study. *Journal of Child Psychology and Psychiatry, 13,* 107-114.

Koluchova, J. (1976). A report on further development of twins following severe and prolonged deprivation. In A. M. Clarke & A.D.B. Clarke (Eds.), *Early experience: Myth and evidence* (pp. 56-66). London: Open Books.

MacDonald, K. B., & Ginsburg, B. E. (1981). Induction of normal prepubertal behavior in wolves with restricted rearing. *Behavioral and Neural Biology, 33,* 133-162.

Maier, I., & Muller, D. G. (1986). Sexual pheromones in algae. *Biological Bulletin, 170,* 145-175.

Margulis, L. (1982). *Early life.* Boston: Science Books International.

Moon, A., & Ginsburg, B. E. (1985, August). *Genetic factors in the selective expression of species-typical behavior of coyote ×* beagle hybrids. Invited paper presented at the 19th International Ethological Conference, Toulouse, France.

Moyer, K. E. (1968). Kinds of aggression and their physiological bases. *Communications in Behavioral Biology, 2,* 65-87.

Panksepp, T. (1982). Toward a general psychobiological theory of emotions: With commentaries. *Behavioral and Brain Sciences, 5,* 407-467.

Rabb, G. B., Woolpy, J. H., & Ginsburg, B. E. (1967). Social relationships in a group of captive wolves. *American Zoologist, 7,* 305-311.

Redican, W. K. (1982). An evolutionary perspective on human facial displays. In P. Ekman (Ed.), *Emotion in the human face* (2nd ed.). New York: Cambridge University Press.

Richards, R. J. (1987). *Darwin and the emergence of evolutionary theories of mind and behavior* (pp. 309-310). Chicago: University of Chicago Press.

Ryan, M. J. (1990). Signals, species, and sexual selection. *American Scientist, 78,* 46-52.

Schopf, A. W. (1980). The evolution of the earliest cells. In P. C. Hanawalt (Ed.), *Molecules to living cells* (pp. 20-36). San Francisco: W. C. Freeman. (Reprinted from *Scientific American,* 1978, September)

Schotté, C. S., & Ginsburg, B. E. (1987). Development of social organization and mating in a captive wolf pack. In H. Frank (Ed.), *Man and wolf* (pp. 349-374). Amsterdam: Dr. W. Junk.

Scott, J. P. (1983). A systems approach to research on aggressive behavior. In E. C. Simmel, M. E. Hahn, & J. K. Walters (Eds.), *Aggressive behavior: Genetic and neural approaches* (pp. 1-18). Hillsdale, NJ: Lawrence Erlbaum.

Scott, J. P. (1989). *The evolution of social systems.* New York: Gordon and Breach Science Publishers.

Spencer, H. (1893). *The principles of ethics.* Indianapolis: Liberty Classics. (Reprinted in 1978)

Suomi, S. J., & Harlow, H. F. (1972). Social rehabilitation of isolate-reared monkeys. *Developmental Psychology, 6,* 487-496.

Trivers, R. (1971). The evolution of reciprocal altruism. *Quarterly Review of Biology, 46,* 35-57.

Wilkinson, G. S. (1990). Food sharing in vampire bats. *Scientific American, 262*(2), 76-83.

Williams, G. (1966). *Adaptation and natural selection: A critique of some current evolutionary thought.* Princeton, NJ: Princeton University Press.

Wilson, E. O. (1975). *Sociobiology: The new synthesis.* Cambridge, MA: Belknap.

7

The Cultural Relativity of
Selfish Individualism
ANTHROPOLOGICAL EVIDENCE THAT HUMANS
ARE INHERENTLY SOCIABLE

ALAN PAGE FISKE

Alan Page Fiske is a psychological anthropologist whose research and teaching focus on how psychology and culture jointly shape social relations. He is the son of one psychologist and the brother of another. He received his B.A. from Harvard and Ph.D. from the University of Chicago. In between, he worked in public health and economic development programs and did ethnographic research in East, Central, and West Africa for eight years. He is currently a member of the psychology faculty at the University of Pennsylvania studying how people interpret and respond to misfortune in diverse cultures, the nature of sex and food taboos in relation to group solidarity, and the marking and cognitive representation of social relationships.

THE MYTH OF THE ASOCIAL
(OR ANTISOCIAL) INDIVIDUALIST

Many Americans, including many psychologists and other social scientists, assume that people are by nature selfish individualists. Whether couched in material terms or with respect to some broader concept of utility, the assumption is that people care only about their own personal welfare and treat others only as means to their selfish ends. Given this presupposition, altruism is problematic: It either is anomalous or is an illusion people perpetrate to advance private ulterior ends. However, the axiom of the primacy of selfish individualism is contradicted by numerous cross-cultural studies and historical analyses and by examination of ethnographic evidence from a wide variety of cultures, including my own participant-observation fieldwork in

AUTHOR'S NOTE: The ideas in this chapter and the ethnographic evidence on which it is based are discussed in much more detail in a book, *Structures of Social Life: The Four Elementary Forms of Human Relations*, 1990, New York: Free Press (Macmillan). The research on which this chapter is based was supported in part by NIMH Grant 1 R29 MH43857-01. Jon Baron, Margaret Clark, Barbara Fiske, Donald Fiske, Nick Haslam, Nancy Littke, John Sabini, Deborah Stearns, and Steven Walters all read an earlier draft and made very useful comments that helped me to eliminate some, but not all, of the muddles it contains.

West Africa. Ethnographic evidence usually does not permit strong inferences about psychological mechanisms, but it provides crucial evidence about the range of forms of human relations and the modal tendencies. What the ethnographic evidence shows is that prosocial behavior is universal, helping is the mode, and altruism is very common. Furthermore, the ethnographic evidence suggests that if altruism means a genuine concern for some good beyond the self, motivated by a deep sense of personal connection or moral obligation to others, then altruism is inherent in human nature.

Theory and data from diverse fields of social science indicate the existence of four elementary forms of social relationships: Communal Sharing, Authority Ranking, Equality Matching, and Market Pricing. People regularly provide distinctive kinds of help and are often appropriately altruistic in the context of these relationships. But they do so in strikingly different ways in different societies, as a function of the cultural rules for implementing each of the relationships. Consequently, considering the entire human population, culture is probably the largest source of variance in altruism and other forms of helping.

This chapter argues that four basic relational models organize most human interaction, and none of the four types of relationship entails selfishness. In the first place, people in all cultures generously share some things—especially cooked food—with some other people (including but not limited to kin) and are kind to them *without expecting specific reciprocation*. This form of social interaction is titled here *Communal Sharing*.[1] Second, in various contexts, people in virtually all cultures provide work, goods, and other tribute to higher ranking people, out of a sense of deference and respect, and obey their superiors dutifully. Conversely, authorities commonly feel a sense of pastoral responsibility (noblesse oblige), looking out for their subordinates and protecting them *simply because they are subordinates*. When people treat such privileges of power and the duties of status as legitimate, this asymmetrical relationship is termed *Authority Ranking*. Third, in every culture, people seek to distribute some things equally among peers and, in certain contexts, voluntarily make equal contributions, want to take turns, seek balanced exchanges, and feel obliged to restore equality by compensating for harm: People find equality and evenly matched relationships *rewarding for their own sake*. We can call this form of interchange *Equality Matching*. In most cultures, people also make *some* kinds of exchanges according to a ratio principle, often comparing alternatives and bargaining with reference to prices or some other intermodal standard of utility. But this fourth form of social interchange, which I call *Market Pricing,* is no more natural, no more basic, and no more universal than the other three kinds of interaction. Indeed, in most cultures and in most historical periods that have been studied, this kind of "rational" benefit/cost assessment is *less* prevalent and less highly regarded than at least one of the three other basic forms of social relations. Moreover, while some cultures (like our own) value and take for granted various sorts of Market Pricing commoditization of relationships, competitive entrepreneurial behavior, selfish individualism, and rational maximization of personal welfare through the exercise of free choice and contractual commitments, other cultures consider such orientations pathological, despicable, or illegitimate. In such cultures, very few people aim to accumulate individual wealth, much less keep it for themselves. Most people do not want to "succeed" alone and in isolation from others, and people ridicule or feel ashamed of those few who do.

The relational-models theory postulates—and the evidence reviewed below indicates—not only that people actually share, seek to maintain equality and balance, defer to authority, and look out for subordinates in practice, but that people value these forms of social relations *ideologically* and are committed to them as *moral* standards they impose on themselves and others. Furthermore, each of the four basic modes of relating to other people is intrinsically *motivating:* People seek to engage in social relationships of each kind because the relationships themselves are intrinsically satisfying. Relationships thus reflect inherent social dispositions. There appear to be significant individual differences in the relative strength of these four kinds of social motivation. But there are even larger cultural differences in the relative prevalence of the four types of relationship, in ideological and moral valuation of them, and probably also in average levels of motivation to engage in each of them. And there are enormous differences in the contexts and the manner in which people implement the basic relational models. Thus, if we want to know how and when people will be altruistic or otherwise prosocial, we have to understand the culture of the people in question.

This chapter illustrates with Market Pricing how the relational models are all socially constructed and culturally constituted. Market Pricing is a culturally informed mode of relating to other people, not a kind of asocial solipsism. Each culture defines such variables as the circumstances in which Market Pricing is appropriate (for obtaining hoes but not for sex), what the exchange ratios are (an hour of unskilled labor is worth three pounds of ground beef), how to define the commodity and how to negotiate ("the painting goes to the lady who nodded her head"), what defines a valid contract ("you signed your name"), and who may engage in such relationships ("He can't sell you his dog—he's only three!"). Even when your orientation is competitive, selfish, and individualistic, you can only engage in Market Pricing behavior in a socially constructed context, in relation to other people, and with respect to culturally defined ends.

The anthropological evidence shows that people act prosocially or altruistically primarily in the context of significant ongoing social relationships of the four basic types. People seem to value these relationships for themselves, not primarily as means to selfish, asocial ends. In the terms of Clary and Snyder (this volume), most helping is sustained and "nonspontaneous" behavior whose value-expressive and social-adjustive functions are inseparable. So altruism and helping are truly pro*social*—people are compassionate and concerned for others because the social *relationship*, which encompasses and often entails altruism, is an end it itself.[2] In many cultures, people acknowledge that in some respects everyone is socially related to everyone else, so that in some limited degree and in some defined circumstances people help others whether or not they happen to know the particular person. For example, in many African cultures, people are extremely hospitable and generous to strangers and casual acquaintances as well, within the bounds of recognized norms.

In short, this chapter reviews the anthropological evidence and concludes that—in varying manifestations and degrees—altruism is salient in every culture. This chapter thus inductively complements and supports the deductive arguments from experimental evidence advanced in the chapters in this volume by Batson and Oleson and by Buck and Ginsburg and reaches a similar conclusion: Human nature is *social* in the most fundamental sense of the term.

THE ELEMENTARY FORMS OF
SOCIAL RELATIONS

Basic Forms

Recent research in social psychology on altruism and helping behavior has been one component of a growing recognition in the social and behavior sciences that it is invalid to assume that all human behavior is driven by selfish individualism. Recently, there have been several cogent and far-ranging critiques of this Hobbesian assumption in a variety of fields (e.g., Etzioni, 1986, 1988; Palmer, 1988; Peters, 1989; Schwartz, 1986; Wellar, 1986; Westen, 1984). But there has been less progress in defining what other natural, basic forms of social interaction exist. Yet, virtually all the major classical theorists and many recent thinkers have recognized the existence of two or more basic forms of human social interaction. A synthesis of social theory in social psychology, sociology, anthropology, and allied disciplines, together with a reading of diverse ethnographies, suggests that humans relate to each other in four basic modes (Fiske, 1990a). The first is *Communal Sharing,* a relationship in which there is a sense of community, solidarity, and identity within a group, often in contrast to outsiders. Individuality is unmarked, some dimensions of selves are merged, and people show compassion and generosity to members of their group. The relationship is characterized by kindness toward one's own kind, especially kin.[3] Intense examples include relations between people who define themselves as close and trusting kin, especially those of parental care and sacrifice for children, deep romantic attachment, intimate friendships, and loyalty to comrades in battle. But (like all four kinds) this relationship can vary in intensity and breadth of application, and, in very attenuated form, Communal Sharing is evident in sharing drinking water, public space, or any other recognized commons. The relations and operations that have social meaning in Communal Sharing relationships are the same ones that have meaning in a nominal or categorical scale of measurement: Group identity is all that matters.

The second basic mode of human relationship is *Authority Ranking,* in which people are linearly ordered in precedence, prerogative, or power. Some people come before or above others, controlling access to resources, making decisions, and giving commands to their inferiors. Subordinates pay tribute, show respect, and defer to their superiors but are entitled to protection: Leaders should be responsible for their subordinates. (Participants' implicit belief in the legitimacy of the social asymmetry of Authority Ranking contrasts with interactions governed by purely exploitive power in which only fear or physical coercion is involved.) Notable examples are military relations across ranks in wartime, charismatic leaders and their disciples, or chiefs and commoners in hierarchical political systems. The axiomatic structure of Authority Ranking relations corresponds to the mathematics of an ordinal scale: Rank order is all that is important, and intervals between ranks are undefined.

The third basic type of relationship is *Equality Matching,* manifested most often in turn-taking rotations, evenly balanced in-kind reciprocity, equal-share distributions or contributions (or distributions evenly matched to contributions), matched eye-for-an-eye, tooth-for-a-tooth retaliatory vengeance, or equalizing compensation. People in such a relationship construe each other as separate and distinct but on a par with each other. Typical examples are relations among equal-status associates or acquaintances, members of a car pool, of a baby-sitting co-op, or of a rotating credit association, or voters in an election. Mathematically, the socially intelligible properties and processes defined under Equality Matching relationships correspond roughly to those defined for an interval scale: Quantities may be compared, matched, and combined by concatenation on a single dimension. But proportions have no meaning.

The fourth elementary structure for social relations is *Market Pricing.* Here people relate to each other with reference to some universal standard of value, prototypically money, by means of which all commodities can be valued in ratio terms. People can compare any two unlike commodities that are encompassed in the relationship (objects, land, work, skills, time, knowledge, rhetoric, attractiveness) with reference to this common standard of value. Hence people relating in this way conceive of themselves as making "*rati*onal" (i.e., according to ratios) decisions based on efficient cost-benefit, means-ends considerations. Common manifestations are a joint-stock corporation or limited partnership, a stock or commodity exchange, an anonymous employer-employee relationship, or the impersonal interaction between any vendor and customer. Market Pricing social interaction has the same formal relational structure as a ratio scale: A price (or other utility metric) is a measure of the value of one commodity in proportion to all other commodites. Market Pricing in itself is *not* asocial or antisocial—it is socially oriented and can be realized only in one or another particular, culture-specific social form, as we shall see below.

It is important to note that these models are sources and structures for both prosocial and agonistic behavior. These models govern anger, envy, and jealousy as well as aggression and conflict: People scapegoat ethnocentrically, commit genocide "to purify the race," or defend their sullied honor to the death (Communal Sharing); a king executes those guilty of lèse-majesté, while citizens are entitled to commit tyranicide (Authority Ranking); injured parties make reprisals to revenge their losses or destroy those who presume to an unequal share (Equality Matching); people maim and kill in response to perceptions of breach of contract and fraud or merely in the quest to open up new territories and markets, exploit new sources of slaves, or make a quick buck selling crack (Market Pricing). These violent acts may even be prosocial or altruistic in the sense that soldiers, terrorists, martyrs, and freedom fighters are construed as willingly and nobly sacrificing themselves for the sake of country or ethnic group, out of loyalty, for religion, honor, or principle.

In most interactions, people use one or more of these four implicit elementary models to generate action, coordinate what they do with other people, anticipate and make sense of what other people do, and evaluate their own and others' actions and reactions. In contrast to these four types of sociality, however, there are other kinds of encounters in which people do not coordinate and evaluate action with reference to a common model that specifies what they should do and what their actions mean. The relatively rare interactions that are not motivated by and oriented toward such a shared model fall into a fifth *asocial null category*. For example, people may treat others as mere things, as when prisoners in a concentration camp huddle up to other prisoners purely for warmth, without knowing or caring who the others are or what the consequences are for them.

The relational-models theory synthesizes a wide range of research and theory across the social sciences, postulating that these four elementary models organize social action and thought in many domains (Fiske, 1990a). The relational-models theory posits that the four models constitute the elementary alternative forms of transfer (organizing bilateral exchange, contribution, and distribution)—as well as the primary standards of social justice. For example, people may consider it just to divide things equally, following the Equality Matching model. Or they may think it right to divide in proportion to some standard, according to Market Pricing. Or they may use the Communal Sharing model and treat their resources as a commons, belonging to the group as a whole. Or they may distribute perquisites and privileges according to Authority Ranking, allocating superiors more than their subordinates. The relational-models theory hypothesizes that the same four models generate the four basic forms of making group decisions and of influencing people. The theory postulates that they are the basic mechanisms of constituting and structuring groups, while providing the basic forms of social identity and the relational self. They are the four fundamental modes of organizing labor and the sources of the social meaning of objects, land, and time. They are the four irreducible standards by which people make moral judgments and that give rise to moral emotions as well as the ideological options for legitimating social order (see Fiske, 1990b). People also respond to misfortune and suffering by interpreting it in terms of one or more of these models. At the same time, each model comprises an autonomous motivational goal: People commonly seek to engage in each kind of social relationship for its own sake (although people may sometimes have extrinsic instrumental motives as well). The same four models appear to operate at all levels of social intercourse, from interactions among individuals to the relations among nations. Moreover, as Fiske (1990a) shows, these four models emerge in cross-cultural studies of all kinds as well as in ethnographies describing particular societies around the world. So they appear to be universal, natural, and elementary forms of social relations.

However, according to the relational-models theory, people rarely construct social relationships using only a single one of the four basic models; pure types are rare. More commonly, people concatenate them and nest them hierarchically in various combinations. Thus the personal relationship between two individuals, the specifications for a pair of complementary roles, the organization of groups, and the relations among groups are typically composed of distinct phases and aspects based on two, three, or all four of the models.

The Irreducible Multiplicity of Motives and Values

This relational-models framework has an important consequence for the issue of altruism and prosocial behavior. The calculatingly rational, cost/benefit, supply/demand orientation of Market Pricing commonly assumed[4] to underlie all human interaction is actually only one of four fundamental orientations. There are three other distinct, independent kinds of motives and evaluative standards governing social interaction. Each of the four is an autonomous directive force in human social life. They are coequal goals, at the same level in the motivational hierarchy, none is inherently or commonly subordinated as a means to any of the others. Teleologically, none of the four is superordinate to the others.

Under some conditions, Market Pricing itself may impel people to prosocial behavior, for example, when an employer wishes to pay employees a fair wage, defined in terms of the market, even if he or she could pay less. Thus there are four separate kinds of prosocial orientations: The motives, the moral standards, and the ideological values of the four elementary models are qualitatively different in nature. As directive forces, they are incommensurable; there is no common currency or convertible metric for comparing, trading off, or choosing among them. People make choices among social goals, for example, by participating in one kind of relationship to the exclusion of another. But this does not mean that the choices are systematic, rationally consistent, and logically coherent. Thus making choices does not imply commensurability of goals, much less an intention to maximize. For the most part, people simply follow the implementation rules of their culture, taking for granted the application of each model where it is culturally appropriate.

This diversity of autonomous motives and values has three consequences. First, people cannot maximize across the four motives if they are subjectively incommensurable. This contradicts the common assumption that people are globally maximizing. Second, if there are four fundamental motives and evaluative standards impelling people to altruistic or prosocial behavior, then presumably they have four different sets of causes, conditions, and mechanisms. We should not look for a unitary explanation for altruistic behavior if there are actually four totally distinct kinds of altruism. The diversity of kinds of prosocial motives alerts us to the existence of a number of interests (often noneconomic and nonmaterial) that people do not reduce to any unitary metric of utility; in other words, reasons for social action that are *not* encompassed in the Market Pricing framework. Third, when helping takes place in the context of enduring Communal Sharing, Authority Ranking, or Equality Matching relationships, as it usually does, people do *not* calculate the benefit/cost price of helping (pace rational net cost models like those presented in this volume by Nadler and by Dovidio,

Piliavin, Gaertner, Schroeder, and Clark). Only among strangers and others relating in Market Pricing terms should cost/benefit ratio assessments determine whether people extend help or ask for help. In this respect, the relational theory presented here converges with the conclusion of Dovidio, Piliavin, Gaertner, Schroeder, and Clark that the decision to help another is crucially affected by the Communal Sharing sense of "we-ness" or other relationships between victim and potential helper.

How do individuals and societies differ in their use and valuation of the four modes of social relationships? There are well-validated research instruments to measure individual differences in motives that correspond fairly closely to three of the four basic models. To a first approximation, intimacy motivation is the proclivity to seek out and engage in Communal Sharing relationships that are based on the sharing of ideas and feelings about the self (McAdams, 1984, 1988, 1989). Clark, Powell, Ouellette, and Milberg (1987) have devised another measure to assess communal orientation, a similar trait. Power motivation is essentially the motive to participate in ranked relationships and to structure relationships hierarchically (McClelland, 1975; Murray, 1938; Uleman, 1972; Veroff, 1957; Winter, 1973). Achievement motivation is, in effect, the desire to make the most of resources by comparing the alternative means and choosing the one with the best cost-effectiveness ratio (Atkinson, 1958; McClelland, 1976; McClelland, Atkinson, Clark, & Lowell, 1953; Murray, 1938). Achievement motivation leads people to engage in Market Pricing social relationships, because global maximizing requires a price-like ratio metric of utility and because monetary profit is a felicitous tool for assessing the real-world outcomes of expected-utility calculations. Thus we already know quite a bit about how three of these basic social motives vary across persons and contexts, particularly in the U.S. population. Furthermore, it is well established in this line of research that these three motives are discrete, autonomous, and orthogonal traits, with qualitatively distinct relational goals.

Anthropologists also know a lot about between-culture differences in prosocial behavior and—by inference—motives. The following section, which makes up the body of this chapter, summarizes what is known about the key questions: What is the range and relative prevalence of each of the basic social orientations in the world's cultures? Is the self-interested Market Pricing individualism that is so prominent and seems so pervasive in our own society today typical of the world's cultures and historical epochs? The evidence shows that all four forms of prosocial behavior are common in diverse societies and that they typically entail helping others and often involve altruism. Yet the relative prevalence and valuation of these models, and of the prosocial behaviors they involve, vary greatly from culture to culture—any of the four models may predominate in any particular social domain in any given culture.

CULTURAL VARIATIONS IN PREVALENCE AND VALUATION

Anthropological research in non-Western cultures and historical research on nonmodern societies (including cultures ancestral to our own) shows that people often help others out of a sense of solidarity and identification with the common interests of the collectivity—that is, people relate to others in a Communal Sharing mode. The same research shows that people often give to others or work for them out of a sense of respect, homage, or deference; conversely, people look after subordinates and protect them out of a sense of pastoral responsibility or noblesse oblige—that is, Authority Ranking often is the directive force governing social relationships. There is also ample evidence that people frequently initiate helping in the expectation of getting the "same thing" back in return and that people are responsive to obligations to maintain even balance in their relationships. Western observers of traditional societies are often struck by the fact that reciprocal aid organized in this Equality Matching framework can be inefficient, uneconomical, and irrational in Market Pricing terms: From a selfish, cost/benefit perspective, each individual would be better off avoiding many such Equality Matching exchanges. Often, the same thing is true of participation in Communal Sharing and Authority Ranking relationships. The relational-models theory posits that people participating in these relationships are not doing so to maximize their material welfare or individual utility: They are engaged in the relationships for their own sake.[5] Each of these basic modes of relating to people is intrinsically rewarding, and people experience distress at the prospect of violating, disrupting, or terminating the relationships.

Cross-Cultural Studies

Margaret Mead (1937/1961) coordinated one of the earliest systematic comparative studies to show the cross-cultural diversity in social orientations. Her group found that six of the thirteen traditional cultures they studied were characterized by *cooperative* social relationships—that is, by Communal Sharing. Only three were *competitive* in a self-interested, Market Pricing sense.[6] In their small sample, there was no evident relationship between the predominant social orientation and ecology, technology, or means of subsistence. Mead's group was concerned with the overall ethos of entire societies, but research focused on specific social domains has confirmed that selfish Market Pricing orientations are less common than other forms of relationships. Studying the organization of production in a world sample of 150 societies, Udy (1959) found that by far the most common form of recruiting people into a permanent work force is along *familial* kinship lines: The core work group is the family working together in a Communal Sharing mode. Work is also very commonly organized by Authority Ranking relationships (Udy calls this arrangement *custodial*). Udy also discovered that familial work groups commonly make use of Equality Matching *reciprocal* arrangements to supplement the labor of the core kin group, but that Equality Matching relationships are rarely the *primary* basis for organizing production. People organize primary work groups in Market Pricing *(contractual)* form more commonly than in Equality Matching but less commonly than in either Communal Sharing or Authority Ranking forms.

Research on systems of exchange shows that, in most societies throughout most of history, people have engaged in Market Pricing transactions less frequently, and have valued them less, than they have any of the other three forms of interchange. The economic anthropologist Karl Polanyi (1944/1957, 1968; Polanyi, Arensberg, & Pearson, 1957) demonstrated that the dominance of Market Pricing relations in the ideology and practice of modern Western societies is a relatively recent and atypical phenomenon. He shows that, in most societies, the transfer of most goods and the organization of the means of material subsistence are embedded in Communal Sharing, Authority Ranking, and Equality Matching social relations (his terms are *householding, redistribution,* and *reciprocity,* respectively). He shows how economists and other social theorists have conflated economics (the production and distribution of the means of subsistence) with economizing (rationally efficient, selfish, benefit/cost maximization in the Market Pricing mode). All societies have mechanisms of producing and distributing food, clothing, housing, and so forth, but the primary mechanisms are not usually markets and neither is exchange usually based on prices. On the basis of ethnohistorical materials, Polanyi argues that people typically contribute, distribute, and transfer goods and services to others to enact and sustain social relationships. Polanyi and many other anthropologists (e.g., Mauss, 1925/1967, and Malinowski, 1922/1961) show that the symbolic social value of goods and services in creating, sustaining, or changing social relationships is often more important than their material-use value (see also Veblen, 1899/1934). In effect, the social relationship is the goal, and the exchange is merely a means—the inverse of the linkage often assumed by Western social scientists.

Sahlins (1965) extended this analysis by exploring the contexts in which people transfer goods back and forth with varying degrees of self-interest and generosity. People give to close kin and neighbors without expecting anything particular in return (*generalized reciprocity:* Communal Sharing). With friends and associates with whom they interact regularly, but not continuously, people expect *balanced,* even reciprocity: They expect to get the same thing back that they gave, but not immediately, and they trust others to judge when and what to return (Equality Matching). People also typically use balanced exchanges to initiate friendly relations with new groups or to end hostilities with enemies. In more distant relations, as with strangers, people give only when they can obtain favorable terms and think it is to their personal advantage—and, when social distance becomes extreme, if people can take without giving, they do so (*negative reciprocity:* Market Pricing). In traditional societies, people often give goods in obeisant tribute to superiors, who nobly and ostentatiously *redistribute* the goods to their retainers and subordinates (Authority Ranking). Sahlins provides many ethnographic illustrations that amply prove the thesis that we have to understand the cultural meaning and, in particular, the social context of transactions to understand when and how people give and what, if anything, they seek to get in return. Goods (and services) are a medium of creating, sustaining, and repairing social relations.

Cultures vary greatly in the value they place on each of the four forms of social relations and in the particular social domains in which they implement each of them. Although they did not study actual behavior, Kluckhohn and Strodtbeck's (1961/1973) research illustrates this. Their pioneering work compared social-relational values and expected practices among Texans, Mormons, Spanish-Americans, Zunis, and Navahos. Informants from the five Southwestern cultures gave very different answers to questions about what kinds of transfers (including inheritance), what modes of organizing work, and what forms of decision making they expected and thought appropriate in specific contexts. Some informants in some cultures preferred *individualistic* (Market Pricing) modes of interaction or expected them in certain domains, but *collateral* (Communal Sharing) and *lineal* (Authority Ranking) orientations predominated among responses in several of these cultures. Subsequently (and independently), Triandis (1972, 1987) and his associates (Triandis, Bontempo, Villareal, Asai, & Lucca, 1988; Triandis, Vassiliou, & Nassiakou, 1968) have shown that *collectivism* is a common orientation in many individuals and predominates over *individualism* in many cultures. In other words, people often put the collective interests of the group ahead of their individual self-interest.

These cross-cultural surveys show that Communal Sharing, Authority Ranking, and Equality Matching forms of prosocial behavior are common around the world. In many cultures, "rational" Market Pricing is restricted to certain kinds of transactions with strangers, and it is often exhibited only toward enemies. Altruistic helping is expected in many domains of social activity in many cultures, and in practice various kinds of helping behavior are highly prevalent in most traditional societies (see Fiske, 1990a; Fortes, 1963/1970, 1983). Because this sort of sociability is literally foreign to many Western readers, it may be helpful to illustrate with a detailed description of how it operates in one culture, supplemented by briefer examples from other traditional societies. These ethnographic materials indicate the pervasiveness of altruistic and other helping behavior and give the flavor of life in one very communal culture. They also attest to the motives of people who care about their social relationships more than about their individual interests. As Clary and Snyder (Chapter 5 of this volume) point out, long-term helping relationships and sustained altruism often reflect motivational dispositions—dispositions, it appears, to participate in the four basic social relationships.

A West African Example

Between the rain forest and the desert, in the bend of the Niger River in West Africa, a number of societies maintain their traditional cultures with remarkable conservatism. The following account describes the Moose (pronounced MOH-say), who live in the villages of central Burkina Faso (as they were in 1979-1982), but most of it also applies to the Tallensi of Ghana (Fortes, 1945, 1949/1969), the Bambara

(Lewis, 1981) and Dogon (Paulme, 1940) of Mali, and many other rural peoples in this culture area and elsewhere in Africa, including, for example, the Bemba of Zambia (Richards, 1939/1969). It shows how Moose exhibit highly altruistic behavior with regard to the things that are most important in their culture. Communal Sharing is the predominant orientation, followed by the complementary deference and pastoral responsibility of Authority Ranking relations.

COMMUNAL USE OF RESOURCES

The Moose live on eroded, overgrazed, leached clay soils, and, due to a population density that is unusually high for Africa, there is a severe shortage of arable land. Yet Moose are extremely generous with their land, and they freely give any land that is not currently in use to anyone who asks for it. Indeed, a very high proportion of the fields under cultivation are on land that has been given to the people farming it. People in the village never pay rent or other compensation, never sharecrop, and never sell land. Borrowers have no explicit or significant obligations to those who lend them land, although they may make small, voluntary gifts from time to time in appreciation. People are somewhat reluctant to ask for the return of land that is still in use, and borrowers may transmit the land de facto to their heirs; so borrowed land often remains with the borrowers. People lend land to kin and in-laws, but they also give land to neighbors and even strangers. Indeed, Moose who are forced by land pressures to emigrate to other, more fertile and less crowded regions of Burkina Faso inhabited by other ethnic groups (who speak different languages) have only to request farmland from their hosts and they are granted whatever they need. Despite rather massive migrations and the evident extreme needs of migrants, this practice continues unabated in rural areas.

The most productive fields are on the manured land in and around the village, on which people grow maize. Yet Moose welcome anyone who wishes to join the community and move into the village. New arrivals have only to say where they wish to build their homes, and the user of the land in question gives it up for the newcomer's residence. I experienced this myself when I moved into the village and arranged to build huts and a living compound for my family: No one expected any compensation, and, indeed, we were gradually assimilated into the family of our hosts. Moose treat all land as a commons: It is not the private property of anyone but is available to meet the needs of everyone. Moose are among the very poorest people in the world, living a very precarious existence, and land is a scarce resource limiting production. But this does not result in selfish individualism or an avaricious, calculating attitude toward interpersonal relations. Water is even scarcer than land. It does not rain at all for six months of the year, and, during another three months or more, the rains are sparse and unpredictable. The villagers work together to dig catchment basins that collect runoff, and they share freely the water in these ponds: People drink and bathe in the water, water their stock, haul water for construction and make bricks with it, according to their various needs and initiative. When the water in these ponds runs out, for five or six months, the 700 inhabitants of the village have to draw all their water from a single hand-dug well, 140 feet deep. Yet they continue to share this water among themselves and with Fulani pastoralists and their cattle. Everyone simply helps her- or himself to whatever is needed. Each of the two years that I lived there, the well ran dry and villagers had to walk miles to get water for themselves and their stock from other villages, carrying it home on their heads. Each of these other villages shared their water until their wells were nearly dry, without expecting any reciprocation for the water. Even in these circumstances, any stranger who comes into the village may ask for a drink, and any visitor is offered water.

COLLECTIVE LABOR AND CONSUMPTION

In the village, Moose virtually never work for pay. Like land and water, labor is simply not a commodity. Moose cultivate their sorghum and millet fields in communal groups of close kin, working together without keeping track of the input of any individual. They work their land with short hoes, everyone in the group simply hoeing as much as he or she can. Young children do relatively little work (and probably damage the crops some when they try to weed); pregnant women and the old do what they can—everyone tries to contribute. Early in the morning and in the evening, the principal cultivating group breaks into small groups (and some individuals) who cultivate separate fields. However, people also help each other with these separate fields when needed. Thus Moose organize the primary core of agricultural production according to Communal Sharing. From time to time, people may also invite their "lineagemates,"[7] friends, neighbors, and in-laws to "cultivating bees" at which people get together to hoe someone's field. Attendance at these bees, and much of the organization of work in them, follows Equality Matching. People attend the cultivating bees of those who have attended their own bees. At such a bee, people work together, cultivating side by side in a line abreast across the field, often to the beat of drums. The result is that each person hoes a strip of equal length, matching the work of each other cultivator.

After the harvest, people take turns holding bees to thresh their millet. Again, attendance is reciprocated, and the work is also organized by Equality Matching. Men stand in a line abreast on the threshing ground, beating in unison to the rhythm of drums and moving slowly across the ground. Men rotate by turns through the line, passing off the threshing flails without missing a beat. Of course, no one has any idea how many blows of the flail anyone makes—but all know that they have matched each other's work blow for blow. Young men dig the catchment basins in just the same way, striking the earth with their picks in unison to the beat of drums. Women use this same system to compact floors and courtyards by pounding them to the rhythm of work songs.

Women prepare beer (or flavored flour water) and usually food to feed the workers after any kind of bee or communal work. The most senior men get the first and largest shares, and their juniors get subsequent, smaller shares, according to the principle of Authority Ranking. People wait for the eldest male present to start, and he takes a bite only after tossing a morsel of food on the ground for the ancestors, who are senior to him. The workers eat in groups of peers from common bowls and drink out of a gourd they pass around. No one keeps track of who eats or drinks how much, although people exercise restraint if the quantities are not ample enough to permit all to eat and drink their fill. People encourage their fellows to take choice morsels of meat (if there is any) and to drink up. Communal Sharing like this, in conjunction with Authority Ranking, always governs Moose eating and drinking.

Moose work together in small groups of neighbors to build huts and animal shelters, and a neighborhood or the whole village usually teams up to dig a well. The elders direct the work and do less physical labor than younger people, but all try to participate. Villagers pool their sheep and goats with their kin, with one or two children tending the combined herd. Although there are markets where any locally produced product can be bought, Moose families make for themselves most of the things they need. Even when Moose make craft products to sell for money,

Communal Sharing, Authority Ranking, and sometimes Equality Matching tend to govern the work itself and sometimes the transactions. For example, men of the Blacksmith clan forge and sell iron implements, taking turns day by day using a forge belonging to the sublineage. Younger men work the bellows and assist their elders. When an implement breaks, its owner brings it to a Blacksmith to repair, giving him whatever cash or goods he feels inclined to give in appreciation. Blacksmith men also do virtually all the woodworking, selling most objects; but they contribute gratis the flails used for threshing, which are passed from bee to bee as needed.

A shortage of land forces all Moose men to go off to the Ivory Coast to work as wage laborers for long periods, and some buy small tracts there to establish cocoa or coffee plantations. So Moose are well aware that labor, land, and goods can be sold according to Market Pricing. Indeed, they know that in economic terms they would be better off in the Ivory Coast or in the more fertile and less crowded regions of Burkina Faso. But they generally prefer to return to live communally in their villages, resuming their places in the age hierarchy of the lineage. When they return (and often while they are away), they distribute much of what they have saved from their wages, making gifts to kin, in-laws, friends, and neighbors. Most Moose would rather work and share collectively at home than stay in the external labor market.

People generally take goods to the market when they need money for a specific purpose. They sell something and more or less immediately take the proceeds and buy what they need. However, people also use an alternative Equality Matching mechanism of even-quantity exchange (called *tekre*). A woman who needs, say, cotton to spin takes a calabash of, say, peanuts to someone and asks to trade even up. She empties out the calabash full of peanuts into her neighbor's container, fills the same calabash full of cotton, and takes it home. Both people are aware in some sense that the *monetary* values of the two items, their market price as commodities, differ. But this is irrelevant in the context of *tekre*. The intent of each person is to make an even exchange, balanced in terms of the quantities given and received. In other words, people may choose to apply Equality Matching and not Market Pricing.

After the harvest, each cultivating group places the millet and sorghum from the collectively cultivated main field into corporate granaries under the control of the senior male of the group. During the rainy season, and if possible all year round, he takes grain from this granary every day to feed the people who have cultivated together. In the rainy season especially, the wives of the men in these polygynous households often take turns cooking for everyone, although they tend to share the arduous work of grinding the grain, helping each other communally. In the dry season, each separate cultivating group takes grain from its granary and prepares food separately. But, in either case, people tend to pool their food, bringing it out to share with other people of cooking groups in the same or neighboring compounds. Men eat together and women eat in a separate group, each group gathered around bowls into which they all dip. Women grow vegetables in their separate fields and collect leaves and roots from wild plants, drying them and storing them in their houses. If a woman runs out of such condiments, she goes to her cowives or neighbors, who give her what she needs—and a woman who fails to ask is chided for not relying on her peers. If grain runs out (as it may), people go to their kin or in-laws, who give what they can. The only valid excuse one can make for refusing to give others what they need is that one has nothing to give. People expect a certain amount of restraint and moderation in the demands that are made, but they try hard to meet genuine needs.

On the manured fields in the village, men grow maize, which usually ripens in the hungry season before the millet and sorghum harvest. Men pick the ears of corn, tie them in bundles, and send most of the bundles to the wives of all their neighbors and friends, keeping very little for themselves. Maize fields are not the same size, their yields differ, and things do not necessarily even out in the long run. Nor is there any particular reason to assume that this works to individuals' long run economic advantage or that Moose believe that it does. As in the other nonmarket forms of organizing labor and consumption, the intent of the Moose appears to be to observe Communal Sharing, Authority Ranking, and Equality Matching primarily for their own sake, simply because these forms of relationship seem both intrinsically good and inevitable. Moose say they act in these ways because "it is what we found when we were born"; it is Moose tradition, it is natural to them, and it is what makes them Moose.

Rather than consuming their own harvest, Moose devote much of it to collective rituals at which they lavishly feed large numbers of guests. When someone dies, many people come to pay their respects to the mourners, who feed them all. Visitors to these mortuary rituals give money to the assembled elders and to the principal mourners, who later give gifts to the drummers who play during certain stages of the ritual. The principal mourners and other closely connected people make major offerings (money; a chicken, goat, or sheep) to the dead person, offerings that (as all Moose know) go to the burial party. The burial party is composed of members of a particular clan that is responsible for religious matters, especially those relating to the earth. They acquire substantial amounts of goods and money in this way, which they are free to consume or use as they wish so long as they do not sell them. Some months later, the bereaved hold an even larger commemorative funeral at which people distribute money and offerings in a similar fashion. Hundreds or even thousands of people may attend, and their hosts provide them all with lots of beer and ample food. The amounts of money and foodstuffs that change hands in these rituals are quite substantial, especially for a population where the per capita income is estimated at around $200 a year.

Much of the food that Moose produce is consumed in religious acts of communion. Moose religion revolves around animal sacrifices, libations, and analogous nonbloody offerings. Moose sacrifice collectively to the spirit of the earth, to their ancestors, to the protective forces that guard their lineages and enforce truth and morality, to sacred masks, to beings that resemble elves or fairies, and to the spirits of mountains and trees.[8] They sacrifice at certain calendrical rituals, at major life cycle transitions, at harvest and threshing, and in the event of misfortunes or when undertaking perilous projects. When Moose sacrifice, the officiant pours libations of water, flavored flour water, and beer on the altar or the earth and lets the blood of the sacrifical animals flow over the altar. Then they pass the sacramental beer around, roast the sacrificial animals, and the officiant tosses token bits of the animal onto the altar. Then they distribute the meat to the participants, often sending beer and meat to village leaders who are absent. At this point, they go home and drink more beer, distributing beer and some sacrificial meat to high ranking people who are connected to the event but did not attend the sacrifice. Moose consume only modest quantities of vegetable protein, and they eat very little meat outside of the context of these sacrifices, so the sacrificial meat they share within and across lineages comprises the bulk of their protein intake. By any measure of worth, the animals sacrificed are also very valuable to them. Furthermore, the nutritional value of the beer is significant, and it represents a substantial portion of the grain they grow.

Moose sacrifice is an act of Communal Sharing and Authority Ranking, at two levels of analysis. First, Moose construe sacrifice as feeding the beings to whom it is addressed, who consume the soul or essence of the animal, while the sacrificers eat the substantial meat. So it is a commensal act, the sharing of food with sacred beings. Most of the beings are hierarchically superior to the sacrificers, and various aspects of the rituals mark human subordination to these beings. Second, the sacrificers and their families share the meat and beer among themselves. The rank of the participants determines the order and quantities of the shares received. But the actual consumption of the meat tends to be communal, and the beer is always distributed within the drinking group out of a shared pot and drunk from a calabash passed around among the people present. The sacramental pot of beer is reserved for the participants, but people offer other beer to anyone who comes by—as they always offer food and drink to anyone who happens to be present.

Both Authority Ranking and Communal Sharing structure many other kinds of distribution, exchange, and consumption in Moose society. For example, when Moose women brew beer to sell, all the cowives and neighboring women come by and make a token contribution by stoking the fire. When the beer is ready, they all come by for a drink. Before selling any beer, a brewer sends a small pot to the chief and usually one to the head of the lineage and/or the head of the household. Whether in everyday meals, or in funerals and sacrificial rites, Moose consume most of what they produce in altruistic acts of Communal Sharing or Authority Ranking.

Although coping, victimization, and social support are a separate dimension from resource allocation, there is an important issue worth mentioning here because it relates to a central problem explored in this volume by Midlarsky (Chapter 9), by Wills (Chapter 10), and by Nadler (Chapter 11). These Moose funerary and sacrificial rituals manifest the ways in which death and suffering affect Communal Sharing relationships and how Communal Sharing in turn shapes responses to misfortune. Moose respond to death and other forms of misfortune by an impressive show of Communal Sharing solidarity and concern, massing in great numbers and eating together. This kind of response to death is common to many cultures, but why? What psychosocial functions are served by this kind of support? In any culture, I think, serious misfortune marks both direct and vicarious victims with a taint that potentially changes their implicit social identity and sets them apart from nonvictims (see Ricoeur, 1967, and funerary rituals across Africa and Asia). Both victims and nonvictims perceive victims as somehow defiled or sullied (and as having a distinctive, embarrassing, perhaps liminal identity), and consequently victims often wish to avoid contact with nonvictims who, conversely, shun them. In the United States, victims often are socially isolated de facto and people tend to treat the misfortune as a taboo topic. Thus misfortune threatens to disrupt victims' Communal Sharing relationships with nonvictims. Victims need to sustain their sense of belonging and being enfolded in Communal Sharing relations with someone. So they seek out victims of similar misfortunes (e.g., in support groups) or others with whom the misfortune is a common, unifying feature that reinforces the sense of oneness that is the core of Communal Sharing. This may explain why some forms of helping are beneficial for coping, as Midlarsky argues.

At the same time, because victims tend to feel separated and cut off from most nonvictims, they are especially dependent on maintaining their previously existing primary Communal Sharing relationships, if any. Victims need these primary Communal Sharing relationships, which they must successfully restore or reinforce—or replace—if they are to cope effectively. This potentially helps clarify some of the issues concerning the varied effects and underlying mechanisms of different sorts of social support that Wills brings out in his review (Chapter 10). Note also that support may be aversive if it is extended in a context that makes salient the contrast between victim and nonvictim, thereby constituting a gulf that breaks down existing Communal Sharing relationships or renders them problematic. Support may also be aversive if the consequence is that the victim in a non-Communal Sharing relationship is now beholden under Equality Matching or Authority Ranking obligations to reciprocate in burdensome ways (see Clark, 1983). This may explain some of the paradoxical consequences of receiving help that Nadler describes (Chapter 11). In sum, misfortune threatens and disrupts Communal Sharing relationships but can also be the basis for creating new Communal Sharing relationships built on the similarity born of suffering in common or on empathic support that transcends the separating particularity of misfortune.

COMMUNAL COURTSHIP

Land, water, labor, and food are all scarce, critical resources essential to Moose survival. But Moose care more about having children, leaving descendants, and perpetuating the lineage than about these material things. For Moose men, this means obtaining wives. Because, in this polygamous society, older men and chiefs, especially, have multiple wives, there is a scarcity of brides. But as Margaret Mead (1937/1961, pp. 464-466) points out, a situation like this need not be culturally defined as competitive. In fact, Communal Sharing, together with Authority Ranking, organizes the Moose pursuit of brides and the transfer of women in marriage.

For the most part, Moose men do not choose their wives, and women do not choose their own husbands. The principal system of Moose marriage is based on collective courtship of a prospective wife-giving lineage. A man may begin courtship at any age from boyhood to old age. He selects a senior man or chief in another lineage and visits him from time to time, especially at certain calendrical festivals, bringing gifts of money, a chicken, or kola nuts for the elder. When he sees the elder at the market, he buys him beer, and, if the elder falls ill, the courting man will come (unasked) and cultivate his field for him, often with the aid of his lineagemates and friends. He will also give gifts to other elders in the lineage and to their senior wives. This goes on for a long time, usually many years, but the courting man never says why he does these things.

Men do not court exclusively for themselves; they often seek wives for their sons or dependent younger lineage brothers. Conversely, if the wife seeker dies or goes to the Ivory Coast, his brothers, sons, or other lineagemates continue the courtship. If (as often happens), the elder being courted dies, then the wife seeker continues to give gifts and services to his successor. Eventually, the elder may say to the wife seeker, "You are a good man. You are just like a son to me. If only I had something to give to you, I would show you how much I appreciate your kindness." Some months or years after this acknowledgment, the elder (or one of his successors) may express his affection and gratitude and promise to give the wife seeker a bride. Or he may not. No amount of time, no quantity of gifts, no fixed expenditure of effort ever *entitles* a wife seeker to receive a wife, and indeed sometimes wife seekers give up and never do receive a bride, after years of gifts and work. A disappointed suitor has no claim for compensation for his kindnesses and gets nothing back for his effort except friendship and gratitude.

Even when a lineage promises a bride, they do not say who she is. At a subsequent ceremony, they invite the wife seekers to bring beer and announce the gift of the bride. But the announcement is conveyed through two or more intermediaries and spoken so softly that the wife seekers may go home unsure of the name of their promised bride. In any case, even if they know her name, they are unlikely to know who she is. And typically she is still only a young girl at this point, perhaps 6 or 8 years old. The wife seekers, now operating even more definitely as a corporate lineage, make many ritual visits, bringing beer, money, poultry, and kola nuts, which the wife-giving lineage distributes according to Authority Ranking, Equality Matching, and Communal Sharing principles (see Fiske, 1990b). There is no fixed amount for these gifts, and the wife-giving lineage accepts what they get. They also provide the wife seekers with a very large meal, from which the visitors eat what they can and then return the rest.

The morning before each of these visits, the wife-seeking lineage invites its neighbors and friends to come and drink some beer, and the visitors all contribute whatever they can to the funds being collected to present to the wife givers. There is no fixed amount, but visitors all try to chip in. The members of the wife-seeking lineage then all contribute what money they have, and ordinarily they raise a substantial sum.

There are a number of other rituals, until eventually the bride, aged 17 or 19, comes to take up residence with her new husband's lineage. However, at some stage, the head of the lineage of the wife receivers has to decide who among them will be her husband. Often the wife givers have specified a particular man who has led the courtship efforts as the husband, but sometimes they do not, giving the bride to the lineage head to allocate as he sees fit. And often the senior man to whom the wife is given already has wives and decides to pass the bride on to a younger brother or a son. Sometimes this decision is not announced until after the bride has taken up residence in her marital lineage, where she initially shares a hut with a senior wife.

A woman calls all the men in the lineage from about her own age to her husband's age, "My husband," and they all call her, "My wife."[9] Despite these forms of address and reference, however, Moose have a very strong taboo against sexual relations between a woman and her husband's lineagemates. Because men usually are 10 to 50 years older than their wives, women are often widowed at least once. When this happens, after the husband's funeral, the widow chooses which of his younger brothers, sons by other wives, or close lineagemates she will marry.[10] The result is that the men of a lineage not only share in the efforts to obtain wives, they tend to share the wives in serial succession.

One other variant way of obtaining wives demonstrates the same attitudes toward interpersonal relations. Moose make friends in various ways with men of other lineages, either informally or by explicitly agreeing to a more formal bond of friendship. A man who has a daughter may give her to a close friend; if the friend has a daughter,[11] he will probably give her in marriage to the first man (the father of his wife). More generally, if a man is especially kind or generous or does a particular service to another man, that man may give him a bride in thanks. I was able to help out people in a number of ways, including obtaining medical care in some cases, and several men told me that, if I had been a polygynous Moose man, they would have given me a wife to express their appreciation. In any case, whenever Moose give a wife, they say they do so because they "like" the recipient; they indignantly reject the idea that giving a wife might be a trade (*tekre*) or purchase. In the past, some Moose men did obtain wives by purchasing slaves, and women sometimes do run away with their lovers, but these are recognized as completely different processes from the way most men have always been given most of their wives.

In sum, Moose seek and obtain wives in a Communal Sharing idiom of filial piety or personal friendship. Coordinately with this, men give and receive wives in Authority Ranking mode through hierarchic channels, and lineage leaders allocate wives to their juniors. Unlike many African societies, Moose do not have a bride price system, and so giving a wife is never obligatory. They give a wife as a Communal Sharing expression of affection, as a free gift to someone who has helped them generously. No set amount of goods or work "earns" a wife, and Moose never "owe" anyone a wife in return for any quantity of kindnesses received. They do not quantify kindness or filial piety in the first place—neither help nor wives are commodities.

INTRINSIC MOTIVES: NOT MERELY EXPEDIENT MEANS OR EXTERNAL CONSTRAINTS

Although it would be possible to construct a hypothetical Market Pricing account (egoistic, individualistic, maximizing, competitive, voluntary, contractual, or otherwise) of this pervasive cultural pattern of Communal Sharing, Authority Ranking, and Equality Matching, there is no evidence for the validity of such an account. It would be entirely gratuitous to assume that Moose are covertly thinking in terms of selfish personal advantage while they conform to these sociable norms. Nor are there good grounds for arguing that, whatever their proximate *motives,* these prosocial patterns of sharing, precedence, and matching actually *result* in the long-run maximization of individual self-interest—anyone making that argument would have a hard task to show that this is in fact the case. If Moose share virtually everything of great material or moral value to them, then *what* ulterior individualistic ends are they each maximizing? When Moose give deferentially to their superiors, when they match and balance their peers, shall we assert that the respect and amity they exhibit is merely sham? Although such ethnographic evidence does not permit irrefutable inferences about motives (especially unreportable motives), it clearly demonstrates the prevalence of prosocial behavior that is phenomenologically embedded in these social relationships.

Indeed, Moose motives and attitudes are more complex than this brief summary can convey. Beneath their courtly and gracious manners lie deep mutual suspicion and fundamental distrust. Anyone, even your wife, may be a witch who is killing you and your children. Anyone may be using dangerous, possibly deadly, magic to harm you out of envy or spite. Partly as a consequence of these dangers, while Moose share their work, their food, their living space, and their resources, they do not share feelings, experiences, personal histories, or plans; they are rarely *intimate* in the American sense of the term. But perhaps self-disclosure and emotional trust are not suitable measures of the nature of Moose relationships. The appropriate, culturally sensitive gauge is the utilization of the things people value. Moose fear each other, yet, as we have seen, they continually place their land, their livelihood, their marriages, and their descendants in the hands of the lineage, submerging their separate interests in the greater good of the encompassing collectivity.[12]

To explain Moose Communal Sharing, Authority Ranking, and Equality Matching relations in terms of either "external" or "internal" normative constraints alone does not really work either. For we have to ask why Moose are sensitive to these particular norms, and why they impose these norms on each other. Norms are the legitimating expression of shared evaluative standards. Moose value Communal Sharing, Authority Ranking, and Equality Matching *relationships* and demand that their fellows respect their relationships. As in any society, people's enforcement of these relational norms is sometimes disinterested: People take into account other people's relationships with third parties and sanction them when they deviate from the prescribed model for social relations.

The relational-models theory shows that motives, morals, norms, social structure, and cultural representations have a common source in the four elementary models. There may be discrepancies and discord when, for example, a person's motives derive from one model while the applicable norms come out of another model. But there is no *necessary* conflict among motives, morals, norms, social structure, and cultural representations, and—contrary to the view implicit in much of Western social science—they are often in harmony.

To explain Moose helping in terms of self-benefit or benefits to others also misses the crucial fact that social relationships encompass self and other in an emergent whole whose importance for the participants often transcends their separate interests. The preeminent motive of Moose coincides with their predominant ideological, legal, and moral values: They seek to create, sustain, and repair social relationships for their own sake. More than anything else, Moose want to belong to an enduring collectivity that defines their identity (Communal Sharing), to have a definite rank in a hierarchical system of precedence and authority (Authority Ranking), and to be evenly matched and balanced with their coequal peers (Equality Matching). Sometimes they act in calculatingly rational ways, evaluating the ratio of rewards to costs (Market Pricing), but this orientation rarely seems to be dominant in Moose life.

Social Relations Around the World

Although every culture is unique in many respects, in general terms, the Moose are not unrepresentative of the world's contemporary and historical cultures. If we want a universal theory of human nature, then we have to recognize that Communal Sharing as well as Authority Ranking and Equality Matching (or some other modes of relationships like them) are pervasive forms of human relations. This has been evident from the earliest professional ethnographic reports. In a seminal classic of economic anthropology, Firth (1938/1965) describes the system of production among the Tikopia in Polynesia in terms that correspond to what I term *Communal Sharing*. It is well known that kinship is the governing idiom structuring most traditional societies. Fortes (1963/1970, 1983) shows that the essence of kinship is prescriptive altruism, the obligation to care for others and work for the collective good.

But Communal Sharing is more than a norm, it is simultaneously a motive to engage in intrinsically rewarding relationships. For example, Doi's (1962, 1971/1981) analysis reveals that the desire to depend on others to nurture and empathically anticipate one's needs is the crux of Japanese culture and personality. A corollary of this is that Japanese often do not *want* autonomy, freedom, and individual choice; they want to belong to enveloping, totally encompassing Communal Sharing groups. To varying degrees, most people in most societies probably want similar kinds of solidarity and senses of belonging. Japanese culture highlights the universal fact that, in a Communal Sharing, Authority Ranking, or even Equality Matching relationship, people often value help seeking as an index of trust and solidarity that affirms the relationship. Seeking help is an appropriate and expected component of these relationships. This contrasts with the Market Pricing situation Nadler (Chapter 11 of this volume) describes in which help seeking is culturally defined as threatening to autonomy and demeaning of individualistic self-esteem.

Of course, Authority Ranking is prominently manifest in many societies in Africa, Asia, and elsewhere (e.g., Brown, 1951; Geertz, 1959/1974; Llewelyn-Davies, 1981). Equality Matching is also salient in many cultures: People may go on perilous voyages and focus their entire culture on the equal exchange of objects that have no practical use value at all, as Malinowski (1922/1961) first showed (not to mention dinner parties or birthday and Christmas cards and presents). Indeed, this kind of evenly balanced Equality Matching relationship is the dominant mode of interaction in New Guinea and other parts of Melanesia (Forge, 1972). Even when money is involved, people often prefer to make balanced, even interest-free, exchanges rather than operating in terms of ratios or seeking a profit. This is evident in the worldwide phenomenon of rotating credit associations, in which a group of people meets at regular intervals, each member contributing an equal sum to a pool that a different member takes home at each meeting (Ardner, 1964; Firth & Yamey, 1964; Vélez-Ibañez, 1983). At the end of a full round of meetings, each person has contributed and received exactly the same amount of money. Rotating credit associations probably predate, and certainly continue to coexist with, modern banks based on Market Pricing principles. Although Market Pricing is common in most societies, people in many societies disdain cost/benefit bargaining and disparage people who exhibit such selfishness (e.g., Bohannan, 1955, on the Tiv of Nigeria; Marshall, 1961, on the !Kung of Botswana). In most cultures, including Europe before the modern era, people take sociable motives for granted, and it may be something of a peculiarity of our own modern culture that we think it plausible to imagine that rational self-interest might be the ultimate motive underlying even the most compassionate sociable acts. Are these sociable motives and values reflected in our own individualistic, materialistic culture? Gilligan (1982) maintains that the morality of caring in personal relationships is very much alive in the United States. Clary and Snyder (this volume) review evidence that the widespread practice of volunteering in the United States is motivated by the value-expressive desire to help others, probably inseparably combined with the social-adjustive desire to create or enhance social relationships. Despite the objective and ideological dominance of a selfish Market Pricing mentality in the United States, everyday observation shows that Americans are still motivated by the need to belong, the need to rank, and the need to be equal. Altruism, helping, and prosocial behavior are usually manifestations of these relationships. Among strangers in our society of autonomy, people may often be reluctant to help or to acknowledge dependency, but, with close friends, romantic partners, and family, the desire to relate to others is unmistakable.

THE SOCIOCULTURAL NATURE OF THE
IMPLEMENTATION OF COST/BENEFIT MODELS

In the analysis of social interaction, it is easy to conceptually confuse *a*social behavior and Market Pricing. The asocial null case is action in which people take others into account only as expedient means or impediments to nonsocial goals. Such behavior does occur, but it is relatively rare except among sociopaths and the autistic. Much of what we describe as selfish, individualistic, competitive, or aggressive behavior actually is socially oriented, culturally formulated action in the framework of Market Pricing. Market Pricing is an implicit model (a "grammar") for relating to other people through the medium of a commoditizing system of ratio values. As equity theory suggests, this kind of ratio-comparing orientation is inherently social (see Adams, 1965; Walster, Walster, & Berscheid, 1978). Failure to help is not an asocial act (see Lerner, 1975, 1980), neither is exploitation of others or even aggression—when people justify it or think it justifiable. Vengeance, letting someone suffer who deserves it, or punishing a transgressor are socially oriented, prosocial acts (from the point of view of the actor). To understand when people act so as to benefit specific others and when they do not, we need to discriminate between action that is beneficial and action that is socially oriented: Socially oriented behavior may well involve harm to others. This is true with respect to all four models, but the greatest confusion surrounds Market Pricing.

Furthermore, we tend to treat Market Pricing as somehow inherent, fundamental, internal, natural, and presocial, while we often regard Communal Sharing, Equality Matching, and deferential subordination under Authority Ranking as extrinsic, artificial, external, imposed, and acquired. But the relational-models theory asserts that, while all the models are equally elementary, people can enact them only in culturally defined ways. Hence we need to understand how the basic models are socially enacted and culturally constituted. Let me illustrate a few of the dimensions of how people realize Market Pricing goals by participating in culturally constituted practices embedded in a matrix of social relationships and institutions.[13]

People can be selfish only vis-à-vis other people. People can bargain and compete only with people, make a profit only from dealings with people, and succeed only in comparison with people (or, in each case, with socially constructed quasi persons like corporations). Achievement may be measured against nominally "private" standards, but people usually assess success in terms of money, promotions, recognition, or the production of socially significant products. In short, the calculus of Market Pricing must be realized in a social-relational context; its goals are certain forms and outcomes of interactions with other people.

Moreover, people can implement Market Pricing interaction only through the medium of culturally defined implementation rules that specify *who* can act this way with regard to *what* sorts of entities, *what counts* as such an entity, and what the actual *parameters* are for such interactions. Let me briefly sketch what this entails about the cultural constitution of Market Pricing.

First, there are culture-specific person and domain application rules that determine when and with whom it is appropriate, or even conceivable, to interact in a Market Pricing mode. In our society, it is degrading and illegal to sell or to buy sex or even to bargain for it. In contrast, a Moose woman would be insulted if her lover failed to offer her money when he wanted to have sexual relations with her, and she would refuse him. In our society, it is now anathema to buy or sell persons. But many societies used to capture and sell slaves, selling them for the best price they could get and buying as cheaply as they could, like any other commodity. In any given culture, alcohol and various drugs may or may not be considered salable to various categories of persons or even to anyone at all. In our society, minors and mentally incompetent people cannot make certain kinds of Market Pricing contracts, but there is nothing in nature that defines who can make a valid contractual commitment; this is a cultural rule. *Some* rules are needed to specify when Market Pricing can operate, but the *particular* content of the rules is largely arbitrary and actually quite variable across cultures. Is it prosocial to have sexual relations with a man because he loves you, but egoistic (or antisocial) to do so because he pays you? Yes, in our own culture, but not among Moose. If someone you know dumps a load of firewood by your house, should you offer him money in payment or would this be an insult? Which is the prosocial action?

Second, there are constitutive rules that define what is going on and what is what. If you offer a price for something in a Moose market and someone replies, "Bless you," do you have a deal or a refusal? If bean leaves are spread out on a grinding platform, is this an offer of sale? If you order a door at a given price and, after delivery, the maker of the door explains that you owe him more than you originally agreed, what is your obligation? And does it matter which hand you use to give him the money? Even such fundamental matters as property and theft are quite culturally relative. In Moose culture (as in many other cultures in Africa and elsewhere), people in specified kin relationships, as well as in some intervillage and interethnic relationships, are expected to tease and provoke each other with lewd remarks, without ever taking offense. People in these joking relationships are entitled, indeed expected, to come in and appropriate the possessions of certain joking partners, without asking or even informing them. Joking partners should derogate, insult, blow sparks at, or try to throw dirty water on each other. Doing these things is prosocial, and failing to do so in the appropriate circumstances would be disparaged as antisocial.

Finally, there must be culturally specified parameters that determine the actual values of things. What is the ratio of the price of baobab leaves to the price of drop-spindles? How many bundles of thatch is one basket of red millet worth? It depends on the culture (and the historical period, the season, the place, and so on). Is it selfish or altruistic to offer eight kola nuts to someone who gave you a chicken yesterday?

In these and other ways, Market Pricing actions, like other ways of relating to people, are necessarily carried out in social interactions and organized with reference to cultural implementation rules. Market Pricing behavior is informed by cultural definitions and amplified or attenuated by cultural values. In consequence, we cannot understand or predict people's motives or intentions without examining the cultural meanings of their actions. If you are away, is it helping behavior when someone disposes of a pheasant that has been hung up in your garden for three days? Is it aggressive or prosocial to put red pepper grounds in your guest's drinking water? The meaning of the acts differs in different cultures. Knowing the culture makes it possible to understand and predict to what *extent* people will relate to others in a Market Pricing framework, the degree to which they will share communally, how often they will realize Authority Ranking, and when they will operate in an Equality Matching mode. The culture also largely controls with *whom* people will relate in each of these ways and *how* they will do so. If we wish to explain altruistic helping in the human species on a worldwide scale, most of the variance is in cultural implementation rules.

A culture may specify the application of any of the models in any kind of transient interactions among strangers or between people and putative beings like gods, ancestors, spirits, witches, corporations, or computers. Thus the implementation of any model does not require an ongoing, preexistent "personal" relationship with a tangible, biologically defined human being. Furthermore, a person's orientation toward any of these forms of social relationships is in no way dependent on the direct perception or the immediate presence of the other person; a relationship in this sense effectively exists so long as any person acts with reference to a putatively shared model for social relations. The relational-models theory thus contrasts with theories that explain helping in terms of direct perception of another's distress, mediated by some kind of empathic emotion or personal discomfort (see Chapter 2 by Eisenberg and Fabes, Chapter 4 by Dovidio, Piliavin, Gaertner, Schroeder, and Clark, and Chapter 3 by Batson and Oleson in this volume, together with the theories of Cialdini and Hoffman that they discuss). The relational-models theory states that people's immediate purpose in most altruism and other helping is to initiate, sustain, reinforce, or repair social relationships. People routinely help when they apply one of the elementary social models to the interaction. The person helped is often not in any perceptible distress, and in general people will not help a person in distress unless they apply one of the relational models to the interaction. In this respect, the Communal Sharing component of the relational-models theory converges specifically with the we-ness component of the arousal: cost-reward model (discussed in Chapter 4) and more generally with its "impulsive" mode of helping based on the existence of a prior relationship instead of cost/reward calculations. But according to the relational-models theory, people only make cost/reward calculations when they are operating in a Market Pricing mode.

The socialization of altruism, discussed in this volume by Grusec (Chapter 1), can be understood as the learning of such cultural implementation rules for each of the four models (particularly Communal Sharing). My hypothesis is that each endogenous mode of relating to others emerges during ontogeny as a form of motivated social cognition that the child seeks to enact. Children do not need to learn the elementary relational forms, which are "built in" by evolution (see the parallel position of Buck and Ginsburg, Chapter 6). But the child *must* learn the culture-specific rules for implementing them. For example, sharing and some form of empathic concern with others' needs appear, apparently spontaneously, very early in childhood (Grusec, and Eisenberg and Fabes, this volume; also Blum, 1987; Gilligan & Wiggins 1987), but the child has to learn with whom it is culturally appropriate to share what and how help should be given.

Finally, there is one other major cultural issue that we need to consider here. In modern Western culture, at least, there is an association and a conceptual conflation among Market Pricing and seven other aspects of interaction: individualism, selfishness (egoism), competitiveness, intent to maximize, material subsistence activities, freedom of choice, and voluntary contractualism. The Market Pricing orientation toward ratios of rewards and benefits calculated in terms of an intermodal metric of utility or price does not logically entail any of these other qualities of interaction, and most of them are analytically independent of the others. People can engage in Market Pricing relations in which they orient to a social unit transcending the individual, in which they may not try to benefit the self (or the in-group) or try to outdo or come out ahead of others. Disinvestment in firms that do business in morally repugnant ways is a common example of this. People relating in a Market Pricing mode need not be trying to maximize; they may just want to be fair in terms of proportional equity, as social justice research illustrates (Bierhoff, Cohen, & Greenberg 1986; Mikula, 1980). Even when people structure their interaction in a framework of prices and markets, they may not be trying to exploit others or get the most advantageous possible terms (see Kahneman, Knetsch, & Thaler 1986). As we have seen in our look at the Moose, subsistence activities are often organized around models other than Market Pricing. And people may structure their actions with reference to socially significant ratios of costs and benefits without having freedom of choice and without making collective choices and rules by subscribing to a social contract: consider taxation under a dictatorship. I cannot go into all the possible combinations of these features here, but let me illustrate with one more example. Tithing is based on a Market Pricing ratio model for contributions, but it does not necessarily involve individualism, selfishness (egoism), competitiveness, intent to maximize, material subsistence activities, freedom of choice, or voluntary contractualism.

To understand altruism, helping, and other forms of prosocial behavior, wc ccrtainly nccd to discriminate among these concepts and disentangle them empirically. Our own culture has tended to obscure these important distinctions, but we can overcome our cultural handicap by defining our terms more precisely and explicitly. Then we can determine empirically to what extent these eight aspects of social relations actually are correlated around the world.

In this chapter I have tried to show that human nature is sociable in four distinct ways. People are inherently motivated to establish and sustain four basic kinds of social relationships: Communal Sharing, Authority Ranking, Equality Matching, and Market Pricing. Market Pricing is no more natural and no more fundamental than any of the other modes of relating to others. Indeed, the Moose of Burkina Faso exemplify many traditional cultures in which Market Pricing is the least prevalent of the four forms of social interaction. Inevitably, people enact each kind of social relationship according to the implementation rules of their particular culture. The relational-models theory says that people engage in all four of the basic relationships largely for the intrinsic rewards of the relationships themselves. Except for sociopaths, people help others primarily to initiate, maintain, reinforce, or repair social relationships, not simply because of extrinsic constraints or because helping is merely an expedient means to some ulterior end. In the absence of any recognized, at least nominal, social relationship, people may be asocially oblivious to the needs of others. But, when people interact in the framework of any of these forms of social relationships, they are always prosocial, usually helpful, and often altruistic.

NOTES

1. My concept of Communal Sharing relationships builds on related conceptions developed by many social theorists over the last century, especially Tönnies's (1887-1935/1988) Gemeinschaft, Durkheim's (1893/1933) mechanical solidarity, Weber's (1922/1978) traditional authority, and the anthropological concept of generalized reciprocity (see Fiske, 1990a, for more details and many other references). It is similar to Clark and Mills's concept (1979; Mills & Clark, 1982), except that, where they define *Communal* relationships in terms of an orientation toward others' needs, I define *Communal Sharing* as a sense of equivalence of some aspect of the self in which individual identity is unmarked: what's mine is yours, and what's yours is mine.

2. Ironically, the arousal: cost-reward model of Dovidio, Piliavin, Gaertner, Schroeder, and Clark (Chapter 4, this volume), uses the term *spontaneous* for helping that is embedded in and motivated by a *preexistent* social relationship.

3. It is not by chance that these three English words have a single etymological source.

4. See Fiske (1990a, Part III) for references to this assumption in diverse social science literatures. Westen (1984), Schwartz (1986), Wellar (1986), Etzioni (1986, 1988), Palmer (1988), and Peters (1989) cite many other manifestations of it.

5. This relational theory suggests that it may be misleading to ask whether people help others with the empathic goal of benefiting others *or* to reward the self and reduce aversive arousal (see Chapter 3 by Batson and Oleson, Chapter 2 by Eisenberg and Fabes, and Chapter 4 by Dovidio, Piliavin, Gaertner, Schroeder, and Clark). In the context of a social relationship that is intrinsically rewarding for the participants, these may not be distinct alternatives: creating, sustaining, or reinforcing the relationship is often the encompassing goal. Engaging in the social relationship has secondary consequences of benefiting both participants individually, but often the participants' intention is to carry on the relationship itself.

6. They also characterized four societies as *individualistic* in the asocial null type sense that people tended to act without reference to others, disregarding any kind of social relationships. This contrasts with the socially oriented "rationalism" of Market Pricing relations, even when they are associated with individualism or competitiveness.

7. *Lineagemates* are people descended through the male line from a common ancestor and others assimilated to such a kin group.

8. They also make some private sacrifices to magical entities that they use to protect themselves and their families and to pursue personal ends.

9. Men and women of the oldest generation in her husbands' lineage call her "My child," and she calls them "My father" and "My mother."

10. Technically, this is called *leviratic widow inheritance.*

11. That is, if he has a daughter by another wife.

12. This is a striking illustration of the impact of cultural implementation rules: Moose in a Communal Sharing relationship share living space, food, work, and courtship, while Americans maintain much more separation and individual autonomy in these domains. Americans in a Communal Sharing relationship share emotions, personal histories, frustrations, hardships, wishes, hopes, and plans, while Moose maintain much more privacy and individuality about these subjective matters.

13. See Fiske (1990a) for further elaboration and parallel discussions of the cultural implementation and social realization of the other three models.

REFERENCES

Adams, J. S. (1965). Inequity in social exchange. In L. Berkowitz (Ed.), *Advances in experimental social psychology* (Vol. 2). New York: Academic Press.

Ardner, S. (1964). The comparative study of rotating credit associations. *Journal of the Royal Anthropological Institute, 94,* 201-209.

Atkinson, J. W. (Ed.). (1958). *Motives in fantasy, action, and society.* Princeton, NJ: Van Nostrand.

Bierhoff, H. W., Cohen, R. L., & Greenberg, J. (Eds.). (1986). *Justice in social relations.* (Critical Issues in Social Justice). New York: Plenum.

Blum, L. (1987). Particularity and responsiveness. In J. Kagan & S. Lamb (Eds.), *The emergence of morality in young children.* Chicago: University of Chicago Press.

Bohannan, P. (1955). Some principles of exchange and investment among the Tiv. *American Anthropologist, 57,* 60-70.

Brown, P. (1951). Patterns of authority in West Africa. *Africa, 21,* 261-278.

Clark, M. S. (1983). Some implications of close social bonds for help-seeking. In B. M. DePaulo, A. Nadler, & J. D. Fisher (Eds.), *New directions in helping: Vol. 2. Help seeking.* New York: Academic Press.

Clark, M. S., & Mills, J. (1979). Interpersonal attraction in exchange and communal relationships. *Journal of Personality and Social Psychology, 37,* 12-24.

Clark, M. S., Powell, M. C., Ouellette, R., & Milberg, S. (1987). Recipient's mood, relationship type, and helping. *Journal of Personality and Social Psychology, 53,* 94-103.

Doi, L. T. (1962). *Amae:* A key concept for understanding Japanese personality structure. In R. J. Smith & R. K. Beardsley (Eds.), *Japanese culture: Its development and characteristics.* Chicago: Aldine. (Reprinted in R. A. LeVine, Ed., 1974, *Culture and personality: Contemporary readings;* Chicago: Aldine)

Doi, L. T. (1981). *The anatomy of dependence* (2nd ed.; J. Bester, Trans.). Tokyo (New York and San Francisco): Kodansha. (Original edition published 1971)

Durkheim, E. (1933). *The division of labour in society* (G. Simpson, Trans.). New York: Free Press. (Original work published 1893, republished 1926)

Etzioni, A. (1986). The case for a multiple-utility conception. *Economics and Philosophy, 2,* 159-183.

Etzioni, A. (1988). *The moral dimension: Toward a new economics.* New York: Free Press; London: Collier Macmillan.

Firth, R. (1965). *Primitive Polynesian economy* (2nd ed.). New York: Norton. (Original edition published 1938)

Firth, R. W., & Yamey, B. S. (1964). *Capital, saving and credit in peasant societies: Studies from Asia, Oceania, the Caribbean and Middle America.* Chicago: Aldine.

Fiske, A. P. (1990a). *Structures of social life: The four elementary forms of human relations.* New York: Free Press.

Fiske, A. P. (1990b). Relativity within Moose ("Mossi") culture: Four incommensurable models for social relationships . *Ethos, 18,* 180-204.

Forge, A. (1972). The golden fleece. *Man*(n.s.), *7,* 527-540.

Fortes, M. (1945). *The dynamics of clanship among the Tallensi.* Oxford: Oxford University Press.

Fortes, M. (1969). *The web of kinship among the Tallensi: The second part of an analysis of the social structure of a Trans-Volta tribe.* Oosterhout N. B., the Netherlands: Anthropological Publications; Oxford: Oxford University Press. (Original work published 1949)

Fortes, M. (1970). *Kinship and the social order: The legacy of Lewis Henry Morgan.* Chicago: Aldine. (Original work published 1963)

Fortes, M. (1983). *Rules and the emergence of society* (Occasional paper No. 39). London: Royal Anthropological Institute of Great Britain and Ireland.

Geertz, H. (1959). The vocabulary of emotion: A study of Javanese socialization process. *Psychiatry, 22,* 225-237. (Reprinted in R. A. LeVine, Ed., 1974, *Culture and personality: Contemporary readings;* Chicago: Aldine)

Gilligan, C. (1982). *In a different voice: Psychological theory and women's development.* Cambridge, MA: Harvard University Press.

Gilligan, C., & Wiggins, G. (1987). The origins of morality in early childhood relationships. In J. Kagan & S. Lamb (Eds.), *The emergence of morality in young children.* Chicago: University of Chicago Press.

Kahneman, D., Knetsch, J. L., & Thaler, R. H. (1986). Fairness and the assumptions of economics. *Journal of Business, 59,* S285-S300.

Kluckhohn, F., & Strodtbeck, F. (1973). *Variations in value orientation.* Evanston, IL: Row, Peterson. (Reprinted by Greenwood Press, Westport, CT, 1961)

Lerner, M. J. (1975). The justice motive in social behavior: Introduction. *Journal of Social Issues, 31,* 1-19.

Lerner, M. J. (1980). *The belief in a just world: A fundamental delusion.* New York: Plenum.

Lewis, J. Van D. (1981). Domestic labor intensity and the incorporation of Malian peasant farmers into localized descent groups. *American Ethnologist, 8,* 53-73.

Llewelyn-Davies, M. (1981). Women, warriors, and patriarchs. In S. B. Ortner & H. Whitehead (Eds.), *Sexual meanings: The cultural construction of gender and sexuality.* Cambridge: Cambridge University Press.

Malinowski, B. (1961). *Argonauts of the Western Pacific: An account of native enterprise and adventure in the archipelagoes of Melanesian New Guinea.* New York: Dutton. (Original work published 1922)

Marshall, L. (1961). Sharing, talking, and giving: Relief of social tensions among !Kung Bushmen. *Africa, 31,* 231-246.

Mauss, M. (1967). *The gift: Forms and functions of exchange in archaic societies* (Ian Cunnison, Trans.). New York: Norton. (Original work published 1925)

McAdams, D. P. (1984). Human motives and personal relationships. In V. J. Derlega (Ed.), *Communication, intimacy, and close relationships.* New York: Academic Press.

McAdams, D. P. (1988). *Power, intimacy, and the life story: Personological inquiries into identity.* New York: Guilford.

McAdams, D. P. (1989). *Intimacy: The need to be close.* New York: Doubleday.

McClelland, D. C. (1975). *Power: The inner experience.* New York: Irvington (Halsted Division of John Wiley).

McClelland, D. C. (1976). *The achieving society*. New York: John Wiley. (Original work published 1967)

McClelland, D. C., Atkinson, J. W., Clark, R. A., & Lowell, E. L. (1953). *The achievement motive*. New York: Irvington.

Mead, M. (Ed.). (1961). *Cooperation and competition among primitive peoples*. Boston: Beacon. (Original work published 1937)

Mikula, G. (Ed.). (1980). *Justice and social interaction: Experimental and theoretical contributions from psychological research*. New York: Springer-Verlag; Bern: Hans Huber.

Mills, J., & Clark, M. S. (1982). Exchange and communal relationships. In L. Wheeler (Ed.), *Review of personality and social psychology* (Vol. 3). Beverly Hills, CA: Sage.

Murray, H. A. (1938). *Explorations in personality*. New York: Oxford University Press.

Palmer, H. (1988). Deeming everyone selfish. *International Journal of Moral and Social Studies, 3*, 113-125.

Paulme, D. (1940). *Organization Sociale des Dogons (Soudan Français)*. Institut de Droit Comparé, Études de Sociologie et D'Ethnologie Juridiques 32. Paris: F. Loviton (Éditions Domat-Montchrestien).

Peters, P. E. (1989). *Rational choice, agency and meanings: Notes toward a critique of Bates*. Paper presented in a session on the "Rational Man in Africa" approach of Robert Bates, at the African Studies meetings, Atlanta.

Polanyi, K. (1957). *The great transformation: The political and economic origins of our time*. New York: Rinehart. (Original work published 1944)

Polanyi, K. (1968). *Primitive, archaic, and modern economies: Essays of Karl Polanyi* (G. Dalton, Ed.). Garden City, NY: Anchor.

Polanyi, K., Arensberg, C. M., Pearson, H. W. (1957). *Trade and market in the early empires: Economies in history and theory*. Glencoe, IL: Free Press.

Richards, A. I. (1969). *Land, labor and diet in Northern Rhodesia: An economic study of the Bemba Tribe*. London: Oxford University Press for the International African Institute. (Original work published 1939)

Ricoeur, P. (1967). *The symbolism of evil* (Emerson Buchanan, Trans.). Boston: Beacon.

Sahlins, M. (1965). On the sociology of primitive exchange. In M. Banton (Ed.), *The relevance of models for social anthropology* (Association of Social Anthropologists, Monograph 1). London: Tavistock. (Reprinted in M. Sahlins, 1972, *Stone age economics;* New York: Aldine)

Schwartz, B. (1986). *The battle for human nature: Science, morality, and modern life*. New York: Norton.

Tönnies, F. (1988). *Community and society (Gemeinschaft und Gesellschaft)* (Charles P. Loomis, Trans., with an introduction by John Samples). Oxford: Transaction. (Original work published 1887-1935)

Triandis, H. C. (1972). *The analysis of subjective culture*. New York: Wiley-Interscience.

Triandis, H. C. (1987). Collectivism vs. individualism: A reconceptualization of a basic concept in cross-cultural psychology. In C. Bagley & G. K. Verma (Eds.), *Personality, cognition and values: Cross-cultural perspectives of childhood and adolescence*. London: Macmillan.

Triandis, H. C., Bontempo, R., Villareal, M. J., Asai, M., & Lucca, N. (1988). Individualism and collectivism: Cross-cultural perspective on self-ingroup relationships. *Journal of Personality and Social Psychology, 54*, 323-338.

214   *Cultural Relativity of Selfish Individualism*

Triandis, H. C., Vassiliou, V., & Nassiakou, M. (1968). Three cross-cultural studies of subjective culture. *Journal of Personality and Social Psychology, 8*(Monograph Supp. No. 4, part 2).

Udy, S. H. (1959). *Organization of work: A comparative analysis of production among nonindustrial peoples.* New Haven, CT: Human Relations Area Files Press.

Uleman, J.S.A. (1972). The need for influence: Development and validation of a measure, and comparison with the need for power. *Genetic Psychology Monographs, 85,* 157-214.

Veblen, T. (1934). *The theory of the leisure class: An economic study of institutions.* New York: Modern Library. (Original work published 1899, republished 1918)

Vélez-Ibañez, C. (1983). *Bonds of mutual trust: The cultural systems of rotating credit associations among urban Mexicans and Chicanos.* New Brunswick, NJ: Rutgers University Press.

Veroff, J. (1957). Development and validation of a projective measure of power motivation. *Journal of Abnormal and Social Psychology, 54,* 1-8.

Walster, E., Walster, G. W., & Berscheid, E., in collaboration with Austin, W., Traupmann, J., & Utne, M. K. (1978). *Equity: Theory and research.* Boston: Allyn & Bacon.

Weber, M. (1978). *Economy and society* (G. Roth and C. Wittich, Trans.). Berkeley: University of California Press. (Original work published 1922)

Wellar, R. (1986, December 4). Discussion paper at the SPA-, AES- and SCA-sponsored session, "The Directive Force of Cultural Models," at the American Anthropological Association Meetings, Philadelphia.

Westen, D. (1984). Cultural materialism: Food for thought or bum steer? *Current Anthropology, 25,* 639-653.

Winter, D. G. (1973). *The power motive.* New York: Free Press; London: Collier Macmillan.

8

Mood and Helping

MOOD AS A MOTIVATOR OF HELPING AND HELPING AS A REGULATOR OF MOOD

PETER SALOVEY
JOHN D. MAYER
DAVID L. ROSENHAN

Peter Salovey received his Ph.D. in clinical psychology from Yale University, where he is currently Associate Professor contributing to both the social/personality and the clinical psychology programs. His major research interest is the functions of human emotion, especially how emotions direct cognition, motivate social behavior, and color close relationships. Most recently, he has been concerned with complex emotions such as envy and jealousy and the influence of emotions on perceptions of health and illness.

John D. Mayer received his Ph.D. in psychology from Case Western Reserve University. He next moved to Stanford University as a postdoctoral fellow and is currently Assistant Professor of personality psychology at the University of New Hampshire. His research interests include models of mood and mood-related processes and their relation to cognitive processes and personality.

David L. Rosenhan is Professor of Psychology and Law at Stanford University. He received his Ph.D. from Columbia University. His research interests concern altruism, affect, and the psychology of religious conviction. He also works in the area of mental health law and is a major proponent of the legal rights of mental patients. His 1973 "pseudopatient" study remains a major demonstration of the effects of labeling on perceptions of psychopathology.

This chapter describes the ways in which moods motivate helping and how helping subsequently serves to regulate moods. We first review the literature on how positive and negative moods motivate helping. We

AUTHORS' NOTE: We wish to thank Ellen S. Cohn, Paula M. Niedenthal, and an anonymous reviewer for their comments on early drafts of this manuscript. We are especially appreciative of Margaret S. Clark's careful and extensive editing on several versions of this chapter. Chloé Drake and Stephanie Fishkin provided assistance in the preparation of this chapter, and we are grateful for their help. Preparation was facilitated by the following grants to Peter Salovey, NIH BRSG S07 RR07015, NCI CA 42101, NCHS 200 88 7001, and an NSF Presidential Young Investigator Award; to John D. Mayer, NIH BRSG S07 RR07108 and NIMH MH44038; and to David L. Rosenhan, a grant from the Kenneth and Harle Montgomery Fund. Please address correspondence to Peter Salovey, Department of Psychology, Yale University, Box 11A Yale Station, New Haven, CT 06520-7447.

next discuss the possible mechanisms by which moods exert their influence on helping and examine the evidence supporting those mechanisms. Then, we evaluate the proposition that helping influences mood by, for example, prolonging joy, preventing guilt, or relieving sorrow. Although this proposition seems almost self-evident, it has accrued mixed empirical support. We argue that such mixed support may result from an overly narrow conceptualization of emotional self-regulation rather than a flaw in the proposition itself. In part, experiments have only explored helping's short-term affective consequences. Although these short-term consequences are important, helping also has long-term affective ramifications that may transcend immediate mood repair or maintenance. Such long-term consequences may contribute to understanding why current moods may motivate helping. We conclude by speculating about the role that long-range affective regulation may play in understanding traditional "cold" motives for helping, in particular, social norms, and social learning.

MOOD-INDUCED HELPING

Much of the literature on mood and helping considers mood as an antecedent to helping. That is, the most common experiments manipulate mood as the independent variable and examine subjects' behaviors in response to a helping opportunity. Experiments involving the laboratory induction of mood states followed by opportunities to help another person have been conducted for the better part of three decades. Systematic reviews of this literature can be found elsewhere (Carlson, Charlin, & Miller, 1988; Carlson & Miller, 1987; Rosenhan, Karylowski, Salovey, & Hargis, 1981; Salovey & Rosenhan, 1989; Schaller & Cialdini, 1990), so we will not attempt a detailed treatment of it here. Rather, in the following sections, we review the consistent trends in mood and helping. Then, relying heavily on two recent meta-analyses (Carlson, Charlin, & Miller, 1988; Carlson & Miller, 1987), we consider the mechanisms that are the likely mediators of mood-induced helping for the pleasant and unpleasant affects. In discussing these mechanisms, we focus particularly on two that involve the regulation of mood: the maintenance of pleasant moods and the repair of unpleasant moods.

Essential Findings

The pleasant affects. The pleasant affect that has been studied most frequently in the helping area is happiness. And there is a joyful consistency to the findings. Happy moods, induced in a variety of ways, consistently motivate helping behaviors. The phenomenon has been called "the glow of good will" (Berkowitz & Connor, 1966), "the warm glow of success" (Isen, 1970), and "feel good, do good" (Rosenhan, Salovey, & Hargis, 1981). Positive feelings have been induced in a robust variety of ways: by having subjects succeed on, or receive bogus success feedback regarding, their performance on a laboratory task or game (e.g., Berkowitz & Connor, 1966; Isen, 1970; Isen, Horn, & Rosenhan, 1973; Weyant, 1978; Yinon & Bizman, 1980), think happy thoughts (e.g., Barden, Garber, Duncan, & Masters, 1981; Manucia, Baumann, & Cialdini, 1984; Moore, Underwood, & Rosenhan, 1973; O'Malley & Andrews, 1983; Rosenhan, Underwood, & Moore, 1974), find money or receive a gift (e.g., Cunningham, Steinberg, & Grev, 1980; Isen, Clark, & Schwartz, 1976; Isen & Levin, 1972), listen to pleasant music (e.g., Fried & Berkowitz, 1979), or simply experience sunny weather (e.g., Cunningham, 1979). In all of these studies, positive feelings motivated helping in a broad array of contexts that included picking up dropped books and papers, looking for contact lenses, contributing money, participating in another experiment, tutoring a needy student, and donating blood to the Red Cross.

There is, however, one interesting exception to these findings. Happy moods experienced *empathically,* rather than for self-relevant reasons, do not seem to engender helping. In laboratory experiments, when attention is focused upon the joyful experiences of *others,* either because the joy is attributed to the other's good fortune (e.g., Rosenhan, Salovey, & Hargis, 1981) or because experimental procedures discourage self-attending (e.g., Berkowitz, 1987), helping is inhibited. Given the nature of empathy, these findings are puzzling. They suggest that empathic good moods may be contaminated by envy (see Salovey & Rodin, 1984). We say more about the important role of attentional focus in mood-induced helping shortly.

The unpleasant affects. The negative moods studied most systematically as motivators of helping have been guilt and sorrow. Guilt was once thought to be the primary motivator of all altruistic behaviors (Freud, 1937; Glover, 1925). Psychoanalytic theorists argued that the motive of relieving guilt was served by redirecting psychic energy to the needs of others. Empirical evidence is consistent with psychoanalytic theory and suggests that guilt expiation motivates helping. For example, individuals are more likely to donate money to charities prior to attending confession with a priest than afterward, when guilt has presumably been reduced (Harris, Benson, & Hall, 1975). Indeed, confessing transgressions, even outside of religious contexts, seems to reduce motivation to help others by diminishing the need to expiate (Regan, 1971).

In the absence of confession, transgression creates a strong motivation to help others. That motivation seems to be mediated by the arousal of guilt rather than shame (Dienstbier, Hillman, Hillman, Lehnhoff, & Valkenaar, 1975). The belief that one has transgressed is typically induced in the laboratory by making subjects feel responsible for breaking a piece of equipment (e.g., Cunningham, Steinberg, & Grev, 1980; D. Regan, Williams, & Sparling, 1972; Wallace & Sadalla, 1966), directly or indirectly causing harm to another person (e.g., Darlington & Macker, 1966; Harris & Samerotte, 1976; Rawlings, 1968) or an animal (e.g., J. Regan, 1971), or lying to another person (e.g., Freedman, Wallington, & Bless, 1967; McMillen, 1970, 1971). When individuals believe they have transgressed, they are especially receptive to opportunities to help.

Even witnessing a person harm another can, at times, motivate helping (e.g., J. Regan, 1971). Individuals who have witnessed such transgressions but who have not transgressed themselves may experience guilt because they did not intercede on behalf of the victim. Alternatively, witnessing harm may lead to a generalized sense that the world is an unfair, harmful place, which, in turn, leads to sympathy for the victim and increased helping. Sympathy is a strong motivator of helping, as is clear in studies in which sympathy is encouraged by allowing subjects to observe the suffering of the victim (Konecni, 1972; J. Regan, 1971). Thus, when victims do not appear to suffer (or their suffering is hidden—perhaps by ghetto or concentration camp walls), helping is much less likely (Carlsmith & Gross, 1969; Freedman, Wallington, & Bless, 1967; Milgram, 1974).

In contrast to guilt, sadness appears to exert very inconsistent effects on helping. Experiences that create sadness in the laboratory— task failure, bogus feedback, thinking sad thoughts—have, in different studies, motivated helping (e.g., Cialdini, Darby, & Vincent, 1973; Donnerstein, Donnerstein, & Munger, 1975), inhibited helping (e.g.,

Moore, Underwood, & Rosenhan, 1973; Underwood, Froming, & Moore, 1977; Underwood et al., 1977), or not affected helping one way or the other (e.g., Harris & Siebal, 1975; Holloway, Tucker, & Hornstein, 1977; Isen, 1970; Rosenhan, Underwood, & Moore, 1974). In a later section of this chapter, we will discuss some of the mechanisms that might help to explain when sadness promotes or inhibits helping. For now, we would simply note that, as was the case with positive feelings, attentional focus seems to mediate the effect of sadness on helping responses. Sadness that is focused on the self is much less likely to result in helping than is sadness focused on others (Carlson & Miller, 1987; Thompson, Cowan, & Rosenhan, 1980).

Accounting for Pleasant Mood—Helping Links

Although positive mood consistently promotes helping, there is some disagreement about the mechanism that underlies this relationship. Here we review some proposed mechanisms as well as the weight of empirical evidence in their favor.

Mood affects attentional focus and thoughts about the self. One explanation for the relationship between positive mood and helping arises from the fact that most positive mood states involve positive cognitions about the self. Thus the induction of a positive mood may often carry with it shifts in attention toward the self (Salovey, 1990; Salovey & Rodin, 1985). This increased self-attention may have three consequences. First, it may make salient one's relatively advantageous resources and good fortune (Rosenhan, Salovey, & Hargis, 1981). This, in turn, may lead to a desire to help others who seem less fortunate. Second, individuals in such a self-focused state may also be more likely to conform to salient behavioral norms and ideals, if only to avoid the negative affective consequences that arise from failing to act on an obvious helping obligation (Duval & Wicklund, 1972; Gibbons & Wicklund, 1982; Vallacher & Solodky, 1979; Wicklund, 1975). Finally, the self-focus itself may amplify the affective state (Scheier & Carver, 1977), thereby intensifying the first and second effects just noted.

The idea that self-focus may play an important mediating role in the effects of positive mood on helping is supported in a recent study by Berkowitz (1987). He found that adding a manipulation of self-focused attention to a mood induction enhanced the facilitative effect of positive moods on helping. Moreover, the results of a recent meta-analysis of the positive mood and helping literature (Carlson, Charlin, & Miller,

1988) showed that, when self-focused attention was heightened, the positive mood-helping link was reliably enhanced. In contrast, when the induced happiness arose from focusing on another's good fortune, the link between positive moods and helping was attenuated, perhaps because such mood inductions recruit cognitions about one's relative *deficits,* thereby creating feelings of deprivation, resentment, or envy (Rosenhan, Salovey, & Hargis, 1981).

Mood improves perceptions of situations and of others. Another explanation for the relationship between mood and helping has been termed the *concomitance hypothesis* (Cialdini, Kenrick, & Baumann, 1982; Manucia, Baumann, & Cialdini, 1984). This hypothesis holds that happy people help more than others because good moods produce helping-relevant thoughts that motivate helping independent of the mood itself. Thus the effect of mood on helping is indirect. Positive moods increase liking toward others because happy individuals generate more positive evaluations of others than do sad individuals (Forgas & Bower, 1987; Gouaux, 1971; Griffitt, 1970; Mayer, Mamberg, & Volanth, 1988; Mayer & Volanth, 1985; Veitch & Griffitt, 1976). In addition, people in positive moods tend to see the positive side of social interactions (Forgas, Bower, & Krantz, 1984). Given that one likes another more and sees the positive side of interactions with the other, one is more likely to offer help.

Second, and closely related to the first point, positive moods may cue positive aspects of the helping situation itself (Clark & Waddell, 1983). For instance, people who are in a good mood may expect that their helpfulness will evoke gratitude and appreciation. Therefore, they are more likely to help.

Finally, positive moods may facilitate thoughts about the positive aspects of one's social community and of human nature more generally. In fact, some investigators contend that, even in the absence of mood changes, positive events produce help-engendering cognitions (Holloway, Tucker, & Hornstein, 1977; Hornstein, LaKind, Frankel, & Manne, 1975). Supporting this idea is the evidence that changes in social outlook (that may or may not be instigated by mood changes) were reliably associated with helping in the Carlson, Charlin, and Miller (1988) meta-analysis.

Mood maintenance. Still another explanation for the link between positive mood and helping is that people may help in order to maintain their positive moods. The mood maintenance hypothesis states that pleasant moods can be best maintained by making responses, including altruistic responses, that foster further pleasant feelings (Clark & Isen, 1982; Isen, Shalker, Clark, & Karp, 1978; Isen & Simmonds, 1978). In short, helping prolongs positive moods. Evidence supporting this idea comes from several sources. In two field experiments, Harris (1977) found that some forms of interpersonal helping lead to mood improvement. In another study, high school students who accepted the opportunity to help by participating in an experiment felt better than those who did not (Yinon & Landau, 1987). Helping led to enhanced mood in three studies reported by Williamson and Clark (1989), especially if the helper desired a communal relationship with the help seeker. Finally, giving advice improved the mood of advice givers in a study by Mayer, Gottlieb, Hernandez, Smith, and Gordis (1990).

Helping, however, does not invariably produce good feelings. Helpers burdened by helping tasks that are chronic and unchanging, such as caring for a family member with Alzheimer's disease, may be at risk for depression (Maslach, 1982). Also, helping those who do not seem to deserve help (such as panhandlers) may not lead to improvement in mood (Harris, 1977). We will confine our discussion, however, to those situations in which helping is likely to be experienced positively.

In addition to showing that helping improves moods, two other types of support for the mood maintenance hypothesis are found in the literature. First, some have argued that, if the mood maintenance explanation is correct, then happy people should prefer helping opportunities that are comparatively pleasant and not stressful. Support for this deduction seems rather consistent. Happy subjects who believe their moods might deteriorate through helping are less willing to offer help (Forest, Clark, Mills, & Isen, 1979; Harada, 1983; Isen & Levin, 1972; Isen & Simmonds, 1978; Shaffer & Graziano, 1983).

Second, the Carlson, Charlin, and Miller (1988) meta-analysis confirmed two predictions that support the mood maintenance hypothesis. The first prediction was that, because pleasant tasks enable better maintenance of pleasant moods, the overall pleasantness of the helping task should correlate positively with the obtained effect size. The second prediction was that intermediate levels of positive affect should lead to more helping than either very low or high levels of positive affect. The rationale for this prediction is that individuals at intermediate levels have a greater opportunity to maintain their moods than those who are either so happy they do not need to or so miserable that improvement would be difficult. Both hypotheses were supported. A correlation of .34 was obtained between the pleasantness of the helping task and the degree to which positive mood motivated helping, while a correlation of .38 was found between moderate degrees of pleasantness and helping (reported as a lack of deviation of mood from an average value).

Accounting for Unpleasant Mood—Helping Links

The influence of negative moods on helping is more complex than that for positive moods. Guilt generally facilitates helping behavior, but sorrow evokes mixed results. Three mechanisms have been posited to explain the pattern of results obtained in the negative mood literature. First, sadness may influence attentional focus, which, in turn, may influence helping. Second, negative mood manipulations may influence felt responsibility to help. And, finally, helping may serve to relieve all negative states because helping makes one feel good (Carlson & Miller, 1987).

Mood influences the content of thoughts and attentional focus. Sadness may influence helping by increasing the salience of negative thoughts while simultaneously influencing focus of attention. If sadness is induced in a self-relevant way, such as recalling the sad events of the past, attention may well drift to other mood-congruent thoughts. Thoughts of deprivation, helplessness, and uselessness may become especially available, rendering such sad and self-focused individuals less likely to help because they are preoccupied with self and/or with perceptions that they are disadvantaged compared with others. Supporting this idea is evidence that the self-preoccupation of sad individuals (see, for example, Pyszczynski & Greenberg, 1987; Wood, Saltzberg & Goldsamt, 1990) retards helping unless the request for help is made extremely salient and cannot be ignored (Mayer, Duval, Holtz, & Bowman, 1985; McMillen, Sanders, & Solomon, 1977; but see Wegner & Schaefer, 1978). In contrast, sad individuals become *more* helpful if their sadness is felt in conjunction with attention directed externally to the plight of others. In an experiment in which subjects experienced sadness by hearing a description of a friend dying from cancer, helping increased if subjects attended to the pain and suffering of their dying friend but decreased if they thought about their own feelings of loss (Thompson, Cowan, & Rosenhan, 1980; see also Barnett, King, & Howard, 1979; Kidd & Marshall, 1982).

There has been some confusion in the literature between self versus other and internal versus external foci of attention (Carlson & Miller,

1987). Although these two dimensions seem conceptually similar, they are not. One can attend to one's own thoughts (internally focused) regarding another (other focused). In the cancer study described above, for example, self versus other focus, not internally versus externally directed attention, was manipulated. The Carlson and Miller (1987) meta-analysis suggested that the self/other distinction is critical: The partial correlation between concern for another person and helping after negative mood induction was .30. On the other hand, internal versus external focus was unrelated to altruism following negative mood induction.

Felt responsibility. Still another explanation for observed links between negative moods and helping has to do with the way in which certain negative moods, guilt in particular, influence a person's felt responsibility for aiding another. Guilt is increased when one feels responsible for the welfare of someone else who is suffering. Thus, when a child entrusted to your care becomes ill, you help. When such felt responsibility is minimized by preoccupation with one's own negative feelings, helping is inhibited, especially when requests for help are not salient or legitimate (Aderman & Berkowitz, 1983; Gibbons & Wicklund, 1982; Rogers, Miller, Mayer, & Duval, 1982).

Negative-state relief. Individuals who wish to terminate their negative mood may be helpful to others as a way of repairing their bad mood. Helping, in this sense, is an instrumental motive in the service of improving mood (Manucia, Baumann, & Cialdini, 1984). This is the so-called negative-state relief account of altruistic behavior. Cialdini and his colleagues (e.g., Cialdini & Kenrick, 1976; Schaller & Cialdini, 1990) have proposed that individuals are motivated to relieve negative feeling states and use helping as a strategy to this end. This view is based on the idea that helping serves a self-reinforcing function (Weiss, Boyer, Lombardo, & Stitch, 1973; Weiss, Buchanan, Alstatt, & Lombardo, 1971) and that helping and self-gratification are functionally equivalent as a means of alleviating sad moods (Baumann, Cialdini, & Kenrick, 1981).

The primary evidence for mood repair as the motivator of helping comes from studies in which sadness is induced and avenues other than the helping opportunity to improve mood are made available. For example, if subjects are rewarded following negative mood induction but before they have an opportunity to help, they are no more likely to help than neutral mood control subjects (Cialdini, Darby, & Vincent, 1973; Cunningham, Steinberg, & Grev, 1980). Moreover, if subjects do not believe their moods can be improved by helping, they do not help following negative mood induction (Manucia, Baumann, & Cialdini, 1984).

The literature on guilt as a motivator for helping is also taken as evidence for negative-state relief. Guilty individuals help rather consistently. For instance, shoppers in a mall were asked to take a photo of an experimental confederate. Those in the guilt condition who were made to feel as if they had broken the camera were later more willing than the controls to help a second shopper (actually, a second confederate) who lost candy through the torn corner of her shopping bag (D. Regan, Williams, & Sparling, 1972). These studies indicated that guilty individuals attempt to repair their guilt through helping others. (The positive findings concerning the repair of guilt, however, did not clearly generalize to relieving other negative moods.)

We should mention as well that theory and findings discussed earlier in the section on positive mood maintenance and helping are just as relevant to the negative-state relief hypothesis. The positive mood enhancement generated by helping in studies by Harris (1977), Yinon and Landau (1987), Williamson and Clark (1989), and Mayer, Gottlieb, Hernandez, Smith, and Gordis (1990) could be also expected to relieve the mood of sad subjects.

Nevertheless, the findings regarding the negative-state relief hypothesis are by no means uniformly supportive. Carlson and Miller's (1987) meta-analysis tested three hypotheses regarding negative-state relief. First, they suggested that, because socialization leads to greater recognition of how helping others results in feeling better, subject age should correlate with effect size. Second, the sadder or more depressed the initial mood (as generated by a given negative mood induction), the more helping should be motivated. Third, the distastefulness of helping should correlate negatively with the effect size on the grounds that distasteful (e.g., effortful, costly) helping should be less apt to improve one's mood.

Carlson and Miller found no support for any of the three hypotheses. The relation between sadness and helping was nonsignificant ($r = .08$), as was that for age ($r = -.13$). Distastefulness of the helping task was significant in the wrong direction ($r = .33$), suggesting that greater unpleasantness might lead to greater feelings of virtue. It is interesting that guilt *did* predict effect size, correlating significantly and highly ($r = .50$) with helping behavior. The authors concluded that negative-state relief is inadequate to explain the increased helping behavior of saddened subjects, but they suggested an exception be made specifically for guilt.

Although the Carlson and Miller (1987) meta-analysis did not provide much evidence for the negative-state relief model of helping (but see Cialdini & Fultz, 1990; Miller & Carlson, 1990), some promising findings have been reported in the subsequent literature (Batson et al., 1989; Cialdini et al., 1987; Schaller & Cialdini, 1988). Schaller and Cialdini (1988), for example, found that altruistic behavior on the part of sad subjects declined if alternative cheering-up situations, such as exposure to humorous, mood-enhancing information, were available as alternatives to helping. On the other hand, the evidence for negative-state relief provided by the Manucia, Baumann, and Cialdini (1984) study was not replicated in a recent experiment by Schroeder, Dovidio, Sibicky, Mathews, and Allen (1988), who found beliefs about the lability of one's mood did not mediate the relationship between the arousal of empathy and helping.

MOOD REGULATION AND ALTRUISM

A Long-Term Perspective

We have examined the ways in which moods influence helping, and now we wish to shift gears a bit and look at the connections between mood and helping from a broader perspective. When we discussed mood maintenance explanations for the impact of positive moods on helping and mood repair explanations for some of the impact of negative moods on helping, we already touched on how helping may influence moods. That is, people may often help in order to maintain their immediate positive moods, and they may also help in order to alleviate their immediate negative states (or, at least, their guilt). But is that the end of the story of links between helping and mood? We think not. We believe the impact of helping on moods goes further. Despite the Carlson and Miller (1987) failure to find support for a mood repair explanation of the relationship between negative mood and helping, we are not quite ready to give up on the idea that helping may serve to regulate moods (and neither are Cialdini & Fultz, 1990). In particular, in this section, we wish to argue, first, that people may help in order to regulate their moods over *quite long periods of time* (in addition to the immediate boost in moods helping may provide) and, second, that this is possible because humans may be unique in their ability to see the possibility of strategically delaying short-term pleasure for greater long-term good and, in fact, often do so.

By *long-term regulation,* we mean habitual ways of organizing life's experiences such that long-term outcomes generate satisfaction and positive feeling. People have many goals in their lives, some of which are long term and unfold over time (e.g., seeing one's children grow to be responsible, independent citizens). These goals can often be met by helping others. We may help others in order to obtain these long-term goals (and their associated satisfactions) *even when the short-term consequences may be quite negative.* Indeed, one of the paradoxes of altruism—that it seems to be a behavior that is persistent, on one hand, but is often unpleasant and unrewarded, on the other (Rosenhan, 1978)—is resolved in this analysis. Christians who rescued Jews from the Nazis probably experienced little immediate pleasure and may well have suffered considerable costs and negative affect (London, 1970; Stein, 1988). Nonetheless, by providing haven for Jews, they also achieved a longer-term goal of being able to reflect on their actions later with great satisfaction. Oliner and Oliner (1988), in this regard, conducted intensive interviews with rescuers of Jews in Nazi Europe. The reflections of these rescuers, subject to all of the biases of retrospectivity, suggest that altruistic behaviors do have long-term affective influences with consequences that often extend even beyond the helper. Indeed, one daughter said of her mother, "It is so important to know that people like my mother, who did not blow up trains or shoot people in the dark, did what she was really cut out to do—to sustain life rather than destroy it. People like her have made such a difference in the world" (Oliner & Oliner, 1988, p. 230).

The kind of altruism of which we write need not be so dramatic as rescue behavior. Consider a more commonplace example: a mother's willingness to allow herself to be interrupted from a pleasurable task to help her daughter and contribute to the child's long-term well-being. The immediate consequence to the mother might well be aversive, but, later, the child's superior self-confidence might reward the mother in many ways. Even current annoyance might be tempered by the positive feelings arising from anticipated future pleasures associated with having met the altruistic goals. Thus helping immediately may serve a long-term mood-regulatory function.

Much as long-term goals can be facilitated by helping, they can be harmed by not helping. Parents who fail to help their children at crucial times, for example, may not experience negative consequences immediately but may well experience negative consequences in the long run (e.g., by raising a child who cares little about them). Helpers often anticipate such consequences. They know that, if they do not help, they will feel bad in the present and, perhaps, even worse in the future.

Thus, when we talk about helping as a form of mood regulation, we take a broader perspective than has been done in the past. Such a long-term perspective seems to clarify some of the initial perplexing findings that are already available in the literature. Consider, for instance, the prediction of Carlson and Miller (1987) that more helping will occur when the helping task is positive, presumably because distasteful helping should be less apt to improve one's mood. This prediction did not receive support in their meta-analysis. But the prediction makes sense only if one considers the immediate, salient consequences of helping. What if one thinks about the helper's long-term goals? If one's long-term goal is to be a person who lives up to one's moral standards, and if striving toward that goal brings pleasure, then helping in a distasteful task may well be more reinforcing than helping in a pleasant one. After all, if one does something especially risky or costly such as saving Jews from Nazis, then one can find consolation in being an especially good person.

The reason that helping serves a long-term mood-regulatory function is that people think strategically about the future. But do people necessarily think about the positive impact of helping on long-term happiness each and every time they help? They may, which may motivate some acts of helping. And, they may not. They may simply help to facilitate a long-term goal, without thinking about the consequences for mood. Or they may simply help out of habit. But, in all three cases, helping will have positive implications for their current and future moods because a long-term goal was facilitated.

The Strategic Regulation of Mood

There is little research on the ways in which helping serves longer-term goals. But it may be useful to examine a related literature for clues about the direction of future research. This literature concerns the ways in which individuals think about and attempt to regulate their *ongoing* mood states.

There is a set of secondary, reflective experiences of mood, called *meta-experiences of mood,* that regulate mood by monitoring, evaluating, and often changing it (Mayer & Gaschke, 1988). For example, some people think positive thoughts to alleviate a bad mood or remind themselves of reality to bring down a mood that is too happy or out of control. Thinking positive thoughts or reminding oneself of reality are meta-experiences of mood whose central function is regulatory.

Individuals often regulate mood through plans and associated actions that are quite deliberate and involved. For example, mood can be regulated by choosing the people with whom we associate or situations we enter. If we would like to experience pride, we can invite a famous (but not too similar) friend for dinner, or we can leaf through the photograph album of our daughter's bat mitzvah (Tesser, Millar, & Moore, 1988). We are often motivated to seek information that maintains a positive view of ourselves (Tesser, 1986, 1988). Moreover, when individuals help others, their moods improve (Harris, 1977; Mayer, Gottlieb, Hernandez, Smith, & Gordis, 1990). For example, Mayer, Gottlieb, Hernandez, Smith, and Gordis (1990) randomly assigned the role of advice giver and advice seeker to undergraduates. Those who *gave* advice showed improvements in mood.

In previous work (Mayer, DiPaolo, & Salovey, 1990; Salovey & Mayer, 1990), we identified a set of skills concerning the appropriate recognition of emotions in the self and others and the use of emotional information to solve problems and motivate behavior. We label these skills *emotional intelligence.* One aspect of emotional intelligence is the recognition, first, that one can regulate mood by behaving in certain ways and, second, that behavior may have long-term as well as short-term affective consequences. Future research may discover that the tendencies to self-regulate moods and to think about long-term affective consequences arise from reliable individual differences. The identification of individuals with such skills may help to clarify the mixed support that, for example, the negative-state relief model of helping has received.

EMOTIONAL INVOLVEMENT IN TRADITIONAL
EXPLANATIONS FOR HELPING BEHAVIOR

In this discussion of moods as motivators for helping behavior and the role of helping behavior in mood regulation, the traditional social psychological explanations for helping behavior—social learning and adherence to norms—have been conspicuously absent. The reason is that such social psychological explanations have not employed affect as a significant determinant. In this final section, we suggest that affective processes can be integrated into traditional explanations for helping. Little data supporting such an integration exist yet. Nevertheless, these ideas are offered as suggestions for further work.

Social Learning

Social learning theories explain helping and altruism in terms of personal assessment of the likely consequences of the behavior and one's capacities to carry out the required actions. For instance, individuals evaluate the costs associated with helping versus not helping in any situation (Piliavin, Dovidio, Gaertner, & Clark, 1981; Piliavin, Piliavin, & Rodin, 1975). Observation of the helpfulness of others also motivates the individual to offer help. Models can make helping salient, demonstrate what appropriate helping would be, and increase self-efficacy on the part of would-be helpers (Bandura, 1973; Krebs, 1970; Latané & Darley, 1970; Rosenhan & White, 1967). Reinforcement history associated with prior helping acts may also motivate subsequent helping. Individuals who have experienced the gratitude of previous recipients of their help may be more likely to seek such gratitude in the future (Moss & Page, 1972).

Although social learning formulations have not emphasized emotional processes as motivators of helping, recent research suggests that perceptions of helping efficacy, for example, may be profoundly influenced by mood. Salovey (1987-1988) constructed a helping self-efficacy scale and asked subjects to indicate their confidence in their ability to carry out required helping behaviors in 20 different situations (such as helping a roommate with homework for several hours, calling the police after hearing a scream, or donating money to the annual office charity drive). Helping self-efficacy was very mood sensitive. After a laboratory mood induction procedure, happy subjects viewed themselves as much more capable of performing helping acts than control subjects. And helping self-efficacy scores were lowest among sad subjects.

Affect is implicated in other social learning explanations for helping. The idea that helping can be used to regulate mood, and especially to relieve negative states, is probably learned both vicariously (by

watching significant others become happier after helping) and through
repeated, positively reinforced experiences (see Weiss, Buchanan,
Alstatt, & Lombardo, 1971). Consistent with this view are findings
that older children who had the benefit of social learning experiences
are more likely to help following negative moods than younger children (Cialdini, Baumann, & Kenrick, 1981; Cialdini & Kenrick, 1976;
Kenrick, Baumann, & Cialdini, 1979).

Societal Norms

Another traditional explanation for helping and altruism concerns
the internalization of various helping norms. One such norm is *reciprocity* (Gouldner, 1960), the idea that giving help involves a quid pro quo,
an equitable exchange of resources. Another is *social responsibility,* a
helping norm that refers to an obligation or civic duty to help others in
certain situations (Berkowitz & Daniels, 1963; Schwartz, 1977). The
selflessness norm refers to the performance of charitable acts with
no expectation of extrinsic gain.

Norm-based explanations for helping behavior have not generally
included affect as a motivator. Yet, affect may be implicated in the
operation of helping norms in two ways. First, different emotions may
facilitate the accessibility of different helping norms, and, second,
conformity to helping norms may help to regulate mood. By presenting subjects with descriptions of helping acts and then asking them to
generate the reasons for helping in each situation, we ascertained that
happiness, for example, increased the saliency of norms concerning
selflessness and charity, decreased the saliency of reciprocity motives,
and had no influence at all on social responsibility (Salovey, 1987-
1988).

Moreover, individuals may conform to helping norms to regulate
their emotions. Selflessness-inspired helping may elicit or maintain
great joy and relieve guilt. Not adhering to norms of social responsibility can produce shame; pride emanates from doing one's civic duty.
When reciprocity is operating, individuals may feel confident and
capable and, when it breaks down, helpless. Furthermore, a strong belief in a just and cooperative world that is maintained by doing good
works may be an excellent way to strategically maximize one's positive mood.

CONCLUSION

In reviewing the literature on the mood-helping relationship, it is important that attention be directed to the regulatory mechanisms that maintain pleasant moods and relieve unpleasant ones. It is clear that individuals may use helping opportunities to regulate their moods over the long term. Long-term regulation looks to maximize pleasure globally over time. An examination of the time frames for mood regulation may enrich theoretical work on the affective consequences of helping and clarify conflicting findings about its importance. Finally, affective processes may well be hidden in traditional social psychological explanations. These processes remain to be explicated.

REFERENCES

Aderman, D., & Berkowitz, L. (1983). Self-concern and the unwillingness to be helpful. *Social Psychology Quarterly, 46,* 293-301.

Bandura, A. (1973). *Aggression: A social learning analysis.* Englewood Cliffs, NJ: Prentice-Hall.

Barden, R. C., Garber, J., Duncan, S. W., & Masters, J. C. (1981). Cumulative effects of induced affective states in children: Accentuation, inoculation, and remediation. *Journal of Personality and Social Psychology, 40,* 750-760.

Barnett, M. A., King, L. M., & Howard, J. A. (1979). Inducing affect about self or other: Effects on generosity in children. *Developmental Psychology, 15,* 164-167.

Batson, C. D., Batson, J. G., Griffitt, C. A., Barrientos, S., Brandt, J. R., Sprengelmeyer, P., & Bayly, M. J. (1989). Negative-state relief and empathy-altruism hypothesis. *Journal of Personality and Social Psychology, 56,* 922-933.

Baumann, D. J., Cialdini, R. B., & Kenrick, D. T. (1981). Altruism as hedonism: Helping and self-gratification as equivalent responses. *Journal of Personality and Social Psychology, 40,* 1039-1046.

Berkowitz, L. (1987). Mood, self-awareness, and willingness to help. *Journal of Personality and Social Psychology, 52,* 721-729.

Berkowitz, L., & Connor, W. H. (1966). Success, failure, and social responsibility. *Journal of Personality and Social Psychology, 3,* 664-669.

Berkowitz, L., & Daniels, L. R. (1963). Responsibility and dependency. *Journal of Abnormal and Social Psychology, 66,* 427-436.

Carlsmith, J. M., & Gross, A. E. (1969). Some effects of guilt on compliance. *Journal of Personality and Social Psychology, 11,* 232-239.

Carlson, M., Charlin, V., & Miller, N. (1988). Positive mood and helping behavior: A test of six hypotheses. *Journal of Personality and Social Psychology, 55,* 211-229.

Carlson, M., & Miller, N. (1987). Explanation of the relationship between negative mood and helping. *Psychological Bulletin, 102,* 91-108.

Cialdini, R. B., Baumann, D. J., & Kenrick, D. T. (1981). Insights from sadness: A three-step model of altruism as hedonism. *Developmental Review, 1,* 207-223.

Cialdini, R. B., Darby, B. L., & Vincent, J. E. (1973). Transgression and altruism: A case for hedonism. *Journal of Experimental Social Psychology, 9,* 502-516.

Cialdini, R. B., & Fultz, J. (1990). Interpreting the negative mood-helping literature via "mega"-analysis: A contrary view. *Psychological Bulletin, 107,* 210-214.

Cialdini, R. B., & Kenrick, D. (1976). Altruism as hedonism: A social development perspective on the relationship of negative mood state and helping. *Journal of Personality and Social Psychology, 34,* 907-914.

Cialdini, R. B., Kenrick, D. T., & Baumann, D. J. (1982). Effects of mood on prosocial behavior in children and adults. In N. Eisenberg (Ed.), *The development of prosocial behavior.* New York: Academic Press.

Cialdini, R. B., Schaller, M., Houlihan, D., Arps, K., Fultz, J., & Beaman, A. L. (1987). Empathy-based helping: Is it selflessly or selfishly motivated? *Journal of Personality and Social Psychology, 52,* 749-758.

Clark, M. S., & Isen, A. M. (1982). Toward understanding the relationship between feeling states and social behavior. In A. H. Hastorf & A. M. Isen (Eds.), *Cognitive social psychology* (pp. 73-108). New York: Elsevier.

Clark, M. S., & Waddell, B. A. (1983). Effects of moods on thoughts about helping, attraction, and information acquisition. *Social Psychology Quarterly, 46,* 31-35.

Cunningham, M. R. (1979). Weather, mood, and helping behavior: The sunshine samaritan. *Journal of Personality and Social Psychology, 37,* 1947-1956.

Cunningham, M. R., Steinberg, J., & Grev, R. (1980). Wanting to and having to help: Separate motivations for positive mood and guilt-induced helping. *Journal of Personality and Social Psychology, 38,* 181-192.

Darlington, R. B., & Macker, C. E. (1966). Displacement of guilt-produced altruistic behavior. *Journal of Personality and Social Psychology, 4,* 442-443.

Dienstbier, R. A., Hillman, D., Hillman, J., Lehnhoff, J., & Valkenaar, M. C. (1975). An emotional-attribution approach to moral behavior: Interfacing cognitive and avoidance theories of moral development. *Psychology Review, 82,* 299-315.

Donnerstein, E., Donnerstein, M., & Munger, G. (1975). Helping behavior as a function of pictorially induced moods. *Journal of Social Psychology, 97,* 221-225.

Duval, S., & Wicklund, R. A. (1972). *A theory of objective self-awareness.* New York: Academic Press.

Forest, D., Clark, M. S., Mills, J., & Isen, A. M. (1979). Helping as a function of feeling state and nature of the helping behavior. *Motivation and Emotion, 3,* 161-169.

Forgas, J. P., & Bower, G. H. (1987). Mood effects on person-perception judgments. *Journal of Personality and Social Psychology, 53,* 53-60.

Forgas, J. P., Bower, G. H., & Krantz, S. E. (1984). The influence of mood on perceptions of social interactions. *Journal of Experimental Social Psychology, 20,* 497-513.

Freedman, J. L., Wallington, S. A., & Bless, E. (1967). Compliance without pressure: The effects of guilt. *Journal of Personality and Social Psychology, 7,* 117-124.

Freud, S. (1937). *The ego and the mechanisms of defense.* London: Hogarth.

Fried, R., & Berkowitz, L. (1979). Music hath charms . . . and can influence helplessness. *Journal of Applied Social Psychology, 9,* 199-208.

Gibbons, F. X., & Wicklund, R. A. (1982). Self-focused attention and helping behavior. *Journal of Personality and Social Psychology, 43,* 462-474.

Glover, E. (1925). Notes on oral character formation. *International Journal of Psychoanalysis, 6,* 131-154.

Gouaux, C. (1971). Induced affective states and interpersonal attraction. *Journal of Personality and Social Psychology, 20,* 37-43.

Gouldner, A. (1960). The norm of reciprocity: A preliminary statement. *American Sociological Review, 25,* 161-178.

Griffitt, W. B. (1970). Environmental effects of interpersonal behavior: Ambient effective temperature and attraction. *Journal of Personality and Social Psychology, 15,* 240-244.

Harada, J. (1983). The effects of positive and negative experiences on helping behavior. *Japanese Psychological Research, 25,* 47-51.

Harris, M. B. (1977). Effects of altruism on mood. *Journal of Social Psychology, 102,* 197-208.

Harris, M. B., Benson, S. M., & Hall, C. (1975). The effects of confession on altruism. *Journal of Social Psychology, 96,* 187-192.

Harris, M. B., & Samerotte, G. C. (1976). The effects of actual and attempted theft, need, and a previous favor on altruism. *Journal of Social Psychology, 99,* 193-202.

Harris, M., & Siebal, C. (1975). Affect, aggression, and altruism. *Developmental Psychology, 11,* 623-627.

Holloway, S., Tucker, L., & Hornstein, H. (1977). The effect of social and nonsocial information in interpersonal behavior of males: The news makes news. *Journal of Personality and Social Psychology, 35,* 514-522.

Hornstein, H. A., LaKind, E., Frankel, G., & Manne, S. (1975). Effects of knowledge about remote social events on prosocial behavior, social conception, and mood. *Journal of Personality and Social Psychology, 32,* 1038-1046.

Isen, A. M. (1970). Success, failure, attention and reaction to others: The warm glow of success. *Journal of Personality and Social Psychology, 15,* 294-301.

Isen, A. M., Clark, M., & Schwartz, M. F. (1976). Duration of the effect of good mood on helping: "Footprints in the sands of time." *Journal of Personality and Social Psychology, 34,* 385-393.

Isen, A. M., Horn, N., & Rosenhan, D. L. (1973). Effect of success and failure on children's generosity. *Journal of Personality and Social Psychology, 27,* 239-247.

Isen, A. M., & Levin, P. F. (1972). The effect of feeling good on helping: Cookies and kindness. *Journal of Personality and Social Psychology, 21,* 384-388.

Isen, A. M., Shalker, T. E., Clark, M., & Karp, L. (1978). Affect, accessibility of material in memory, and behavior: A cognitive loop? *Journal of Personality and Social Psychology, 36,* 1-12.

Isen, A. M., & Simmonds, S. F. (1978). The effect of feeling good on a helping task that is incompatible with good mood. *Social Psychology, 41,* 345-349.

Kenrick, D. T., Baumann, D. J., & Cialdini, R. B. (1979). A step in the socialization of altruism as hedonism: Effects of negative mood on children's generosity under public and private conditions. *Journal of Personality and Social Psychology, 37,* 747-755.

Kidd, R. F., & Marshall, L. (1982). Self-regulation, mood, and helpful behavior. *Journal of Research in Personality, 16,* 319-334.

Konecni, V. J. (1972). Some effects of guilt on compliance: A field replication. *Journal of Personality and Social Psychology, 23,* 30-32.

Krebs, D. L. (1970). Altruism: An examination of the concept and review of the literature. *Psychological Bulletin, 73,* 258-302.

Latané, B., & Darley, J. (1970). *The unresponsive bystander: Why doesn't he help?* New York: Appleton-Century-Crofts.

London, P. (1970). The rescuers: Motivational hypotheses about Christians who saved Jews from the Nazis. In J. Macaulay & L. Berkowitz (Eds.), *Altruism and helping behavior.* New York: Academic Press.

Manucia, G. K., Baumann, D. J., & Cialdini, R. B. (1984). Mood influences on helping: Direct effects or side effects? *Journal of Personality and Social Psychology, 46,* 357-364.

Maslach, C. (1982). *Burnout: The cost of caring.* Englewood Cliffs, NJ: Prentice-Hall.

Mayer, F. S., Duval, S., Holtz, R., & Bowman, C. (1985). Self-focus, helping request salience, felt responsibility, and helping behavior. *Personality and Social Psychology Bulletin, 11,* 133-144.

Mayer, J. D., DiPaolo, M., & Salovey, P. (1990). Perceiving affective content in ambiguous visual stimuli: A component of emotional intelligence. *Journal of Personality Assessment, 54,* 772-781.

Mayer, J. D., & Gaschke, Y. N. (1988). The experience and meta-experience of mood. *Journal of Personality and Social Psychology, 55,* 102-111.

Mayer, J. D., Gottlieb, A., Hernandez, M., Smith, J., & Gordis, F. (1990). *Advice and self-regulation.* Manuscript in preparation.

Mayer, J. D., Mamberg, M. H., & Volanth, A. J. (1988). Cognitive domains of the mood system. *Journal of Personality, 56,* 453-486.

Mayer, J. D., & Volanth, A. J. (1985). Cognitive involvement in the emotional response system. *Motivation and Emotion, 9,* 261-275.

McMillen, D. L. (1970). Transgression, fate control and compliant behavior. *Psychonomic Science, 21,* 103-104.

McMillen, D. L. (1971). Transgression, self-image and compliant behavior. *Journal of Personality and Social Psychology, 20,* 176-179.

McMillen, D. L., Sanders, D. Y., & Solomon, G. S. (1977). Self-esteem, attentiveness, and helping behavior. *Personality and Social Psychology Bulletin, 3,* 257-261.

Milgram, S. (1974). *Obedience to authority.* New York: Harper & Row.

Miller, N., & Carlson, M. (1990). Valid theory-testing meta-analyses further question the negative state relief model of helping. *Psychological Bulletin, 107,* 215-225.

Moore, B., Underwood, B., & Rosenhan, D. L. (1973). Affect and altruism. *Developmental Psychology, 8,* 99-104.

Moss, M. K., & Page, R. A. (1972). Reinforcement and helping behavior. *Journal of Applied Psychology, 2,* 360-371.

Oliner, S. P., & Oliner, P. M. (1988). *The altruistic personality: Rescuers of Jews in Nazi Europe.* New York: Free Press.

O'Malley, M. N., & Andrews, L. (1983). The effect of mood and incentives on helping: Are there some things money can't buy? *Motivation and Emotion, 7,* 179-189.

Piliavin, J. A., Dovidio, J. F., Gaertner, S. L., & Clark, R. D. (1981). *Emergency intervention.* New York: Academic Press.

Piliavin, I. M., Piliavin, J. A., & Rodin, J. (1975). Costs, diffusion, and the stigmatized victim. *Journal of Personality and Social Psychology, 32,* 429-438.

Pyszczynski, T., & Greenberg, J. (1987). Self-regulatory perseveration and the depressive self-focusing style: A self-awareness theory of depression. *Psychological Bulletin, 102*, 122-138.

Rawlings, E. I. (1968). Witnessing harm to others: A reassessment of the role of guilt in altruistic behavior. *Journal of Personality and Social Psychology, 10*, 337-380.

Regan, D. T., Williams, M., & Sparling, S. (1972). Voluntary expiation of guilt: A field experiment. *Journal of Personality and Social Psychology, 24*, 42-45.

Regan, J. W. (1971). Guilt, perceived injustice, and altruistic behavior. *Journal of Personality and Social Psychology, 18*, 124-132.

Rogers, M., Miller, N., Mayer, F. S., & Duval, S. (1982). Personal responsibility and salience of the request for help: Determinants of the relations between negative affect and helping behavior. *Journal of Personality and Social Psychology, 43*, 956-970.

Rosenhan, D. L. (1978). Toward resolving the altruism paradox: Affect, self-reinforcement, and cognition. In L. Wispé (Ed.), *Altruism, sympathy and helping* (pp. 101-113). New York: Academic Press.

Rosenhan, D. L., Karylowski, J., Salovey, P., & Hargis, K. (1981). Emotion and altruism. In J. P. Rushton & R. M. Sorrentino (Eds.), *Altruism and helping behavior* (pp. 233-248). Hillsdale, NJ: Lawrence Erlbaum.

Rosenhan, D. L., Salovey, P., & Hargis, K. (1981). The joys of helping: Focus of attention mediates the impact of positive affect on helping. *Journal of Personality and Social Psychology, 40*, 899-905.

Rosenhan, D. L., Underwood, B., & Moore, B. S. (1974). Affect moderates self-gratification and altruism. *Journal of Personality and Social Psychology, 30*, 546-552.

Rosenhan, D. L., & White, G. (1967). Observation and rehearsal as determinants of prosocial behavior. *Journal of Personality and Social Psychology, 4*, 253-259.

Salovey, P. (1987-1988). *The effects of mood and focus of attention on self-relevant thoughts and helping intention* (Doctoral dissertation, Yale University, 1986). *Dissertation Abstracts International, 48*(10), 3121B.

Salovey, P. (1990). *Mood-induced self-focused attention*. Unpublished manuscript, Yale University.

Salovey, P., & Mayer, J. D. (1990). Emotional intelligence. *Imagination, Cognition, and Personality, 9*, 185-211.

Salovey, P., & Rodin, J. (1984). Some antecedents and consequences of social-comparison jealousy. *Journal of Personality and Social Psychology, 47*, 780-792.

Salovey, P., & Rodin, J. (1985). Cognitions about the self: Connecting feeling states and social behavior. In P. Shaver (Ed.), *Self, situations, and social behavior: Review of personality and social psychology* (Vol. 6, pp. 143-166). Beverly Hills, CA: Sage.

Salovey, P., & Rosenhan, D. L. (1989). Mood states and prosocial behavior. In H. L. Wagner & A. S. R. Manstead (Eds.), *Handbook of psychophysiology: Emotion and social behavior* (pp. 371-391). Chichester, England: John Wiley.

Schaller, M., & Cialdini, R. B. (1988). The economics of empathic helping: Support for a mood management motive. *Journal of Experimental Social Psychology, 24*, 163-181.

Schaller, M., & Cialdini, R. B. (1990). Happiness, sadness, and helping: A motivational integration. In R. M. Sorrentino & E. T. Higgins (Eds.), *Handbook of motivation and cognition: Foundations of social behavior* (Vol. 2). New York: Guilford.

Scheier, M. F., & Carver, C. S. (1977). Self-focused attention and the experience of emotion: Attraction, repulsion, elation, and depression. *Journal of Personality and Social Psychology, 35*, 625-636.

Schroeder, D., Dovidio, J. F., Sibicky, M. E., Mathews, L. L., & Allen, J. L. (1988). Empathic concern and helping behavior: Egoism or altruism? *Journal of Experimental Social Psychology, 24,* 333-353.

Schwartz, S. H. (1977). Normative influences on altruism. In L. Berkowitz (Ed.), *Advances in experimental social psychology* (Vol. 10). New York: Academic Press.

Shaffer, D. R., & Graziano, W. G. (1983). Effects of positive and negative moods on helping tasks having pleasant or unpleasant consequences. *Motivation and Emotion, 7,* 269-278.

Stein, A. (1988). *Quiet heroes: True stories of the rescue of Jews by Christians in Nazi-occupied Holland.* Toronto: Lester and Orpen Dennys.

Tesser, A. (1986). Some effects of self-evaluation maintenance on cognition and action. In R. M. Sorrentino & E. T. Higgins (Eds.), *Handbook of motivation and cognition: Foundations of social behavior* (pp. 435-464). New York: Guilford.

Tesser, A. (1988). Toward a self-evaluation maintenance model of social behavior. In L. Berkowitz (Ed.), *Advances in experimental social psychology* (Vol. 21, pp. 181-227). San Diego, CA: Academic Press.

Tesser, A., Millar, M., & Moore, J. (1988). Some affective consequences of social comparison and reflection processes: The pain and pleasure of being close. *Journal of Personality and Social Psychology, 54,* 49-61.

Thompson, W. C., Cowan, C. L., & Rosenhan, D. L. (1980). Focus of attention mediates the impact of negative affect on altruism. *Journal of Personality and Social Psychology, 38,* 291-300.

Underwood, B., Berenson, J. F., Berenson, R. J., Cheng, K. K., Wilson, D., Kulik, J., Moore, B. S., & Wenzel, G. (1977). Attention, negative affect and altruism: An ecological validation. *Personality and Social Psychology Bulletin, 3,* 54-58.

Underwood, B., Froming, W. J., & Moore, B. S. (1977). Mood, attention, and altruism: A search for mediating variables. *Developmental Psychology, 13,* 541-542.

Vallacher, R. R., & Solodky, M. (1979). Objective self-awareness, standards of evaluation, and moral behavior. *Journal of Experimental Social Psychology, 15,* 254-262.

Veitch, R., & Griffitt, W. (1976). Good news-bad news: Affective and interpersonal effects. *Journal of Applied Social Psychology, 6,* 69-75.

Wallace, L., & Sadalla, E. (1966). Behavioral consequences of transgression. I. The effects of social recognition. *Journal of Experimental Research in Personality, 1,* 187-194.

Wegner, D. M., & Schaefer, D. (1978). The concentration of responsibility: An objective self-awareness analysis of group size effects in helping situations. *Journal of Personality and Social Psychology, 36,* 147-155.

Weiss, R. F., Boyer, J. L., Lombardo, J. P., & Stitch, M. H. (1973). Altruistic drive and altruistic reinforcement. *Journal of Personality and Social Psychology, 25,* 390-400.

Weiss, R. F., Buchanan, W., Alstatt, L., & Lombardo, J. P. (1971). Altruism is rewarding. *Science, 171,* 1262-1263.

Weyant, J. M. (1978). Effects of mood states, costs, and benefits on helping. *Journal of Personality and Social Psychology, 36,* 1169-1176.

Wicklund, R. A. (1975). Objective self-awareness. In L. Berkowitz (Ed.), *Advances in experimental social psychology* (Vol. 8, pp. 233-275). New York: Academic Press.

Williamson, G. M., & Clark, M. S. (1989). Providing help and desired relationship type as determinants of changes in moods and self-evaluations. *Journal of Personality and Social Psychology, 56,* 722-734.

Wood, J. V., Saltzberg, J. A., & Goldsamt, L. A. (1990). Does affect induce self-focused attention? *Journal of Personality and Social Psychology, 5,* 899-908.

Yinon, Y., & Bizman, A. (1980). Noise, success, and failure as determinants of helping behavior. *Personality and Social Psychology Bulletin, 6,* 125-130.

Yinon, Y., & Landau, M. O. (1987). On the reinforcing value of helping behavior in a positive mood. *Motivation and Emotion, 11,* 83-93.

9

Helping as Coping

ELIZABETH MIDLARSKY

Elizabeth Midlarsky is Professor in the Department of Clinical Psychology at Columbia University, Teachers College. Her research is on altruism and helping in persons of diverse ages and particularly under conditions of extreme stress.

Prosocial behavior, or helping, refers to actions undertaken on behalf of others. As in the case of all interpersonal transactions, helping not only consists of a motive and a series of motoric acts but also includes outcomes—for the helper as well as for the recipient. Most of the existing literature on prosocial behavior, however, focuses on the antecedents of helping and, in some cases, on reactions to help by recipients. In contrast, this chapter explores the impact of prosocial behavior upon the helper. In it, I argue that helping others can be a means for productive and successful coping with a variety of life stresses.

Within the current literature on stress and coping, the spotlight is on the role of social support by others as a moderator of stress (Bell, LeRoy, & Stephenson, 1982; Gottlieb, 1981; Kaplan, 1983). When one takes the perspective of the recipient, however, support from others is far from an unmixed blessing (Fisher, Nadler, & Whitcher-Alagna, 1982), particularly when the help cannot readily be reciprocated (Clark, Gotay, & Mills, 1974; Gross & Latané, 1974). For instance, being the recipient of help can lower self-esteem or create a sense that one is in debt to the donor of the help. Thus, at least in some instances, when support is provided to the person under stress, the "cure" may be worse than the disease.

Why should this be the case? The answer may lie, in part, in the roles of "victim" or "recipient" and "helper." The recipient typically is viewed in a quite negative light, as one whose plight is attributable to the stress associated with some disturbing event—whether the demands associated with chronic disability, traumatic events during wartime, or, in some instances, the losses and declines associated with aging. When

AUTHOR'S NOTE: I thank Margaret S. Clark, editor, and the anonymous reviewers for their suggestions and help in revising this manuscript. I also acknowledge the support of the AARP Andrus Foundation as well as that of the National Institute on Aging (AG6535).

one is a recipient, there is often an implicit demand that one show some improvement in the future, thus reflecting negatively on one's current state (Miller, Brickman, & Bolen, 1975). There is also a tacit assumption that help is needed from others because the recipient is facing a situation whose demands overwhelm his or her competence to meet them. Indeed, when one occupies a recipient role, as in the case of the institutionalized elderly, efforts to help others or oneself may be virtually ignored (Baltes & Werner-Wahl, 1987). The perceived imbalance between demands and capabilities may come from the appraisal of the situation as a threat or a loss rather than as a challenge (Lazarus & Launier, 1978). In sharp contrast to the recipient role, the role of a helper seems to be viewed in a quite positive light—that is, helpers are typically viewed as competent and good people.

What do these two divergent roles—a recipient role with at least some negative consequences and a helper role with some positive consequences—imply for a person under stress? Well, to the extent to which that person adopts the recipient role, stress might actually increase. However, to the extent to which the individual is able to interpret that situation as a positive challenge, to be met by instrumental problem solving (such as self-help or the helping of others), then stress reduction may occur. Indeed, according to Lawton (1987), people may experience stress when environmental demands either exceed their abilities *or* fail to challenge them, with the concomitant assumption that they lack the competence to meet a challenge. In other words, in this treatment, the individual under stress is viewed not merely as a potential victim but as a potential agent who continues to have the capacity to act as well as to react. As an agent, the person can help him- or herself *or* may provide help to others. Either may benefit the person under stress, although this chapter emphasizes the less obvious strategy of helping others as an effective coping strategy.

The remainder of this chapter is divided into three sections. In the first, conceptual and empirical perspectives on the relationship between helping and coping are presented. Helping will be depicted as a behavior that may plausibly predict positive psychosocial sequelae to stress. The second section presents empirical evidence on the nature and degree of helping by individuals presumed to be exposed to stress, including siblings of children with disabilities and elderly persons. The purpose of this second section is to show that contrary to stereotypes of people presumed to be under stress, many such people *do* help others despite their own troubles. Such evidence, I argue, increases the plausibility that helping may serve as a form of coping among members of such populations. Finally, a third section is devoted to describing the results of two of my own emerging field studies, the results of which, when taken in combination with evidence presented in the first section, should increase the plausibility that helping serves as an effective coping mechanism.

CONCEPTUAL AND EMPIRICAL PERSPECTIVES

There are five analytically distinguishable reasons that helping others may benefit the helper, even—or perhaps especially—when the help is given by an individual who is experiencing stress but helps, nevertheless, from other-centered motives. These include the capacity of helping (a) to provide distraction from one's own troubles, (b) to enhance the sense of meaningfulness and value in one's life, (c) to increase perceived competence, (d) to improve mood tone, and (e) to promote social integration—all of which can be disrupted by exposure to stressful events.

First, on an a priori basis it seems plausible that helping others may serve as a *distraction* from one's own troubles. In the course of many life stresses one experiences a range of emotional reactions, including anxiety, embarrassment, and anger. These feelings and one's behavioral responses to them may be distressing, over and above the impact of the stress-producing event. If, however, one turns from the cauldron of one's own reactions to the other-orientation inherent in altruism, the sense of despair may decrease. An egocentric, "turning inward" may be a natural tendency for some people. Yet, it may be hypothesized that an allocentric orientation may be more *effective* in restoring equanimity during times of stress.

Although systematic data on the capacity of altruistic activity to distract one from one's troubles are largely unavailable or inaccessible, preliminary results of a study on rescue during the Holocaust suggest the possible relevance of distraction as an antidote to self-concern. In this ongoing study, in-depth interviews are being conducted with rescuers of Jews during World War II in comparison with nonrescuers. In addition, letters and diaries written during the war are being examined. These interviews, letters, and diaries reveal the power of active helping as a distraction. Overall, the letters and diaries of the rescuers are filled with details of activities necessary to accomplish their goals for others; the nonrescuers generally reported less activity and more preoccupation with their own concerns. Furthermore, in interviews conducted more than 40 years after the war's end, the nonrescuers still presented detailed lists of their wartime deprivations, losses, threats, and adverse emotional reactions. The rescuers, conversely, tended to *minimize* personal privations. Rescuers recalled fewer adverse personal reactions. When disturbing episodes were reported, they pertained largely to the suffering of those around them, perceived inability to help *enough,* and horror over the brutality of the perpetrators. These differences remain even after controlling for objective wartime circumstances (Midlarsky, 1989a, 1989b). Are these results attributable to the rescuers' prewar personalities or to the impact of their helpfulness? No retrospective correlational study can provide the definitive answer to this question. Nevertheless, the results are at least suggestive regarding the power of altruistic involvement to serve as a source of positive distraction.

A second hypothesis is that helping has the capacity to enhance *the sense of meaningfulness and value* in one's own life.[1] Helping others may be not merely a way to keep busy but also a way to occupy oneself in activities that are designed to produce important outcomes. In American society, there is a tendency to judge people on the basis of what they do, not what they are. The older person who is "roleless" may feel useless and outmoded (MacDonald, 1973). The usefulness inherent in helping contradicts the stereotyped view of retired older adults as "useless." Altruistic activities may also preserve one's sense of meaning even under the most extreme circumstances. For many citizens of Europe during World War II, the savage brutality observed or experienced posed a major threat to their value system and sense of justice. For such individuals, whether bystanders or concentration camp inmates, the expression of moral values through the help proferred to others reportedly had the potential to restore their faith in humankind.

In an account based on his own firsthand experience, Frankl (1963) emphasized the great importance of the meaning attributed to their experience by inmates of the Nazi camps. Focusing specifically on cooperative behavioral responses, Des Pres (1976) presents a descriptive analysis of documents indicating that helping and sharing were among the measures used to preserve the sense of humanity among concentration camp inmates. One Treblinka survivor was quoted as saying, "In our group, we shared everything; and the moment one of the group ate something without sharing it, we knew it was the beginning of the end for him" (Des Pres, 1975, p. 110). In their description of responses by rescuers of Jews during World War II, Oliner and Oliner (1988) noted that several reported being thankful that they had behaved in accordance with their system of values. Others said that, through their helping, they experienced a sense of vital attachment to broader humanity, in almost a spiritual sense.

In another context, grandparents over the age of 60 who help others indicate that they are performing a meaningful role (Bengtson, 1985), as do older volunteers (Midlarsky, 1989b). Kahana and Kahana (1983) reported that elderly people preparing to migrate to Israel often expressed a desire to have the chance, at last, to make contributions to others outside their families. Ultimate satisfaction with the move was related to helping opportunities and professed altruistic activities. There are also recorded self-reports that at least some members of families of children with disabilities feel that they have found a new meaning in life—in the form of a religious or quasi-religious experience—as a result of helping the disabled child (Grossman, 1972).

Third, involvement in helping activities is also postulated to have a *positive impact on self-evaluations*. The relevant literature in this area too is limited. Therefore, the literature regarding three related constructs will be summarized under the rubric of "perceived competence." These constructs are personal control orientations (e.g., Schulz, 1976): self-esteem, which includes the global feeling of self-worth (Coopersmith, 1967), and self-efficacy (Bandura, 1986), defined as the performance-based cognition that one has the ability to control behavioral outcomes. According to Pearlin, Menaghan, Lieberman, and Mullan (1981), the process of dealing with stress has the capacity to threaten one's sense of self-esteem. Indeed, Thoits (1983) has written that it is the decrement in positive self-regard, which is considered by many theorists to be a fundamental human need (Mecca, Smelser, & Vasconcellos, 1989), that is a primary cause of the difficulties that occur subsequent to stress. Even in situations that have the potential to undermine self-esteem, positive self-regard can be restored through effective helping; and, even under extreme stress, people can emerge as effective helpers (Kahana, Kahana, Harel, & Segal, 1986). Of course, it can be argued that helping may be just a behavior that covaries with self-esteem, in that those evaluating themselves most highly are the ones who emerge as helpers. However, it seems likely that, in the process of behaving as a competent helper, the individual gains perspective on his or her abilities and thus is reassured that he or she has the ability to overcome a negative life experience.

Congruent with the hypothesized relationship between successful helping and perceived competence (Midlarsky, 1984) is Bandura's (1986) finding that what he calls "enactive attainment" is an important source of information about one's effectiveness. When one performs successfully on behalf of others (i.e., when there is "enactive attainment"), then one's efficacy appraisals are enhanced. The enhanced self-efficacy is likely to generalize. In connection with this third way of viewing helping as a means for coping with stress, it is noteworthy that, according to Bandura, the generalization of enhanced self-efficacy is *most* likely where prior decrements in performance resulted from concern with one's own perceived inadequacies. Consider the person under stress who may feel ineffective as demands and obstacles exceed his or her perceived capacities to meet or remove them. It is this very individual whose enactive attainment, perhaps through effective helping, will generalize to a greater extent than if no perceived deficiencies had existed. A second source of critical input to one's self-esteem consists of the appraisals and esteem of others. In contrast to the recipient's implied lack of worth, the prevailing image of the helper is as a powerful and active figure.

Consonant with the "helper-therapy" principle (Riessman, 1976, p. 41), helping may serve as an alternative to perceived helplessness. Even in the event that one can no longer accomplish goals for oneself, one still may be able to accomplish goals for others. It is interesting that when people succeed in accomplishing their goals under adverse circumstances—because they are assumed to have less ability, to be receiving less supervision, or to be experiencing stress or hardship—they are typically given more credit for their success (e.g., Kipnis, 1972; Taynor & Deaux, 1973). A third consideration comes from social comparison theory (Suls & Miller, 1977). Successful helping may lead to increased self-esteem because those whose helping behavior constitutes a productive outlet are in the position to make favorable comparisons between themselves and others.

There is a paucity of research that has attempted to systematically link helping behavior or altruistic attitudes with perceptions of self-worth. Anecdotal reports, based primarily on case studies, indicate that children who serve as caretakers and teachers of their handicapped siblings express self-evaluations of competence and mastery. Those taking less responsibility, usually male siblings, report higher anxiety and embarrassment about a sibling's handicap (Grossman, 1972). Bank and Kahn (1982), psychotherapists who based their conclusions on interviews conducted in the context of individual and family therapy over an eight-year period, claim that, at least in some cases, siblings of children with impairment assume a competent and masterful identity as the result of helping. They further assert, on the basis of their clinical case reports, that the helper role may extend into late life. That is, their in-depth interviews with members of the mental health professions revealed that a sizable number of these individuals were caretakers of siblings with disabilities in their families of origin. In a systematic study employing home interviews and daily telephone interviews with families of mentally retarded children, siblings who reportedly engaged in higher amounts of helping—in regard to both sibling caregiving and the performance of household chores—obtained higher scores on a measure of perceived competence (McHale & Gamble, 1989).

In regard to helping patterns among older adults who receive services from others, Wentowski (1981) found a significant correlation between opportunities to engage in helping and the maintenance of self-esteem. Significant relationships among altruistic orientations, self-esteem, and perceived control were found in a study of attitudes expressed by residents of Florida retirement communities (Midlarsky & Kahana, 1981). In a study evaluating the effectiveness of the Senior Companion Program (Fogelman, Roberts, & Dunbar, 1983), a program authorized by Congress in 1973, the elderly companions expressed concern primarily with the effectiveness of the program in meeting the needs of the people they served rather than with its effects on their own well-being. It also is interesting that the companions rated the program as being more valuable and even necessary for the survival of their clients than did the clients themselves.

Experimental research on the improvement of self-evaluations following helping has yielded mixed results. As Williamson and Clark (1989, p. 724) pointed out, following their review of some of the existing evidence, "Although the results of some research efforts are consistent with the idea that providing help improves self-evaluations, the evidence is not conclusive. In addition, some researchers have failed to find support for the effect." In two of their own experiments designed to directly assess the effects of helping, Williamson and Clark found that both self-evaluations and moods became more positive subsequent to responding to a request for help. In a third experiment, unmarried men desiring a communal relationship with the recipient of their efforts were found to respond in a significantly more positive way than those desiring a communal relationship but who did not help. Although, in contrast to some of the populations just discussed (the elderly and members of families that include a disabled child), the Williamson and Clark work did not involve subjects likely to be under stress; the work, nonetheless, does show that helping can improve self-evaluations. And if helping can raise the self-evaluations of people whose self-evaluations do not seem likely to be threatened, it seems plausible that the impact of helping would only be greater among stressed individuals whose self-evaluations may start off at a lower point.

Initial results of an interview study of World War II rescuers and nonrescuers indicate that those whose self-esteem is highest today were helpers in the past, and they report that they continue to help others today as well (Midlarsky, 1989a). Some of the rescuers interviewed by Oliner and Oliner (1988) said that their altruistic activity helped to reinforce their self-esteem—to preserve their sense of identity and integrity. Even more striking are the many comments by nonrescuers that reveal a sense of powerlessness—the perception that conditions in the war, during which they took no proactive role, left them feeling drained and impotent (Midlarsky, 1989a; Oliner & Oliner, 1988).

Similarly, the few men who were able to help others and to repair their own homes following the Buffalo Creek disaster gave verbal reports of higher levels of self-confidence than did men who did not help. According to Gleser, Green, and Winget (1981), self-reports following the Buffalo Creek disaster indicated that the most adverse psychological effects were experienced by those thrust into a position of childlike dependency—and who, therefore, were not in a position to help themselves or others. As a case in point, women who were married and for whom it was not normative to help themselves or others coped less well than did those not residing with spouses. Huerta and Horton (1978) found that among elderly flood victims, those living with their children reported feeling less competent, and more insecure, in comparison with those living independently.

Results of experimental studies underscore the importance of the sense of control—whether exercised on one's own behalf or for another—for the maintenance of psychological and physical well-being. Schulz (1976) determined that, when institutionalized older adults were either told when they would be visited by college students or could control the duration and frequency of visits, their well-being was significantly enhanced relative to the well-being of comparison groups.

Hypothesizing that the curtailment of autonomy may lead to the rapid deterioration and decline of elderly individuals in nursing homes, Langer and Rodin (1976) investigated the effects of self-care and a form of nurturance on health of the aged. Of the older adults given the opportunity to become more involved in their own care, and given a plant to cultivate, only half were found to have the 18-month mortality rate of a comparison group. Congruent with these results is Taylor's (1979) finding, based on a review of the literature, that patients given a wider role in caring for themselves and other participants recover more rapidly than do patients who are not given such roles.

The giving of help may also result in *positive moods*. This prediction is based on the notion that altruism is reinforcing, with investigators arguing for its status as either a primary reinforcer (Weiss, Buchanan, Alstatt, & Lombardo, 1971) or a secondary reinforcer (Cialdini, Baumann, & Kenrick, 1981). It also may be argued that altruism leads to self-reward, particularly when the provision of assistance to others is congruent with the relatively high level of moral values expressed by older people (Midlarsky, Kahana, & Corley, 1986) and by individuals during wartime (Midlarsky & Oliner, 1987). The sense of rightness resulting from involvement in altruistic activities may lead people to reward themselves with good moods for helping. This tendency may be further reinforced among those who are open to new, preferably communal, relationships (Williamson & Clark, 1989).

In addition to augmenting positive moods, helping may result in the alleviation of negative moods. In the negative-state relief model advanced by Cialdini and his associates (Cialdini, Baumann, & Kenrick, 1981), altruism is viewed as a behavior that acquires the capacity, through the process of socialization, to dispel bad moods as well as to produce good moods.

Evidence for the relationship of helping and moods comes from the experimental research reviewed and conducted by Williamson and Clark (1989). In nonexperimental field studies of the psychosocial adjustment of adults, "feeling good" also has been cited as a benefit of helping others. Similarly, older volunteers in the Foster Grandparents program reported increases in morale following service in the program (Gray & Kasteler, 1970). Recent research by Karuza and his associates (in press) indicates that, when older persons adhere to prevailing stereotypes that portray them as dependent and ill (Carver & del la Garza, 1984)—by attributing low responsibility to themselves for solving their own problems—then their overall mood tone is less favorable than if they had accepted responsibility. That is, older adults tend to accept the "medical model" assigned to them by society, very much to their own detriment. Among elderly adults who do help others, increased helping appears to diffuse negative affect but *not* to augment positive moods, according to these investigators.

An additional source of benefit may come from enhanced *social integration* with others within one's own milieu. Altruism is a concept associated with solidarity, or the sense of "we-ness" (Hornstein, 1976). Just as the sense of we-ness may lead to altruism, continued involvement in generous acts may promote social integration or a sense of community among people who are initially strangers to one another as well as among people who are kin (Clark, 1983). Indeed, the nurturance of infants by their mothers is often taken as a prototype for altruism, and mutual concern may cement love relations; both may bring with them a vital sense of connectedness. Furthermore, evidence suggests that social skills obtained through involvement in helping interactions within one's own social or familial domain may lead to enhanced bonding and increased social integration within the family or the wider community (Zahn-Waxler, Iannotti, & Chapman, 1983).

However, unlike the other reasons that helping may serve as an effective coping strategy discussed thus far, caution is in order when discussing the effect of helping on social integration and consequently on coping. Although, as I have argued thus far, helping may well enhance coping by promoting social integration, it also seems possible that it could interfere with social integration under certain circumstances. For example, under conditions of high cost for the helper and a less than salutory outcome for the recipient, the sense of social integration may be threatened. A frequent complaint by siblings of the handicapped is that the increased family responsibilities thrust upon them as the result of having a disabled child in the family leads to a reduction in the amount of time available for friendships with peers outside the family (Hannah & Midlarsky, 1985). Furthermore, at least in the short run, relationships with parents are described as negative, despite the effort expended in caretaking and household responsibilities (McHale & Gamble, 1989). Or, to give another example, what of the adult who is caretaker of a loved one with whom a strong bond has already been established?

It may well be the case that in adult life, helping within families can reinforce communal relationships. But what if the one whom one is helping is seriously, even terminally, ill? In considering elderly caretakers of people with Alzheimer's disease, for example, an important facet of "caretaker burden" may be—according to self-reports—the gradual loss of a lifetime of shared memories that eventually ends in the loss of the corporal person as well (Midlarsky, 1989b). Unless the older person then becomes involved in other social relationships, social isolation may follow, despite a lengthy period—or even a lifetime—of involvement in family caretaking. Adults who survive to old age may indeed become increasingly isolated as they experience the series of losses associated with late life. In addition to the possibility of widowhood, colleagues and friends may be lost upon retirement, adult children and grandchildren disperse, and relocation and deaths of peers may disrupt existing ties to lifelong neighbors and friends. Kalish and Knudtson (1976) have speculated that the elderly may become disengaged from social relationships because of the perception that they have made, or are soon to make, a transition to dependency and are unable to help others (or themselves). Thus, during the very time of life when losses of friends and family members may necessitate the development of new relationships, perceived resources—such as health and finances—may be at their lowest ebb.

Nevertheless, it seems that helping often can promote coping by increasing social integration. There is growing evidence that even those whose resources are objectively low do help others (Midlarsky & Hannah, 1989). Among those who become involved in helping others, social integration may be enhanced. There is research, for example, indicating that people who give willingly, in a supportive way and without reciprocation of benefits, are liked by others (Greenberg & Frisch, 1972; Hartup, 1983) and that those who value altruism receive social support (Aldwin & Revenson, 1985). In a study of friendship, 67% of elderly people considered "caring" to be the most important characteristic of their friends (Shenk & Vora, 1985). Moreover, even when helping does not promote *immediate* social integration, it may still promote long-term improvements in social integration. For instance, helping by child and adolescent siblings of the disabled may ultimately be found to lead to the development of social skills, which, in turn, may enhance bonding during adult life. There is, therefore, a modicum of evidence that helping roles have the potential to lead to the sense of integration (or reintegration) in the social milieu.

In sum, it appears plausible that helping may benefit the person under stress for the five analytically distinguishable reasons presented above. The positive psychosocial sequelae of helping outlined here are not, however, intended to be viewed as entirely discrete. Indeed, it is very difficult in practice to separate positive moods from self-evaluations, and both may be related to perceived control and self-efficacy. The impact of helping on negative moods may well be mediated through social integration, in some cases, and self-esteem, in others. Similarly, the sense of meaning derived from helpfulness to others is related to both congruence and mood tone, and all five of the hypothesized sequelae appear to be both conceptually and empirically related to well-being (Liang, 1985).

In addition to recognizing the possible interrelationships among the positive outcomes of helping, it is also likely that the relationships between helping and its outcomes are reciprocal rather than unidirectional. The relationship between helping and well-being may well be mutually reinforcing, once their benign cycle is set in motion. In the case of the relationships to helping of other facets of well-being, such as positive moods and self-esteem, it is possible that, just as they promote the tendency to help others, they may also represent outcomes of benevolence for the helpful person. This set of hypothesized relationships is depicted, in its most general form, in Figure 9.1.

This diagram depicts a set of reciprocal relationships wherein each of the variables has the capacity to predict that which follows in the cycle. It reflects an assumption that the causes and effects of much of human adaptation are reciprocal and can best be represented as benign or vicious cycles. Furthermore, in this view, the cycle of relationships between helping and coping may theoretically be set in motion at any of the three main points. Hence, an individual motivated to help may provide the help requested, which, in turn, may result in the augmentation of one or more of the facets of well-being. In contrast, enforced rehearsal as a helper, or a volunteer pressed into service, may theoretically lead to positive outcomes. The experience of these outcomes may then lead to the development of motives that have the capacity to promote future, self-directed helping. It is further hypothesized that the set of relationships depicted above may be useful in comprehending helping both by people in general and by people who are currently being exposed to certain objective life stresses, such as siblings of the disabled and the elderly.

It is proposed, then, that helping may provide a means for dealing with stress, for the reasons enumerated above. Do people under stress help others, though? This is an important question, for if no objective evidence is found that people presumed to be under stress *do* help, it

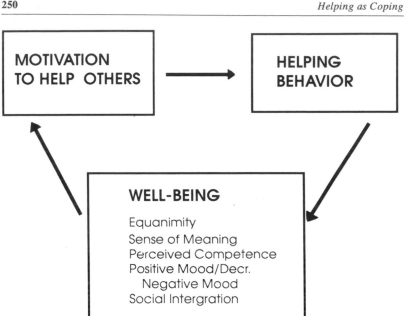

Figure 9.1. The conceptual model of the reciprocal relationships among helping motives, helping behavior, and positive psychosocial outcomes.

makes little sense to argue that helping actually serves as an effective coping strategy for such groups (even if, theoretically, it could). Thus, in the next section, I briefly present evidence that two groups often presumed to be exposed to stress—siblings of the disabled and older adults—do provide significant amounts of help to others.

HELPING BY PEOPLE UNDER STRESS

To examine whether people under stress do help, one must first select a group or groups to examine who *are* under stress. Unfortunately, for the specific purposes of this chapter I do not have both objective stress data and helping data on the same group or groups of subjects. However, I do have helping data for two groups, the elderly and siblings of the disabled—groups that are widely perceived to be under stress. First, consider the siblings of the disabled, who are often described as saddled with problems not of their own making, as exposed to a difficult and generally unsatisfying family life (Featherstone, 1980), and, therefore, as being at risk for psychiatric problems (e.g., Poznanski, 1969; San Martino & Newman, 1974). Furthermore, siblings of the disabled are portrayed as being simultaneously deprived of parental attention and "burdened" with caretaking responsibilities (e.g., Seligman, 1983). A recurring theme in the literature regarding families of the disabled is that these siblings need to be "protected" from such caretaking responsibilities (e.g., Bank & Kahn, 1982), thereby suggesting that experts in this area share the opinion that these children are indeed under stress.

Next, consider the elderly. This group also is widely believed to have to deal with increased problems. As people age, they have a greater chance of encountering such high stress events as poor health, problems in paying for costly medical care (Harris and Associates, 1981), enforced (rather than voluntary) relocation (Moos & Lemke, 1985), death of a close friend, death of a spouse, and retirement (Eisdorfer & Wilkie, 1979). With the decline in physical abilities (e.g., as with heart problems and arthritis), for some older people, even the simple act of climbing stairs may produce stress (Lawton & Nahemow, 1973). Moreover, the choice of this group comes, in part, from the position that additional stress may come from the *removal* of certain responsibilities from this group—often combined with the reinforcement of dependency (Lawton, 1987). The anomie that may result, for some aged adults, from the view of themselves as unchallenged (because seen as unable to meet challenges) can be viewed as diametrically opposite a helper identity. Thus I believe it reasonable to at least suggest that these two groups are under increased stress. The next question then becomes, do they help?

Helping Among Siblings

The literature on altruism and helping often includes suggestions about ways to model helping behavior or to attribute responsibility to children to teach them what is considered a very important social behavior—prosocial/moral action (e.g., Rushton, 1980; and see Grusec's chapter in this volume). Yet, the literatures of social and developmental psychology rarely indicate any recognition of naturally occurring situations within U.S. society in which helping and caretaking by siblings are highly salient daily occurrences, that is, in families in which there is a handicapped child. Indeed, the recurrent emphasis on helping relationships within such families (McHale & Gamble, 1989; Midlarsky, Hannah, & Chapin, 1987; Seligman, 1983) may occur because, unlike the situation for the U.S. population at large (Whiting & Whiting, 1973), opportunities for helping and attributions of responsibility to well siblings may abound. Indeed, Seligman (1983) found that one of the conditions most frequently leading to caretaking by siblings is the presence within the family of a disabled child. McAndrew (1976) reports that 75% of the siblings of children with cerebral palsy or spina bifida, who were themselves over the age of 7, were expected to provide help. Responsibilities included dressing, toileting, feeding, supervising, and amusing the siblings as well as putting on the braces. Similarly, all of the teenage participants in the research by Graliker, Fishler, and Koch (1962) assumed considerable responsibility for a sibling with Down syndrome.

Do siblings of children with handicaps help more than the "typical" American child? In most of the research on siblings of the handicapped, comparison groups were not included, so that it is difficult to determine whether or not responsibilities exceeded those typically given to siblings. However, two studies indicate that such may be the case. Swirean (1976) compared siblings of hearing impaired or normal 4-year-olds on their child care responsibilities. He found that siblings of the hearing impaired had significantly greater child care and home responsibilities in comparison with siblings of nonimpaired children. In a recent study comparing siblings of retarded and nonretarded children, girls with a retarded sibling helped the most, and boys with nonretarded siblings helped the least. In general, findings indicated that siblings of the retarded do help more, on the average, than siblings of nonretarded children (McHale & Gamble, 1989).

Helping by the Elderly

Investigators of interpersonal relationships among older adults are, by and large, social gerontologists. In the literature of social gerontology there appears to be little expectation of altruism by the elderly. The elderly are generally viewed as giving less than they receive. When they do help others, they are perceived as being motivated by the anticipation of resources or favors that they will receive or by the desire to reciprocate for resources already received (Dowd, 1980; Wentowski, 1981). Although helping by others directed *toward* the elderly has been the subject of numerous investigations, studies in which the older adult helps others without anticipation of reward or reciprocation have been rare (Stewart & Smith, 1983). In general then, older adults are viewed as a needy, recipient class, a "handicapped population dangling at the end of the life span" (Ehrlich, 1979)—a view that itself may serve as a source of stress (Lawton, 1987).

The literature provides suggestive evidence, however, that the elderly are willing helpers of others (Kahana, Midlarsky, & Kahana, 1987). In a number of survey research projects, the elderly have reported that they provide help to others and that the recipients of their efforts consist of family, friends, acquaintances, and neighbors as well as the wider community (the latter served primarily in the course of volunteer participation; Midlarsky & Kahana, 1983; Streib & Streib, 1978). In a survey of several hundred community dwelling elderly, for example, 55% reported that they regularly provide assistance to others (Chappell & Havens, 1983). Even older people who are currently receiving assistance report that they continue to provide help (Prohaska & McAuley, 1984). In a study that set out to explore the service needs of the urban aged (Kahana & Felton, 1977), community dwelling older adults reported that they provide more help than they receive.

In an investigation of variations in generosity across the life span (Midlarsky & Hannah, 1989), a donation task was set up in which funds were solicited, in randomly selected shopping malls and parks, to help infants with birth defects. As all of the study sites were known to be frequented by people across a wide age span, we were able to compare monetary donations by individuals aged 5 through 75+. Older people were generally retired and, objectively, have more time for participation in charitable endeavors. Consequently, the study was conducted on weekends, when all participants were presumably at leisure. Results indicated that there was an increase in numbers of persons donating with age. For example, 48% of those 15-24 years old donated, and 60% of those 25-34. There was an even larger increase in midlife, with an average of 73% giving to charity among those aged 35 to 44. The percentages of people donating remained stable through age 64, followed by a jump to 91% in the number of donors aged 65 and above. A different picture emerged, however, when *amount* donated was the dependent variable. Here, donation size showed a continual trend upward until about the age of 65, followed by a significant decline. Because this finding was thought possibly to reflect the possession of differential financial resources rather than generous tendencies, a second experiment was conducted.

The methodology of Study 2 was essentially identical to that of Study 1, with the exception that the donation task required effort rather than money. People approaching the donation booth were told that, if they wished to make a contribution to the fund for infants with birth defects, they should operate the lever labeled "for the children" and that, for each lever pull, 5¢ would be donated to the fund by local merchants. Results of Study 2 indicated that the numbers of people donating was very similar to the numbers in Study 1 and that elderly people pulled the donation lever more than persons at younger ages. Hence, with financial costs controlled, the relationship between age and helping was maintained, with the highest donations given by the older adults. Results of this experiment lend support to the notion that generosity may increase through life, particularly when resources for helping are available.

DOES HELPING BY THE ELDERLY AND BY SIBLINGS OF THE DISABLED LEAD TO MORE EFFECTIVE COPING?

In this section I present evidence from research conducted with my colleagues Mary Elizabeth Hannah and Eva Kahana. In our work, we chose to study siblings of the disabled and older adults because of the general tendency noted above to view them as groups with a higher than average exposure to stressful events and who, therefore, are generally expected to suffer from impairments in mental and physical health (Dohrenwend & Dohrenwend, 1974).

It is interesting, however, that the literature regarding the *actual* well-being of these groups does not support the notion that their life situations result in across-the-board psychiatric impairment. Research studies conducted on the mental health of siblings of the retarded, employing comparable groups of siblings of the nonretarded and psychometrically adequate instruments, did discern somewhat higher levels of maladjustment. But, despite the differences, the average scores fell within the normal range (Hannah & Midlarsky, 1988, 1989; McHale & Gamble, 1989). The research on life satisfaction among the older adult population also indicates that although objective life circumstances may change, chronological age is not, in itself, a significant predictor of psychological distress or of morale (George, 1981). However, a focus on average group differences tends to obscure the fact that there is wide variation in the adjustment of individuals within the groups. What this may indicate is that other factors—whether status variables (such as sex), resources (such as health), or coping strategies (such as helping)—

may combine with objective stress in its impact on outcomes, even possibly superseding its effects.

Research on Siblings of the Disabled

To explore the relationship between sibship with a handicapped child and mental health, 50 siblings of individuals with mental retardation were contrasted with a demographically comparable group of 30 siblings of nonhandicapped individuals. Both parents and teachers rated the siblings' competence and adjustment in regard to schoolwork, learning, behavior, and happiness (Achenbach & Edelbrock, 1983). Each child was interviewed to determine self-esteem (Coopersmith, 1967) and general happiness (Viet & Ware, 1983). Initial findings from this project indicate that the siblings of the retarded help more than do siblings of individuals who are not retarded and that neither group is psychiatrically impaired (Hannah & Midlarsky, 1988) or judged as having serious problems in school (Hannah & Midlarsky, 1989). In a further investigation of siblings of blind versus siblings of normally sighted individuals, no significant average differences were found on indices of psychiatric impairment. On the other hand, descriptions of objective demands associated with the handicapping condition were indirectly related to the indices of mental health, and high levels of voluntary caretaking were directly related to those same indices. Specifically, siblings of the blind who described themselves as effective helpers showed significantly higher levels of positive affect and self-esteem.

Further evidence for the value of competent helping as an effective coping strategy comes from an experimental study conducted in a naturalistic setting. Several orthopedists in a major metropolitan area cited serious problems in managing the treatment of children suffering from a hip condition. The treatment for this potentially crippling disorder required that these youngsters wear a heavy and unattractive brace. Problems in compliance occurred even though failure to comply could result in serious lifelong disability. The majority of families in the orthopedic practices included a sibling who was cast into a helping role. Many of these siblings were described as having problems adjusting to the multifaceted difficulties and deprivations that the disability imposed on them. Results of interviews with medical personnel working with several of the normal siblings suggested that these children were not just expressing concern about the impact of the disability on

themselves but were frustrated about their perceived inability to miti-
gate the strain felt by the family. Most felt that even though they were
always having to "do things," they were usually not *effective* helpers—
capable of "making a difference" in their expenditure of effort.

To alleviate the strain observed among the siblings of the disabled,
county funds were allocated for a two-week summer camp. Three camps
and a waiting list were established for the first season. As the provision
of a camping experience was viewed as an experiment in community
preventive intervention, it was designed to permit a systematic evaluation of the results of alternative camp experiences in comparison with
those of waiting list controls.

The children, who represented a wide spectrum of backgrounds in
regard to socioeconomic status and ethnicity, were then randomly
assigned to one of four groups. In Group 1, recreational activities and
excursions filled each day. In the other two camps, in addition to the recreational activities, two hours each day were spent working directly
with the nonhandicapped children on issues salient to their sibship
with a handicapped child. In Group 2, information was provided about
the disability, the rationale and importance of the prescribed treatment,
and the importance of taking a supportive role within the family. These
campers were also given information about how they could obtain help
for themselves if they felt overburdened by the care of their brothers or
sisters. In Group 3, the two hours spent each day dealing with the
disability were designed to provide concrete training in how to effectively provide help within the family. In addition, they were given
practice in the use of the skills and information about how to help and
also how to obtain help if the need arose. Individuals in the fourth group
were placed on a waiting list.

The siblings and mothers of the children with disabilities, along with
all other mother-sibling pairs in the medical settings sampled, filled
out a set of measures designed to assess mood, self-esteem, and family
helping behavior (Midlarsky, Hannah, & Chapin, 1987). These instruments were administered as a "standard procedure" several weeks
before the camping opportunity was announced. The effects of the camp
experience were assessed by self-report measures on the last day of
camp and by data from structured, in-depth interviews with the siblings
one week, one month, and one year following the end of the camp. Other
data came from systematic interviews in small groups held during
"family camp days," which were also held one week, one month, and
one year after the end of camp.

In brief, results of the investigation indicated, first, that there were no significant differences among the groups in demographic variables, psychosocial functioning, or helping before the initiation of the camps. On the last day of camp, the children generally manifested elevations in positive mood in comparison both with their prior levels and with the second set of scores obtained from the waiting list controls. Moreover, the participants in Camp 3, and their parents, also reported increased rates of helping after the camp experience, and a linear trend was observed over the three observation points. No such trend was observed in any of the other groups. Camp 3 participants also were the most vocal in expressing an increased satisfaction in their roles as able helpers to the younger siblings. Most important, children who participated in the helping-skills camp (Camp 3) manifested significantly higher levels of positive affect and self-esteem than all other groups; this difference was greater at one month and one year after camp than at one week following the end of the camp. Taken together, these results are viewed as support for the position that siblings of disabled children who achieve active mastery through helping within the family are, concomitantly, contributing to their own self-esteem.

Research on Older Adults

To determine the relationship between helping behavior and mental health in older adults, interviews were conducted with 400 community dwelling older persons who had been randomly chosen from voter registration lists in the Detroit metropolitan area (Midlarsky & Kahana, 1985). We found, first of all, that after controlling for health and demographic variables, a primary predictor of self-reported helping was a set of values wherein service to others was viewed as highly important. Also significantly related to self-reported helping were emotional empathy, social responsibility, and a situational variable—perceived opportunity to help. At variance with the predictions from social exchange theory (Dowd, 1980), the most helpful persons were also least likely to be recipients of services from formal or informal sources, even after controlling for health and finances.

As predicted, the degree to which the older individual gives help to others was found to be significantly related to the three facets of well-being studied—subjective social integration, morale, and self-esteem. The most powerful predictor of social integration was helping, followed by internal locus of control, perceived health, and altruistic values. Predictors of morale included two of the personality variables associated with helping—internal locus of control and social responsibility. Helping was an indirect predictor. In regard to self-esteem, even after controlling for health, finances, and other salient demographic variables, helping emerged as an important predictor. Also interesting was the fact that being a recipient of assistance from formal helpers was inversely related to self-esteem in this sample of community dwelling elderly.

Results of this investigation provided support for the hypothesized relationships among personality and situational variables, helping, and psychosocial benefits such as morale, self-esteem, and subjective integration. However, this research was cross-sectional, so that the direction of causation could not be directly ascertained.

An experiment was conducted, therefore, to discover whether reported increases in helping and volunteering were related to psychosocial well-being (Midlarsky, 1989b). The project had two aims. First, it was designed to evaluate the impact on helping behavior of fully informing older adults about volunteer opportunities, in contrast to not informing them. The hypothesis was that the provision of detailed information about volunteer opportunities would result in an increase in volunteer behavior. Moreover, it was expected that because of the sensitization effect of exposure to information about volunteer opportunities (e.g., as a Foster Grandparent, hospital volunteer), even people not volunteering through formal agencies would report increases in the help given in other domains (e.g., neighbor and family contexts), in comparison with subjects in the control group. Second, the study investigated the impact on psychosocial well-being of self-reported helping. The hypothesis here was that people who engage in more helping also show higher levels of well-being. This study also was designed to determine whether helping of different kinds—such as volunteer participation versus helping of friends and neighbors—differentially affects indices of well-being.

In this study, two groups of respondents were selected at random from the 400 adults interviewed four years earlier as part of the study described above. The interview administered to those people—which included questions about personal and situational variables (e.g., perceived opportunities), helping and volunteering behavior, and psychosocial well-being—was treated as a "pretest" for purposes of the new analysis. One of the two pretested groups, as well as a third group, received the experimental intervention. The fourth group was exposed neither to the pretest nor to the intervention. The intervention provided in-depth, personalized information about volunteer activities coupled with encouragement to volunteer. Posttests six months after the intervention phase asked the respondents about their volunteering and helping in considerable depth and detail and assessed their well-being on a series of standardized instruments.

Results of this experiment indicated, first, that the pretest and the intervention each led to independent increases in perceived opportunities to volunteer, in helping (e.g., of family and neighbors), and in volunteer activities. Also, the greatest increase in perceived opportunities and in helping occurred in the group that received the intervention after first having been sensitized to the pretest. The study also provided support for the hypothesis that helping and volunteering are causally linked to psychosocial well-being. Both helping and volunteering were significant predictors of most of the indices of well-being employed. (But, of the types of prosocial behavior studied, only volunteering was linked to all four indices—positive affect, morale, self-esteem, and social integration.) Support for the causal relationship also comes from the finding that both self-esteem and positive affect increased more among people exposed to the intervention than it did among people in the other groups.

Summary and Conclusions

To summarize, the central thesis expressed here is that human beings—most notably those who hold membership in "recipient" or "victimized" groups within society—have the potential to move beyond avoidance or passivity to become the architects of their own lives. Learning to express compassion and exercising the discipline, fortitude, and control necessary to help others effectively may ultimately serve as a pathway to successful coping, which may have long-lasting positive consequences both for others and for oneself. I argue that this may occur because it is possible that helping makes one feel happy enough, and/or competent enough, to lead to the reappraisal of stress as a challenge rather than as a threat or a loss. I argue that it also is possible that this may occur because helping restores or maintains well-being by distracting oneself from one's current troubles, increasing or maintaining social integration, and/or lending a sense of meaning to one's life.

Is there evidence for this thesis? I think the answer must be yes, but accompanied by a cautionary note that far more evidence is needed. The study of helping as coping is still clearly in its infancy. More questions, by far, remain than have been answered. Nonetheless, it certainly can be said that there is considerable anecdotal evidence that helping serves as an effective coping strategy, that there is evidence that helping is high at least among two groups of people widely assumed to be under stress, and that among these two groups, helping seems to be associated with some positive psychosocial sequelae. Moreover, we have reviewed a few experimental studies (two of my own in the third section of the chapter and a few others in the first section) that support the claim of a positive causal relationship between providing help and subsequent positive psychological outcomes for the helper.

Clearly, more is needed. In particular, research is needed in which objective measures of stress, of helping, and of outcomes are combined in a single study. A convincing case for helping as an effective coping strategy can best be made if helping is found to lead to positive outcomes in groups demonstrably under stress. The most powerful pattern of findings would be one wherein helping others would lead to greater increases in well-being among people under stress than it would in other, nonstressed people. That is, we need a demonstration of the capacity of helping to "buffer" stress, with a concomitant exploration of the possible mediating processes in this relationship. If helping is, indeed, found to be a significant coping mechanism, its stress-buffering effect compared with other forms of interchange—such as receiving social support from others—needs to be explored as well. An important aim for future research may be to investigate the conditions under which the giving of help may be equally, or even more, effective than other forms of exchange in alleviating psychological distress and enhancing well-being.

NOTE

1. This is conceptually very similar to the "value-expressive function" of helping discussed by Clary and Snyder in Chapter 5 of this volume.

REFERENCES

Achenbach, T., & Edelbrock, C. (1983). *Manual for the child behavior checklist and revised behavior profile*. Burlington: University of Vermont.

Aldwin, C., & Revenson, T. (1985, November). *Cohort differences in stress, coping, and appraisal*. Paper presented at the meeting of the Gerontological Society of America, New Orleans.

Baltes, M., & Werner-Wahl, B. (1987). Dependence in aging. In L. Carstensen & B. Edelstein (Eds.), *Handbook of clinical gerontology* (pp. 204-221). New York: Pergamon.

Bandura, A. (1986). *Social foundations of thought and action*. Englewood Cliffs, NJ: Prentice-Hall.

Bank, W., & Kahn, M. (1982). *The sibling bond*. New York: Basic Books.

Bell, R., LeRoy, J., & Stephenson, J. (1982). Evaluating the mediating effects of social support upon life events and depressive symptoms. *Journal of Community Psychology, 10*, 325-340.

Bengtson, V. (1985). Diversity and symbolism in grandparental roles. In V. Bengtson & J. Robertson (Eds.), *Grandparenthood* (pp. 11-25). Beverly Hills, CA: Sage.

Bryant, B., & Crockenberg, S. (1980). Correlates and dimensions of prosocial behavior. *Child Development, 51*, 529-544.

Carver, C., & del la Garza, N. (1984). Schema-guided information search in stereotyping of the elderly. *Journal of Applied Social Psychology, 14*, 69-81.

Chappell, N., & Havens, B. (1983). Who helps the elderly person? In W. Peterson & J. Quadragno (Eds.), *Social bonds in later life* (pp. 21-227). Beverly Hills, CA: Sage.

Cialdini, R., Baumann, D., & Kenrick, D. (1981). Insights from sadness. *Developmental Review, 1*, 207-223.

Clark, M. (1983). Reactions to aid in communal and exchange relations. In J. Fisher, A. Nadler, & B. DePaulo (Eds.), *New directions in helping* (Vol. 1, pp. 281-304). New York: Academic Press.

Clark, M., Gotay, C., & Mills, J. (1974). Acceptance of help as a function of similarity of the potential helper and the opportunity to repay. *Journal of Applied Social Psychology, 4*, 224-229.

Coopersmith, S. (1967). *Antecedents of self-esteem*. San Francisco: Freemont.

Des Pres, T. (1976). *The survivor*. New York: Washington Square.

Dohrenwend, B., & Dohrenwend, B. (1974). *Stressful life events*. New York: John Wiley.

Dowd, J. (1980). Exchange rates and old people. *Journal of Gerontology, 35*, 596-602.

Ehrlich, P. (1979). *Mutual help for community elderly* (Final report, Vol. 1). Carbondale: Southern Illinois University.

Eisdorfer, C., & Wilkie, F. (1979). Research on crisis and stress in aging. In H. Pardes (Ed.), *Issues in mental health and aging: Research* (Vol. 3, pp. 512-537). Rockville, MD: Department of Health, Education, and Welfare.

Featherstone, H. (1980). *A difference in the family: Life with a handicapped child*. New York: Basic Books.

Fisher, J., Nadler, A., & Whitcher-Alagna, S. (1982). Recipient reactions to aid. *Psychological Bulletin, 91*, 27-54.

Fogelman, C., Roberts, J., & Dunbar, M. (1983). Volunteering, helping yourself, and helping others. In M. Smyer & M. Gatz (Eds.), *Mental health and aging* (pp. 231-241). Beverly Hills, CA: Sage.

Frankl, V. (1963). *Man's search for meaning*. New York: Washington Square.

Gath, A. (1973). The school-age siblings of Mongoloid children. *British Journal of Psychiatry, 123*, 161-167.

George, L. (1981). Sibling well-being. In C. Eisdorfer (Ed.), *Annual review of gerontology and geriatrics* (Vol. 2, pp. 345-384). New York: Springer.

Gleser, G., Green, B., & Winget, C. (1981). *Prolonged psychosocial effects of disaster*. New York: Academic Press.

Gottlieb, B. (Ed.). (1981). *Social networks and social support*. Beverly Hills, CA: Sage.

Graliker, B., Fishler, K., & Koch, R. (1962). Teenage reaction to a mentally retarded sibling. *American Journal of Mental Deficiency, 66*, 838-842.

Gray, R., & Kasteler, J. (1970). An evaluation of the effectiveness of a Foster Grandparent project. *Sociology and Social Research, 54*, 181-189.

Greenberg, M., & Frisch, D. (1972). Effect on intentionality on willingness to reciprocate a favor. *Journal of Experimental Social Psychology, 8*, 99-111.

Gross, A., & Latané, J. (1974). Receiving help, giving help, and interpersonal attraction. *Journal of Applied Social Psychology, 4*, 210-221.

Grossman, F. (1972). *Brothers and sisters of retarded children*. Syracuse, NY: Syracuse University Press.

Hannah, M., & Midlarsky, E. (1985). Siblings of the handicapped. *School Psychology Review, 14*, 510-520.

Hannah, M., & Midlarsky, E. (1988, August). *Mental health and competence in siblings of the retarded*. Paper presented at the meeting of the American Psychological Association, Atlanta.

Hannah, M., & Midlarsky, E. (1989, August). *School performance of siblings of the retarded*. Paper presented at the meeting of the American Psychological Association, Washington, DC.

Harris, L., & Associates. (1981). *Aging in the eighties*. Washington, DC: National Council on the Aging.

Hartup, W. (1983). Peer relations. In P. Mussen (Ed.), *Handbook of child psychology* (4th ed., pp. 37-81). New York: John Wiley.

Hornstein, H. A. (1976). *Cruelty and kindness*. Englewood Cliffs, NJ: Prentice-Hall.

Huerta, F., & Horton, R. (1978). Coping behavior of elderly blood victims. *The Gerontologist, 18*, 541-546.

Kahana, E., & Felton, B. (1977). Social context and personal needs. *Journal of Social Issues, 33*, 56-74.

Kahana, E., & Kahana, B. (1983). Environmental continuity, discontinuity, futurity and adaptation of the aged. In G. Rowles & R. Ohta (Eds.), *Aging and milieu* (pp. 205-228). New York: Academic Press.

Kahana, B., Kahana, E., Harel, Z., & Segal, M. (1986). The victim as helper: Prosocial behavior during the Holocaust. *Humboldt Journal of Social Relations, 13*, 357-373.

Kahana, E., Midlarsky, E., & Kahana, B. (1987). Beyond dependency, autonomy and exchange. *Social Justice Research, 1*, 439-459.

Kalish, R., & Knudtson, F. (1976). Attachment vs. disengagement. *Human Development, 19*, 171-181.

Kaplan, J. (Ed.). (1983). *Psychosocial stress*. New York: Academic Press.

Karuza, J., Zevon, M., Gleason, T., Karuza, C., McArdle, J., & Nash, L. (in press). Models of helping and coping among community based elderly and their helpers. *Psychology and Aging*.

Kipnis, D. (1972). Does power corrupt? *Journal of Personality and Social Psychology, 24*, 33-41.

Langer, E., & Rodin, J. (1976). The effects of choice and enhanced personal responsibility for the aged. *Journal of Personality and Social Psychology, 34*, 191-198.

Lawton, M. P. (1987). Environment and the need satisfaction of the aging. In L. Carstensen & B. Edelstein (Eds.), *Handbook of clinical gerontology* (pp. 33-41). New York: Pergamon.

Lawton, M. P., & Nahemow, L. (1973). Ecology and the aging process. In C. Eisdorfer & M. P. Lawton (Eds.), *The psychology of adult development and aging* (pp. 619-674). Washington, DC: American Psychological Association.

Lazarus, R., & Launier, R. (1978). Stress-related transactions between person and environment. In L. Pervin & M. Lewis (Eds.), *Perspectives in interactional psychology.* New York: Plenum.

Liang, J. (1985). A structural integration of the Affect Balance Scale and the Life Satisfaction Index. *Journal of Gerontology, 40,* 552-561.

MacDonald, M. (1973). The forgotten American. *American Journal of Community Psychology, 1,* 272-294.

McAndrew, I. (1976). Children with a handicap and their families. *Child, 2,* 213-237.

McHale, S., & Gamble, W. (1989). Sibling relationships of children with disabled and nondisabled brothers and sisters. *Developmental Psychology, 25,* 1-5.

Mecca, A., Smelser, N., & Vasconcellos, J. (Eds.). (1989). *The social importance of self-esteem.* Berkeley: University of California Press.

Midlarsky, E. (1984). Competence and helping. In E. Staub, D. Bar-Tal, J. Karylowski, & J. Reykowski (Eds.), *Development & maintenance of prosocial behavior* (pp. 291-308). New York: Plenum.

Midlarsky, E. (1989a, June). *Helpers and heroes in late life.* Paper presented at the meeting, "Altruism in Extreme Situations," Warsaw, Poland.

Midlarsky, E. (1989b, November). *Helping and volunteering by the elderly.* Paper presented at the meeting of the Gerontological Society of America, Minneapolis.

Midlarsky, E., & Hannah, M. (1989). The generous elderly. *Psychology and Aging, 4,* 346-351.

Midlarsky, E., Hannah, M., & Chapin, K. (1987, August). *Assessing children's helping behavior.* Paper presented at the meeting of the American Psychological Association, New York.

Midlarsky, E., & Kahana, E. (1981, August). *Altruism and helping among the elderly.* Paper presented at the meeting of the American Psychological Association, Los Angeles.

Midlarsky, E., & Kahana, E. (1983). Helping by the elderly. Interdisciplinary Topics in Gerontology, 17, 10-24.

Midlarsky, E., & Kahana, E. (1985). *Altruism and helping among the elderly* (Final report, NIA grant AG03068-01). Detroit: University of Detroit.

Midlarsky, E., Kahana, E., & Corley, R. (1986, November). *Altruistic moral judgment among the elderly.* Paper presented at the meeting of the Gerontological Society of America, Chicago.

Midlarsky, E., & Oliner, S. (1987, November). *Enduring compassion.* Paper presented at the meeting of the Gerontological Society of America, Washington, DC.

Miller, R., Brickman, P., & Bolen, D. (1975). Attribution vs. persuasion as a means of modifying behavior. *Journal of Personality and Social Psychology, 31,* 430-441.

Moos, R., & Lemke, S. (1985). Specialized living environments for older people. In J. E. Birren & K. S. Schaie (Eds.), *Handbook of the psychology of aging* (2nd ed., pp. 212-247). New York: Van Nostrand Reinhold.

Oliner, S., & Oliner, P. (1988). *The altruistic personality.* New York: Free Press.

264 Helping as Coping

Pearlin, L., Menaghan, E., Lieberman, M., & Mullan, J. (1981). The stress process. *Journal of Health and Social Behavior, 22,* 337-356.

Poznanski, E. (1969). Psychiatric difficulties in siblings of handicapped children. *Pediatrics, 8,* 232-234.

Prohaska, P., & McAuley, W. (1984). Turning the tables on assistance. *Academic Psychology Bulletin, 6,* 191-202.

Riessman, F. (1976). How does self-help work? *Social Policy, 7,* 41-45.

Rushton, J. P. (1980). *Altruism, socialization, and society.* Englewood Cliffs, NJ: Prentice-Hall.

San Martino, M., & Newman, M. B. (1974). Siblings of retarded children: A population at risk. *Child Psychiatry and Human Development, 4,* 168-177.

Schulz, R. (1976). Effects of control and predictability on the physical and psychological well-being of the institutionalized aged. *Journal of Personality and Social Psychology, 33,* 563-573.

Seligman, M. (1983). Siblings of handicapped persons. In M. Seligman (Ed.), *The family with a handicapped child.* New York: Grune & Stratton.

Shenk, D., & Vora, E. (1985, July). *Friendship patterns of the elderly.* Paper presented at the meeting of the International Congress of Gerontology, New York.

Stewart, B., & Smith, C. (1983). Prosocial behavior by and for older persons. In D. Bridgman (Ed.), *The nature of prosocial development.* New York: Academic Press.

Streib, G., & Streib, B. (1978, July). *Retired persons and their contributions.* Paper presented at the meeting of the International Congress of Gerontology, Tokyo.

Suls, J., & Miller, R. (Eds.). (1977). *Social comparison processes.* Washington, DC: Hemisphere.

Swirean, P. (1976). Effects of the presence of a hearing impaired preschool child in the family on behavior patterns of older normal siblings. *American Annals of the Deaf, 121,* 373-380.

Taylor, W. E. (1979). Hospital patient behavior. *Journal of Social Issues, 35,* 156-184.

Taynor, R., & Deaux, K. (1973). When women are more deserving than men. *Journal of Personality and Social Psychology, 28,* 360-367.

Thoits, P. (1983). *Dimensions of life events that can influence psychological distress* (pp. 33-103). New York: Academic Press.

Viet, C., & Ware, J. (1983). The structure of psychological distress and well-being in general populations. *Journal of Consulting and Clinical Psychology, 51,* 730-742.

Weiss, R., Buchanan, W., Alstatt, L., & Lombardo, J. (1971). Altruism is rewarding. *Science, 171,* 1262-1263.

Wentowski, G. (1981). Reciprocity and the coping strategies of older people. *The Gerontologist, 21,* 600-609.

Whiting, J., & Whiting, B. (1973). Altruistic and egoistic behaviors in six cultures. In L. Nader & T. Maretzki (Eds.), *Cultural illness and health* (pp. 112-131). Washington, DC: American Anthropological Association.

Williamson, G., & Clark, M. (1989). Providing help and desired relationship type as determinants of changes in mood and self-evaluations. *Journal of Personality and Social Psychology, 56,* 722-734.

Zahn-Waxler, C., Iannotti, R., & Chapman, M. (1983). Peers and social development. In K. Rubin & H. Ross (Eds.), *Peer relationships and social skills in childhood* (pp. 133-162). New York: Springer-Verlag.

10

Social Support and Interpersonal Relationships

THOMAS ASHBY WILLS

Thomas Ashby Wills is Associate Professor of Psychology, Epidemiology and Social Medicine at the Ferkauf Graduate School of Psychology and the Albert Einstein College of Medicine. His research interests are in social support, help seeking, social comparison theory, coping processes, and adolescent drug use.

This chapter discusses recent research on social support. Several themes in findings on social support and linkages to social psychological theory will be noted. The general finding in field studies is that persons perceive a high level of available support from informal sources, that social support is related to higher levels of well-being, and that support reduces the impact of life stressors such as unemployment or illness. Social support research raises a number of theoretical questions about how informal helping relationships contribute to well-being and which functions of relationships are responsible for the observed effects. These questions bear on theories of close relationships, coping processes, and helping. The purpose of the chapter is to discuss these issues from the perspective of field research on social support, suggesting what social support research has to contribute to social psychology and what social psychological studies on helping and relationships can offer to social support research.

The chapter begins with a brief review of social support research, giving attention to substantive findings and methodological issues. Then I consider several theoretical issues posed by field studies of social support. First, there is a basic question concerning what aspects of social relationships contribute to well-being and how they do so. Second, I consider what kinds of help provided by supportive relationships are most relevant for well-being. Third, I consider how personality factors influence the formation of networks and the utilization of help. In a final section, I draw on the preceding material to consider the

AUTHOR'S NOTE: This work was partially supported by grant #R01-DA-05950 from the National Institute on Drug Abuse. Thanks to Margaret Clark and an anonymous reviewer for their comments on a draft.

relation between helping as studied in laboratory research and in field research.

REVIEW OF SOCIAL SUPPORT RESEARCH

Research on social support has typically used the methods of social epidemiology, studying the association between social relationships and well-being in representative samples of the general population. In the typical study, questionnaire measures are administered to a sizable sample of respondents, who may be followed over time. Measures of social ties may index structural aspects of the social network (e.g., number of friends, proportion of kin in network, membership in community organizations) or may determine the perceived availability of supportive functions provided through social relationships (e.g., confiding, advice and guidance, tangible assistance). Outcome measures of psychological well-being are obtained from survey scales that index symptoms of anxiety or depression. Studies of physical health status use measures that include self-reports of physical conditions or mortality status as determined from long-term follow-up. Univariate procedures or multiple regression analyses are then used to determine the statistical relationship between social ties and outcome measures, either cross-sectionally or longitudinally.

Initial studies examined how social ties were related to the distribution of disease in the community, and several lines of investigation suggested that social ties might be an underlying factor in reducing risk for illness (see, e.g., Cassel, 1976; Cobb, 1976). From this point, several questions about social support were raised. One was whether social support is beneficial primarily for persons with a high level of life stress or whether support is beneficial irrespective of stress level. The first position was termed the *buffering hypothesis* because it posits that social support serves to reduce (buffer) the potentially adverse impact of negative life events on well-being. To test this hypothesis, it is necessary to have as predictors measures of both social support and stressful life events and to examine whether a significant Stress × Support interaction is detected. Evidence for buffering is shown by an interaction in which life stress has a considerable effect for increasing psychological symptomatology among persons with low support, but the relationship between stress and symptomatology is significantly reduced among persons with high support. S. Cohen and Wills (1985) reviewed a variety of studies showing the existence of stress-buffering effects of supportive relationships for outcome measures of psychological symptoms. Buffering effects have been observed in representative community samples as well as in work site settings, such that the adverse impact of life stressors on psychological adjustment is considerably (or completely) reduced for persons with a high level of support from interpersonal relationships. Recent studies have provided evidence of stress-buffering in other contexts. In addition to findings from college students (Roos & L. Cohen, 1987) and community samples (Lin, Woelfel, & Light, 1985; Phifer & Murrell, 1986), buffering effects have been observed among elderly persons (Cutrona, Russell, & Rose, 1987; Krause, 1987b) and adolescents (Greenberg, Siegel, & Leitch, 1983; Newcomb & Bentler, 1988; Wills, 1986). Buffering effects have been found for specific stressors such as unemployment (Atkinson, Liem, & Liem, 1986), warfare (Hobfoll, London, & Orr, 1988; Solomon, Mikulincer, & Hobfoll, 1987), and medical conditions (Fontana, Kerns, Rosenberg, & Colonese, 1988; C. Hanson, Henggeler, & Burghen, 1987; Pilisuk, Boylan, & Acredolo, 1987; VanderPlate, Aral, & Magder, 1988; Varni, Wilcox, & V. Hanson, 1988).

A methodological issue in many of these studies is whether support is related to increased well-being over time, as findings of longitudinal effects strengthen the interpretation of a causal relationship between support and well-being. Prospective findings from early studies (Cohen & Wills, 1985) continue to be demonstrated in recent longitudinal research (Cutrona, Russell, & Rose, 1987; Monroe, Bromet, Connell, & Steiner, 1986; Newcomb & Bentler, 1988; Tompkins, Schulz, & Rau, 1988), thus indicating that support processes are temporally antecedent to changes in well-being. Inclusion of demographic controls in multivariate analyses also has served to rule out the suggestion that the effects of social support are simply attributable to persons with high support also being of higher socioeconomic status.

Epidemiological studies have also shown that social ties are related to physical health. In the typical epidemiological study, a measure of social ties is obtained at a baseline point and determination of health status is made five to ten years subsequently (see S. Cohen, 1988; House, Landis, & Umberson, 1988). Evidence is currently available from six prospective studies of large community samples, using mortality as the end point measure. For example, a prospective study by Berkman and Syme (1979) used a social network inventory with items about marriage, contacts with friends and relatives, church or temple membership, and group memberships. Results indicated that persons low on social ties showed an increased mortality rate over the follow-up period, and each of the four types of social ties predicted mortality independently of the other three. Comparable studies in Michigan (House, Robbins, & Metzner, 1982), Georgia (Schoenbach et al., 1986), North Carolina (Blazer, 1982), Finland (Kaplan et al., 1988), and Sweden (Orth-Gomer & Johnson, 1987; Welin et al., 1985) have found similar evidence for mortality being substantially reduced among persons with a high level of social ties. Detailed analyses show an effect of social ties on mortality from all causes, indicating that effects are not specific to any one disease entity. Control analyses indicate that the effect of social ties is not attributable to baseline health status, socioeconomic status, or a variety of health behaviors.

In summary, a considerable body of evidence indicates that social support is related to well-being. In the following sections, I discuss questions of how social support operates and how the effect of social networks can be understood in relation to current social psychological theory.

SOCIAL INTEGRATION VERSUS FUNCTIONAL SUPPORT

A first question, relevant to several theoretical perspectives, is this: What aspect of social membership is relevant for psychological well-being and/or physical health? One perspective is that well-being is determined by the total number of social ties or, put differently, by a person's overall integration into a social system. In this model, social integration may contribute to well-being because it provides a feeling of predictability and coherence in life, increases access to useful resources in the community, or has a prevailing effect on mood states because of regular social interaction. A second perspective is that well-being is determined by the availability of psychological functions that are useful for coping with stressful events. From this perspective, relationships contribute to well-being because they help persons deal with emotional distress, provide communications that enhance self-esteem and self-acceptance, or provide useful advice and information that help to guide more effective coping efforts. While these models are not mutually exclusive, each presents a different view of how social ties contribute to well-being (see Antonovsky, 1979; Diener, 1984; Taylor, 1983).

Each model has some confirmation, but from different bodies of evidence. This situation derives from the coexistence of two traditions of research that use different conceptualizations of support. Research based on models of social integration tends to obtain detailed measures of the size and structure of social networks and relate these to measures of health and well-being (see, e.g., Hall & Wellman, 1985). Research based on models of supportive functions obtains psychometrically refined measures of the availability of emotional support and other functions and examines how these functions are useful for adaptation to life stressors (see, e.g., Kessler & McLeod, 1985). The current evidence shows that each aspect of social ties (social integration and functional support) is related to increased well-being, but knowledge of the mechanism of the effects is limited.

The theoretical interest of this work is increased by the fact that measures of social integration and functional support are not highly related. Although one might expect that persons with more social relationships would receive more help and hence experience greater availability of intimacy and guidance, empirical data show this is not really the case. For example, Schaefer, Coyne, and Lazarus (1981) correlated an index of total social network size with a measure of perceived emotional and informational support with a middle-aged sample and found correlations of about $r = .23$. Cutrona (1986) administered a measure of general emotional support together with four social network indices tapping the number of kin and nonkin relationships; here the multiple correlation between structural and functional indices was $R = .22$ with a sample of younger mothers and $R = .34$ with a sample of elderly persons. B. Sarason, Shearin, Pierce, and Sarason (1987) administered a social network list together with several functional measures to a college student sample and found correlations ranging from .08 to .17. Although the correlations are positive, the magnitude is modest in absolute terms, indicating that having a larger number of social relationships does not guarantee high perceived support.

Given that structural and functional aspects of social membership are not strongly related, is there clear evidence that one aspect is important for well-being? No; instead, each aspect is found to be related to well-being but in different ways. Measures of social integration predict lower rates of mortality over long time spans (House, Landis, & Umberson, 1988). Over shorter time periods, measures of social integration are related to higher psychological well-being but the effect is not related to stress level, that is, there is no buffering effect; in contrast, measures of functional support relate over shorter time spans to increased psychological well-being and typically operate as stress buffers (Cohen & Wills, 1985). Thus it has been established that social integration is related to well-being but is not necessarily helpful under stress. The questions then become these: What are the mechanisms for the two types of effects? How can these mechanisms be clarified in terms of social psychological theory?

One suggestion from theories of subjective well-being is that social integration increases prevailing levels of positive affect. In this sense, the benefit of social ties derives not from receiving any particular form of help but from regular participation in social activities. A variety of correlational studies have, in fact, shown that positive affect is strongly linked to social interaction (e.g., Diener, 1984; Okun, Stock, Haring, & Witter, 1984). The structural measures used in epidemiological studies of physical health (e.g., visiting with friends and relatives, social leisure activities, attendance at clubs and social organizations) may be tapping into this domain of experience; but these studies have not included measures of prevailing positive or negative affective levels, so the linkage remains inferential. Here, theoretical models of how social interaction influences positive affect may help to clarify how this aspect of social membership operates. For example, Rook (1987b) found that social companionship served to buffer the effect of minor daily stressors and suggested that positive affect generated by social activity served to offset the impact of negative affect generated by daily hassles. Because positive and negative affect are independent in daily life (Diener, 1984; Wills & Shiffman, 1985), this is a plausible mechanism, but there is little direct evidence on how social integration relates to positive affect in community samples (see P. Cohen et al., 1982; Schaefer, Coyne, & Lazarus, 1981).

An alternative or additional explanation is that persons with high social integration have greater awareness of available resources, which, in turn, influences coping effectiveness (e.g., Granovetter, 1973; Thoits, 1986). In this model, a person with a more diverse social network will, through casual interaction, become familiar with persons and organizations in the community that may be helpful for certain types of problems; the suggestion is that there is little explicit help seeking but, instead, a gradual absorption of information through social contacts in everyday life. Social support research provides some evidence for this position, showing, for example, that higher social integration is related to greater effectiveness in obtaining child care

(Kessler & Essex, 1982; Powell & Eisenstadt, 1983) and both formal and informal support services (Birkel & Repucci, 1983; Wilcox & Birkel, 1983). Again, there is little direct evidence for this model and few tests of whether persons with larger social networks actually have more knowledge of available resources. A theory-testing study might obtain measures of relevant coping knowledge together with measures of affective states and perform a test of whether effects of social ties on well-being are mediated through knowledge or affect. This represents one area in which social psychological theories of coping and well-being may guide the direction of field research on social support.

Turning to studies of functional social support, a quite different theoretical model is suggested. To begin, the low correlation between structural and functional measures implies that the majority of direct helping (in the form of confiding, sharing, and guidance) occurs in a few close relationships. Together with the consistent finding of stress-buffering effects for functions such as emotional support, the suggestion is that close relationships help a person cope with major life stressors because, in such a relationship, he or she can disclose and discuss problems, share concerns and anxieties, and receive advice that is accurately keyed to his or her needs.

This hypothesis is aided by the fact that measures indexing the existence of a confidant relationship (one that provides these same qualities) show the most consistent correlations with outcomes (see Cohen & Wills, 1985). A specific test was provided by Lin, Woelfel, and Light (1985), who compared the effects of close versus distant relationships in relation to major negative events and found that only close relationships provided a buffering effect for life events. In this model, the quality or intimacy of the interpersonal relationship is the crucial factor in helping persons cope with stressors, and studies that compare different measures find that intimacy is the primary factor in accounting for stress-buffering effects (Kessler & Essex, 1982; Stemp, Turner, & Noh, 1986), a conclusion subject only to the qualification that confidant relationships may have more impact for women than for men (Henderson, Byrne, Duncan-Jones, Scott, & Adcock, 1980; Reis, Wheeler, Kernis, Spiegel, & Nezlek, 1985).

The functional support model thus suggests that close relationships contribute to well-being through an influence on emotion-focused coping and negative-affect reduction. The availability of confiding relationships and intimacy seems to be most relevant for persons facing a current life crisis and is demonstrably related to lower levels of anxiety and depression. Close relationships may also be helpful in other ways (e.g., advice, practical assistance, companionship), and the typically high correlation among subscales in functional support measures (Cutrona & Russell, 1987; B. Sarason, Shearin, Pierce, & Sarason, 1987) suggests that a close relationship provides greater levels of various support functions.

To summarize, studies of social support have suggested two somewhat different models of how interpersonal relationships contribute to adaptation and well-being. The perspective of social integration proposes that a larger and more diverse social network increases prevailing levels of positive affect and may increase overall knowledge of available community resources. The perspective of functional support suggests that the availability of a close relationship enables persons to cope better with life stressors because they can confide about problems and receive help in dealing with negative emotions, thus resulting in lower anxiety and depression. It should be noted again that these perspectives are not mutually exclusive; for example, Rook (1987b) found that social companionship served to buffer the effect of minor daily stressors, whereas emotional support served to buffer the impact of major life events. Again, there have been few direct tests of the mechanism of action for these different aspects of social support. A theory-testing study might obtain multidimensional measures of social support, together with outcome measures of both positive and negative affective states, to test for differential effects of support dimensions on affective outcomes. In this manner, social psychological theory may contribute to designing precise tests of how structural and functional aspects of social networks influence affective states and coping abilities.[1]

WHAT SUPPORT FUNCTIONS ARE IMPORTANT?

An understanding of how interpersonal relationships contribute to well-being involves examination of which kinds of help are most important. What aspects of relationships do persons perceive as central for helping them cope with life stressors, and what implications does this have for social psychological theory? In the following section, I discuss this question from the perspective of social support research.

In theory, there are several helpful functions provided by relationships that could be of differential importance for coping and adjustment. Analyses of support functions (e.g., Cutrona, Russell, & Rose, 1987;

Wills, 1985) converge in proposing at least four distinct types of func- tions that can be provided through interpersonal relationships. First, relationships may contribute to well-being because they provide a source of acceptance, intimacy, and confiding about emotions; this has been variously termed *emotional support, confidant support, esteem support, appraisal support,* or *reassurance of worth.* Second, support persons may provide useful information, advice, and guidance; this is termed *informational support, advice,* or *cognitive guidance.* Third, persons may help with instrumental problems by providing financial assistance, goods, or services; this is termed *instrumental support, tangible aid,* or *material support.* Fourth, one can distinguish the function of interpersonal relationships for providing social companion- ship, termed *companionship support* or *belonging.* Measures indexing the extent to which respondents perceive these functions to be available have been used in several studies of stress and support. The crucial test is a multivariate analysis in which individual scores for several func- tions are entered together as predictors of symptomatology to determine which function(s) show a unique contribution to well-being, net of the other functions.

Here, results from field studies are notably consistent in finding one function to be important across a broad range of life stressors: emotional support. Global functional support inventories, which primarily index emotional support, show strong contributions to well-being across a variety of settings (e.g., Billings & Moos, 1985; Holahan & Moos, 1987; Phifer & Murrell, 1986; Russell, Altmaier, & Van Velzen, 1987; I. Sarason, Levine, Basham, & Sarason, 1983). Further, analyses with multidimensional functional inventories have typically shown emo- tional support to make the strongest unique contribution to well-being when analyzed with other functions (S. Cohen & Hoberman, 1983; Constable & Russell, 1986; Krause, 1987a; Roos & Cohen, 1987; Schaefer, Coyne, & Lazarus, 1981). It is noteworthy that emotional support has beneficial effects not only for the broad range of life stressors but also for specific stressors such as financial strain (Kessler & Essex, 1982; Krause, 1987a).

From a theoretical standpoint, this suggests that, for persons facing life stressors, supportive relationships are helpful because they provide maintenance of self-esteem (Taylor, 1983; Wills, 1983). Close relation- ships may serve this function because the distressed person can talk to someone who is accepting, can be told about negative aspects of the self without rejection, and can be reassured about his or her worth as a person. It is noteworthy that this aspect of social support is conceptually similar to dimensions of formal helping relationships, as derived in psychotherapy research (Elliott et al., 1982; Wills, 1982). Hence the social support literature provides significant external validation for social psychological theories that construe esteem maintenance as a basic determinant of adjustment (e.g., Swann, 1987; Taylor & Brown, 1988; Tesser, 1990). The findings of field studies suggest that the most valued aspect of helping in field settings is that which supports and maintains a person's self-esteem.

The theoretical import of the research, however, depends on whether the effects of social support are mediated through an impact on recipients' self-esteem. Here, field studies provide only a little elucidation of the process. The crucial test is one in which the effect of a supportive relationship (e.g., a confidant) is analyzed together with individual-level measures of psychological attributes, such as self-esteem, in predicting depressive symptomatology. One example is by Kessler and Essex (1982), who used cross-sectional data from a community sample to test whether the buffering effect of a supportive function (intimacy) for specific stressors (chronic life strains) was mediated by an impact on the respondent's self-esteem and self-efficacy. Results indicated that the effect of intimacy was mediated through these psychological attributes, but this was true primarily for economic strain and not for household or parenting strains. Pearlin, Menaghan, Lieberman, and Mullan (1981) analyzed four-year longitudinal data from the same sample to test whether the effect of intimacy support for a specific stressor (unemployment) was mediated through impact on changes in self-esteem or self-efficacy. Results suggested that the effect of support was mediated through impact on both self-esteem change and self-efficacy change. Using a similar analytic approach with data from an elderly sample, Krause (1987b) found that a compound measure of emotional support was related to increase in self-esteem, which, in turn, was related to a reduction in depressive symptomatology.

Thus data from field studies provide some evidence for a theoretical model in which social support operates through an effect on self-esteem. However, the available tests are restricted to two samples and a few specific stressors. Further, some data suggest an operation of social support through an impact on self-efficacy; Cutrona and Troutman (1986) found mediation through parenting efficacy with data from a sample of new mothers, and Pearlin, Menaghan, Lieberman, and Mullan's (1981) analysis suggested that changes in self-efficacy may have been more important than changes in self-esteem.[2] Hence there is a need for more specifically designed tests that examine how social support affects a number of dimensions, including self-esteem, but also tapping specific knowledge and efficacy, social competence, and related psychological attributes. Such research would help to develop theories of helping and coping based on self-control or self-esteem (e.g., Carver & Scheier, 1990; Scheier & Carver, 1988; Taylor, 1983). This discussion has emphasized the importance of emotional support across a range of settings, but the role of other functions should not be minimized. In some studies, informational support is found to make a unique contribution to well-being, and this has been demonstrated both with new parents (Cutrona, 1984) and with elderly persons (Cutrona, Russell, & Rose, 1987; Krause, 1987b). Instrumental support has been found to have unique effects among new parents (Paykel, Emms, Fletcher, & Rassaby, 1980) and college students (Roos & Cohen, 1987), possibly reflecting specific coping needs in these populations. Social companionship has been shown to produce a stress-buffering effect in some studies (Cohen & Hoberman, 1983; Rook, 1987b), and social integration buffers the effect of parenting strain (Cutrona, 1984; Kessler & Essex, 1982), possibly because persons with more social contacts have greater access to child care. In theory, the functions that are most helpful will depend on the coping demands of the population studied, but tests of the match between coping needs and help provided are still minimal (see Cutrona, 1990).

PERSONALITY AND SUPPORT RECEIPT

In field research, there has been some investigation of how helping is influenced by the personality characteristics of the recipient. Two processes are possible in theory. First, members of social networks are reluctant to help persons who are depressed, hence depression will lead to a decrease in support over time. Second, persons with particular personality attributes may be more able to form networks and utilize available support. The field research generally has provided confirmation for the second proposition, but not the first. Relevant evidence is discussed in the following section.

The first question is whether depressive affect makes the recipient less grateful for help received, which, then, makes persons less likely to help (Barnett & Gotlib, 1988). This issue is addressed in field studies by longitudinal analyses in which level of support at follow-up is predicted from symptomatology at baseline, controlling for level of support at baseline; this analysis tests whether high symptomatology leads to decrease in support over time. Available evidence shows little confirmation for this type of process (Aneshensel & Frerichs, 1982; Billings & Moos, 1982; Mitchell & Moos, 1984), that is, failing to find that depressive symptomatology decreases support. Thus, with the measures and models used in current research, there is little evidence to support the hypothesis that neuroticism leads to reduction in support over time.

The second question concerns whether persons with certain personality characteristics show more benefit from support. The relevant analytic model uses personality and support, plus the Personality × Support interaction, as predictors of symptomatology; a significant interaction indicates that the effect of support is stronger for persons high on the personality attribute. Here, the evidence is confirmatory for locus of control: Several investigators have found beneficial effects of social support occurring primarily among persons with internal locus of control (e.g., Caldwell, Pearson, & Chin, 1987; Lefcourt, Martin, & Saleh, 1984; Riley & Eckenrode, 1986). Research using Pearlin's self-efficacy scale has indicated also that persons with high efficacy show greater beneficial effects from available support (Hobfoll & Lerman, 1988; see Husaini, Neff, Newbrough, & Moore, 1982). The suggestion has been made that persons with internal control and high competence are better able to utilize support resources because they are better able to involve others in a problem-solving process.

Longitudinal data complement this picture. S. Cohen, Sherrod, and Clark (1986) showed that high self-disclosure and social competence were related to increases in perceived support over time, controlling for change in number of friends, which suggests that high competence persons were able to derive more effective support from the networks they established. Similarly, Newcomb (1990) found, in an adolescent panel, that self-esteem was related to increases in peer support over time (see I. Sarason, Sarason, & Shearin, 1986). The data thus indicate that persons with internal control or greater social competence are more effective in obtaining needed help from support networks.

SOCIAL SUPPORT AND HELPING

Field studies of social support serve to extend laboratory research on helping behavior because they provide a test of how processes demonstrated in the laboratory may apply in naturalistic settings. In this section, I consider the similarities and differences between the two bodies of literature. I note that levels of help seeking and perceived support in field settings are quite high, in contrast to typical data from laboratory studies, and offer some explanations for this. I also consider how the nature of helping in natural settings may differ from the type of helping interaction studied in laboratory paradigms and discuss relevant psychological processes.

Prevalence of Help Seeking

Data on the prevalence of help seeking show considerable divergence. In laboratory settings where a help-seeking opportunity is provided, the typical finding is that the majority of subjects do not seek help (e.g., DePaulo, Nadler, & Fisher, 1983). Laboratory research has identified a number of factors that may deter help seeking, including self-esteem concerns, imposition on the helper, and values concerning achievement and independence (Ames, 1983; Rosen, 1983; Wills & DePaulo, in press; see also Nadler, this volume). Similarly, laboratory studies of reactions to help have found a widespread occurrence of negative reactions to being helped (e.g., Fisher, Nadler, & Whitcher-Alagna, 1982). This research has also identified several factors that influence negative reactions to help, which include similarity to the helper and ego-centrality of the task (e.g., Nadler & Fisher, 1988). Another replicated finding is that persons with high self-esteem are less likely to seek help and react more negatively if they do receive help (Nadler, 1986).

These data contrast with typical findings from field research, which show the majority of respondents seeking help for personal problems (Wills & DePaulo, in press). Data on preferred sources of help show a marked preference for informal help in general and for help from spouses and friends in particular (e.g., Norcross & Prochaska, 1986; Tinsley, de St. Aubin, & Brown, 1982; Veroff, Kulka, & Douvan, 1981). This preference for informal help is observed not only for emotional problems but also for instrumental, achievement, and vocational problems (DePaulo, 1982; Tinsley, de St. Aubin, & Brown, 1982). Correspondingly, in field settings, people perceive a high level of support functions available. For example, with the scales for emotional and instrumental support from the Interpersonal Support Evaluation List, mean scores approximate 10-11 on a 12-point scale (Brookings &

Boulton, 1988); with the Social Provisions Scale, subscale means approximate 12-13 on a 16-point scale (Cutrona, Russell, & Rose, 1987); and for the Social Support Questionnaire, mean support satisfaction scores are about 145 on a 162-point scale (Sarason, Levine, Basham, & Sarason, 1983; Sarason, Sarason, & Shearin, 1986). Even making some allowance for social desirability, the level of available emotional and other support is high. Moreover, the available evidence on self-esteem indicates that persons with high esteem or competence get more help from social networks.

How is the difference between these various findings about help seeking and social support to be understood from a theoretical standpoint? Beyond the basic observation that naturalistic settings involve long-term interactions between friends while laboratory work has typically involved interactions between strangers, I think it is possible to delineate some specific processes that may be differentially relevant in the two settings.

Esteem Threat

Results from laboratory settings indicate that persons react more negatively to receiving help when helpers are similar to themselves, a phenomenon that has been linked to esteem-threat concerns and is magnified when the amount of help received is large (Fisher, Nadler, & Whitcher-Alagna, 1982; Nadler & Fisher, 1988). In studies of social support in natural settings, it is often virtually guaranteed that the helper and recipient are highly similar to each other because they are in self-selected relationships as friends or marriage partners. Moreover, in social support interactions, the participants may be discussing highly threatening, emotional events. Nonetheless, it is apparent that, in naturalistic helping relationships, the element of esteem threat that is dominant in laboratory studies is not highly relevant. Why would this be so?

While there is probably no single answer to this question, one approach is to consider the role of intimacy in ongoing relationships. By definition, *intimacy* involves a mutual disclosure of negative as well as positive aspects of the self, with the additional assumption that the helper is nonjudgmental and accepting when he or she listens to the recipient's problems (e.g., Reis & Shaver, 1987). With the addition of intimacy as a process in naturalistic relationships (or at least in those that are perceived as highly supportive), the element of esteem threat may be minimized because persons know they can disclose problems or personal limitations and still be accepted. The history of mutual self-disclosure, which appears to be a crucial component in supportive relationships (Clark & Reis, 1988), may play a large role in minimizing the role of esteem concerns in the settings studied in social support research. Reciprocal self-disclosure between partners also shows that problems and concerns occur for both persons, so perceived deviance becomes less of an issue than in interactions with strangers (Nadler & Porat, 1978; Snyder & Ingram, 1983).

Interdependence and Reciprocity

Close relationships as studied in field settings involve a basic element of interdependence and reciprocity (Kelley et al., 1983). In theory, reciprocal helping relationships should be more satisfying than ones that are not reciprocal, and this is generally found to be true in laboratory settings (M. S. Greenberg & Westcott, 1983). In the kinds of enduring relationships studied in field settings, the long-term interaction between partners allows ample opportunities for reciprocal help giving and help receiving. This should act to reduce concerns about indebtedness that are found to provide a barrier to help seeking in some laboratory interactions and may account for the fact that people are more likely to seek help from friends than from strangers even in laboratory situations (DePaulo, 1982; Nadler, Fisher, & Ben-Itzhak, 1983; Shapiro, 1980). Although the role of reciprocity has been established in the laboratory, there is surprisingly little data on this issue from field research. Antonucci and Israel (1986) did note data showing a high degree of reciprocity in social support relationships, and Rook (1987a) found that persons were more satisfied with reciprocal relationships, compared with either underbenefited or overbenefited relationships.

The process of reciprocal helping in daily life also minimizes the visibility of help seeking. In laboratory settings, results show that persons are less likely to ask for help when they must make an explicit help-seeking request and the request is highly visible (e.g., Shapiro, 1978). In naturalistic relationships, partners typically do things for each other as part of regularized interaction, so that explicit help seeking is minimized (Coyne & Bolger, 1990). In an intimate relationship, moreover, partners are more likely to be aware of each other's needs through both verbal and nonverbal cues (DePaulo & Fisher, 1981) so the probability of explicit help-seeking requests is further reduced.

Relationship Norms

A final consideration is that people's schemas for relationships may be basically different. At least one relationship model (Clark & Mills, 1979) proposes that people hold different schemas for strangers or acquaintances (exchange relationships) than for such intimate relationships as friendships and romantic partners (communal relationships). This model suggests that, in a close relationship, a person is motivated by concern for the other's needs and his or her subjective well-being is linked to the other's affective state. Data from laboratory studies indeed show quite different results for conditions in which subjects have a communal orientation; for example, they are less likely to keep track of the other's inputs, they respond more positively as the amount of help given increases, and they respond more positively when the other is experiencing negative affect (Clark, Mills, & Powell, 1986; Clark, Ouellette, Powell, & Milberg, 1987; Williamson & Clark, 1989). Thus the basic meaning of help may be fundamentally altered as a function of relationship type, so that it is essentially negative in an exchange relationship (because it incurs indebtedness, must be kept track of, and leaves the helper subject to nonreciprocation), whereas, in a communal relationship, it is essentially positive because of a sense of shared fate and concern for the other's needs.

Convergence of laboratory and field research is suggested by data on social support: The high levels of perceived support, the manifest willingness to expend energy in helping, and the perception that help is available in many domains all point to a relationship schema resembling the communal model. In laboratory settings, strangers participating in short-term interactions may instead be following exchange norms. Yet there is little evidence from field studies on how various relationships differ in orientation or on how cognitive and normative factors affect perceived support. This remains an avenue of interest for understanding support relationships in natural settings.

SUMMARY

This chapter has made two basic points about research on social support and its bearing on theories of helping. First, evidence from field studies shows that interpersonal relationships have a major role in contributing to well-being, and this applies not only for psychological adjustment but also for physical health outcomes. Second, the mechanisms for these effects are not well delineated. Models of social support effects that involve cognitive, affective, and coping-based mechanisms are plausible, and each addresses some aspect of the evidence; but there has been little research to delineate the mechanism of how either social integration or functional support contributes to well-being. Thus this is an area in which social psychological theory may contribute to the design of social support research by suggesting mediators and mechanisms through which support may influence well-being.[3]

At the same time, field research on social support provides an important arena in which findings from laboratory research on helping can be checked and cross-validated. Because of the size and representativeness of samples that are typical of epidemiological studies, plus the relevance of outcome measures of psychological and physical health, the results of field research are high on external validity and hence have strong bearing for suggesting how helping operates in naturalistic settings. Thus the results of social support research are significant for both social psychology and health psychology.

On the first point, it is noteworthy that one major mechanism through which social ties influence well-being is through confiding and intimacy, apparently through the effect of intimacy on self-esteem. However, little is understood about how interpersonal relationships provide esteem support. It is apparent from the preceding discussion that self-disclosure and intimacy are basic elements for emotional support (Clark & Reis, 1988), and this is an area in which the theory of close relationships may lead to better understanding of the mechanisms of social support. For example, the presence of intimacy may enhance the value of a close relationship for providing guidance because persons are more aware of one another's capabilities and limitations and hence provide more appropriate advice (Reis, 1990). This model is consistent with the observation in social support research of high correlations among the availability of different support functions, but currently there is no basic theoretical account of this phenomenon or the low correlation between structural and functional measures. Theories of close relationships may help lead toward this goal.

In a broader sense, there is the question of why self-esteem is so important for adjustment, and how self-esteem, self-efficacy, and actual competence mutually develop and influence each other. It is apparent from the social support research that emotional support from relationships enhances adjustment to a wide range of problems, including financial stressors, but there is little understanding of how this works. It is possible that intimacy between partners increases communication of relevant information and modeling and hence contributes to the coping effort through increasing actual competence. These issues remain to be investigated in studies on daily interaction in ongoing relationships.

Also, there is little understanding of the conditions that influence perceived support or of the types of interpersonal transactions that foster a sense of being accepted and supported (Melamed & Brenner, 1990; Sarason, Sarason, & Shearin, 1986). There is a large body of literature on communication and satisfaction in marital relationships (e.g., Bradbury & Fincham, 1988), and, because marital relationships appear to be one of the major sources of functional support, this represents another avenue for bridging between fields. As yet, there has been little application of theory on marital relationships and marital interaction to a more general understanding of the helping process.

On the second point, I have noted that findings from field studies are inconsistent with laboratory research on helping in several respects, and this discussion has suggested several ways in which the paradigms of the two traditions differ. For one, the sensitivity to esteem threat that is present in interactions between strangers may be less salient in natural support relationships, a factor that may be attributable to intimacy or to other considerations. Another difference is that laboratory studies typically involve situations in which there is a direct request for help, whereas, in naturalistic settings, the character of helping may be quite different because it frequently occurs without direct requests (Coyne & Bolger, 1990). I have also suggested that some of the benefits of social membership may occur through social activity, which is not readily construed as helping at all. So, in this respect, the nature of helping as it occurs in natural settings may be substantially different from the kind of helping studied in laboratory paradigms. This observation may have implications for the design of further laboratory research as well as for field studies that would examine how specific variables from laboratory research operate in naturalistic settings.

NOTES

1. It should be noted that other mechanisms are possible, for example, social integration may influence health outcomes through encouraging desirable health behaviors or discouraging undesirable ones (S. Cohen, 1988; Umberson, 1987). A full discussion of this issue is beyond the scope of this chapter.

2. This issue has another source of ambiguity because measures of self-efficacy and self-esteem are themselves highly correlated. This raises intriguing questions for the theory of self-esteem but, at the same time, makes it statistically difficult to obtain a clear differential test.

3. At the same time, it is recognized that interpersonal relationships in natural settings involve conflictual or rejecting interactions as well as supportive experiences (e.g., Henderson, Byrne, Duncan-Jones, Scott, & Adcock, 1980; Manne & Zautra, 1989; Rook, 1984). Here, laboratory research on reactions to help (e.g., Fisher, Nadler, & Whitcher-Alagna, 1982) may help to clarify why relationships are not always supportive.

REFERENCES

Ames, R. (1983). Help-seeking and achievement orientation. In B. M. DePaulo, A. Nadler, & J. D. Fisher (Eds.), *New directions in helping: Vol. 2. Help seeking* (pp. 165-186). New York: Academic Press.

Aneshensel, C. S., & Frerichs, R. R. (1982). Stress, support, and depression: A longitudinal causal model. *Journal of Community Psychology, 10,* 363-376.

Antonovsky, A. (1979). *Health, stress, and coping.* San Francisco: Jossey-Bass.

Antonucci, T. C., & Israel, B. A. (1986). Veridicality of social support. *Journal of Consulting and Clinical Psychology, 54,* 432-437.

Atkinson, T., Liem, R., & Liem, J. H. (1986). The social costs of unemployment: Implications for social support. *Journal of Health and Social Behavior, 27,* 317-331.

Barnett, P. A., & Gotlib, I. H. (1988). Psychosocial functioning and depression: Distinguishing among antecedents, concomitants, and consequences. *Psychological Bulletin, 104,* 97-126.

Berkman, L. F., & Syme, S. L. (1979). Social networks, host resistance, and mortality. *American Journal of Epidemiology, 109,* 186-204.

Billings, A. G., & Moos, R. H. (1982). Social support and functioning among community and clinical groups: A panel model. *Journal of Behavioral Medicine, 5,* 295-311.

Billings, A. G., & Moos, R. H. (1985). Life stressors and social resources affect posttreatment outcomes among depressed patients. *Journal of Abnormal Psychology, 94,* 140-153.

Birkel, R. C., & Repucci, N. D. (1983). Social networks, information seeking, and the utilization of services. *American Journal of Community Psychology, 11,* 185-205.

Blazer, D. G. (1982). Social support and mortality in an elderly community population. *American Journal of Epidemiology, 115,* 684-694.

Bradbury, T. N., & Fincham, F. D. (1989). Behavior and satisfaction in marriage. In C. Hendrick (Ed.), *Review of personality and social psychology* (Vol. 10, pp. 119-143). Newbury Park, CA: Sage.

Brookings, S. B., & Bolton, B. (1988). Confirmatory factor analysis of the Interpersonal Support Evaluation List. *American Journal of Community Psychology, 16,* 137-147.

Caldwell, R. A., Pearson, J. L., & Chin, R. J. (1987). Stress-moderating effects of social support in the context of gender and locus of control. *Personality and Social Psychology Bulletin, 13,* 5-17.

Carver, C. S., & Scheier, M. S. (1990). Principles of self-regulation: Action and emotion. In E. T. Higgins & R. M. Sorrentino (Eds.), *Handbook of motivation and cognition* (Vol. 2, pp. 3-52). New York: Guilford.

Cassel, J. C. (1976). The contribution of the social environment to host resistance. *American Journal of Epidemiology, 104,* 107-123.

Clark, M. S., & Mills, J. (1979). Interpersonal attraction in exchange and communal relationships. *Journal of Personality and Social Psychology, 37,* 12-24.

Clark, M. S., Mills, J., & Powell, M. C. (1986). Keeping track of needs in communal and exchange relationships. *Journal of Personality and Social Psychology, 51,* 333-338.

Clark, M. S., Ouellette, R., Powell, M. C., & Milberg, S. (1987). Recipient's mood, relationship type, and helping. *Journal of Personality and Social Psychology, 53,* 94-103.

Clark, M. S., & Reis, H. T. (1988). Interpersonal processes in close relationships. *Annual Review of Psychology, 39,* 609-672.

Cobb, S. (1976). Social support as a moderator of life stress. *Psychosomatic Medicine, 38,* 300-314.

Cohen, P., Struening, E. L., Muhlin, G. L., Genevie, L. E., Kaplan, S., & Peck, H. B. (1982). Community stressors, mediating conditions, and well being in urban neighborhoods. *Journal of Community Psychology, 10,* 377-391.

Cohen, S. (1988). Psychosocial models of the role of social support in the etiology of physical disease. *Health Psychology, 7,* 269-297.

Cohen, S., & Hoberman, H. (1983). Positive events and social supports as buffers of life change stress. *Journal of Applied Social Psychology, 13,* 99-125.

Cohen, S., Sherrod, D. R., & Clark, M. S. (1986). Social skills and the stress-protective role of social support. *Journal of Personality and Social Psychology, 50,* 963-973.

Cohen, S., & Wills, T. A. (1985). Stress, social support, and the buffering hypothesis. *Psychological Bulletin, 98,* 310-357.

Constable, J. F., & Russell, D. (1986). The effect of social support and work environment on burnout among nurses. *Journal of Human Stress, 12,* 20-26.

Coyne, J. C., & Bolger, N. (1990). Doing without social support as an explanatory concept. *Journal of Social and Clinical Psychology, 9,* 148-158.

Cutrona, C. E. (1984). Social support and stress in the transition to parenthood. *Journal of Abnormal Psychology, 93,* 378-390.

Cutrona, C. E. (1986). Objective determinants of perceived social support. *Journal of Personality and Social Psychology, 50,* 349-355.

Cutrona, C. E. (1990). Stress and social support: In search of optimal matching. *Journal of Social and Clinical Psychology, 9,* 3-14.

Cutrona, C. E., & Russell, D. W. (1987). The provisions of social relationships and adaptation to stress. In W. H. Jones & D. Perlman (Eds.), *Advances in personal relationships* (Vol. 1, pp. 37-67). Greenwich, CT: JAI.

Cutrona, C. E., Russell, D., & Rose, J. (1986). Social support and adaptation to stress by the elderly. *Psychology and Aging, 1,* 47-54.

Cutrona, C. E., & Troutman, B. R. (1986). Social support, infant temperament, and parenting self-efficacy: A mediational model of postpartum depression. *Child Development, 57,* 1507-1518.

DePaulo, B. M. (1982). Social-psychological processes in informal help-seeking. In T. A. Wills (Ed.), *Basic processes in helping relationships* (pp. 255-279). New York: Academic Press.

DePaulo, B. M., & Fisher, J. D. (1981). Too tuned-out to take: The role of nonverbal sensitivity in help-seeking. *Personality and Social Psychology Bulletin, 7,* 201-205.

DePaulo, B. M., Nadler, A., & Fisher, J. D. (Eds.). (1983). *New directions in helping: Vol. 2. Help-seeking.* New York: Academic Press.

Diener, E. (1984). Subjective well-being. *Psychological Bulletin, 95,* 542-575.

Elliott, R., Stiles, W. B., Shiffman, S., Barker, C. B., Burstein, B., & Goodman, G. (1982). The empirical analysis of help-intended communications. In T. A. Wills (Ed.), *Basic processes in helping relationships* (pp. 333-356). New York: Academic Press.

Fisher, J. D., Nadler, A., & Whitcher-Alagna, S. (1982). Recipient reactions to aid. *Psychological Bulletin, 91,* 27-54.

Fontana, A. F., Kerns, R. D., Rosenberg, R. L., & Colonese, K. L. (1989). Support, stress, and recovery from coronary heart disease. *Health Psychology, 8,* 175-193.

Granovetter, M. S. (1973). The strength of weak ties. *American Journal of Sociology, 78,* 1360-1380.

Greenberg, M. S., & Westcott, D. R. (1983). Indebtedness as a mediator of reactions to aid. In J. D. Fisher, A. Nadler, & B. M. DePaulo (Eds.), *New directions in helping* (Vol. 1, pp. 85-112). New York: Academic Press.

Greenberg, M. T., Siegel, J. M., & Leitch, C. J. (1983). The nature and importance of attachment relationships to parents and peers during adolescence. *Journal of Youth and Adolescence, 12,* 373-386.

Hall, A., & Wellman, B. (1985). Social networks and social support. In S. Cohen & S. L. Syme (Eds.), *Social support and health* (pp. 23-41). Orlando, FL: Academic Press.

Hanson, C. L., Henggeler, S. W., & Burghen, G. A. (1987). Social competence and parental support as mediators of the link between stress and metabolic control in adolescents with insulin-dependent diabetes mellitus. *Journal of Consulting and Clinical Psychology, 55,* 529-533.

Henderson, S., Byrne, D. G., Duncan-Jones, P., Scott, R., & Adcock, S. (1980). Social relationships, adversity and neurosis: A study of associations in a general population sample. *British Journal of Psychiatry, 136,* 574-583.

Hobfoll, S. E., & Leiberman, J. R. (1987). Personality and social resources in immediate and continued stress resistance among women. *Journal of Personality and Social Psychology, 52,* 18-26.

Hobfoll, S. E., & Lerman, M. (1988). Personal relationships, personal attributes, and stress resistance: Mothers' reactions to their child's illness. *American Journal of Community Psychology, 16,* 565-589.

Hobfoll, S. E., & London, P., & Orr, E. (1988). Mastery, intimacy, and stress resistance during war. *Journal of Community Psychology, 16,* 317-331.

Holahan, C. J., & Moos, R. H. (1987). Risk, resistance, and psychological distress: A longitudinal analysis with adults and children. *Journal of Abnormal Psychology, 96,* 3-13.

House, J. S., Landis, K. R., & Umberson, D. (1988). Social relationships and health. *Science, 241,* 540-545.

House, J. S., Robbins, C., & Metzner, H. L. (1982). The association of social relationships and activities with mortality. *American Journal of Epidemiology, 116,* 123-140.

Husaini, B. A., Neff, J. A., Newbrough, J. R., & Moore, M. C. (1982). The stress-buffering role of social support and personal competence among the rural married. *Journal of Community Psychology, 10,* 409-426.

Kaplan, G. A., Salonen, J. T., Cohen, R. D., Brand, R. J., Syme, S. L., & Puska, P. (1988). Social connections and mortality: Prospective evidence from Finland. *American Journal of Epidemiology, 128,* 370-380.

Kelley, H. H., Berscheid, E., Christensen, A., Harvey, J. H., Huston, T. L., Levinger, G., McClintock, E., Peplau, L. A., & Peterson, D. R. (1983). *Close relationships.* New York: Freeman.

Kessler, R. C., & Essex, M. (1982). Marital status and depression: The role of coping resources. *Social Forces, 61,* 484-507.

Kessler, R. C., & McLeod, J. D. (1985). Social support and mental health in community samples. In S. Cohen & S. L. Syme (Eds.), *Social support and health* (pp. 219-240). Orlando, FL: Academic Press.

Krause, N. (1987a). Chronic financial strain, social support, and depressive symptoms among older adults. *Psychology and Aging, 2,* 185-192.

Krause, N. (1987b). Life stress, social support, and self-esteem in an elderly population. *Psychology and Aging, 2,* 349-356.

Lefcourt, H. M., Martin, R. A., & Saleh, W. E. (1984). Locus of control and social support as interactive moderators of stress. *Journal of Personality and Social Psychology, 47,* 378-389.

Lin, N., Woelfel, M. W., & Light, S. C. (1985). The buffering effect of social support consequent to an important life event. *Journal of Health and Social Behavior, 26,* 247-263.

Manne, S. L., & Zautra, A. J. (1989). Spouse criticism and support: Their association with coping and psychological adjustment among women with rheumatoid arthritis. *Journal of Personality and Social Psychology, 56,* 608-617.

Melamed, B. G., & Brenner, G. F. (1990). Social support and chronic medical stress: An interaction-based approach. *Journal of Social and Clinical Psychology, 9,* 104-117.

Mitchell, R. E., & Moos, R. H. (1984). Deficiencies in social support among depressed patients: Antecedents or consequences of stress? *Journal of Health and Social Behavior, 25,* 438-452.

Monroe, S. M., Bromet, E. J., Connell, M. M., & Steiner, S. C. (1986). Social support, life events, and depressive symptoms: A 1-year prospective study. *Journal of Consulting and Clinical Psychology, 54,* 424-431.

Nadler, A. (1986). Self-esteem and the seeking and receiving of help. In B. Maher & W. Maher (Eds.), *Progress in experimental personality research* (Vol. 14, pp. 115-163). New York: Academic Press.

Nadler, A., & Fisher, J. D. (1986). The role of threat to self-esteem and perceived control in recipient reaction to help: Theory development and empirical validation. In L. Berkowitz (Ed.), *Advances in experimental social psychology* (Vol. 19, pp. 81-122). New York: Academic Press.

Nadler, A., Fisher, J. D., & Ben-Itzhak, S. (1983). With a little help from my friends: Effects of single or multiple-act aid as a function of donor and task characteristics. *Journal of Personality and Social Psychology, 44,* 310-321.

Nadler, A., Mayseless, O., Peri, N., & Chemerinski, A. (1985). Effects of self-esteem and ability to reciprocate on help-seeking behavior. *Journal of Personality, 53,* 23-36.

Nadler, A., & Porat, A. (1978). Effects of anonymity and locus of need attribution on help-seeking behavior. *Personality and Social Psychology Bulletin, 4,* 624-626.

Newcomb, M. D. (1990). Social support and personal characteristics: A developmental and interactional perspective. *Journal of Social and Clinical Psychology, 9,* 54-68.

Newcomb, M. D., & Bentler, P. M. (1988). Impact of adolescent drug use and social support on problems of young adults: A longitudinal study. *Journal of Abnormal Psychology, 97,* 64-75.

Norcross, J. C., & Prochaska, J. O. (1986). The psychological distress and self-change of psychologists, counselors, and laypersons. *Psychotherapy, 23,* 102-114.

Okun, M. A., Stock, W. A., Haring, M. J., & Witter, R. A. (1984). The social activity-subjective well-being relation. *Research on Aging, 6*(1), 45-65.

Orth-Gomer, K., & Johnson, J. V. (1987). Social network interaction and mortality: A 6-year follow-up study of a random sample of the Swedish population. *Journal of Chronic Disease, 40,* 949-957.

Paykel, E. S., Emms, E. M., Fletcher, J., & Rassaby, E. S. (1980). Life events and social support in puerperal depression. *British Journal of Psychiatry, 136,* 339-346.

Pearlin, L. I., Menaghan, E. G., Lieberman, M. A., & Mullan, J. T. (1981). The stress process. *Journal of Health and Social Behavior, 22,* 337-356.

Phifer, J. F., & Murrell, S. A. (1986). Etiologic factors in the onset of depressive symptoms in older adults. *Journal of Abnormal Psychology, 95,* 282-291.

Pilisuk, M., Boylan, R., & Acredolo, C. (1987). Social support, life stress, and subsequent medical care utilization. *Health Psychology, 6,* 273-288.

Powell, D. R., & Eisenstadt, J. W. (1983). Predictions of help-seeking in an urban setting: The search for child care. *American Journal of Community Psychology, 11,* 401-422.

Reis, H. T. (1990). The role of intimacy in interpersonal relations. *Journal of Social and Clinical Psychology, 9,* 15-30.

Reis, H. T., & Shaver, P. (1987). Intimacy as an interpersonal process. In S. Duck (Ed.), *Handbook of personal relationships* (pp. 367-389). Chichester: John Wiley.

Reis, H. T., Wheeler, L., Kernis, M. H., Spiegel, N., & Nezlek, J. (1985). On specificity in the impact of social participation on health. *Journal of Personality and Social Psychology, 48,* 456-471.

Riley, B., & Eckenrode, J. (1986). Social ties: Subgroup differences in costs and benefits. *Journal of Personality and Social Psychology, 51,* 770-778.

Rook, K. S. (1984). The negative side of social interaction: Impact on psychological well-being. *Journal of Personality and Social Psychology, 46,* 1097-1108.

Rook, K. S. (1987a). Reciprocity of social exchange and social satisfaction among older women. *Journal of Personality and Social Psychology, 52,* 145-154.

Rook, K. S. (1987b). Social support versus companionship: Effects on life stress, loneliness, and evaluations by others. *Journal of Personality and Social Psychology, 52,* 1132-1147.

Roos, P. E., & Cohen, L. H. (1987). Sex roles and social support as moderators of life stress adjustment. *Journal of Personality and Social Psychology, 52,* 576-585.

Rosen, S. (1983). Perceived inadequacy and help-seeking. In B. M. DePaulo, A. Nadler, & J. D. Fisher (Eds.), *New directions in helping: Vol. 2. Help-seeking* (pp. 73-107). New York: Academic Press.

Russell, D., Altmaier, E., & Van Velzen, D. (1987). Job-related stress, social support, and burnout among classroom teachers. *Journal of Applied Psychology, 72,* 269-274.

Sandler, I. N., & Lakey, B. (1982). Locus of control as a stress moderator: The role of control perceptions and social support. *American Journal of Community Psychology, 10,* 65-80.

Sarason, B. R., Shearin, E. N., Pierce, G. R., & Sarason, I. G. (1987). Interrelations of social support measures. *Journal of Personality and Social Psychology, 52,* 813-832.

Sarason, I. G., Levine, H. M., Basham, R. B., & Sarason, B. R. (1983). Assessing social support: The Social Support Questionnaire. *Journal of Personality and Social Psychology, 44,* 127-139.

Sarason, I. G., Sarason, B. R., & Shearin, E. N. (1986). Social support as an individual difference variable. *Journal of Personality and Social Psychology, 50,* 845-855.

Schaefer, C., Coyne, J. C., & Lazarus, R. S. (1981). The health-related functions of social support. *Journal of Behavioral Medicine, 4,* 381-406.

Schoenbach, V. J., Kaplan, B. H., Fredman, L., & Kleinbaum, D. G. (1986). Social ties and mortality in Evans County, Georgia. *American Journal of Epidemiology, 123,* 577-591.

Shapiro, E. G. (1978). Effects of visibility of task performance on seeking help. *Journal of Applied Social Psychology, 8,* 163-173.

Shapiro, E. G. (1980). Is seeking help from a friend like seeking help from a stranger? *Social Psychology Quarterly, 43,* 259-263.

Scheier, M. S., & Carver, C. S. (1988). A model of behavioral self-regulation: Translating intention into action. In L. Berkowitz (Ed.), *Advances in experimental social psychology* (Vol. 21, pp. 303-346). New York: Academic Press.

Snyder, C. R., & Ingram, R. E. (1983). The impact of consensus information on help-seeking for psychological problems. *Journal of Personality and Social Psychology, 45,* 1118-1136.

Solomon, Z., Mikulincer, M., & Hobfoll, S. E. (1987). Objective versus subjective measurement of stress and social support: Combat-related reactions. *Journal of Consulting and Clinical Psychology, 55,* 577-583.

Stemp, P. S., Turner, R. J., & Noh, S. (1986). Psychological distress in the postpartum period: The significance of social support. *Journal of Marriage and the Family, 48,* 271-277.

Swann, W. B., Jr. (1987). Identity negotiation: Where two roads meet. *Journal of Personality and Social Psychology, 53,* 1038-1051.

Taylor, S. E. (1983). Adjustment to threatening events. *American Psychologist, 38,* 1161-1173.

Taylor, S. E., & Brown, J. D. (1988). Illusion and well-being: A social psychological perspective on mental health. *Psychological Bulletin, 103,* 193-210.

Thoits, P. A. (1986). Social support as coping assistance. *Journal of Consulting and Clinical Psychology, 54,* 416-423.

Tesser, A. (1990). Emotion in social comparison and reflection processes. In J. Suls & T. A. Wills (Eds.), *Social comparison: Contemporary theory and research* (pp. 115-145). Hillsdale, NJ: Lawrence Erlbaum.

Tinsley, H. E. A., de St. Aubin, T. M., & Brown, M. T. (1982). College students' help-seeking preferences. *Journal of Counseling Psychology, 29,* 523-533.

Tompkins, C. A., Schulz, R., & Rau, M. T. (1988). Post-stroke depression in primary support persons: Predicting those at risk. *Journal of Consulting and Clinical Psychology, 56,* 502-508.

Umberson, D. (1987). Family status and health behaviors: Social control as a dimension of social integration. *Journal of Health and Social Behavior, 28,* 306-319.

VanderPlate, C., Aral, S. O., & Magder, L. (1988). The relationship among genital herpes simplex virus, stress, and social support. *Health Psychology, 7,* 159-168.

Varni, J. W., Wilcox, K. T., & Hanson, V. (1988). Mediating effects of family social support on child psychological adjustment in juvenile rheumatoid arthritis. *Health Psychology, 7,* 421-431.

Veroff, J. B., Kulka, R. A., & Douvan, E. (1981). *Mental health in America: Patterns of help-seeking 1957-1976.* New York: Basic Books.

Welin, L., Tibblin, G., Svardsudd, K., Tibblin, B., Ander-Peciva, S., Larsson, B., & Wilhelmsen, L. (1985). Prospective study of social influences on mortality. *Lancet, i,* 915-920.

Wilcox, B. L., & Birkel, R. C. (1983). Social networks and the help-seeking process: A structural perspective. In A. Nadler, J. D. Fisher, & B. M. DePaulo (Eds.), *New directions in helping* (Vol. 3, pp. 235-253). New York: Academic Press.

Williamson, G. M., & Clark, M. S. (1989). Providing help and desired relationship type as determinants of changes in moods and self-evaluation. *Journal of Personality and Social Psychology, 56,* 722-734.

Wills, T. A. (1982). Nonspecific factors in helping relationships. In T. A. Wills (Ed.), *Basic processes in helping relationships* (pp. 381-404). New York: Academic Press.

Wills, T. A. (1983). Social comparison in coping and help seeking. In B. M. DePaulo, A. Nadler, & J. D. Fisher (Eds.), *New directions in helping: Vol. 2. Help-seeking.* (pp. 109-141). New York: Academic Press.

Wills, T. A. (1985). Supportive functions of interpersonal relationships. In S. Cohen & L. Syme (Eds.), *Social support and health* (pp. 61-82). Orlando, FL: Academic Press.

Wills, T. A. (1986). Stress and coping in early adolescence: Relationships to substance use in urban school samples. *Health Psychology, 5,* 503-529.

Wills, T. A., & DePaulo, B. M. (in press). Interpersonal analysis of the help-seeking process. In C. R. Snyder & D. R. Forsyth (Eds.), *Handbook of social and clinical psychology.* Elmsford, NY: Pergamon.

Wills, T. A., & Shiffman, S. (1985). Coping and substance use: A conceptual framework. In S. Shiffman & T. A. Wills (Eds.), *Coping and substance use* (pp. 3-24). Orlando, FL: Academic Press.

11

Help-Seeking Behavior
PSYCHOLOGICAL COSTS AND
INSTRUMENTAL BENEFITS

ARIE NADLER

Arie Nadler is Professor of Psychology at Tel Aviv University, Ramat Aviv, Israel. In addition to his interests in the study of help seeking and recipient reactions to help, he has written on interpersonal relations and Holocaust survivors and their families.

It has been well documented by past research that individuals often do not seek needed help. This is true in community (e.g., Brown, 1978), mental health (e.g., Dew, Dunn, Bromet, & Shulberg, 1988), educational (e.g., Ames & Lau, 1982), and work (e.g., Burke, Weir, & Duncan, 1976) settings. Moreover, this differential willingness to seek help is affected by situational (e.g., Nadler & Porat, 1978), personality (e.g., Nadler, Mayseless, Peri, & Tchemerinski, 1985), and demographic variables (e.g., Asser, 1978). The reason for this variability is that seeking help involves instrumental benefits *and* psychological costs. From an *instrumental perspective,* seeking outside assistance often is important for easing suffering or for further task completion. However, relying on outside help may threaten a person's feelings of independence and competence.

An understanding of the help-seeking phenomenon has important conceptual and applied implications. Conceptually, it broadens the outlook of social psychological research on *helping behavior* to the study of *helping relationships,* which commonly begin when an individual seeks help. Further, specification of the variables and processes involved in willingness to seek help will shed light on the role of dependence and independence in interpersonal relations. On the applied level, an understanding of the help-seeking process should result in the design of more effective helping programs, which would foster better utilization of available resources and better personal coping.

AUTHOR'S NOTE: Support for the preparation of this manuscript was provided by grant 86-00082 from the Israel-U.S.A. BINSF.

Paradigmatically, the help-seeking interaction involves three entities: a *person in need of help, a source of help,* and a specific *need for help.* These categories serve as an organizing framework for this chapter. Data regarding the effects of the characteristics of (a) the person in need, (b) the helper, and (c) the help on help seeking are reviewed. Within each of these three categories, the organizing question concerns the perceived psychological costs and instrumental benefits in help seeking.

Field studies and laboratory experiments are relevant to this topic. One line of relevant field research is the "epidemiological research" that examined *actual* help seeking such as in visits to a mental health clinic (e.g., Dew, Dunn, Bromet, & Schulberg, 1988). Also relevant are "coping studies" that have asked individuals what they would do (e.g., Hobfoll & Lerman, 1988) or have done (e.g., Tausig & Michello, 1988) in one or a number of stressful events. Here, help seeking is viewed as one possible coping response. The epidemiological line of research relies on sociological concepts and methodologies, while the coping studies are associated with research on social support and clinical or counseling psychology.

Experimental social psychological research views help seeking as a general phenomenon and is concerned with theory building. It views the type of problem for which help is sought as a moderator within a larger conceptual scheme. The current review of the psychological costs and instrumental benefits associated with help seeking draws on all these lines of study.

CHARACTERISTICS OF THE PERSON NEEDING HELP

The demographic variables most frequently studied as affecting help have been gender, age, and socioeconomic status. The personality variables most frequently studied have been self-esteem, achievement motivation, and shyness.

Demographic Variables

(1) Gender. Epidemiological studies indicate that, on the whole, females seek more help than males. Veroff (1981) suggested a rate of two to one favoring women over men in seeking help. This is true in both medical (Verbrugge, 1981) and psychiatric contexts (Fischer,

Winer, & Abramowitz, 1983). Also, females are overrepresented among callers to radio counseling programs (Raviv, Raviv, & Yunovitz, 1989) and among clients of counseling centers on college campuses (Robertson, 1988). A controlled observation of children in the classroom also indicates that girls seek more help than boys (Nelson LeGall & Glor-Scheib, 1985).

The greater willingness of women to seek help is also found in the social support literature. Butler, Giordano, and Neren (1985) report that, relative to females, males perceived the environment as offering less help and saw themselves as seeking less help and support. Finally, *psychological* gender (i.e., self-perceived femininity and masculinity) also appears to predict help seeking. Femininity scores are positively related to willingness to seek help (Nadler, Maler, & Friedman, 1984), especially when the task is defined as feminine (Wallston, 1976).

A number of studies indicate that both males and females prefer seeking help from a same-sex helper (Nelson-LeGall, 1987). The reason for this preference may be due to the fact that help seeking normally occurs between friends (Clark, 1983) and that the young adults who were studied are likely to have closer same- than other-sex friends. This, however, does not hold when females encounter a physically attractive male. Under these conditions, self-presentation concerns appear to motivate young females to seek more help, thereby presenting themselves as more "feminine" to the attractive male helper (Nadler, Shapira, & Ben-Itzhak, 1982).

The link between helper and recipient gender becomes more complex when help-seeking patterns of married individuals are considered. Whereas married females continue relying on friends for help, males rely on their wives (Veroff, 1981). These data coincide with analyses showing the greater role of intimate same-sex friendships in the lives of women as compared with men (Reis, Senchak, & Solomon, 1985). Research on the issue of naturally occurring help seeking within the family, however, is still largely missing.

Another moderator of the gender-help-seeking relationship is the nature of the need. The higher ratio of females to males among helpseekers is more evident in seeking help for problems of a personal-emotional nature than for problems of an instrumental nature (Robertson, 1988; Veroff, 1981). This preference of males for instrumental-informational help also characterizes help-seeking behavior of male and female children (Belle, Burr, & Cooney, 1987). The reason for this consistent finding is most likely associated with the fact that, relative to the feminine sex role, the masculine sex role puts a premium on instrumental goal achievement (Chafetz, 1978). Therefore, males may view emotional difficulties as more stigmatizing and threatening. In support of this view, Philips (1964) reports that men felt more stigmatized than women when displaying emotional symptoms.

The most often quoted explanation for this consistent sex difference in help seeking has been in terms of the definitions of the masculine and feminine sex roles. Because males are supposed to be strong and independent and females are allowed, and sometimes encouraged, to be weak and dependent (Meeker & Weitzel-O'Neill, 1977), seeking help is more consistent with the feminine than the masculine sex role. The data linking help seeking to differences in "psychological gender" (e.g., self-perceived femininity) lend important support to this view.

Yet, this explanation does not tell us what these sex differences mean. They may reflect different labeling processes such that, given a similar difficulty, females are more likely than males to label it as a "problem" with which to deal. Alternatively, both sexes may define the difficulty of a problem similarly, but, relative to males, females may show greater preference to use external sources to solve it. The data suggest that these are not mutually exclusive explanations. Supporting the position that sex differences reflect a different "problem" definition, Wills and DePaulo (in press) indicate that the sex difference in help seeking occurs only in mild states of need. In extreme states of need, which are defined as a "problem" by all, males actually tend to seek more help than females. Supporting the position that males prefer to rely on themselves rather than seeking help, Mitchell (1987) has found that, relative to females, males see themselves as more able to control situations on their own.

(2) Age. Because this chapter is concerned with the help-seeking behavior of adults, only help seeking in adult years is considered here. A number of studies indicate that older adults tend to cope with problems by relying on themselves rather than by seeking outside help. Veroff (1981) notes that older men and women are particularly unlikely to seek help. In a similar vein, Brown (1978) reports that the proportion of troubled individuals who seek help drops markedly after the age of 60. The same phenomenon also is apparent in the relatively low number of older people in mental health settings (e.g., Fox, 1984). The relative reluctance of older people to seek help seems best explained by the importance older individuals attach to personal independence (Lieberman & Tobin, 1983). This suggests that, as the issue of

independence becomes more ego-central in older age, the psychological costs associated with losing it, even temporarily, by seeking help are high, and help seeking is not favored.

(3) Socioeconomic status. On the whole, there is a positive relationship between socioeconomic status and the seeking of psychological help. This relationship holds when socioeconomic status is operationalized by education or income and when the dependent measure is actual visits to mental health professionals or attitudes people hold toward such help (Fischer, Winer, & Abramowitz, 1983). Further, important evidence for the positive link between socioeconomic status and help seeking is reported by Tessler and Schwartz (1972). In their study, the only demographic variable positively related to help seeking in a laboratory setting was father's income.

Asser (1978) distinguished between "negotiating" and "didactic" styles of help seeking. The didactic style reflects a request for the solution of the problem. In contrast, in the negotiating style, individuals retain responsibility for the solution. They seek partial help that will allow them to find the problem's solution on their own. This distinction sheds light on the socioeconomic status-help-seeking relationship. Asser found that individuals with lower socioeconomic status employ a didactic style, while higher socioeconomic status individuals use a negotiating style. This suggests that higher socioeconomic status individuals make *more requests for help,* but, in each of these help-seeking encounters, *they seek less help* than individuals with lower socioeconomic status.

Personality Variables

The personality variables most frequently studied reflect the two sides of the help-seeking dilemma: self-esteem and achievement motivation. (a) Self-esteem has been linked to psychological costs in help seeking; (b) achievement motivation has been linked to instrumental aspects of seeking help.

(1) Self-esteem. In general, the data indicate that individuals high in self-esteem seek less help than those low in self-esteem. Turning first to field studies, women with lower self-acceptance scores were more willing to join women's counseling groups than those with higher self-acceptance score (Gross, Fisher, Nadler, Stiglitz, & Craig, 1979). Miller (1985) suggested that low self-esteem may increase help-seeking and dependent compliant behavior in alcoholics, and Burke et al. (1976)

noted that low self-esteem employees seek more job-related advice than high self-esteem employees. Finally, Nadler and Wolmer (1989) correlated individuals' preferred coping responses to a variety of need states. They found that self-esteem was negatively correlated with willingness to seek help in a variety of need states.

Yet, as noted by Miller (1985), the links between self-esteem and help seeking may indicate that low self-esteem individuals either have a generally greater need for help or are more willing to seek help. On the basis of field data, one cannot answer this question, because need situations vary freely between individuals. The fact that in laboratory studies, where state of need is held constant, high self-esteem individuals also sought less help (for a review, see Nadler, 1986a) substantially weakens the possibility that different levels of need are responsible for this effect.

This reliable self-esteem effect has been interpreted in terms of the self-consistency approach. It has been argued that, for high self-esteem individuals, seeking help is inconsistent with their positive self-image (Nadler, 1986a). An examination of some of the moderators of the help-seeking/self-esteem relationship supports this interpretation. Specifically, high self-esteem individuals are reluctant to seek help only when situational conditions cause threat to be high in seeking help. This is the case when the need for help reflects on an ego-central dimension (Tessler & Schwartz, 1972), when the helper is a peer who arouses a high level of comparison stress (Nadler, 1987), or when there is no perceived opportunity to reciprocate (Nadler, Mayseless, Peri, & Tchemerinski, 1985).

Yet, the nature of the threat to the self involved in this relationship is not clear. It may reflect unwillingness to expose weakness to another person or a desire to maintain a positive view of oneself. The first possibility suggests that threat to one's social esteem (i.e., desire to maintain a positive public image) is responsible for this self-esteem/help-seeking relationship. The second possibility suggests that self-esteem concerns (i.e., desire to maintain a positive view of oneself) are a more parsimonious explanation for this relationship.

To study this, Nadler and Fux (described in Nadler, 1986a) examined whether or not help seeking is affected when the helper is aware of the subject's prior failure at the onset of help seeking. The rationale for this variation was that, if threat to social esteem is a more parsimonious explanation, then these effects should be weaker when the helper knows that the person failed before the help-seeking encounter. The finding that high self-esteem individuals sought less help in both "prior" and "no prior knowledge of failure" conditions suggest that self- rather than social esteem concerns are responsible for the self-esteem/help-seeking relationship. Further, in this study, the data indicate that the effects of self-esteem on help seeking were evident when subjects' social desirability scores were partialed out. This finding indicates that the lower willingness of high self-esteem individuals to seek help is not accounted for by differential levels of ego-defensiveness (see Dion & Dion 1985).

In contrast to the above findings, a number of studies have found that low self-esteem individuals are more reluctant to seek help than high self-esteem individuals. These contradictory findings (Morris & Rosen, 1973; Nadler, Sheinberg, & Jaffe, 1981) have been explained (e.g., Nadler, 1986a) as reflecting the fact that, when the need for help is non-ego-central, the instrumental benefits in seeking help are paramount. In this situation, high self-esteem individuals, for whom success is more expected and valued, use external help to ensure task completion.

The meaning of the relationship between self-esteem and help seeking should be considered in light of the distinction between under- and overutilization of helping resources (Nadler, 1986a). Some authors suggest that high self-esteem individuals underutilize available help and that this may be detrimental to performance. In support of this, Weiss and Knight (1980) demonstrated that high self-esteem individuals perform more poorly than low self-esteem individuals on tasks that require reliance on others' assistance. They labeled this phenomenon "the utility of humility." On the other hand, low self-esteem individuals may overutilize helping sources. It may be that, relative to high self-esteem persons, low self-esteem individuals label themselves more readily as dependent on others. This self-labeling may lead to an overutilization of help and lower reliance on one's own resources (for links between self-labeling and performance, see Langer & Benevento, 1978). This suggests that, while the high self-esteem person's view of self as competent and independent is threatened by the need for outside assistance, the low self-esteem person's view of self as dependent and incompetent is validated by the reliance on outside help. The consequences of this is that high self-esteem individuals face the danger of underutilization of help, and low self-esteem individuals face the danger of overutilizing it.

(2) Achievement motivation. Studies focusing on achievement motivation have centered on the instrumental benefits of help seeking in facilitating task completion. From this perspective, it has been reasoned

that, because task completion is more important for high than low achievers, high achievers would be more likely to seek help. In support of this rationale, Nadler (1986b) found that need for achievement was positively correlated with willingness to seek help. Moreover, this link was moderated by the importance of task completion. Achievement motive predicted help seeking for subjects from a communal culture (i.e., the kibbutz) when the task was presented as a group task. For individuals from the city, for whom personal rather than group achievement is more important, achievement motive predicted help seeking in individual task conditions.

An opposite link between achievement motive and help seeking, however, might be expected in view of the fact that the need to achieve is associated with a desire for "individual achievement" and not task completion per se. This motivational force may discourage the high achiever's willingness to seek help. In support of this, Tessler and Schwartz (1972) found a negative correlation between achievement motivation and help seeking.

Ames's (1983) attributional analysis of help seeking suggests a resolution to this conceptual and empirical controversy. Ames suggested that individuals adopt an instrumental perspective and seek help when the ego-threatening aspects of help seeking are minimal and perceptions of control are high. Low threat to the self is said to be associated with attributing the need for help to the lack of a specific ability while maintaining perceptions of adequate overall ability (see Abramson, Seligman, & Teasdale, 1978). Perceptions of control are maintained by attributing prior failure to lack of effort. Under these conditions, help seeking is encouraged. In support of this analysis, Ames and Lau (1982) found that, under these two conditions, failing students were more likely to seek help by attending help sessions.

Applying Ames's analysis to the link between achievement motivation and help seeking, a positive relationship may be expected when perceptions of adequate overall ability and control are maintained. Under these conditions, the instrumental aspects of help seeking are paramount, and the high achiever is more inclined to utilize any available resources that would guarantee task completion. When, however, the seeking of help threatens perceptions of adequate overall ability, the high achiever may be especially sensitive to maintaining "self-achievement" and view achievement through help as threatening.

Here too the distinction between negotiating and didactic help seeking seems to be of special importance. Given the importance attached by high achievers to individual achievement, it seems likely that these individuals would be (a) more sensitive to variations in the "negotiating" versus "didactic" nature of help seeking and (b) prefer negotiating rather than a didactic seeking of help.

(3) Other moderators: Shyness and self-consciousness. Another personality variable that moderates help-seeking behavior is shyness. Almost by definition, the relative unwillingness to seek others' assistance is the shy person's major behavioral attribute (Zimbardo, 1977). In addition, shy students were less likely than nonshy students to approach advisers with a request for help (Wills & DePaulo, in press). Another recent experimental study found that this effect of shyness on seeking others' assistance is most pronounced when the other individual is of the opposite sex (DePaulo, Dull, Greenberg, & Swaim, 1989). Yet, this reluctance to rely on others may have its positive side as well. Wills and DePaulo (in press) noted that the motivation to avoid interpersonal contacts with others may motivate the shy person to invest more in self-help efforts and result in better mastery of a given problem area.

Although shyness is negatively correlated with self-esteem (Cheek, Malchior, & Carpentieri, 1986), the processes that govern the link between self-esteem and help seeking are different than those that underlie the links between shyness and help seeking. Because shyness relates to the interpersonal domain, shy individuals may be willing to seek help when the source of help is impersonal (e.g., a computer). This is not the case with self-esteem. Here, because high self-esteem people are motivated to maintain a positive self-image, they are likely to refrain from seeking help even when the source of help is impersonal.

Other personality variables are also relevant in this context. One such variable is self-consciousness. Individuals who are self-aware are also more self-critical (Carver & Scheier, 1981). Applied in this context, this suggests that, when self-aware, people may be more sensitive to the threat to the self involved in seeking help. Because self-consciousness is the personality analogue of self-awareness (Fenigstein, Scheier, & Buss, 1975), the self-evaluative elements of seeking help may be more salient for people high in self-consciousness. In support of this, LaMorto-Corse and Carver (1980) found that individuals high in self-consciousness sought less help than those characterized as low in self-consciousness.

A final group of personality variables relevant to this topic is related to willingness to seek psychological help. These variables tap various facets of conservatism and rigidity and are also related to negative attitudes toward the seeking of psychological help (e.g., liberal versus conservative orientation or authoritarianism scores; Fischer, Winer, & Abramowitz, 1983).

CHARACTERISTICS OF THE HELPER

The first issue discussed is the individual's preference to seek help from a personal or an impersonal source of help. After this issue is considered, research concerning the effects of the specific characteristics of the helper will be discussed.

Personal Versus Impersonal Source of Help

Controlled experimental studies have found that individuals prefer seeking help when they are allowed the safety of anonymity (e.g., Nadler & Porat, 1978; Shapiro, 1978). Although the specific concept used to explain these findings may vary (e.g., threat to self-esteem, embarrassment), the rationale underlying these findings is that public help seeking increases the threat to feelings of esteem by making one's dependency and failure known to others.

The implications of this principle have been extended to a number of applied settings. Hill and Harmon (1976) note that the success of various "hot line" counseling programs is due to the fact that the person seeking help remains anonymous. Raviv, Raviv, and Yunovitz (1989) viewed the relative success of radio counseling programs as reflecting individuals' preference for anonymous helping sources, especially when the nature of the problem is personal and embarrassing. In yet another application, Karabenick and Knapp (1988a) showed that, because seeking help from a computer allows the help-seeking event to remain private, individuals sought more help from a computer than from another person. Finally, Shapiro (1983) suggested that the failure of various food stamp programs is due to the fact that using food stamps is analogous to a public request for help.

These discouraging effects of visibility on help seeking may not occur when the need is perceived as severe. Under such conditions, individuals may not want to rely on an anonymous source of help. In support of this, Raviv, Raviv, and Yunovitz (1989) found that the two major reasons given for calling a radio counseling program were (a) that people need not identify themselves and (b) that they did not perceive the problem they called about as serious. When the need is viewed as serious, forsaking thorough attention from another person (e.g., a close friend, a professional) may be too costly.

Preferred Sources of Help: Similarity and Intimacy

Epidemiological studies on seeking psychological help indicate that individuals who experience emotional difficulties seek professional help only after having first approached someone in their close network (e.g., Brown, 1978; Wills, 1983; Wills & DePaulo, in press). In a similar vein, Knapp and Karabenick (1988) reported that students needing academic assistance approach friends more often than institutional sources of help (e.g., advisers). Yet, other data indicate that this help-seeking sequence is moderated by severity of need (Neighbors & Jackson, 1984) and by interpersonal preferences for personal or institutional sources of help (Amato & Saunders, 1985).

The experimental studies that have investigated this issue suggest an opposite conclusion. Clark, Gotay, and Mills (1974) found that individuals seek less help from a similar other when they do not foresee an opportunity to reciprocate the help. Also, in the research context of recipients' reactions to help, recipients felt uneasy about receiving help from a similar other or a friend, especially when the task was ego-central (Nadler, Fisher, & Ben-Itzhak, 1983; Nadler & Fisher, 1986). In a more direct demonstration, Nadler (1987) found that, when the task was presented as ego-central, individuals were more reluctant to seek help from a similar than a dissimilar other. Explaining these data, Nadler (1986a) reasoned that, in line with social comparison theory (Festinger, 1954) and related formulations (e.g., Tesser, 1988), admitting inferiority to a similar other by seeking help induces a negative comparison that individuals try to avoid. Yet, this reluctance to seek help from a close other occurs only when there is potentially high threat to the self.

In general then, the epidemiological and social support literatures indicate a preference for help from a socially close other, whereas the experimental literature suggests that such help is more self-threatening. A number of reasons can account for this empirical inconsistency. First, in the social support and epidemiological literatures, a close helper usually was an intimate other (e.g., a spouse). In the experimental studies, the close helper was a similar other or an acquaintance. By the nature of the definition, an intimate other is one with whom one shares one's weaknesses without loss of esteem (Jourard, 1971). In contrast, a similar other or an acquaintance serves as a frame of reference for self-judgments. The display of weakness to such an individual may be self-threatening. In support of this, a recent study (Nadler & Kramer, 1989) found that students are more willing to approach someone described as an "intimate friend" than a "friend from class" with a request for help. This analysis suggests that willingness to seek help on an ego-relevant dimension may be an important behavioral manifestation of intimacy.

Another reason for the above empirical inconsistency may be the nature of the helping interaction in the two contexts. In the case of psychological help, individuals often approach an intimate other with the intent of "airing" the problem and discussing possible solutions (e.g., Horwitz, 1977). Here, the greater responsiveness and empathy of an intimate other is instrumental (Clark, 1983). Furthermore, in ongoing relationships, the individual may employ various tactics to minimize the psychological costs associated with seeking help, such as by describing the problem as something that happened to another individual (Glidewell, Tucker, Todt, & Cox, 1983). This is not the case in the experimental studies in which the need is concrete and well defined and the person *decides either to seek or not to seek help.* Applying the concepts of "negotiating" and "didactic" help seeking, the social support literature looks at individuals who could "negotiate" the seeking of help, while the experimental literature examines help-seeking encounters of a "didactic" nature.

This suggests a two-stage process regarding the link between social proximity and help seeking. When the problem is not well defined, as is the case with psychological difficulties, the person is first motivated to "air" the problem and consider possible solutions. For this purpose, social proximity is instrumental. Once a problem is well defined, seeking help implies dependency. Then, the psychological costs associated with seeking help from a close other dominate the psychological scene and discourage help seeking from a close other. Individuals may then prefer to protect their self-esteem by not seeking help or, if given the opportunity, negotiate the seeking of help.

Helper's Attractiveness

A number of investigators have suggested that, because attractive others serve as a more potent source for self-evaluation (Zanna & Pack, 1975), individuals may be more reluctant to seek help from an attractive other rather than an unattractive other. Stokes and Bickman (1974) found that female subjects were more willing to seek help from a physically unattractive rather than an attractive helper. A clearer demonstration of the role of evaluation apprehension in this context was furnished by Nadler (1980), who found that, when it was clear that no future interaction would take place with the helper, attractiveness did not affect help seeking.

The relationships between helper's attractiveness and willingness to seek help become more complex when cross-sex interactions are concerned. In a study of cross-sex interactions, female subjects sought more help from a physically attractive rather than an unattractive male helper (Nadler, Shapira, & Ben-Itzhak, 1982). These results were interpreted in line with prevailing sex role stereotypes in which a female's dependency on a male may be seen as constituting a positive self-presentation, and the male's attractiveness may have increased this motivation. On the basis of these data, Nadler, Shapira, and Ben-Itzhak (1982) suggested that the help-seeking interaction can be viewed from a self-presentational perspective. If the norms surrounding the helping context dictate that the person will benefit from a self-presentation of independence, esteem saving concerns discourage help seeking. If, however, the person benefits from presenting him- or herself as weak and dependent, ingratiation concerns motivate the seeking of help.

The viewing of physical attractiveness as a private case of social status (see Berger, Rosenholtz, & Zelditch, 1980) suggests that helpers of higher status may arouse esteem saving or ingratiation concerns. Data regarding increased help seeking from a physically attractive cross-sex other document the operation of ingratiation in help seeking. The individual acknowledges the status discrepancy by seeking help. Data showing the reluctance to seek help from an attractive same-sex other reflect greater esteem saving concerns with a higher status other.

CHARACTERISTICS OF THE NEED FOR HELP

A third category of variables that affect willingness to seek help are characteristics of the need for help. Three such variables have received systematic research attention: (a) ego-centrality, (b) level of need, and (c) consensus of need.

Ego-Centrality of Need for Help

Distinctions between different kinds of help-seeking situations can be made on numerous dimensions (e.g., medical, psychological, or financial needs; instrumental versus psychological needs). But a distinction that cuts across many other distinctions is whether the need for help reflects an ego-central or an ego-peripheral dimension. When need for help is said to reflect inadequacy on central dimensions (e.g., intelligence), individuals seek less help than when it is not (e.g., Tessler & Schwartz, 1972). Amato and Saunders (1985) noted that, when need states are viewed as stigmatizing and embarrassing, subjects are least likely to seek help. In fact, many of the relationships reported in previous sections of this chapter are determined by the ego-centrality of the help. High self-esteem individuals seek less help than low self-esteem people only when the need for help reflects ego-central qualities (Nadler, 1987). Similarly, the comparison stress inherent in receiving help from a similar other occurs only when the need for help is ego-central (e.g., Nadler et al., 1983). From this perspective, ego-centrality of need is a necessary, but not sufficient, condition for psychological costs to discourage willingness to seek help.

Level of Need and Help Seeking

A number of studies dealing with seeking psychological help indicate that higher levels of need are associated with more help seeking (Fischer, Winer, & Abramowitz, 1983; Mechanic, 1978). In a similar vein, Scot and Roberto (1985) found that, when the need for help is extreme, the elderly increase their help-seeking efforts by approaching professional sources of help. A somewhat different picture emerges from studies of help seeking in educational settings. Karabenick and Knapp (1988b) reported a curvilinear relationship between need for help and help seeking. Students who experienced high and low need for academic assistance sought less help than those reporting a moderate level of need. The reason those with low need for assistance did not seek help is quite evident. They simply did not need it. More puzzling is the finding that those who needed it most sought it least.

A similar phenomenon is reported by Amato and Saunders (1985), who found that the more serious the need, the less the willingness to seek help. They also found that serious states of need were associated with greater levels of threat to self-esteem. This suggests that—at least in the research contexts of the kind used by Karabenick and Knapp (1988b) and Amato and Saunders (1985)—in higher states of need, the person's perceptions of overall ability may be threatened by seeking help. Such conditions discourage the seeking of help (Ames, 1983).

Another interpretation for the reluctance of high need individuals to seek help is that they may *have already made* "lack of overall ability" attributions for their need. This would imply a helplessness-like state where the person neither helps him- or herself nor seeks help (Karabenick & Knapp, 1988b). The available data do not allow a determination of which of the two processes is more valid. Based on Nadler and Fisher's (1986) conception regarding the interactive effects of threat to self and perceptions of control, it may be expected that, when the need for help is high, individuals who enjoy perceptions of control will help themselves and those who do not will enter a helplessness-like state. These perceptions of control may be associated with other personality (e.g., self-efficacy, self-esteem, achievement motivation) and situational (e.g., attributions for failure) variables. Yet, an examination of these two processes in this context remains for future research.

Finally, the empirical inconsistency between the studies on psychological and educational help may be due to the different nature of high need in these two contexts. Extreme psychological need makes normal functioning without help very difficult. The meaning of need in an educational context is less extreme.

Consensus of Need for Help

In line with attribution theories, it has been reasoned that, when the problem is known to be shared by many individuals (i.e., high consensus), the need for help will be attributed externally. When consensus is low, the attribution for the need is likely to be internal and help seeking more self-threatening (Nadler & Porat, 1978; Tessler & Schwartz, 1972).

Snyder and Ingram (1983) have suggested an interesting extension of this relationship. According to Snyder and Ingram, the relationship between consensus of need and help seeking is different for "normals" (i.e., those who do not evidence a particular problem) and problem populations (i.e., those who are experiencing a specific difficulty). The "normals" are said to use consensus information to judge whether or not their difficulty is serious enough to require external assistance. High consensus (i.e., many people suffer from a similar difficulty) leads them to conclude that the difficulty is not serious enough to merit outside help. People in a problem population, on the other hand, have already identified themselves as having a serious problem. If the information is that few others share the same problem (i.e., low consensus), they may react defensively and abstain from seeking help. If consensus is high (i.e., many others have the same problem), individuals in this group may feel that it is safer to "lower" their defenses and seek help.

To test these predictions, Snyder and Ingram invited extremely anxious (i.e., problem population) students and students average in anxiousness (i.e., "normal" population) to an experiment. They then gave these subjects high or low consensus information about the problem (i.e., that test anxiety is common or uncommon among college students). The results indicate that high consensus caused normal individuals to view the problem as less serious and seek less help. In contrast, for "problem" individuals, high consensus information resulted in an increased sense of problem seriousness and greater motivation to seek help.

A consideration of Snyder and Ingram's data, together with other research on the effects of consensus on help seeking, allows an integrative conclusion. If one looks at these findings from the perspective of stage models of help seeking (see Gross & McMullen, 1983), for nonproblem individuals, consensus affects the labeling stage of the help-seeking process. Low consensus leads to a definition of the difficulty as serious enough for a person to consider seeking help. Individuals who have already labeled themselves as having a problem, or were made to face a concrete difficulty (i.e., subjects in experimental studies of help seeking), are beyond the labeling stage. For them, low consensus information lowers the probability of seeking help.

CONCLUSIONS, IMPLICATIONS, AND FUTURE RESEARCH

This chapter conceptualizes the seeking of help as affected by the associated psychological costs and instrumental benefits. The nature of threat to self is related to the centrality of self-sufficiency and independence—two qualities that are violated when one seeks help (Nadler & Fisher, 1986). The *characteristics of need* for help that make this dependency ego-relevant, long lasting (i.e., inability to reciprocate) or public and known to others (i.e., visibility) cause the help-seeking interaction to be a self-threatening event. This threat to self lowers willingness to seek help.

The need to maintain independence varies across people. Consequently, *characteristics of the person* in need of help affect help seeking. Independence is more valued by men and older people than by women and younger individuals, respectively. Therefore, females and younger individuals are more willing to seek outside assistance than males and older individuals, respectively. Also, personality traits like self-esteem, shyness, and self-consciousness are associated with the importance assigned to independence in interpersonal relations. Specifically, maintaining a self- and a public image of independence and self-reliance is related to being high in self-esteem, self-consciousness, and shyness. Finally, *characteristics of the helper* also affect the importance of being self-reliant. The fact that close others serve as a frame of reference for self-judgments makes dependence on such individuals self-threatening and discourages the seeking of help. This, however, may not be the case when the help is from an intimate other.

Regarding the instrumental benefits of seeking help, in general, when threat to self is minimized, instrumental benefits dominate the help-seeking scene. Thus, for example, when the person in need retains a perception of adequate overall ability and control, dependence on others is less self-threatening. Similarly, when the individual in need is able to negotiate the degree of dependence he or she retains when seeking help, seeking help is less threatening. This is so especially when situational conditions (e.g., a relatively high need for help) or personality variables (e.g., a high need for achievement) render the solution of the problem, or completion of the task, important.

A number of important yet relatively neglected aspects of the help-seeking interaction are highlighted in this review. These are general issues that cut across many of the studies presented here and need to be attended to by future research. One aspect concerns the effectiveness of help-seeking behavior. Help-seeking behavior may represent an overutilization, underutilization, or optimal utilization of helping resources. In both of the first instances, seeking help represents a relatively ineffective form of coping. Future research should attend to this issue and specify the links between help seeking and performance, thereby focusing on seeking help as an effective or ineffective coping strategy.

A second aspect relates to the conceptualization of help-seeking behavior. The majority of the literature on help seeking has conceptualized help seeking as a dichotomous behavior (i.e., seek versus not seek). In contrast, this chapter portrays high seeking as a dynamic interpersonal process that unfolds over time. Some requests are "disguised," while others are direct. Some requests for help are didactic, while others are negotiated. These distinctions represent a second avenue for future research that should be directed at the ways in which different individuals in different situations prefer to ask others for assistance.

Finally, the meaning of the decision not to seek help is ambiguous. This decision may reflect a helplessness like passivity or a decision to invest extra efforts in self-help. Although both alternatives are reflected in a behavioral decision not to seek help, they represent diametrically opposite phenomena. It remains for future research to explore this "dual" meaning of the decision not to seek help. In all, the multiple aspects of help-seeking behavior outlined in this chapter highlight the complexity of the help-seeking process. In light of this complexity, it appears that a true understanding of help seeking requires the adoption of a dynamic and multifaceted view of the help-seeking process.

REFERENCES

Abramson, L. Y., Seligman M. E. P., & Teasdale, J. (1978). Learned helplessness in humans: Critique and reformulation. *Journal of Abnormal Psychology, 87,* 49-74.

Amato, P. R., & Saunders, J. (1985). The perceived dimensions of help seeking episodes. *Social Psychology Quarterly, 48,* 130-138.

Ames, R. (1983). Help seeking and achievement orientation: Perspectives from attribution theory. In B. M. DePaulo, A. Nadler, & J. D. Fisher (Eds.), *New directions in helping: Vol. 2. Help seeking* (pp. 165-186). New York: Academic Press.

Ames, R., & Lau, S. (1982). An attributional analysis of help seeking in academic settings. *Journal of Educational Psychology, 74,* 414-423.

Asser, E. S. (1978). Social class and help seeking behavior. *American Journal of Community Psychology, 6,* 465-474.

Belle, D., Burr, R., & Conney, J. (1987). Boys and girls as social support theorists. *Sex Roles, 17,* 657-665.

Berger, J., Rosenholtz, S. J., & Zelditch, M. (1980). Status organizing processes. *Annual Review of Sociology, 6,* 479-508.

308	Help-Seeking Behavior

Brown, R. B. (1978). Social and psychological correlates of help seeking behavior among urban adults. *American Journal of Community Psychology, 6,* 425-439.

Burke, R. J., Weir, T., & Duncan, G. (1976). Informal helping relationships in work organizations. *Academy of Management Journal, 19,* 370-377.

Butler, T., Giordano, S., & Neren, S. (1985). Gender and sex role attributes as predictors of utilization of natural support systems during personal stress events. *Sex Roles, 13,* 515-524.

Carver, C. S., & Scheier, M. F. (1981). *Attention and self regulation: A control theory approach to human behavior.* New York: Springer-Verlag.

Chafetz, J. S. (1978). *Masculine, feminine or human?* Itasca, IL: Peacock.

Cheek, J. M., Malchior, L. A., & Carpentieri, A. M. (1986). Shyness and self concept. In L. M. Hartman & K. R. Blankstein (Eds.), *Advances in the study of communication and affect: Vol. 2. Perception of self in emotional disorder and psychotherapy* (pp. 113-131). New York: Plenum.

Clark, M. S. (1983). Some implications of close social bonds for help seeking. In B. M. DePaulo, A. Nadler, & J. D. Fisher (Eds.), *New directions in helping: Vol. 2. Help seeking.* (pp. 205-233). New York: Academic Press.

Clark, M. S., Gotay, C. C., & Mills, J. (1974). Acceptance of help as a function of similarity of the potential helper and opportunity to repay. *Journal of Applied Social Psychology, 4,* 12-24.

DePaulo, B. M., Dull, W. R., Greenberg, J. M., & Swaim, G. W. (1989). Are shy people reluctant to ask for help? *Journal of Personality and Social Psychology, 56,* 834-844.

DePaulo, B. M., Nadler, A., & Fisher, J. D. (Eds.). (1983). *New directions in helping: Vol. 2. Help seeking.* New York: Academic Press.

Dew, M. A., Dunn, L. O., Bromet, E. J., & Schulberg, H. C. (1988). Factors affecting help-seeking during depression in a community sample. *Journal of Affective Disorders, 14,* 223-234.

Dion, K. K., & Dion, K. L. (1985). Personality gender and the phenomenology of romantic love. In P. Shaver (Ed.), *Review of personality and social psychology* (Vol. 9, pp. 209-239). Beverly Hills, CA: Sage.

Fenigstein, A., Scheier, M. F., & Buss, A. H. (1975). Public and private self consciousness: Assessment and theory. *Journal of Consulting and Clinical Psychology, 43,* 522-527.

Festinger, L. (1954). A theory of social comparison processes. *Human Relations, 1,* 117-140.

Fischer, E. H., Winer, D., & Abramowitz, S. I. (1983). Seeking professional help for psychological problems. In A. Nadler, J. D. Fisher, & B. M. DePaulo (Eds.), *New directions in helping: Vol. 3. Applied perspectives on help seeking and receiving.* New York: Academic Press.

Fox, J. W. (1984). Sex, marital status and age as social selection factors in recent psychiatric treatment. *Journal of Health and Social Behavior, 25,* 394-405.

Glidewell, J. C., Tucker, S., Todt, M., & Cox, S. (1983). Professional support systems: The teaching profession. In A. Nadler, J. D. Fisher, & B. M. DePaulo (Eds.), *New directions in helping: Vol. 3. Applied perspectives on help seeking and receiving.* New York: Academic Press.

Gross, A. E., Fisher, J. D., Nadler, A., Stiglitz, E., & Craig, C. (1979). Correlates of help utilization at a women's counseling service. *Journal of Community Psychology, 7,* 42-49.

Gross, A. E., & McMullen, P. A. (1983). Models of the help seeking process. In B. M. DePaulo, A. Nadler, & J. D. Fisher (Eds.), *New directions in helping: Vol. 2. Help seeking* (pp. 47-73). New York: Academic Press.

Hill, F. E., & Harmon, M. (1976). The use of telephone tapes in telephone counseling program. *Crisis Intervention, 7,* 88-96.

Hobfoll, S. E., & Lerman, M. (1988). Personal relationships, personal attributes and stress resistance: Mothers' reactions to their child's illness. *American Journal of Community Psychology, 16,* 565-589.

Horwitz, A. (1977). Family, kin and friend networks in psychiatric help-seeking. *Social Science and Medicine, 12,* 287-304.

Jourard, S. (1971). *The transparent self.* New York: Van Nostrand.

Karabenick, S. A., & Knapp, J. R. (1988a). Help seeking and the need for academic assistance. *Journal of Educational Psychology, 80,* 406-408.

Karabenick, S. A., & Knapp, J. R. (1988b). Effects of computer privacy on help seeking. *Journal of Applied Social Psychology, 18,* 461-472.

Knapp, J. R., & Karabenick, S. A. (1988). Incidence of formal and informal academic help seeking in higher education. *Journal of College Student Development, 29,* 223-227.

LaMorto-Corse, A. M., & Carver, C. S. (1980). Recipient reactions to aid: Effects of locus of initiation attributions and individual differences. *Bulletin of the Psychonomic Society, 16,* 265-268.

Langer, E. J., & Benevento, A. (1978). Self induced dependence. *Journal of Personality and Social Psychology, 36,* 886-893.

Lieberman, M. A., & Tobin, S. S. (1983). *The experience of old age: Stress, coping and survival.* New York: Basic Books.

Mechanic, D. (1978). Effects of psychological distress on perceptions of physical health and use of medical psychiatric facilities. *Journal of Human Stress, 4,* 26-32.

Meeker, B. F., & Weitzel-O'Neill, P. A. (1977). Sex roles and interpersonal behavior in task oriented groups. *American Sociological Review, 42,* 91-105.

Miller, W. R. (1985). Motivation for treatment: A review with a special emphasis on alcoholism. *Psychological Bulletin, 98,* 84-107.

Mitchell, C. L. (1987). Relationship of femininity, masculinity, and gender to attribution of responsibility. *Sex Roles, 16,* 151-163.

Morris, S. C., & Rosen, S. (1973). Effects of felt adequacy and opportunity to reciprocate on help seeking. *Journal of Experimental Social Psychology, 9,* 265-276.

Nadler, A. (1980). Good looks do not help: Effects of physical attractiveness and expectations for future interactions on help seeking. *Personality and Social Psychology Bulletin, 6,* 378-383.

Nadler, A. (1986a). Self esteem and the seeking and receiving of help: Theoretical and empirical perspectives. In B. Maher & W. Maher (Eds.), *Progress in experimental personality research* (Vol. 14, pp. 115-163). New York: Academic Press.

Nadler, A. (1986b). Help seeking as a cultural phenomenon: Differences between city and kibbutz individuals. *Journal of Personality and Social Psychology, 57,* 976-983.

Nadler, A. (1987). Determinants of help seeking behavior: The effects of helper's similarity, task centrality and recipient's self esteem. *European Journal of Social Psychology, 17,* 57-67.

Nadler, A., & Fisher, J. D. (1986). The role of threat to self esteem and perceived control in recipient reactions to aid: Theory development and empirical validation. In L. Berkowitz (Ed.), *Advances in experimental social psychology* (Vol. 19, pp. 81-123). New York: Academic Press.

Nadler, A., & Kramer, L. (1989). *Help seeking from a friend or an intimate other across three different cultures.* Unpublished manuscript, Tel Aviv University.

Nadler, A., Maler, S., & Friedman, A. (1984). Effects of helper's sex, subject's sex, subject's androgyny and self evaluation on males' and females' willingness to seek and receive help. *Sex Roles, 10,* 327-339.

Nadler, A., Mayseless, O., Peri, N., & Tchemerinski, A. (1985). Effects of self esteem and ability to reciprocate on help seeking behavior. *Journal of Personality, 53,* 23-36.

Nadler, A., & Porat, I. (1978). When names do not help: Effects of anonymity and locus of need attributions on help seeking behavior. *Personality and Social Psychology Bulletin, 4,* 624-628.

Nadler, A., Shapira, R., & Ben-Itzhak, S. (1982). Good looks may help: Effects of helper's physical attractiveness and sex of helper on males' and females' help seeking behavior. *Journal of Personality and Social Psychology, 42,* 90-99.

Nadler, A., Sheinberg, L., & Jaffe, Y. (1981). Coping with stress through help: Help seeking and receiving behavior in male paraplegics. In C. Speilberger, I. Sarason, & N. Milgram (Eds), *Stress and anxiety* (Vol. 8, pp. 375-386). Washington, DC: Hemisphere.

Nadler, A., & Wolmer, L. (1989). *Motivation to change and motivation to receive help: Two related and distinct psychological constructs.* Unpublished manuscript, Tel Aviv University.

Neighbors, H. W., & Jackson, J. S. (1984). The use of informal and formal help: Four patterns of illness behavior in the Black community. *American Journal of Community Psychology, 12,* 629-644.

Nelson-Le Gall, S. A. (1987). Necessary and unnecessary help seeking in children. *Journal of Genetic Psychology, 148,* 53-62.

Nelson-Le Gall, S., & Glor-Scheib, S. (1985). Academic help seeking and peer relations in school. *Contemporary Educational Psychology, 11,* 187-193.

Philips, D. L. (1964). Rejection of the mentally ill: The influence of behavior and sex. *American Sociological Review, 29,* 679.

Raviv, A., Raviv, A., & Yunovitz, R. (1989). Radio psychology and psychotherapy: A comparison of client attitudes and expectations. *Professional Psychology: Research and Practice, 20,* 1-7.

Reis, H. T., Senchak, M., & Solomon, B. (1985). Sex differences in the intimacy of social interaction: Further examination of potential explanations. *Journal of Personality and Social Psychology, 48,* 1204-1217.

Robertson, M. F. (1988). Differential use by male and female students of the counseling services design and counseling models. *International Journal for the Advancement of Counseling, 11,* 231-240.

Scott, J. P., & Roberto, K. A. (1985). Use of informal and formal support networks by rural elderly poor. *The Gerontologist, 25,* 624-630.

Shapiro, G. E. (1978). Help seeking: Effects of visibility of task performance on seeking help. *Journal of Applied Social Psychology, 8,* 163-173.

Shapiro, G. E. (1983). Embarrassment and help seeking. In B. M. DePaulo, A. Nadler, & J. D. Fisher (Eds.), *New directions in helping: Vol. 2. Help seeking* (pp. 143-165). New York: Academic Press.

Snyder, C. R., & Ingram, R. E. (1983). "Company motivates the miserable": The impact of consensus information on help seeking for psychological problems. *Journal of Personality and Social Psychology, 45,* 1118-1126.

Stokes, S. J., & Bickman, L. (1974). The effect of physical attractiveness and role of the helper on help seeking. *Journal of Applied Social Psychology, 4,* 286-294.

Tausig, M., & Michello, J. (1988). Seeking social support. *Basic and Applied Social Psychology, 9,* 1-12.

Tesser, A. (1988). Toward a self-evaluation maintenance model of social behavior. In L. Berkowitz (Ed.), *Advances in experimental social psychology* (Vol. 21, pp. 181-227). New York: Academic Press.

Tessler, R. C., & Schwartz, S. H. (1972). Help seeking, self esteem, and achievement motivation: An attributional analysis. *Journal of Personality and Social Psychology, 21,* 318-326.

Verbrugge, L. M. (1981). Sex differentials in health and mortality. In A. H. Stomberg (Ed.), *Women, health and medicine.* Palo Alto, CA: Mayfield.

Veroff, J. B. (1981). The dynamics of help seeking in men and women. *Psychiatry, 44,* 189-200.

Wallston, B. S. (1976). The effects of sex role ideology, self esteem, and expected future interactions with an audience on male help seeking. *Sex Roles, 2,* 353-365.

Weiss, H. M., & Knight, P. A. (1980). The utility of humility: Self-esteem, information search and problem solving efficiency. *Organizational Behavior and Human Performance, 25,* 216-223.

Wills, T. A. (1983). Social comparison in coping and help seeking. In B. M. DePaulo, A. Nadler, & J. D. Fisher (Eds.), *New directions in helping: Vol. 2. Help seeking* (pp. 109-142). New York: Academic Press.

Wills, T. A., & DePaulo, B. M. (in press). Interpersonal analysis of the help seeking process. In C. R. Snyder & D. R. Forsyth (Eds.), *Handbook of social and clinical psychology.* New York: Pergamon.

Zanna, M. P., & Pack, S. J. (1975). On the self fulfilling nature of apparent sex differences in behavior. *Journal of Experimental Social Psychology, 11,* 583-591.

Zimbardo, P. G. (1977). *Shyness: What it is, what to do about it.* Reading, MA: Addison-Wesley.

12

Altruism and Prosocial Behavior Research
REFLECTIONS AND PROSPECTS

JOHN M. DARLEY

John M. Darley is the Warren Professor of Psychology at Princeton University. With Bibb Latané, he did some of the early studies about bystander responses to emergencies that initially called attention to questions of altruistic behavior and was awarded the Socio-Psychological Essay Prize and the Appleton-Century-Crofts Manuscript Prize. He is a past president of the Society for Personality and Social Psychology and a past associate editor of the *Psychological Bulletin*.

With a remarkable consistency, a major theme emerges from the chapters in this volume. The driving questions behind many lines of research inquiry and underlying many theoretical efforts in the area of prosocial behavior are these: "What is the motive for helping behavior?" "How is that motive to be conceived?" Batson and Oleson (Chapter 3) and Dovidio, Piliavin, Gaertner, Schroeder, and Clark (Chapter 4) centrally address this question. The former suggest that genuinely altruistic motives drive helping behavior, and the latter suggest that attaining maximum rewards at minimum costs drives it. Buck and Ginsburg (Chapter 6) suggest that the origin of the motive lies in evolutionary considerations, and Eisenberg and Fabes (Chapter 2) and Grusec (Chapter 1) trace the socialization of the motive throughout the lives of children—at least children in Western societies. Fiske's chapter also suggests the centrality of socialization, and he makes clear that socialization may result in a variety of different motives driving helping behavior. Salovey, Mayer, and Rosenhan (Chapter 8), Midlarsky (Chapter 9), and Clary and Snyder (Chapter 5) also raise the issue of motives, albeit more indirectly, by discussing what benefits a helper may derive from helping. By suggesting that helping may aid helpers in regulating their moods (Salovey, Mayer, and Rosenhan), in coping with stress (Midlarsky), or in fulfilling various functions such as being able to

AUTHOR'S NOTE: I gratefully acknowledge the support of the National Science Foundation (BNS #87-07412 and BNS #80-11494), the John D. and Catherine T. Mac Arthur Foundation, the John Simon Guggenheim Foundation, the James McKeen Cattell fund, and the thoughtful comments of Margaret Clark, the review series editor.

express their values (Clary and Snyder), these authors are also, albeit more indirectly than the others, addressing the question of what may motivate people to help.

Whereas many of these researchers have chosen to champion a particular motive (e.g., Batson and Oleson, and Dovidio, Piliavin, Gaertner, Schroeder, and Clark), there are dissenters from this approach. Specifically, Fiske, Clary and Snyder, and Midlarsky can be seen as dissenting—gently but firmly in the case of Clary and Snyder and Midlarsky; firmly in the case of Fiske. They are not so much questioning the existence of any particular motive as arguing for including a diverse set of perspectives on the question of sources of helping. The sole chapters that cannot be described as having the analysis of the motives for helping as a central theme are those by Wills (Chapter 10) and by Nadler (Chapter 11). These focus more on the similarities between prosocial behavior and social support (in Wills's case) and on outcomes of helping for the person who has received the help (in Nadler's case). I will begin with several comments about what I see as being the "majority approach" to the issue of why people help. Then I will turn to the dissenters.

THE SELF-INTEREST PERSPECTIVE

In the United States, and perhaps in all advanced capitalistic societies, it is generally accepted that the true and basic motive for human action is self-interest. It is the primary motivation, and it is the one from which other motives derive. Thus it is the only "real" motivation, a fact that some celebrate and some bemoan but most accept. To use currently fashionable vocabulary, the perspective that asserts the primacy of self-interest, and the ideologies within which that primacy is contained and justified, is now the "privileged" perspective in our society. To suggest that human actions could arise for other purposes is to court accusations of naïveté or insufficiently deep or realistic analysis.

This cultural presupposition has shaped the approach of psychologists to the topic of "prosocial behavior."[1] For instance, initially, to study helping was a less than completely acceptable pursuit, an idealistic concern that was out of the main and theoretically acceptable topics of a reinforcement-based psychology. One suspects that each of the current investigators would have stories to tell about times this issue was bluntly or tactfully raised with him or her by concerned colleagues.

There were other consequences as well. To explain the existence of apparently altruistic actions—when "altruism" connotes actions taken to benefit others without benefit, and perhaps even at cost, to self—was seen as the central task of researchers who were working within the background of our society's orienting perspective of self-interest. Thus prosocial researchers struggled with that question early in their investigations.[2] How does the distress of others motivate an individual into helping action? That particular framing of the question leads naturally to the answer: A representation of the distress of the other is created, probably automatically and nonoptionally, within the potential helper. In the next step of the explanation, that representation is given motivational properties. Perhaps because of empathic capacities, the distress of the other is not merely represented but felt emotionally and felt as distress (or some other negative emotional state that is reinforcing to reduce). Thus, when I reduce the distress of the other, I reduce my own distress because my distress is coupled with that of the victim.

In the literature, this "coupled distress" hypothesis is referred to as "the aversive-arousal reduction" explanation for prosocial behavior. It is the mechanism that is explicitly placed at the motivational core of the Dovidio model; it is consistent with what would be produced by many of the socialization processes described by Grusec and by Eisenberg and Fabes. It also is broadly congruent with Cialdini's general account of helping (Cialdini & Kenrick, 1976; Cialdini et al., 1987).

As I read the Salovey, Mayer, and Rosenhan chapter, I think many of their suggestions may fit in here as well. After reviewing the evidence that demonstrates that mood affects helping, they suggest that persons can learn to help because doing so can maintain a positive mood or bring into being a positive mood. What I am unclear about is whether they think that this happens because helping actions live up to various standards that people have internalized, and, therefore, prevent guilt and shame, as well as produce positive emotions. If so, are these positive feelings to be equated with moods? Alternatively, they may be postulating some mood-altering effects of helping that come about independently of self-ideal discrepancy considerations. We will watch with interest as these theoretical considerations are developed.

There are several comments that seem important to make about the aversive-arousal mechanism as an explanation for the motivation of all prosocial behavior. First, it neatly resolves an apparent inconsistency in the self-interest perspective that dominates social analysis in our culture—the introspectively available fact that we do feel empathic distress when others are in pain or difficulty. That fact, an apparent embarrassment for a self-interest perspective, is converted to an argument in its favor. Our affect, because of this tendency to construct internal representations of the other's plight, is coupled with the affect of the other. The internal representation is natural and nonoptional, but the reduction of its effective component, by the act of reducing the distress of the other, is that event that brings the perspective of self-interest to bear. Second, of course, it is consistent with the reward-punishment explanations of behavior that are the generic representation of the self-interest perspective within psychology. Thus a disreputable research area is rendered more acceptable. All that aside, it is possible that the aversive-arousal reduction hypothesis is true.

THOSE ARGUING AGAINST THE SELF-INTEREST PERSPECTIVE

Batson and Oleson argue that it's just not so that all helping derives from self-interest. Instead, helpers sometimes act for the sole purpose of reducing the suffering of others ("the empathic-concern hypothesis"). While benefits to self might accrue, these are not the cause of the helping action. It is interesting that the debate between Batson and Cialdini and others who hold variants of the coupled distress perspective has been carried out over the years via experimentation. Given the way that the initially apparently differing perspectives on helping have converged over time,[3] I would not have been sanguine about the possibilities of experimentally disentangling these positions. However, the experimenters have proved to be remarkably ingenious in constructing experimental conditions that test different predictions of the alternate theories. It has been an interesting debate to watch, and I have frequently been awed by the sustained ingenuity of the researchers as well as by their commitment to the pursuit of this issue.

As I read Ginsberg and Buck, I see them joining in on Batson's side of the debate. Ginsburg and Buck suggest there is a built-in readiness to construct the internal representation of the distress of the other, that there is an evolutionary mechanism in play here. They derive the coupled distress mechanism from evolutionary selection mechanisms. Evolutionary pressures select for individuals who make external their own emotional states and for individuals who are able to accurately read those cues that others make external. What I miss in the Ginsberg and Buck argument, but what it would not be difficult to construct, are the steps that lead from the accurate reception of cues of the distress of others to the internal representation of that distress in a way that motivates action.

Fiske's sentiments seem to lie with Batson as well. Fiske brings a different perspective to bear on the issue of altruism, an anthropological one. From that perspective, he would make us aware that our skepticism about the existence of altruism, and our propensity for finding reward mechanisms that make altruistic actions merely "altruistic," is a culturally conditioned one. Other cultures have no difficulty conceiving of the existence of altruistic acts. More to the point, other cultures organize large domains of their activities in terms of a communal sharing orientation, and this orientation is often applied to exactly those domains that are absolutely essential to the survival of the community members.

From this, two alternate conclusions seem possible to me, as we reflect the analysis back on our own culture. First, our culture has so completely organized itself around the market orientation that any propensities for altruistic sharing have been socialized out of us (distressing, but perhaps true). Second, although our cultural ideology is organized around the market orientation, and many of the spheres of our activities are governed by that thinking, there may still be domains in which all normal members of our culture habitually behave altruistically, and there are some members of our culture who genuinely behave altruistically in other domains as well. By focusing much of our research efforts on doing experimental studies in which interactions between strangers are examined, we may have unintentionally missed situations and relationship types (e.g., parent-child interactions that take place in private) in which people do tend to operate on a more altruistic basis. Moreover, there may be some members of our culture who genuinely behave altruistically in a wide variety of situations. (Note that Clark, our volume editor, has developed a scale that measures some of these differences in orientation within our culture—Clark, Ouellette, Powell, and Milberg, 1987—and Schwartz and Gottlieb, 1981, some years ago developed an Ascription of Responsibility scale that measured a person's tendency to take internal responsibility for the plight of others and predicted an individual's likelihood of helping in several of what Clary and Snyder call "considered" helping situations.)

Clary and Snyder have taken a very different approach to helping behavior, but it is one that can be read as having implications for the general study of prosocial behavior. They begin by pointing out the utility of studying helping in "considered" situations—situations in which the helpers have time to decide when and how to help. Volunteer work, particularly when engaged in on a continuing basis, is one such situation, and one worthy of study from the perspectives of social policy and psychological theory. Their approach is a functional one; they suggest that the functionalist approach previously applied to attitude research can be illuminatingly applied to a person's motives for engaging in volunteer behavior. A functional analysis of helping behavior suggests that a volunteer may help another because of his or her concerns for the other (the "value-expressive" function) or because it fits in with the norms of his or her reference group (the "social-adjustive" function). Helping also may serve "ego-defensive" functions, avoiding the acceptance of negative images of the self or of negative images of the world as a place in which injustice prevails.[4] Even a "knowledge function" may be served, with volunteering being an opportunity to achieve greater understanding of some corners of the social world and to exercise skills at organization and coping.

Two interesting points arise from this analysis. First, an apparently similar act of helping may be engaged in by two individuals for quite different functional reasons. Second, and a characteristic of this perspective that I find attractive, there is a setting aside of the tendency to judge certain kinds of helping behaviors as more desirable or more moral than others. One person volunteers to gain standing in his community or to quiet his own fears. So what? He is helping. Of course, the functionalist perspective suggests that helping engaged in for different functional reasons may have different patterns and intensities and may be vulnerable to disruption by different sorts of changes. Still, it does remind us that, as with so many other times in life, we might "take what we can get," particularly when what we can get may be genuinely helpful, although given for complex motivational reasons.

All of this can and should be studied, as can the conditions under which helping launched to fill one function alters in character and comes to fill other functions. Further analysis of volunteerism may also cause us to discover new functions, and not the ones highlighted when we draw upon those would-be attitude researchers. Thus we might also be able to illuminate the core of the functionalist perspective by examining this domain. What this chapter calls to our attention most squarely is the possibility of altering certain aspects of societal organization to increase the likelihood that helping will occur and be sustained. This is a valuable new question to raise.

RELATIONSHIP ISSUES

Clearly recognized by many of the current writers, and clearly documented within their research projects, is the fact that the propensity to help another is strongly affected by the preexisting character of the relationship between the helper and the one in need of help. This was foreshadowed in the original emergency research in which it was found that the existence of previously established relationships, even fleeting ones, sharply altered the responses of individuals. (So, for instance, Latané and I—Latané & Darley, 1970—found that any acquaintance relations between observers facilitated their communication and, therefore, enabled them to communicate about the meaning of an ambiguous event, to determine whether it was an emergency, and eventually to act jointly.)

Further exploration of relationship issues is of theoretical importance for several reasons. First, it bears on the question of the motives for helping behavior. As most reading this know, it is possible to construct a sociobiological argument for the existence of altruism (Trivers, 1971) if that altruism is displayed toward others with whom one shares genes. Is altruism confined to those with whom we are related or is it extended to others in a way that can be made credible within a sociobiological theoretical structure?

The sociobiological perspective is not the only one that suggests that helping is not randomly distributed across all individuals in distress. A functional account of helping suggests that certain value-expressive functions are best served by helping certain targeted groups of others. I may choose to help those, for instance, children, who I think cannot be the authors of their own plight, rather than the homeless, to whom I might assign responsibility for their plight.[5] Certainly it is likely that people will aim their help-giving efforts in the directions of those in need with whom they most strongly identify, either by reasons of shared dangers or at a more general level. One expects that sailors, for instance, would be disproportionately moved to contribute to homes for distressed sailors and might generalize this to contributing to all those who worked in physically dangerous occupations.

Fiske again pulls away from easy generalizations, particularly the one that we help—those like ourselves or those with whom we can easily empathize. In the culture he observed, the Communal Sharing relation explicitly generalized to strangers from other cultures. For hundreds of years, people observing the Greek culture have commented on its tradition of hospitality to strangers, which often is taken to the point of depriving the immediate family of resources.

THE REFLEXIVE NATURE OF THE
HELPING RELATIONSHIP

Scattered studies of helping behavior were reported in the early social psychological literature, but the rapid emergence of helping research as an empirical research area can be traced to the late 1960s. The initial studies of helping done then concerned emergency responding and generally involved simulated but realistic "emergencies" that arose rapidly and in which the victim of the emergency was usually a stranger to the potential respondent. The standard experiment had the help-demanding event arise during a fleeting encounter between strangers. It is not surprising then that the data that arose from these experiments did not allow for measurements of the ways that the participants in the helping encounter were changed by having been in it.[6] Many of the current research programs continue in this tradition, but others report on longer-term helping situations and touch on questions about how the help offerer and the help recipient are altered by the initial encounter.

The following seems to me to be a systematization of the process. The initial decision to offer or not to offer help can have some immediate consequences for the offerer. For instance, a decision not to help may lead to more negative attitudes toward helping largely through the processes of rationalization, as documented by the dissonance theorists. In general, we would expect these changes in attitudes to be in the direction of legitimating nonhelping in the future. Some aspect of the context, or the other person, is seized on to justify the decision not to help, and when that aspect of the situation recurs in the future, the individual's helping is rendered less likely by the decision not to help that was made in the past. However, decisions to help will also have effects on the helper. Many of these effects are likely to be positive ones. As Salovey, Mayer, and Rosenhan point out, helping may make the helper feel good immediately and perhaps in the future. As Midlarsky points out, the act of helping may reduce stress. And, as Clary and Snyder point out, helping may often fulfill a valuable function for the helper. These things suggest that giving help ought to lead to increased chances of giving help in the future.

However, the picture is more complicated than that. Not all consequences of helping will be positive. For instance, there ought to be effects of helping that are conditioned by the absence of positive things occurring as a result of that offer or even by the presence of negative things. As an example, to the extent that helping does not fulfill the function that motivated it, that sort of helping may become less frequent in the future. Or, to give another example, as Nadler reminds us, the offer of help is not always an unequivocally positive event for the recipient. It may convey with it the suggestion that the potential recipient is in need of help, and there are some circumstances in which that realization might be ego-damaging to the individual. For this reason, the offer of help may be quite emphatically refused, and one would expect that this would make similar offers from the "rejected" help offerer less likely in the future, even if future potential recipients of help would not react in a similar fashion.

There are other reasons that the reception of help, once offered, may lessen the likelihood of help being offered in the future: The negative consequences for the help giver may be greater than anticipated, or the help may be unsuccessful, or the help giver may emerge with the suspicion that the help was fraudulently solicited. Some more subtle points can also be made. As a help-eliciting situation unfolds, the degree of the need for help may not be seen to be as great as it actually is at the end of the unfolding. However, often the bystander offers help before the unfolding is complete. This means that the bystander may sometimes learn that he or she "made the right move" in offering help at a point before the need for it became absolutely clear and thus may gain in confidence in his or her ability to size up ambiguous situations.

From all this, a catalog is emerging of reasons that a person who gives help once may or may not do so again. Social psychologists are looking at helping from a broader perspective than was done in the past. The ongoing interdependence between people involved in the helping process is being considered in a way it was not in the past. This represents a considerable gain in sophistication for the field.

PROSOCIAL BEHAVIOR AND RELATED RESEARCH AREAS

Several chapters in this volume relate prosocial behavior to other research domains. I feel, as do those chapter authors, that this task of comparison should provide illumination for conceptualizations both of helping and of the behavioral determinants of action in the related areas. That is, for instance, I agree with Wills that there are conceptual similarities between the concepts of "helping" and "giving social support" and that we ought to learn a great deal about both from examining them together. But I now realize that the task of establishing these relationships is a more difficult one than could have been foreseen. Perhaps because of methodological concerns, many of the related research areas prove to be more strongly "encapsulated" than they initially seem. As Wills reminds us, the social support researchers have often taken a social epidemiological perspective, using questionnaire and self-report measures, often with physical health measures as their dependent variables. These researchers map community ties and only recently have begun to conceptualize the helping actions that flow along these social network lines (Cohen, 1988; Thoits, 1986).

Then too, different research areas have different sets of preferred theoretical constructs, and the theoretical constructs of one domain are sometimes split and fragmentarily represented among the constructs of another domain. "Stress" is one such concept used within certain research circles that imperfectly maps onto several other concepts in several other research domains.

Midlarsky's chapter draws on work using the concept of stress. In my reading, Midlarsky makes an argument that is somewhat broader than she sometimes frames it, and so it is first important to summarize it. Briefly, helping others can have various positive consequences for the helper, including distraction from his or her own troubles, enhancing his or her sense of meaningfulness, increasing perceived competence and/or mood tone, and promoting integration into society. Individuals whom we refer to as "stressed" are experiencing decrements on one or more of those dimensions and can restore positivity by engaging in the helping of others. Two forms of a hypothesis emerge: first the strong form, which would hold that stressed individuals will engage in more helping behavior that unstressed individuals. Second, and the one that I take Midlarsky to be holding, is that stressed individuals will engage in more helping behavior than we would expect, given their stressed circumstances.

It seems to me, though, that the concept of stress in these hypotheses would at least benefit from being narrowed and further refined. Further, and tentatively, I would suggest that stress is not the best construct to use to predict helping behavior. Stress is an extremely global construct, with respect to its causes. Persons experiencing stress are experiencing some negative state on one of many possible dimensions. But differentiating between the causes of stress may enable us to make more accurate predictions about helping actions. If, for instance, I am stressed because of the multiple demands on my time required to care for my children and my aged parents, it is difficult to see how I am going to find the further resources for helping or benefit from additional helping demands. However, if I am stressed because I have just had a disappointment in love, or a failure of academic competence, then I can see why I might be motivated to help another. Taking on responsibility for helping others may, in that instance, restore some damaged element of my self-esteem, by demonstrating that I am able to play a significant role in at least one other's life or by demonstrating that I have practical competences that I can think of as compensating for the threatened academic ones. Or I suppose that many of my negative conclusions about myself might be altered by social comparison; my plight might be discovered not to be so bad in comparison with the plight of the others to whom I offer help.

I am assuming that Midlarsky is using the conventional conceptualization of stress (that is, the view of stress that is implicitly assumed in the scales measuring stress that descend from Holmes and Rahe's, 1967, "life events scale." This is a quite global conceptualization of stress. So my point is that I am not sure that that implied conceptualization of stress will give us great insight into why people help. I suggest that we will do better, where *better* is defined as the improvement of our understanding of why individuals are more likely to help others, in certain different ways, at different times of their lives, if we use concepts like "threat to an element of self-esteem" rather than "stress." Putting this another way, thinking about research done on stress brings us into the area of several interesting questions about helping, but the concept of stress is not likely to emerge as a central one in our developing theorizing about the kinds of helping that are motivated by negative states.

My sense is that the notion is not something that Midlarsky would disagree with if it is taken as subdividing "stress." I suspect that she would not fall in with this notion if it is taken as suggesting replacing the concept of stress with more familiar social psychological ones. The debate can be an empirical one.

FUTURE DIRECTIONS

One of the tasks of a review volume such as this is to suggest directions in which future empirical research and theoretical exploration profitably can go. Various chapter authors have implied such directions when they highlight the questions that are as yet unresolved in their research programs or suggest research that will resolve tensions between their theoretical formulations and those of others. They also have frequently indicated what they saw as the new directions to address in coming years. Drawing from their lists, it is possible to see the following possibilities.

Homelessness and the Development of Callousness

As mentioned earlier, one is changed by the act of helping—or not helping. In the 1980s, most cities saw an increase in the number of homeless people wandering their streets. In fact, it is probably reasonable to say that a decade ago, people rarely encountered beggars and now routinely do, and not only in New York but in most cities in this country. People cope with this in different ways, but many accounts have appeared in which people describe what might be called the "natural history" of their encounters. For a number of reasons that can be quickly imagined by those reading this, the trend seems to be in the direction of, first, helping these individuals, then, not helping these individuals, and, then, not "noticing" them. But surely this cannot go on without some corresponding attitude change occurring. One suspects that we must either commit ourselves to some ameliorating actions or come to see the homeless as "different from us"—different, undeserving, and perhaps somewhat less than human. Sadly, we may need research on this topic.

Social Structures that Promote Helping

Psychological social psychologists work at the level of the individual and the small group. However, we do that with the sense that we can eventually make contact with those who analyze phenomena at a more macro level. It is now time that we address this connection. Given our understanding of the ways individuals frame helping contexts, and the individual motives for helping, we should be able to say how society might be organized to facilitate help giving. Obviously, this is a task in social engineering rather than social theory building. Nonetheless, it is one that we are able to address and have committed ourselves (in those sections of our grant applications about "relevance") to addressing. Snyder's functional account of the various reasons for help giving provides us with a tool for beginning this task. In my local volunteer fire department, various people get many of the rewards of leadership, which they may not get in the other activities of their day-to-day lives. How can we foster and sustain the hundreds of organizations that do take on help-giving roles in our society? Putting this in more psychological terms, how can we arrange that those organizations continue to provide the rewards that the functional analysis suggests are so important while reducing the frustrations and defeats that the analysis would suggest would drive volunteers out of those settings? This is a remarkably different question. In tandem with organizational psychologists and experts on governmental entities, we need to explore how organizations might be structured, probably of a mixed public-private nature, to provide ego gratifications for workers in the programs.[7] This is a vast task, but it is one to which we have a contribution to make.

Taxonomies as Research Generators

Within many of the chapters, taxonomies of helping actions are suggested or implied. The achievement of some taxonomic clarity on help-giving actions seems to me to be an important task, and one to which energies can increasingly be turned. Still, I do not think that it is ever going to be the case that we will arrive at a single all-purpose taxonomic organization of help-giving actions. Nadler suggests an organization in terms of the impact of the action on the recipient, and a valuable perspective lies behind that. Snyder suggests that we consider the functions of the help-giving act from the perspective of the help giver, and that too is a valuable perspective from which to approach the field. But the taxonomies are generated for different purposes and are unlikely to be identical; taxonomies, as philosophers of science remind us, are instantiations of sorting principles that are not universal or logically given. Instead, they are developed for purposes that are ultimately functional. Different ethnic groups of humans can be sorted by evolutionary closeness or, alternatively, by current organizations of the economic arrangements of their societies; which sorting is of interest to you depends on your scientific purposes.

If it is necessarily the case that we will have different taxonomies of helping behavior, of what value are taxonomies to us? First, they enable us to make various predictions, exactly those predictions that the specific taxonomic system is organized to make. Nadler's distinctions of help-offering actions in terms of their impact on the recipient enable us to predict acceptance of offers. But there is an interesting second benefit of taxonomies in this area as well. Within a culture, we are all socialized into the categorical systems of that culture. This means that we often react to, for instance, a help-giving offer in terms of our categorization of that offer. Thus if we could bring both the help-offering and the help-accepting taxonomies to bear simultaneously, it could lead to interesting discoveries; for instance, it might be the case that certain help-giving acts that provide great public acclaim for the giver are not necessarily well tuned to the recipient and might even cause the recipient distress. Then the two taxonomies, operating jointly, might suggest ways to reorganize the situation so that the functional benefits to the giver might be continued, but, for instance, the privacy of the recipient could be protected. This is perhaps an obvious suggestion, but I suspect that many less obvious ones would arise from a sustained examination of the joint implications of the various taxonomies that are beginning to arise in the field. This may be one of the tools we could use in suggesting the optimal design for helping organizations.

Psychological Conceptualizations of the Urge to Help

One final point: In the late 1960s, when Latané and I had obtained our first bystander results, I had a chance to discuss them with Fritz Heider. At that time, various people had pointed out to us that we had not addressed the question of why, in our experiments, at least some people helped. "Why did they help?" was the question directed to us. I asked Heider this question. Heider made a very interesting suggestion, saying simply that it was his sense that people sometimes experienced what he called an "externally located ought force." There was a gestalt quality to his analysis, reminiscent of Lewin's notion of field forces. The helping response of an individual flowed from the perception that a person was in distress and was experienced as a necessary response to that distress. While I do not think that this is a compelling analysis of those many situations in which we carefully and self-consciously consider what we ought to do in the face of some complex occasion in which help might be given, his comment does strike me as true in the rapidly arising, unequivocal emergency situations that Latané and I originally examined. I mention it here for two reasons. I do not think it is an idea that has ever gotten its due, and I again sense its presence when Fiske is describing the interior character of what he calls the "Communal Sharing" relationship that prevailed in the tribe among whom he did his fieldwork.

SUMMING UP

In conclusion, prosocial behavior has not been a topic of sustained study until quite recently. Yet we see that several well-worked-out research programs have been carried out. We now know a great deal about the socialization of prosocial behavior and the situations that lead to its display—and to its suppression. We begin to have a sense of the motivations that lie behind it, and we begin to see connections between prosocial behavior, the structures that maintain it, and other human actions. Many directions for future research have emerged. These are very reasonable achievements for a field that has been addressed in major and sustained ways only since the 1960s.

NOTES

1. *Prosocial behavior,* by the way, is an interesting example of psychologists' own vocabulary, with the human connotations of *helping* replaced by the more austere phrase *prosocial,* and even that phrase controlled and tamed by the wonderfully distancing and scientizing addition of *behavior.*

2. Actually, not all did. Latané and I finessed the question, creating emergencies in which the "natural" response of anyone observing them was to intervene, and then studying the ways in which the presence and actions of other bystanders inhibited this "natural" response. We never theoretically addressed just why the helping response was "natural."

3. For instance, Batson and Cialdini agree that seeing another in trouble causes both personal distress and empathic concerns. Batson assigns motivational power to empathic concerns; Cialdini does not. Recently, Cialdini has suggested that a third negative-state emotional response is provoked by a person in distress, that of sadness, and that it is the relief of this sadness that motivates helping action.

4. Midlarsky's suggestion, that helping others may sometimes relieve stress felt by the helper, might be classified here as an example of an ego-defensive function of helping. It also may be value expressive.

5. Because of their recognition of exactly this sort of impulse, others, whom we often think of as "saints," make a point of helping all others, regardless of the source of their

distress or its momentary fashionableness. By doing so, they signal their message that the obligation to help has a universal component.

6. This is not completely accurate. Shalom Schwartz (1968) rounded up people who had been in a helping experiment and debriefed them about the situational forces acting on individuals who faced emergencies. He found that their rate of intervention in a second helping situation, staged sometime later, had been elevated by their participation in the first experiment.

7. This is in sharp contrast to what we hear from those who work in current bureaucratic organizations. There, *burnout* is the current term for the ways in which participants lose many of the reinforcements for their work.

REFERENCES

Cialdini, R. B., & Kenrick, D. (1976). Altruism and hedonism: A social developmental perspective on the relationship of negative mood state and helping. *Journal of Personality and Social Psychology, 34*, 907-914.

Cialdini, R. B., et al. (1987). Empathy-based helping: Is it selflessly or selfishly motivated. *Journal of Personality and Social Psychology, 52*, 749-758.

Clark, M. S., Ouellette, R., Powell, M., & Milberg, S. (1987). Recipient's mood, relationship style and helping. *Journal of Personality and Social Psychology, 53*, 94-103.

Cohen, S. (1988). Psychosocial models of the role of social support in the etiology of physical disease. *Health Psychology, 7*, 269-297.

Holmes, T. H., & Rahe, R. H. (1967). The Social Readjustment Rating Scale. *Journal of Psychosomatic Research, 11*, 213-218.

Latané, B., & Darley, J. M. (1970). *The unresponsive bystander: Why doesn't he help?* New York: Appleton-Century-Crofts.

Schwartz, S. H. (1968). Words, deeds, and the perception of consequences and responsibility in action situations. *Journal of Personality and Social Psychology, 10*, 232-242.

Schwartz, S. H., & Gottlieb, A. (1981). Participants' postexperimental reaction and the ethics of bystander research. *Journal of Experimental Social Psychology, 17*, 396-407.

Thoits, P. (1986). Social support as coping assistance. *Journal of Consulting and Clinical Psychology, 54*, 416-423.

Trivers, R. (1971). The evolution of reciprocal altruism. *Quarterly Review of Biology, 46*, 35-37.

NOTES